THE
SIXTIES

BIBLIOTHÈQUE DE
DOCUMENTATION
INTERNATIONALE
CONTEMPORAINE

M U S É E
D' H I S T O I R E
CONTEMPORAINE

This book has been published with the co-operation of the Musée d'Histoire Contemporaine, BDIC

THE SIXTIES

Britain and France, 1962–1973

The utopian years

edited by
David Alan Mellor and **Laurent Gervereau**

with the collaboration of
Sarah Wilson and **Laurence Bertrand Dorléac**

PHILIP WILSON

CULCOM

This book has been published with the co-operation of the British Council

Design: Des Souris et des Pages, Nantes
Make-up for the English edition: Chapman Bounford & Associates, London

This book is edited by David Alan Mellor and Laurent Gervereau with the collaboration of Sarah Wilson and Laurence Bertrand Dorléac, with contributions originally in French by Marianne Amar, Antoine de Baecque, Laurence Bertrand Dorléac, Thérèse Blondet-Bisch, Geneviève Dreyfus-Armand, Laurent Gervereau, Thierry Groensteen, Marie-Françoise Lévy, Jean-Pierre Mercier, Gérard Monnier, Michel Winock, Michelle Zancarini-Fournel and in English by Vicky Allan, Barry Curtis, Philip Dodd, Philippe Garner, Ian Jeffrey, Stuart Laing, Andy Medhurst, David Alan Mellor, Bill Osgerby, Andrew Wilson and Sarah Wilson

The images and works of art reproduced are from the public and private collections mentioned in the captions. The photographs of works or of documents reproduced here were taken, unless otherwise indicated, by Nicholas Sinclair and Jean-Hugues Berrou for the Musée d'Histoire contemporaine-BDIC. Photographs by Kevin Noble, 23; Jacqueline Hyde, 53; Shunk-Kender, 60; Gaillard, 73.
© Adagp, Paris, 1997, for the works of Arman, 32: Eduardo Arroyo, 68; Ben, 42; Peter Blake, 14; Henry Bernard, 118; Daniel Buren, 50; César, 32; Roman Cieslewicz, 64, 156, 244-7; Jean Degottex, 264; Erró, 60, 72; Peter Klasen, 59, 73; Yves Klein, 34; Julio Le Parc, 39; Le Corbusier, 117, 118; Jacques Monory, 62; François Morellet, 38; Bernard Rancillac, 58, 73, 120; Martial Raysse, 35, 56, 57; Siné, 71, 158; Solé, 147, 148; Daniel Spoerri, 33, 63; Peter Stämpfli, 60; Hervé Télémaque, 62; Roland Topor, 63; Clovis Trouille, 67; Claude Viallat, 53; Christian Zeimert, 64.
© Spadem, Paris, 1997, for the works of Alexis, 141; Henri Cueco, 72; Philippe Druillet, 139; Fred, 132, 133, 134; Nicholas Ferguson, 15; Richard Hamilton, 16, 26; Guy Peellaert, 65, 66; Ralph Steadman, 15, 18, 149; Jacques de la Villeglé, 30, 31; Georges Wolinski, 144, 159.

First published in France by Somogy Éditions d'Art, Paris, under the title 'Les Sixties, Années utopies'
© Somogy Éditions d'Art, Paris, 1996
© Philippe Garner for the text 'King's Road to Courrèges: Fashion and fashion photography', 1997
© Philip Wilson Publishers Limited, 1997, for the present edition
Translation by Judith Hayward
First published in the United Kingdom 1997 by Philip Wilson Publishers Limited
143-149 Great Portland Street London WIN 5FB
Distributed in the USA and Canada by
Antique Collectors' Club Limited
Market Street Industrial park
Wappingers' Falls NY 12590 USA

ISBN 0 85667 4672
Printed in Italy by Grafedit, Azzano-San-Paolo
Photoengraving: Fotolito Star, Grassobbio, Italy

11877266

We should like to thank the following for their support:

Max Moulin, Marie-Paule Serre et l'Association française d'action artistique (AFFA)
Catherine Ferbos-Nakov and The British Council
Philip Dodd and the British Film Institute, London
Roger Silverstone and the Culture and Communication Graduate Centre, University of Sussex
Olivier Poivre d'Arvor and the Institut français, London
Marthe Goducheau and FIP, Paris
Nicola Coleby, Jessica Rutherford and the Brighton Museum and Art Gallery
Karen Wraith, University of Sussex
Stuart Laing and the University of Brighton

We are particularly grateful to:
Marcel Alocco; Philip Bone; Philippe Garner; Gerald Gassiot-Talabot; Julie Harrold and l'Ècomusée de Saint-Quentin-en-Yvelines; Jean-Jacques Lebel; François Morellet; Adrian Mibus; Tim Moreton, Terence Pepper, Charles Saumarey-Smith and the National Portrait Gallery; Guy Peellaert; Bernard Plossu; Bernard Rancillac; Nicholas Sinclair; and Robert Whitaker.

In addition, we should like to thank all those without whom this work would never have been published:
Françoise Afoumado and the staff of the Bibliothèque de Documentation et d'Information contemporaine (BDIC), Gérard Aimé, Jackie Akehurst, Eduardo Arroyo, J.G. Ballard, Laure Barbizet, Jean Beauchesne (Paris-Match), Nadine Beauthéac-Bouchart, Ben, Jean-Hugues Berrou, Peter Blake, Thérèse Blondet-Bisch, John Boty, Mark Boyle, Simon Bradford, Claire Bretécher, Daniel Buren, Cabu, Toumany Camara, Zelda Cheatle, Chantal Cislewicz, André Coutelle (Elle), Henri Cueco, Nicolas Davio (Galerie Krief), Francine Deroudille (Agence Rapho), Rita Donagh, Fabienne Dumont, Jacques and Jean Donguy, Phillippe Druillet, Dudley Edwards, Michael and Jacqueline English, Erró, Boris Eizykman, Espace Carole Brimaud, Jacques Faizant, Mathias Fels, Nicholas Ferguson, Marcel Fleiss (Galerie 1900–2000), Jean-Claude Forest, Danièle Fournier, Fred, Gérard Fromanger, Galerie Beaubourg, Galerie Louis Carré, Galerie Éric Fabre, Galerie Jean Fournier, Galerie Jérôme de Noirmont, Galerie Alain Oudin, Galerie Denise René, Galerie Nathalie Seroussi, Pierre Gaudibert, Jean-Claude Gautrand, Gébé, John Gill (South East Arts), Lorraine Gillet, Jean Giraud, Marcel Gotlib, Valérie Goyena, Magali Guyon, Richard Hamilton, Françoise Hardy, Adrian Henri, Joan Hills, Willem Holltrop, Allen Jones, Barry Joule, Françoise Juillard, Peter Klasen, Peter Knapp, Gerald Laing, Peter Lederboer, Julio Le Parc, François Letailleur, Christopher Logue, Roddy Maude-Roxby, Michael McInnerney, Vanessa de Mestiers, Jacques Monory, Lewis Morley, Dominique Murgia, Annette Nebut (Elle), Gérard Neuvecelle, Claude Nori, Sousse Ohana, Jackie Parry, Hervé Poulain, Martial Raysse, Roger Roche, Wanda Romanowski, Jacques Rouxel, François Sage, Christian Schlatter, Siné, Jean Solé, Daniel Spoerri, Peter Stämpfli, Ralph Steadman, Simon Stuart Smith, Hervé Télémaque, Alice Twemlow, Ivan Tyrell, David Vaughan, Jacques Veuillet (Espace Electra), Jacques and Valérie de La Villeglé, Lara Vinci, Robin Vousden (Anthony d'Offay Gallery), Sarah Walker (The British Council, London), Michael Ward, Gabriel Weissman, Colin St John Wilson, Wolinski.

Gérald Laing,
Brigitte Bardot,
1963, oil on canvas.
Private collection

Did the Sixties really happen?

The decade of the Sixties was a generational phenomenon, and there is a similar generational phenomenon today. Thirty years on, the way we regard those years both benefits and suffers from the fact that we lived through them in our youth. To be sure, those vivid memories mean we can avoid gross misunderstandings of this or that aspect of politics or music, but excessive nostalgia can cloud our memories and introduce unwelcome distortions. These can be countered only by meticulous historical cross-checking.

Everyone thinks that they know the Sixties. In the doubt-filled, crisis-ridden mid-1990s they seem like an oasis radiant with hope, an improbable, mythical period, paradise lost, even – or especially – for younger generations. A dream of earlier times, after dreams of times to come. Let us try to get a clearer picture.

Faced with such a profusion of material we had to make choices. For example, we could quite legitimately have talked about the United States, where the search for a life free of social constraints (the 'beat' culture of the Fifties) was allied with political radicalization (Bob Dylan and the protest song, the opposition to armed involvement in Vietnam). But we have chosen Britain and France because each of these two countries came up with a powerful but different response to the aspirations of youth, Britain through its music ,which flooded across the planet, and France through the political crystallization centred on 1968.

Therefore this book is not a general history of the Sixties. It has focused on two countries and the exchanges between them. That is why authors from either side of the Channel respond to one another and alternate, producing a true comparative vision, something which is unfortunately still only too rare. This comparative vision was something we clearly chose to aim for, as it highlights cultural aspects and innovations.

Two symbolic dates have been chosen as landmarks: 1962 and 1973. The Beatles' first 45 rpm record, *Love me do*, was issued on 5 October 1962 (Ringo Starr had only been with the group since 19 August). *That was the week that was*, the BBC's satirical programme which ushered in a new climate, started in November. In France General de Gaulle was in power, the Algerian War was over, and a new period opened with the Assemblée nationale being dissolved on 10 October and the referendum on whether the President of the Republic should be elected by universal suffrage taking place on 28 October. In 1973 (on 17 October) OPEC (Organization of Petroleum-Exporting Countries) made the unilateral decision to restrict its sales and sharply increase its prices. The western countries were rocked by crisis. Edward Heath's government had to introduce strict rationing. In France the Pompidou years came to an end, as did the post-'68 Left-wing impetus. Music moved on from decadent rock (David Bowie, Roxy Music) to punk (in 1976, after earlier intimations). There was a shift in the point of view.

Between 1962 and 1973 a change in individual behaviour patterns (the hippies) and the collective struggle to overthrow the organization of society within countries that were mostly steeped in ancient traditions followed and even mingled: it was a behavioural revolution and a political revolution producing a variety of effects.

This book has been sub-titled 'the utopian years'. In periods of strong economic growth and with demographic factors such as those associated with the post-war baby boom, it would appear that a powerful desire to change everything develops in some people's minds: consumption, dreams, love, public performance, art and life; a desire to do away with barriers, and in particular for life to be art and art to integrate life, and for the distinction between elitist art and mass-produced goods to be eliminated. These ideas travelled along the sound waves of concerts, recordings on vinyl and in particular radio stations which could cross frontiers. They were printed in magazines, on posters and on record sleeves.

And the icons spoke. Imagination, humour, collage, the baroque and diversion were all at work. Peter Blake played a part in creating the record sleeve for the Beatles' *Sergeant Pepper*, Richard Hamilton in creating that of their double white album, and Marc Boyle perfected light shows for Soft Machine. The creative arts merged and mingled – in France too, through happenings, the desire to bring art on to the street, the search for sexual freedom and the influence of political commitments. Photographers, fashion designers, graphic artists, comic-strip writers, architects, designers, musicians and writers set out the terms of a new way of life.

We obviously cannot attempt to describe such ferment in exhaustive detail, but this book is one step along the way. It goes beyond truisms, combining studies in depth with a rich and exceptional iconography.

As the Sixties become more remote, they undeniably take on a sense of unreality and are given undue weight when contrasted with the current crisis. Yet in the Eighties people laughed at the ideas and activities of the decade because of its naivety. But now we are beginning to have a better understanding of how one part of society had moved into such a breakaway position. Its excesses and failures were on a scale proportionate to the huge aspirations that had been generated. Some people died in the process. But the western world was marked by the shock wave of this 'historic period'. As we approach the new millennium it is important to understand all the pieces that have gone into constructing our contemporary world. We hope that this work may contribute to that understanding, engendering astonishment, gaiety, the pleasure of discovery and the warmth of memory.

DO YOU WANT TO KNOW A SECRET (J'ai un secret à te dire)

TWIST AND SHOUT (Twiste et chante)

SHE LOVES YOU

A TASTE OF HONEY (Un homme est venu)

odeon

SOE 3741

THE BEATLES

One of the first 45 rpm records by the Beatles issued in France in 1963 (the song titles have been translated into French).
Private collection

Contents

'Tomorrow
starts NOW'

At the carnival of Pop culture

A festive future beckoned for British Pop art and culture after its inception at Richard Hamilton's seminal 'fun house' in an exhibition at the Whitechapel Art Gallery in London. Entitled *this is tomorrow*, it opened in the autumn of 1956. The pleasures of modernity had yet to arrive in the still authoritarian, post-war, neo-Elizabethan Britain of the late 1950s, but every aspect of Hamilton's contribution to *this is tomorrow*, suggested an imminent advent, an apocalyptic cultural deregulaton of British culture. It was not for nothing, perhaps, that Hamilton presented, as the dominant figure in a giant collage of Pop imagery, Charlton Heston as Moses in *The Ten Commandments*, leading the people of Israel to the Promised Land. But the moment of metaphoric cultural exodus into the land of Pop did not arrive until the next decade, in 1962.

The Beatles materialized in the second, re-painted version of Adrian Henri's *Entry of Christ into Liverpool* (1962–4), filling the empty place around his transcription of Alfred Jarry's Père Ubu, signifier of twentieth-century mis-rule and a definite stranger to the streets of Lancashire. A student of Richard Hamilton, Henri gathered in the genre of the celebratory group portrait some of the insurgent cultural forces that would transform the Sixties in Britain: the impulse of the radical politics of unilateral nuclear disarmament (CND, which claimed the allegiance of Hamilton, Hockney and Henri) in the Ban-the-Bomb banners; the ambivalent embrace of promotional culture (the advertisements); Pop and jazz music personified by the Beatles, Charlie Parker and Charles Mingus (themselves signs of a certain anti-racism). Local Liverpool painters and poets join these culture heroes at the front of a vast demonstration which has echoes of the panoramic Socialist triumph of Pelizza da Volpedo's *Il quatro stato* (1901). Like that painting it is a portent of an inevitable coming-to-power: in the case of Adrian Henri's picture it is the carnival emancipation of representatives of a popular culture, an emancipation which is simultaneously bohemian and media sophisticated; it is adept at juggling citations as it looks back to a sardonic modernity – Ensor as culted figure in sun-glasses – which had never fully arrived to transform imperial and post-imperial British culture. Thus an epochal cultural and social liberation is mimed as a popular, carnivalesque event in Liverpool's city centre in a scene of civic transformation that forecasts Peter Blake's design for *Sergeant Pepper* in 1967.

As he concluded his great gathering painting in 1964, Adrian Henri honoured and centrally inserted the Beatles, not only because they were local celebrities but because they had been the chief agents in effecting cultural liberation on a national and – as 1964 proceeded – an increasingly global scale. By the summer of 1964 the Beatles had definitively re-located from Liverpool to London, in an uncomfortable acknowledgement of British metro-centricity. Peter Blake began his group portrait of them in 1963, their *annus mirabilis*, and it was completed in 1968; it contained an immediate nostalgia for a climactic moment of Pop, arguably at the point of exhaustion of this utopian trajectory in British culture. It invokes, in the circled Art Deco-vernacular centre of the four compartmented composition, their talismanic name and the year 1962, the moment of advent, their unveiled, originating self-constitution and also Year One of the Pop art revolution in London, inaugurated in March by Ken Russell's TV film for the BBC of Blake, Pauline Boty, Peter Phillips and Derek Boshier, *Pop goes the easel*. These artists were depicted by Russell as part of a youthful group, visually and sonically at ease with mass culture, moving through a festive London of parties, circuses, wrestling matches and street markets to the background of Pop music, the first use of such a soundtrack in an arts documentary. Blake's Beatles are manipulated, colour-screened photo-images from their publicity repertoire, painted using the disfiguring pictorial structures of Francis Bacon; they are already a hybrid part of the fine-art/Pop-art continuum, that 'long front of culture' about which Lawrence Alloway had theorized at the turn of the decade. As with Andy Warhol's analogous revolution that used silkscreened promotional photographs in the summer of 1962, the essential vehicle and currency of publicity – the halftone and screened photograph – now acquired centrality within a displaced and drastically redefined field of figurative painting, whose iconography had migrated to the dramas of the zones that were by some regarded as 'low', television, cinema and Pop music.

Photograph by Lewis Morley, *Spotty Muldoon*, 1965. Courtesy National Portrait Gallery, London. © Lewis Morley/Akehurst Bureau

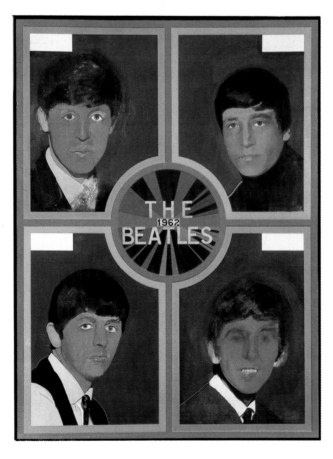

The enigmatic photographer

Adrian Henri had placed the photographer Phillip Jones-Griffiths, a future chronicler of the Vietnam War, on the front row of his *Entry of Christ...*, and the figure of the male photographer – in fashion and reportage – was to take on heroic connotations in the changed landscape of London in the mid-Sixties. Michelangelo Antonioni's *Blow-up* fused the practices and mannerisms of David Bailey's acidic libertinism and Don McCullin's abject horror. Like the Forties' detective of hard-boiled fiction, the Sixties' London photographer was licensed to intrude across cultural and class boundaries with an unprecedented mobility: photographers were perceived to be close to the heart of the new society which was in formation and preoccupied with image-making. The marriage of photographer Antony Armstrong-Jones to Princess Margaret in 1960 confirmed this, as had such literary fictions as Colin MacInnes's *Absolute Beginners* (1959). Ralph Steadman's ironic caricature *New London cries* displayed one such 'class-less', T-shirted photographer abusing his female model: 'I said I'm going to put your face on the front page of *Vogue*, you stupid old cow!' The director Michelangelo Antonioni, shooting the film *Blow-up* in London in 1966, imagined just such a Baileyesque young

observed phenomena, supplemented by photography and the experience of human identity, were brought to a pitch by Hamilton in his painting *People* (1965–6). Here, photomechanical screening processes are blown up – in anticipation of Antonioni's *Blow-up* – to arrive at grotesque and phantasmic forms, where orthodox human representations disappear in the allusive technical veils of the media.

Above:

Nicholas Ferguson,

montage for *Ready, Steady,*

***Go!*, 1964.**

Private collection

photographer thrown into an existential maelstrom, as a 'Swinging London' parkland pastorale became the scenography for a murder that was elusively visible on his 35 mm film – but only as a blurred, fugitive, untrustworthy image. (The painterly homologues used in the film were abstract paintings made by another of Richard Hamilton's ex-students, Ian Stephenson.)

The photographer's view upon the world had become the site of profound ontological enquiry and as a culture hero he became, in the London of the Sixties, the dandified – but remasculinized – heir to the great modernist explorers of visual doubt. Richard Hamilton had been assured of this since 1963, when he apostrophized a colour close-up shot of female lips by Richard Avedon. With his *Fashion plate* series of 1969, Hamilton scrupulously negotiated terrain between the promotional activity of contemporary fashion photography modelling and the deconstructive strategies of early modernist Cubism. But doubts over the coherence and signification of

Richard Hamilton,
People, 1965–6, oil and
mixed media.
Courtesy the artist

The choreographed image

It was the interstitial professionals in image-making areas such as magazine and editorial photography and design – that constituency which Hamilton admired and still belonged to – who surged to the forefront of that triumphant entry into a utopian prospect of youth and modernity in London in 1963–5. Nowhere was this more salient than in the juncture between TV and the Pop music industry exemplified by the ground-breaking Associated Rediffusion TV programme, *Ready, Steady, Go!*, which began in July 1963 and ended in December 1966. The Slade School trained artist Nicholas Ferguson acted as designer for the series, which showcased Pop groups in the surroundings of a small TV studio with a live audience. His acheivements in pressing into service the developing visual languages of the London-based Pop artists for a nationally networked, mass youth audience were crucial to the fashioning of a synaesthetia of TV fragmentation,

Brechtian theatrical space and commercial Pop music. Influenced equally by the East End stage experiments of Joan Littlewood, the Berliner Ensemble and the pictorial collage aesthetic of Peter Blake and Derek Boshier, Ferguson deployed gigantic photomontages amongst *rostra* on which the musicians performed, in the midst of a participating audience. The spectacle, as realized by the TV director, Michael Lindsay-Hogg, was a vivid vision-mixing cyclorama of montaged signs, performers and dynamized dancing consumers – the negation of the established TV Pop music display format, which up to then had regarded as necessary the segregation of the audience from the performers on the stage. Youth was seen to be inextricably attached to media technologies, possessed by a kind of nihilism, according to its detractors, and lampooned by Lewis Morley's portrait of the transistor-radio-clutching teenager with his head stuck in a brown paper bag, the mute and nugatory *Spotty Muldoon* (1965).

Derek Boshier and
Christopher Logue, 'Sex
War Sex Cars Sex,
1966, screenprint.
Private collection

Scandals: Dismantling national roles and identities

Morley worked closely with the main channels of the 'satire industry' in London from 1961 to 1967: for the Establishment Club in Soho (which also utilized Brechtian techniques in its performances); the BBC TV programme *That was the week that was;* and also the key satire magazine *Private Eye*. He photographed Christine Keeler in his studio above the Establishment Club, representing her in the role of a cabaret stripper, before the scandal broke publicly over her liaison with the Secretary of State for War in June 1963. These pictures were pastiches of pin-up and pornographic genres and very soon became contentious, flagrant images which seriously undermined the Conservative government's claims to high moral authority and rectitude. While *Ready, Steady, Go!* announced an intense, hyper-kinetic culture of media-enhanced festivity and consumption, *Private Eye* comically portrayed a certain political elite in anachronistic and monstrous stasis, corrupt and moribund, through the caricatures of Ralph Steadman and Gerald Scarfe. But in fact the entire social spectrum was open to comic graphic satire by Steadman, including the leading paragons of the new 'trendy' culture, photographers and Pop singers. Revivalism and an attachment to the continuities of visual modes across the long centuries of British cultural history marked the sensibility of Sixties satire. Just as Peter Blake reopened the options on Victorian graphic conventions, so William Hogarth's series of prints from the 1730s, *Marriage à la Mode*, was the explicit model for Steadman's updated anatomization of narrative details of contemporary fashionable taste, dress and behaviour in the London suburbs around the North Circular Road in *Private Eye* in 1965. While Morley represented

Ralph Steadman,
Marriage à la mode, **1964.**
Courtesy the artist

excessive and awkward postures in self-fashioning, Steadman concentrated on creating full-blown grotesque images of a range of types from current British society, whose bodily strata bulge and are soiled: the disenchanted middle-aged, as well as the lumpen-rockers.

The *Private Eye* group of satirists – recruited from well-established public schools and old universities – were also fundamentally at odds with the forces of modernization signalled by the arrival in government of Harold Wilson's Labour Party in October 1964, and its avowed creation of an advanced, liberal, technologized consumer culture. In the course of 1965 Prime Minister Wilson was seen, by many Socialist intellectuals and former CND supporters, to be inexcusably supporting the US government's intervention in Vietnam. This aspect of British 'bad conscience' surfaces in the comic-strip poster, 'Sex War Sex Cars Sex', produced by the poet and *Private Eye* contributor Christopher Logue and the Pop painter and *Ready, Steady, Go! habitué* Derek Boshier in 1966. Distributed in an unlimited edition through the fashionable youth clothing shop Gear, as well as via other London boutiques and directly through *Private Eye*, the poster anticipated the ambivalent erotics and horrors of J.G. Ballard's *Crash!* It surveyed a panorama of news-media terrors – on the highways and roads, as well as in Vietnam. The stage was set for Jean-Luc Godard's film *Weekend* of the following year: the 'warfare state' of regulated capitalism is figured in comic-book frames as speeding to catastrophe and inter-personal violence. Derived from Roy Leichtenstein's formalized epics, the poster by Logue and Boshier perpetrated a comic-strip narrative, comparable with Situationist posters of the the following year which offered provocative synoptic narratives of *le décor spectaculaire* and its manifold sites of tension.

(the assertion of the Asian immigrant community's identity) were highly formative: 'We all went to Bradford Art College and I think we have been influenced by the Pakistanis who live there. They like to paint their houses in bright colours,...they have a much better colour sense than most English people'.[1] They became media celebrities in themselves, exhibiting an AC Cobra sports car which they had painted at the Robert Fraser Gallery and collaborating with Paul McCartney on his 'Million Volt Light and Sound Rave' at the Roundhouse in January 1967. It was at this point that Dudley Edwards decorated McCartney's piano with the trademark BEV mix of motifs from Art Deco, Peter Blake, bargees and the circus, in the speciality Flamboyant paint used by fairground artists. In this proto-*Sergeant Pepper* style, BEV, like Peter Blake and the Beatles, were perceived as arcadians of the mythical Swinging London metropolitan landscape, innovative cultural producers who could combine modernity and conservatism; one of their first patrons, an advertising boss, described them as 'brash, arrogant, yet traditional'.[2]

Allen Jones, *Bus*, 1966, colour lithograph. Courtesy the artist

Photograph by Martin Cook of the upright piano for Paul McCartney decorated by BEV (Douglas Binder, Dudley Edwards and David Vaughan), 1966. Private collection

Arcadia

The pleasures rather than the satirized terrors of tomorrow and the future could be realized by the multitude of strategies circulating around Pop art's embrace of media imagery and the great remnants of a utopian visual vernacular of popular festivity and ceremonial from the past and from ethnically diverse signs. The young, male decorative design co-operative known as BEV (Douglas Binder, Dudley Edwards and David Vaughan), which came to prominence in the last months of 1965, revived the early Modernist project of Roger Fry's Omega Workshop of 1913. Their agenda of decorating ready-made furniture possessed the idyllic register of Fry's Bloomsbury and found a similar range of sources: the circus, exotic 'ethnic' motifs and synthetic Fauve colouring; it was for the entertainment of a liberal metropolitan elite – Antony Armstrong-Jones, David Bailey and Henry Moore – whose purchase of BEV decorations reached the gossip columns and feature articles of the national daily papers. BEV, like the Beatles, was composed of northern cultural insurgents from a place where the relics of the industrial revolution (barge paintings) and imperial legacies

Painted Asian
doorways, Bradford,
Yorkshire, 1965.
Courtesy Dudley
Edwards

The epiphany of psychedelia

By late in 1966 that mobility of skills in London – between painting, decoration, poster-making, dress-making, tailoring and Pop musicianship – had resulted in what could be called 'pan-Pop', a situation where individuals could cross over between particular roles, creating across and within a number of networks contexts that became known as the 'underground'. Blake and Jan Haworth's work on the *Sergeant Pepper* tableau; *Private Eye* artist Barry Fantoni's compering of the Pop-chat show, *A whole scene going*; and, equally, Michael English and Nigel Weymouth's careers as poster artists and as members of a Pop group, under the same name – Hapshash and The Coloured Coat – were all examples of this transferability. Particular institutions – boutiques such as Gear, for whom

Photograph by John Claxton for the light show 'The Sensual Laboratory liquid light projection' by Mark Boyle and Joan Hills, 1967. Courtesy Mark Boyle and Joan Hills

Logue and English produced work; the psychedelic clothes shop Granny Takes a Trip; and the UFO Club, all run by enlightened entrepreneurs (Tom Slater, for example, at Gear) – were linked and developed and marketed objects and styles, aided by multi-skilled practitioners. A certain synaesthesia might be identified as the central cultural project, and in the hands of the artists Mark Boyle and Joan Hills light projection was brought to a height of expressivity. Calling themselves the Sensual Laboratory, Boyle and Hills pioneered 'liquid light environments', with sound and music, first at the UFO Club, which opened in London in December 1966, and collaborated with the experimental Pop group the Soft Machine. An animated biomorphism reproduced the flows and palpations of bodily experience on a massive, cinematic scale. The psychedelic style which was being formed in London by early 1967 drew upon a range of referents and codes: the organicism of the supra-individual body; attempted analogues for narcotic experiences; and techniques of excess – such as the use of ultra-violet light, Day-Glo flourescent inks and Flamboyant paint. Finally, psychedelicism, as a distinctive visual style in London, depended upon a flexible scavenging of the archives of a

Michael McInnerney, 'Legalise Pot Rally', 1967, silkscreen print. Private collection

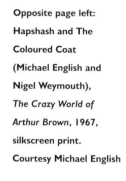

Modernist art history that was beginning to acknowledge Art Nouveau graphics as significant, as at the time of the Victoria and Albert Museum's important Aubrey Beardsley exhibition in the summer of 1966; Nigel Weymouth admitted, 'One of our seminal influences was the Beardsley exhibition ... we'd sit around and look at Mucha and Beardsley in the National Art Library at the V&A'.[3]

The impact of Beardsley's biomorphic designs was apparent across an entire spectrum of contemporary graphics, from Alan Aldridge's editorial art-work for the *Sunday Times* colour magazine to Michael McInnerney's poster advertising the 'Legalise Pot Rally' in July 1967. McInnerney liquified a flat, red, monumental human figure, a patriarch-cum-wizard with a passing resemblence to Karl Marx (McInnerney had been involved in the radical community politics of Notting Hill). In one hand this magician holds a joss stick or an attenuated marijuana cigarette which generates a cloud of hypnagogic sleeping faces, in the other a crystal ball in front of his left eye. Bars of radiance emerge from his eye as a sunburst, which metamorphoses into waves and finally droplets. Winged, angelic creatures and wildly feathered birds ascend from a lower, vegetal world into the upper zone of a Blakeian vision, like one of Phillip Otto Runge's sacred-naive diagrams of the spiritual world.

McInnerney's Merlin-like figure, with smoke, beams and waves in his hair, is a mythic giant (evidence, also, of the poster artists' absorption in the Celticist esotericism of certain Art Nouveau paradigms). He is the equal of that native American in a Sioux chieftan headdress, in the company of fairyland dragons, who appears as a colossal persona for Jimi Hendrix in the Hapshash-designed poster 'Hendrix at the Fillmore'. Hendrix supervised English and Weymouth in this design, insistent that he should be represented at his first appearence at the key US psychedelic venue by a distinctively London poster, rather than by an example of San Francisco-based graphics. Hendrix's links to the artists involved in the London psychedelic vanguard were markedly strong; on his second tour of the United States in the late spring of 1968, he was accompanied by Mark Boyle and Joan Hills, who projected their 'liquid light environments' at his concerts across the continent.

Very possibly the most extraordinary performer of this moment, in 1967, was the musician Arthur Brown. Like BEV and Peter Blake, Arthur Brown effected a combination of urban folkloric sumptuary ornamentation with the decors of contemporary consumption and excess. His *noir* presence fused 'old English' pantomime conventions with the 'destruction in art' tenets of visceral and dangerous presentations of the self. To this he added mythological and occultist narratives – like Blake's parodic portrait of Marianne Faithfull as the Arthurian witch Morgan le Fay, intertwined with dragons, in his unlimited edition poster 'Morgan le Faythfull', which was sold through the broadsheet *Daily Telegraph*. 'The Crazy World of Arthur Brown' poster was an extravagant, satanic, bat's-winged, silkscreen design by Hapshash – English and Weymouth – which also successfully subverted the image of

Mickey Mouse, depicting him in the moment of injecting himself with heroin. The decorous conventions of the graphic world were turned upside down in a tactic similar to contemporary transgressive antics in the USA in the Grove Press publications of *Snow White and the Seven Dwarfs* and in Robert Crumb's reconciliation of genial comic strip figures within a blighted cultural climate. This British variant of Pop unfolded an infantile landscape of gratifications and guignol, with the English sensibility of bizarre whimsy – itself a gentle form of the carnivalesque – as the major structuring device. It was when the London psychedelic *avant-garde* was transplanted across the Channel in the month of November 1967 that they chose the format of a massive event at the Palais des Sport called 'La Fenêtre Rose'. Boyle and Hill's Sensual Laboratory, the Soft Machine, the Pop group Tomorrow, David Medalla's dance ensemble, The Exploding Galaxy and the 'inflatables' performers, Jeffrey Shaw and his Plastic Circus, were all represented by a poster which was the joint work of Michael McInnerney and Dudley Edwards, who had now submerged their identity together as Omtentacle. In a kind of late survival of Tchelitchevian neo-Romanticism, the poster displayed a youthful male head; the physiognomy was composed of a tree trunk and a canopy of leafy hair, an occultly enlightened brain which appeared to be dissolving into a patterned geodesic dome – an iconographic citation of the London underground's fascination for the utopian US architect Buckminster Fuller.

Poster by Omtentacle (Dudley Edwards and Michael McInnerney), 'La Fenêtre Rose', 1967, screenprint. Courtesy Dudley Edwards

Grotesque corporeality
and the decline of the utopian underground

The depiction of outlandish and grotesque versions of the body could have a corrosive, critical and satiric function that was distant from such whimsical utopias as 'La Fenêtre Rose'. Psychedelia depended primarily on visual disturbances, anamorphoses and what could be called the perspectives of narcosis. The debt to a certain satanic English Romanticism of the early nineteenth century, evident in contemporary dandyism and revivals of the occult, could entail a condition which de Quincy had recognized, in visual experience: 'Space swelled and was amplified'.[4] When this occurred, the experiencing body also swelled and fell into component parts. It was dismembered, just as Ralph Steadman and Gerald Scarfe had represented it. In March 1966 the photographer Robert Whitaker dressed the Beatles in white butchers' coats, sat them as if in a group portrait and arranged joints of slaughtered beef and pig about their bodies. He did this in conscious disruption of the conventions surrounding orthodox Pop star promotional photography. John Lennon claimed the Beatles' own input into this session, which resulted in the notorious 'butchers' cover': 'Bob (Whitaker) was into Dali and making Surrealist pictures .... It was inspired by our boredom and resentment at having to do another photo session and another Beatles thing. We were sick to death of it .... That combination produced the cover'.[5] Their manager, Brian Epstein, who had given Whitaker free rein in crafting publicity images for them, had, correctly as it turned out, profound 'misgivings'[6] over this transgression of the codified image, but he was overruled by the Beatles. Printed as the cover for their LP album *Yesterday and today*, an initial 750,000 were produced; but the provocation had succeeded – American disc jockeys were, it was reported to Epstein, 'almost retching',[7] and a decision was made hastily to withdraw the cover. Now banned as a result of the squeamishness of certain US opinion makers, a reporter at a press conference asked Lennon whether it was a gratuitous image. It was, the reply came, '...as relevant as Vietnam'.[8] The larger violence in the world was invoked by Lennon, as it contemporaneously was by Logue and Boshier in 'Sex War Sex Cars Sex', and four months before in Peter Hall's Theatre of Cruelty tableaux about Vietnam, and in his production *US* at the Royal Court

Photograph by Martin Sharp of Peter Draffin holding a Martin Sharp 'Smile on a stick' and Robert Whitaker driving a Mini Moke in Paris, 1966. Courtesy Robert Whitaker

Photograph by Lewis Morley of Catherine Deneuve and David Bailey at a fashion show, London, 1965. Courtesy Lewis Morley and National Portrait Gallery, London. © Lewis Morley/ Akehurst Bureau

The sixties, utopian years

Theatre, which entailed the killing on stage of butterflies as metaphors for the military slaughter.

Here was a visceral and sardonic side to that great saturnalia, that overturning of established British (and American) customs, in the festivities and feasts that constituted 'Swinging London'. Mikhail Bakhtin's claims for the significance of such an iconography revolved around the

celebration of mortality and carnality: '... in an atmosphere of Mardi Gras, revelling, dancing, music were all closely combined with the slaughter, dismemberment, bowels, excrement and other images ....'[9] For Whitaker, another aspect of the 'butchers' cover' was for him to realize the carnality and mortality of those cosmic stars the Beatles. He wished to counter their idealized, spectacularly transcendentalized status by stressing their grimaces, their gross

materiality, their flesh and blood, in order to mock corporate pomp and vanity. Such an abject casting down of social idols and roles was crucial to the contemporary 'Anti-Psychiatry' ideas of the visionary R.D. Laing at the Kingsley Hall community in London in 1966. Gabriel Weissman, then a final year fine art student at the Chelsea School of Art, gravitated to this Mecca of psychedelic and libertarian attitudes to mental health. He exhibited his painting *Brain drain* (a phrase used to denote the flight of talent from English institutions to the USA) there in the following year. In this grotesque portrait, the hyperbolic teeth (like Martin Sharp's clowning 'Smile on a stick') and dissolving facial contours, together with chemically reduced pupils, were indicated by graffiti spray-can lines, a figurative appropriation of Bernard

Cohen's Art Nouveau-derived spray paintings. When Hornsey College of Art rose in revolt in May 1968, its Atelier Populaire-influenced posters presented a similar image of explosive inner illumination within the head – a confined, blooming flower – and the words, 'Tomorrow starts NOW'. This epiphanic seizure of the present, this *jet-zeit*, was not to be sustained. The spectral, hallucinatory scenarios of J.G. Ballard, especially in his novel *The crystal world*

The sixties, utopian years

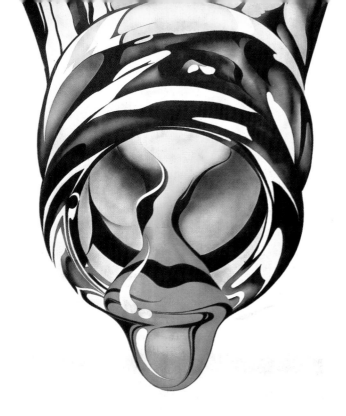

Michael English, *Syrup*, 1970, gouache and ink on board. Courtesy the artist

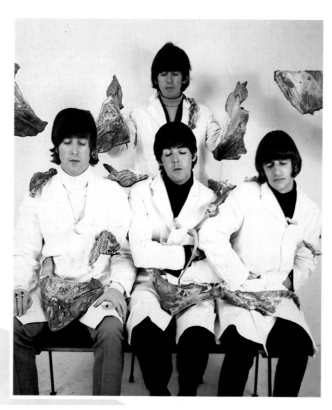

Photograph by Robert Whitaker, censored cover for a Beatles' album called 'the butchers' cover', 1966. Courtesy Robert Whitaker

– bodied forth in Ivan Tyrell's apocalyptic poster design 'The illuminated man' – lapsed. Ballard turned to the automotive fantasies of death and disaster in *Crash*, paralleled by his own, serial photographs of the car crash he had experienced in his Ford Zephyr in 1970. Michael English passed from the artificial paradises of Day-Glo ink and Beardsleyan polymorphous perversity to the harsh fetishes of his photo-realist and spray paintings of 1969 and 1970, where the world of commodities struggles free and stands embellished, nullifying the promises and metaphysics of a radiant future.

David Alan Mellor

1. '81, the story of a street number 10-feet high', *The Sun*, 22 December 1965.
2. Ibid.
3. Nigel Weymouth in conversation with the author, London, 22 February 1992.
4. T. de Quincy, *Confessions of an English opium eater*, 1821, p. 236.
5. Quoted by M. Harrison in *The unseen Beatles: Photographs by Robert Whitaker*, 1991, p.148.
6. P. Norman, *Shout: The true story of the Beatles*, 1982, p. 278.
7. Ibid.
8. Ibid.
9. M. Bakhtin, *Rabelais and his world*, 1984, pp. 223–4.

J.G. Ballard photographs,
*Ford Zephyr after a car
crash*, 1970.
Courtesy J.G. Ballard

The art scene in France, 1960–73

In the nineteenth century, disciples of Saint-Simon had a prophetic vision of art, seeing artists as the guides of civilian society, with their vanguard – or *avant-garde* – being in the best position to change the world. This idea inevitably emerges during consideration of the art scene in France between 1960 and 1973, when it played a very prophetic role, stirred up by a radical protest movement well before the May '68 rebellion. While it is true that other elements in society seemed to presage profound upheavals, the art scene called for action involving very special violence and imagination, opening up a wide range of new *situations*. As the still authoritarian and patriarchal European societies blossomed economically, especially their consumerism, artists and some intellectuals responded by saying that everything had to be rethought, first in the ways in which reality was interpreted along with all the codes, visual and otherwise, of language and communication. This essay aims to disinter some of their *positions*, which will be supplemented in the next chapter by those identified by Laurent Gerverau with reference to different artistic trends.[1]

Some fine happenings in prospect

Between the end of the Fifties and the start of the Seventies, greeting the age of the media, artists of the extreme *avant-garde* took exception to the manipulative function of words and images. Following on from Dada and the Surrealists, and in the footsteps of Marxism, psychoanalysis and the young social sciences, they wanted to get shot of the old terms used in communication, which were seen as vestiges of an outdated world controlled by the Establishment, an Establishment that was disputed whether it took the form of authoritarian Gaullism or the modern democracy of Georges Pompidou. Moreover, the protesters decided to question culture and art, which in a way were acting as parrots for the existing Establishment and employing the same language.

From the end of the Fifties there had been a tremendous reactivation of the plans nurtured by the *avant-garde* at the beginning of the century, plans to metamorphose a world it regarded as intolerable. But whereas earlier the revolution had violently attacked inertia, in the Sixties the cries of rebellion became so effective that the norms were shaken

and the Establishment itself swayed, briefly leaving artists to take command. Too much should not be read into this: there were no coherent troops of artists, strictly representative and acting together, who spelt out any properly predetermined plan. For the most part actions were spontaneous, sporadic, simultaneous and not necessarily visible. Often they seemed to observers, even attentive observers, to have no immediate impact, and they took place more or less all over France, in Paris, in the provinces, in traditional and untraditional locations alike, even on the streets. Those trends that are interesting now, New Realism, GRAV, happenings and Fluxus, Conceptual art, BMPT and Supports-Surfaces, progressed and demonstrated every conceivable difference as well as some definite, converging ideas: breaking with all artistic tradition, including modern artistic tradition, and with the sense that art is unique, sacred and inaccessible to the public; revealing to one and all the condition of the artist; dispensing with the Establishment, and all forms mediating between artists and the public; uncovering the reverse side of art, the 'repressed' side of art, as well as social and individual repression; moving towards an objectivity which would finally end all Romanticism.

It is customary to repeat that nobody foresaw May '68. In fact the stirrings of rebellion were perceptible well before then, even in the national press which served to echo the turmoil of protest. In 1966, in an introduction to a survey by Évelyne Sullerot on the 'mouvement provo' (provocative tendency), Georges Belmont commented ironically on the kind of society being offered to sceptical youth:

> One which is in fact collapsing on every side today? Typified by narrow-minded, outdated capitalism fighting rearguard actions and crossing swords with the Prime Minister himself when he wants to raise the school-leaving age and extend training? A society which is stupid enough not even to be capable of providing housing for young couples? Consisting of middle classes that no longer even have the virtue of pretending they believe in its hypocrisies and taboos? .... Verily, verily, I say unto you that all these things will lead to trouble before they are resolved. We have some fine 'happenings' in prospect.[2]

The aim of the 'provos', new anarchists, was: 'To influence public opinion, to hit out, to force each and every person

Jacques de la Villeglé, *Rue Mayet*, 8 August 1962, torn posters. Artist's collection

Left: Arman,
Poubelle ménagère,
1960, accumulation
of household rubbish
under Plexiglas.
Galerie Beaubourg
collection, Paris

to unmask their latent ideology and their concealed authoritarianism'. Évelyne Sullerot proposed getting to grips with them there and then, or risk ending up one day being 'provoked', forced to react 'in the heat of the moment, during a riot, wearing the highly unattractive mask of narrow-minded authoritarianis'.[3]

Where the future prospect was concerned, the Situationists were in the best position, having ploughed the

extended to all habitable planets'. They wanted to set up an 'art of dialogue' and 'interaction' which would reintegrate the artist into the social fabric. This would surely happen, they believed, as, in this new culture of

total communication ... with everyone becoming an artist at a high level, i.e. inseparably producer and consumer of a total cultural creation, we will soon witness the rapid dissolution of the linear criterion of novelty. Once everyone is, so to speak,

Right: César,
Blanc-rose, 1972,
mural compression
made from Plexiglas.
Galerie Beaubourg
collection, Paris

fields of rebellion in every direction since 1958, the first year when *L'Internationale situationniste* was published. In their manifesto directed against the capitalist world of show business they established the foundations of a new culture based on 'total participation'[4] and a form of 'pure present' that denounced the 'world of deprivation' and 'art preserved', promoting instead 'the directly experienced moment' and temporary situations constructed according to their wishes. The Situationists were opposed to 'compartmentalized art' and in favour of 'collective, no doubt anonymous production (at least as far as is possible, since works will not be stocked like commodities for sale and this culture will not be dominated by the need to leave its spoor)'; and of 'a revolution in behaviour and unitary, dynamic town-planning capable of expanding right across the planet, and then being

a Situationist, we will witness a multi-dimensional inflation of radically different trends, experiments and schools, not in succession but simultaneously.

Well before this revolutionary programme had been implemented, the art scene in France was still an exploration site where every group had to fight for existence.

Modern nature

Since the Fifties artists had been trying to establish new tactics for appropriating reality. Going back only to 1959 when the first Paris Biennale was inaugurated by André Malraux, the Minister for Culture, they caused the ritual scandal always essential for the legitimation of an *avant-*

garde. A year before the official birth of 'New Realism' (1960) Yves Klein had exhibited a large unframed monochrome painting of Jacques de la Villeglé, his posters torn by anonymous passers-by; François Dufrêne had showed his first posters viewed from the wrong side; and Raymond Hains had shown a *Palissade des emplacements réservés* (Stockade of reserved sites). Finally on the forecourt of the Musée d'Art moderne de la Ville de Paris Jean Tinguely had installed his big *Méta-matic 17*, a car-like machine with an engine which spat out drawings cut up by mechanical scissors and exhaust fumes collected by a balloon which exploded, releasing the smell of petrol and violets.

Following this Biennale Tinguely was invited to the *Art, machines and motion* exhibition by the Kaplan Gallery in London, and two days before he arranged to give a lecture entitled 'Static, static, static! Be static' at the Institute of Contemporary Arts. The lecture had been tape-recorded in Paris but was incomprehensible if only because two recordings were superimposed on top of one another at different speeds. During the evening a young woman walked through the audience operating a manual *Méta-matic* and handing out its drawings, while two racing cyclists were pitted against one another on one *Super-cyclo-Méta-matic* which produced one and a half kilometres of paper. That same year Tinguely scattered 1500 tracts over Düsseldorf from an aeroplane proclaiming that 'everything moves' and 'there is no immobility'[,5] advising the people to stop letting themselves be terrorized by outdated ideas, demanding that they should cease 'reaffirming "values" which are collapsing all the same', calling for 'an end to the building of cathedrals and pyramids which nonetheless collapse like cards' and for people to live 'in and on their time for a beautiful, total reality'. At this stage Tinguely's discourse related to the *pure present* but it was soon to shift. Meanwhile his actions and projects, straddling nascent New Realism, happenings and Kinetic art, were couched in the terms of the artistic debate of the Sixties. With exceptional ironic distance, following in the footsteps of Dada, he dismantled the traditional objects of the art world, the unique work of art, the crafted product of the artist's genius, and its traditional presentation. He opened a window on spectacle, the anonymity of the artist, public participation, on the move away from painting, on the belief in permanent movement, on the rejection of all nos-

talgia, on the poetic, on the sarcastic diversion of the machine and on the modern tools of communication.

New Realism was established as an active group in 1960, legitimizing randomly dispersed gestures that were incomprehensible in the still 'pictural' climate of the day. In April 1960 the critic Pierre Restany wrote the preface to the group's first exhibition in Milan, synthesizing the contradictory streams then flowing, especially in the extremely effervescent environment of the social sciences. The group's new perception of reality came from an empirical use of sociology; the actions involved in storing records of reality in all its forms were dependent on neutral sociological observation, heated by an expressive euphoria and renewed, as it were, by galloping modernity. The actions of the New Realists meant turning their backs on what had dominated the art scene in the Fifties: lyrical Abstract Expressionism in the aftermath of the war, thought to embody a regressive flight from reality. In fact the New Realists, for all their confrontation with contemporary daily reality, were far from carrying out cold and objective observation.

Arman produced 'accumulations', made lyrical by repetition, a lyricism enhanced when he used worn-out objects that referred back to an individual or a collective memory. His cups, his sawings, his combustions and especially his *Colères* – violent destructions of symbolic objects such as a grand piano (1962) carried out in public – were saturated with expression. The same is true of César with his

The sixties, utopian years

squashed cars – and Renault made no mistake when they collaborated with him from 1965 (and with Arman in 1967); nor did Rochas perfumes when they bought his monumental breast of a dancing girl from the Crazy Horse Saloon (1966) or the Saint-Cyr Military School when it adopted his huge fist (1969).

Even when the objects were used mockingly, as for example by Gérard Deschamps – the 'bananas' (military decorations transposed on to coloured gratings, 1965) – once they had been made into artistic pieces they achieved a sort of grandeur: the same applies to his enlarged waxed cloths or his iridescent metal sheets which had originally been used to insulate jet engines on planes (1964).

The torn posters by Villeglé, Hains and Rotella, and Dufrêne's back-to-front posters, following on from the Dadaists and the Surrealists, Léo Malet and Johannes Baader, reconstituted the poetry of subverted writing, of towns and their collective memory. This also applies to Villeglé's street walks, his socio-political graphic works (1969) or Hains's puns, his work on the Ultra-lettre, his grooved glass and his *Palissade* ('lapalissade' = self-evident truth), and the torn posters of both men relating to and opposing the Algerian War, which were imbued with political emotion.

Daniel Spoerri straddled New Realism and Fluxus. He was a dancer, stage designer, concrete poet, restorer and haunter of flea markets full of remembered objects who trapped 'situations found by accident', 'as they were, whatever their medium': remains of meals in his *Tableaux-pièges* (1959) or *Multiplicateurs d'art* (1963) where a mirror is the support. When he withdrew in 1966 it was to concentrate

on the magic powers of the object and produce his *Conserves de magie à la noix* (1968). When he invented 'eat art', in 1963 transforming the Galerie J into a restaurant – with himself as chef and the art critics as waiters, with his *Menus-pièges* – it was again with a tremendously expressive, provocative and sometimes horrified sense of reality; or when he caught children's shoes in rat traps (*Les Dangers de la multiplication*, 1971), or dug out his *Investigations criminelles*, horrific police photographs the sight of which 'chilled

Martial Raysse, *Jolie comme tout*, 1962, mixed media on paper with powder-puff. Nathalie Seroussi collection

in worship, on gilded wood. Her monumental *Nanas* (1965), which people could enter (1966), were devouring, purely imaginary *Nana dream houses* (1967).

Klein was the most mystical and lyrical of the group, in the multiplication of his famous blue monochromes (1957) or *Monogold* (1960), his *Peintures-feu* (1957) when he attached flares to a blue monochrome, which he lit at the opening of the show, in his *Immatériels* when the bare walls of his gallery were brought to life solely by his presence (1958), in his experiments with live paint-brushes, when he daubed naked women with blue paint (1958), or his *Cosmogones*, paintings made with atmospheric elements, rain and wind (1960). Martial Raysse with his beauty in 'bad taste' perhaps came closest to chilling the artistic gesture, though his continuing ironic comments on the consumer society, especially in his female portraits, did not fundamentally undermine it as a formidable machine for fantasizing. The same is true of Christo's wrappings, an idea he got from Bulgaria where students like himself were taken on by the department of propaganda to camouflage anything that might sully the landscape on the route of the Orient Express.

In fact rather than aspiring towards neutrality the New Realists set out to transform modern consumer society into an emotional poetic reservoir of so far unexploited wealth. While they had all agreed on the term 'New Realism', it was a 'new realism of pure sensibility',[6] 'immersed in direct expressivity up to its neck and 40° above Dada as zero'.[7]

Their rapid legitimation was ensured by their violent programmatic break with the dominant trend of warm, material-bound abstraction, accompanied by formidable individual

his blood', but which he could not bring himself to part with. Tinguely also had established his interest in 'junk' work, collecting anything that could be used in his Kinetic pieces glorifying the eternal movement of things and fundamental chaos: his monstrous machine *Narva* (1961), *Baloubas, études pour une fin du monde* (1962), *Radio-sculptures* (1963), *Chariots géants* (1964), his big ultra-fast *Copulatrices* and *Masturbatrices* (1965) and *Rotozazas* (1967) which invited the viewer to play ball with them or broke objects. Niki de Saint-Phalle subverted *Autels, Choeurs, Cathédrales* (1962) in *L'Autel OAS* for example, where objects associated with war and violence were mixed up with objects used

energy – they were no exception to the old romantic requirement for artists to be charismatic. The group was composed of strong personalities capable of generating astonishment and diversity. There were thirteen of them (not counting Restany), and they proved capable of playing on a number of registers without going against the initial basic plan of appropriating modern reality. They were intent on conveying cold and heat, the contemporary world and its ludicrous fragility, the pure present and memory, emptiness and fullness, violence and pacifism. Nonetheless the contradictions inherent in the group were obvious: the apologia for the disorder and conflicts of memory of Daniel Spoerri, Tinguely, Niki de Saint-Phalle, Hains or Villeglé, the industrial efficiency of César and Arman and the smooth, harmonious Zen immaterialism of Klein were worlds apart. Klein, a master of judo who had lived in Franco's Spain,[8] called on people to lose themselves in blue, declaring war on the birds which lingered in his azure sky; from December 1958 he was dreaming with Werner Ruhnau of an architecture that would 'condition the air with special geographic spaces', that would end 'the principle of secrecy' and invent a town 'bathed in light and completely open to the outside',[9] where a new atmosphere of intimacy would prevail, the inhabitants would wear no clothes, the patriarchal structure of the primitive family would no longer exist and there would be a perfect community – free, individualist and impersonal. By placing their project under the wing of David Ben Gurion ('anyone who does not believe in miracles is not a realist'), Klein and Ruhnau justified in advance actions the utopianism of which (in the form of 'the best of all possible worlds') was oddly at variance with its period, intoxicated both by progress and the white, almost mystical image of the first cosmonauts.[10]

Cyber-kinetics

The Sixties, caught up in a tremendous acceleration of science, did in fact lend themselves to a marriage between art and technology. In this respect it is symptomatic that Robert Rauschenberg – who had already linked Abstract Expressionism and Pop Art – created the EAT (Experiments in Art and Technology) group in New York in 1966, together with the engineer Billy Klüver, a laser expert who helped him to stage technological spectacles. In France as in other

countries scientific and technological optimism had always been present on the art scene. Just after World War II lovers of high-precision beauty had battled to make their view of the world prevail, in Paris at the Salon des Réalités nouvelles and a few militant locations like the Galerie Denise-René. As they saw it, technology did not produce signs of death – quite the opposite: Auschwitz, Nagasaki and Hiroshima were the products of Establishment primitivism, and that was that. Kinetic art[11] which had never really caught on in France became part of the official scene in the Sixties, in Victor Vasarely in particular; Georges Pompidou, President of the Republic (from 1969 to 1974), a modern-minded art-lover, took a fancy to his work, appreciating his plasticity and his predilection for 'movement'.

Movement had reactivated high-precision beauty from 1955 at the Galerie Denise-René, demonstrating that it could bring together different generations and sensibilities, from Duchamp to Tinguely.[12] Activities close to the Kinetic trend and its Op art[13] variants flourished more or less all over Europe. Shows of Kinetic art now invited viewers to join in the party, in 1967 at the Musée d'Art moderne de la Ville de Paris in particular, at an exhibition organized by Frank Popper that brought together works by Yaacov Agam, Pol Bury, Nicolas Schöffer, Soto, Vasarely and Le Parc as well as Tinguely and Takis. Viewers pressed buttons, set off lights by walking in front of photo-electric cells, or triggered other surprise effects by beginning to speak. They discovered science as much as art, became guinea pigs of *La Ville cybernétique*[14] dreamt up in France by Schöffer, an artist and an engineer. Over and above his sophisticated devices manipulating artificial light, electronics and cybernetics,[15] like his series *Lux* – great prisms equipped inside with mirrors that projected luminous effects into space – Schöffer conducted a missionary campaign, condemning the art scene to extinction if it did not accept the idea of using new technologies. He made an apologia for futurology, a science used by business and military circles and regarded as foretelling the future. According to him art and artists had to claim a leading role on this divinatory scene. Schöffer cogently demanded that they should do professionally what they had successfully done working empirically as amateurs. 'Permanent futurology demands constant effort,' he warned. Henceforth the work of the artist must be directed towards a vision and an idea pointing directly towards the future; he must not look back, nor even stand still.

> The artist's work will be carried out in decreasing intellectual comfort. The artist has to be the active pole of universal consciousness. The more or less inconsequent appearance of art will disappear as its increasingly apparent function grows in importance. The artist must cease to practise art based on the image and create art based on conditioning.[16]

GRAV (Groupe de recherche d'art visuel), 'Une journée dans la rue', 19 April 1966. Private collection

The sixties, utopian years

François Morellet,
Sphère trame,
1962, sculpture.
Artist's collection

This was an assumptionist image of kinetics which was then to be taken over, in its own manner, less 'rigidly', by GRAV (Groupe de recherche d'art visuel – Visual art research group). This group, including Garcia-Rossi, Le Parc, François Morellet, Sobrino, Joël Stein and Yvaral, produced only a very few communal works, although it acted as a generator for anonymous art, encouraging new activity by onlookers, who were invited to a spectacular 'day in the street' in 1966; if it did not jolt them out of their routine it at least prompted a 'simple displacement of situation'.[17] In its archives ORTF (French radio and television) preserves the memory of these strange images dating from two years before 1968 of passers-by throughout Paris being called upon to assemble or dismantle sculptures, and to try out stools made of springs, moving paving-stones, a giant kaleidoscope or a habitable kinetic object. In moving away from the Establishment, turning from the snobbish public composed of the select few, condemning the cult of the artist's personality, GRAV was defending a plan that had wide support on the art scene, following the agitpro logic invented in the Soviet Union. Before 'communication' became commonplace, GRAV's members decided that rather than concentrating exclusively on the work, an artist had to prepare or 'condition' the spectator to make him 'capable of the maximum response to a given aesthetic situation', as Morellet put it; together with François Molnar he established the principle made public at Zagreb in 1963 of preserving an equilibrium between a 'progressivist tendency' and a 'reactionary tendency'.[18] On the side of the former, Morellet and Molnar put reason, logic, progress, art used in the interests of scientific research, sudden qualitative change, the materials of the day, the 'often active' participation 'of the spectator', collective criticism and experimental art. On the side of reaction, they placed the irrational, the denial or relativity of progress, individualism, art with a private or elitist objective, slow development with no real qualitative change, the choice of precious or traditional materials, disdain or an aggressive attitude towards the spectator, mistrust of all criticism, and the unique work of art that could not be altered or regulated. Since artists could not begin conditioning viewers or spectators until they entered an artistic location (family, surroundings, society), they had to concentrate on 'express' conditioning in the short time devoted to visits, taking account of a certain number of given factors: the power of the light, the temperature of the location, noises, smells, the nature of the ground, a straight, curving or broken approach, etc.

Art is life

The staging of happenings that became widespread in Europe at the same period was moving in the same direction, reconciling art and life, art that was not different from life but an activity within life, as John Cage expressed it in terms close to Zen thought. It was now necessary to establish a more direct, primitive relationship with the public that went beyond any scientific materialism, in the context of a libertarian plan outside the Establishment; it would basically be transnational and trans-disciplinary, partly inherited from Italian and Russian Futurism (Marinetti's 'theatre of surprise', the Burliuk brothers, Mayakovsky), Dadaism (Kurt Schwitters's action poetry, Arthur Cravan), close to the Gutai Group (formed in Japan in the 1950s), action poetry, sound poetry and *lettrisme*, and finally the action music of the Black Mountain College artists (in the United States). Centred on John Cage, Merce Cunningham and Robert Rauschenberg,[19] they organized spontaneous actions, most of them improvised, mixing genres and media and traditional and new techniques: poetry, dance, music, theatre, film and slide projection, painting, records, radio.

In 1959 Alan Kaprow,[20] while suggesting a definition of the 'happening' as an action that cannot be transported or reproduced, put on '18 happenings in six parts' at the Reuben Gallery in New York during which spectators were invited to take part in the action in accordance with an initial scenario the limits of which were always exceeded. Following on from Kaprow and at the very beginning of the Sixties the Fluxus Group was formed in New York, affirming that actions could be reproduced, with Dick Higgins, Alison Knowles, La Monte Young, Yoko Ono and Maciunas. In its 1961 manifesto it called on people 'to purge the world of bourgeois life. To promote the REALITY OF NON-ART so that it can be understood by everybody ....To dissolve the structures of the cultural, social and political revolutions into a common front with common actions.'

Fluxus was soon emulated in Europe by Wolf Vostell,

Ben, *Beau-laid*,
1969, acrylic on slate.
Galerie Jérôme de
Noirmont collection

Right:
Photograph by
Georges Maciunas, the
Fluxus group's quest
for new musical and
theatrical creativity.
Gilbert and Lila
Silverman Foundation
collection

Right:
Music for teeth by Ben at
the Fluxus festival in
Nice, 1963. Concert in
the street with Maciunas,
Ben and Bozzi. Ben's
collection

Joseph Beuys and Nam June Paik, with Benjamin Vautier and Robert Filiou in France. In September 1962 the members of Fluxus dismissed five virtuoso violinists at the Städtisches Museum in Wiesbaden and took their place for three hours of 'anti-violin' music, none of the players having touched a violin before in his life. Fluxus's European tour finished in Nice in the summer of 1963, where Maciunas organized another concert with Ben (Vautier). As early as 1958 Ben had opened his *Laboratoire 32* (which later became the Galerie *Ben doute de tout*) in Nice where the Fluxus spirit was very much in the air; it was the only Fluxus centre in France, 'with 'La Cédille qui sourit', a non-school and centre of permanent creativity at Villefranche-sur-Mer, being run by George Brecht, Filiou, Donna Brewer and Marianne Staffeldt from September 1965. Fluxus advocated uninterrupted action in all its forms: concerts, happenings, street spectacles, various objects, and 'mail art' (sent by post) dreamt up by Ray Johnson.[21]

Producing objects that were difficult for the traditional circuits to get hold of, Fluxus, seemingly autarchic, appeared to guarantee its own independence: publications, multiple objects and films were made and distributed by the artists themselves.[22] In the summer of 1965 Ben placed placards around his shop saying 'Everything is art', or 'No art', or 'Dying is a work of art'. His biting irony, directed against everything including himself, gradually gained acceptance as a sign of narcissistic rebellion; it could be immediately perceived by the spectator and could in the long run be taken over by the market – once the artist agreed to sell picture-objects in which his hand-writing would be enough to identify him, even if they were not signed. This was one way of sidestepping the anonymity being demanded on all sides, among others by his friend Serge III (Oldenbourg) who used white vinyl to paint over other artists' canvases as a protest against original work and signature. In 1971, following the same line of reasoning, Ben polished other artists' shoes on the pavement in front of his premises and that same year declared on one of his pictures: 'I sign anything'. His Troupe d'Art total, which he and Pierre Pontani[23] established in Nice in November 1963, promised permanent creation which consisted not of 'talking of what is new' but of breathing it, 'exuding it in spite of oneself'.[24] His sado-masochistic actions were intended to let spectators 'undergo' all sorts of experiences: 'Example 1: The actors disguised as the Riot Squad go down into the stalls and kiss the spectators; 2: A box containing eight rats and another containing eight cats will be left among the public; 3: Saying a theft has taken place and systematically searching all spectators; 4: Preventing the spectators from leaving, by force if necessary.'[25] During Fluxus's European tour in the summer of 1963 Ben swam across Nice harbour, Bozzi signed missals and Maciunas ate a 'mystery food' in public. The acts of provocation by Fluxus artists sometimes resulted in a reaction from the public and the media, and even from the police. At a Fluxus concert at Coaraze (near Nice) Robert Lafont was so annoyed that he stood up and sang *La Marseillaise*.[26] In *Le Figaro* in 1969 Philippe Bouvard made bitter-sweet comments on Serge Oldenbourg's 'action' of hitch-hiking on the Route Nationale 7 with a grand piano;[27] three years earlier Serge had been arrested by the Czechoslovak police after presenting Fluxus happenings and concerts in Prague.[28] He was taken in for questioning again in France in 1970 after diverting a bus in Tours, armed with a pistol, and taking its passengers to the site of an exhibition by Nice artists (Charvolen, Dezeuze, Dolla, Flexner and himself). Pinoncelli also got into trouble in February 1969 for throwing red paint at the Minister André Malraux when he came to open the Marc Chagall museum in Nice. Malraux joined in the game, spraying his attacker, and later declared that it was an act directed against Chagall and that he thought it was marvellous 'that people can still be so passionate about painting in this day and age'.[29] Finally, among other reprisals, the police had already arrested Jean-Jacques Lebel in 1966 at the third Festival de la Libre

Expression after an evening of happenings including the famous '120 minutes dédiées au Divin Marquis' (120 minutes dedicated to the Divine Marquis) in response to the official censorship of the New Wave film *La Religieuse* by Rivette, inspired by Diderot's novel.[30]

Jean-Jacques Lebel, who carried out his first happening, *Anti-Procès,* in Venice in 1960 with Alain Jouffroy, acted as a very active internationalist militant, defending the genre in an essay[31] and a series of provocative demonstrations. He organized the first Festival de la Libre Expression in May 1964 at the American Cultural Center in Paris, with Fluxus happenings, films and actions, a concert by Ben and *Solo pour la mort* by Serge III, who on this occasion played Russian roulette. The event was reported in the national press. In her column 'Les Potins de la commère' in *France-Soir* Carmen Tessier wrote: 'Half-naked men and women sprawled on a heap of papers and daubed themselves with red, green and yellow paint. Then they threw mackerels and a blood-covered chicken at one another's heads. Meanwhile a rotating water jet sprayed the spectators.'[32] These were 300 people invited by Jean-Jacques Lebel, '26 years old, the son of a modern art specialist', to record the birth of 'total art, a relentless bulldozer which has undertaken to rid the world of its cultural ruins'.[33]

At the third Festival de la Libre Expression in 1966 the international stars of happenings and Fluxus again invited spectators to cross over on to the stage – but to no avail, as most of them were glued to their seats in surprise. Though a young Brechtian actress complained of the 'macho' conformism of happenings – with woman 'remaining the object manipulated by men'[34] – it was a waste of time: in France at a time when the sexual and feminist revolutions had not yet exploded, pornography still carried with it the sulphur of liberation. In October 1967 the *Internationale situationniste* called for experiments to be made in misappropriating *photos-romans* (photo-stories) and so-called pornographic photographs;[35] and in fact French-style happenings often included voyeurism that was excoriating for the transfixed spectators who hardly ever dared venture on to the stage. Hence their relative relief when it was suggested they move on to 'body art'. Especially from the end of the Sixties body art became an international spectacle with artists using their own bodies as a medium: a body put to the test, a new tool to measure pain, space and time, and the shared schizophrenia of the art scene and the public, as in the happening thrown back on largely uncontrollable impulses. Here again art and life fused, this time in the actual body of the artist who no longer left any clear space between himself and his object. The spectator in turn was drawn into a logic which no longer left any room for critical distance. In France this genre was represented by François Pluchart, who was in charge of the art page of *Combat*; in 1971 he founded the magazine *Attitudes*, which was devoted to the body as an 'art material' and in it he took on the defence of artists such as Journiac, Gina Pane, Piero Manzoni, Denis Oppenheim and Vito Acconci.

Gestures that were extreme abounded, ranging from the American Chris Burden who got one of his friends to fire a .22 rifle at him in public (1971), to Ben who hit his head against a wall until it bled (1969) or Gina Pane who drew attention to the anthropological violence of her contemporaries and their worsening living conditions; always silent, seeing language as having lost its

VIᵉ CONGRES DE L'INTERNATIONALE SITUATIONNISTE ANVERS DU 12 AU 15 NOVEMBRE 1962

ÉDITÉ PAR:
INTERNATIONALE
SITUATIONNISTE
B.P. 75-06 PARIS

Poster for 6th conference of L'Internationale situationniste, 1962. Private collection

efficacy, she remained hanging in the void, clinging to the parapet of a window, for two and a half hours (*Je*, Bruges, 1972) until the public in a frenzy demanded that she fall. She cut her mouth and mixed milk with her blood (*Sang/lait chaud*, 1972) or swallowed putrid meat (*Nourriture*, 1971). Journiac was more ironic, serving a *Messe pour un corps* (1969) at the Galerie Templon, with the communion consisting of a host made of a blood sausage concocted from

his own blood. Through religious, sexual or nutritional rituals, artists appealed to the public's emotions and primal impulses, including the most extreme ones. Based on psychoanalysis they appealed to memory, or even nostalgia – Christian Boltanski in particular; in 1972 he invented his *Soixante-deux membres du club Mickey*, enlargements of passport photographs sent in by children to their favourite newspaper, with which anyone at all could identify. Whether dealing with happenings, actions, performances (which were more narrative in content) or body art, there was a lot to see – and feel – at the moment and later on at individual level; at the collective level there was generally nothing left at the end, or just a few traces on photographs.

'Live in your head'[36]

The 'loss of visuality', to use Benjamin Buchloh's expression, was the order of the day, or at least the subordination of all 'visuality' to the idea. This loss had already been intimated in France by Yves Klein in April 1958 when he exhibited *Le Vide* at the Iris Clert gallery, and then in 1959 with his 'zones of immaterial pictural sensibility' given in exchange for a specified weight of refined gold. American and British artists who believed in the Concept (from the mid-Sixties) played on several levels, advocating – by turn if necessary – autarchic art, far removed from any Establishment premises, or the opposite, art which would be intimately associated with the gallery or museum setting. In general the linguistic definition alone took precedence,

internationale situationniste

12

From left to right, and from top to bottom:

Daniel Spoerri's meal at the Galerie J, March 1965. Jérôme de Noirmont collection

Cover of the last issue of the magazine *L'Internationale situationniste*, devoted to the events of May '68, no. 12, 1969. Private collection

Meetings of members of *L'Internationale situationniste* centred on Guy Debord, early 1960s. Private collection

and in the final resort the pieces of art did not necessarily have to be 'carried out' after being thought up. In France Conceptual Art[37] in the Sixties was defended by a few artists, Bernar Venet in particular; in 1963 he started his series of *Cartons peints*, setting out to give a new dimension to collage, but mainly to 'produce cold, non-craft works using industrial materials'.[38] That same year he had himself photographed in front of a pile of tar in the Albert I gardens in Nice, knowing that the mound could be taken for a sculpture, then in 1965 he made his first Conceptual works with the help of mathematical diagrams.

Concerning Conceptual art, the most rational alternative was proposed by Daniel Buren. In 'Mise en garde' in 1969 he invited readers to measure the risks of praising concept to the skies: first because what was a means could turn into an end without coming out on any object; secondly because it could flatter mannerism, the anecdotal, academicism and a return to Romanticism (instead of 'depicting the number of gilt buttons on a soldier's tunic down to the very last one' they would 'talk about the number of steps it took to walk a kilometre');[39] and thirdly it would be very easy to 'take any old "idea", turn it into art and call it "concept"'.[40]

At the same time the opposite idea arose, that it was necessary to show that art is first and foremost materiality and 'visuality', which Buren reaffirmed in spring 1970 as follows: 'Painting should no longer be the vision/illusion in any form, even mental, of a phenomenon (nature, the subconscious, geometry ...) but visuality of the painting itself.'[41] Buren in fact insisted – and still insists – on the context of art, its architectural context, but also its social, economic and political context, a context that can be renewed *ad infinitum*. Analysing the methods of artistic production, distribution and reception in detail,

L'Internationale Hallucinex, containing writing by William S. Burroughs and Jean-Jacques Lebel, 1970. Private collection

whether dealing with its individual or collective manifestations, Buren – with Olivier Mosset, Michel Parmentier, Niele Toroni (BMPT, from the first letters of their surnames) – made criticisms on several fronts: of the reductionist interpretation that had been made of Duchamp[42] and of European and American Modernist painting which he knew well. He misappropriated painting, ridding it of the traditional stretcher, preferring a cloth object on which he produced parallel vertical bands (always 8.7 cm wide), adding a layer of white paint over the outermost bands. He flitted from one medium to another, from canvas to printed paper, from the pages of books to poster panels. For the May 1968 Salon, for example, the same papers covered with vertical white and green bands appeared inside the Musée d'Art moderne de la Ville de Paris and on boards carried by two sandwich men, while twenty unlicensed poster-sticking forays took place in Paris and the surrounding area. Buren ended up in prison in Berne in 1969 for this type of action after being reported to the police by local residents who had seen him covering advertising hoardings with pink and white bands.[43]

With Mosset, Parmentier and Toroni, Buren exhibited four times[44] between December 1966 and December 1967 against the illusionism of painting which distanced people from reality, inviting (condemning) the viewer to 'become intelligent' and think about the traditional references of history and art. At the Musée des Arts décoratifs in January 1967 Buren exhibited a canvas with vertical white and red stripes (8.7 cm wide), Olivier Mosset a white canvas with a black circle in the centre (7.8 cm in diameter), Michel Parmentier a canvas covered with white and grey horizontal bands (38 cm wide), and Niele Toroni a white canvas covered with a staggered arrangement of 85 imprints of flat brush no. 50 (at intervals of 30

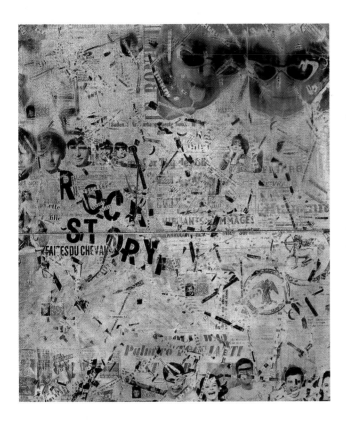

cm). In September 1967 the poster for their last collective exhibition at the Paris Biennale, featuring cheap reproductions of passport photographs of the four men,[45] emphasized the deliberately ludicrous nature of the cult of the artist, thus indicating their refusal to present themselves as a group, an entity that the Establishment and critics could immediately latch on to. It was a waste of time as the critics nonetheless 'launched' BMPT as a coherent group which could be assimilated and consumed – like everything else. When the Biennale was held Buren, Mosset, Parmentier and Toroni responded to the figurative *Mythologies quotidiennes* and the audiovisual device by Pommereulle, Erró and Peter Stämpfli by means of an arrangement of reproductions of the pope, animals or pin-ups accompanied by a tape repeating: 'Art is the illusion of disorientation, art is false. Painting starts with Buren, Mosset, Parmentier, Toroni'. This painting was radically Abstract and reduced to elementary signs that were believed to escape from transmitting images, messages, or 'discourses' about the world.

Dialectical materials

In this sense at least the ideas of Buren, Mosset, Parmentier and Toroni were close to those of the Supports-Surfaces group; in 1970 they exhibited pieces by Daniel Dezeuze, Patrick Saytour, André Valensi, Claude Viallat,

Vincent Bioulès and Marc Devade at the ARC (see below). In Supports-Surfaces (the above artists plus Bernard Pagès, François Arnal, Noël Dolla, Toni Grand, Jean-Pierre Pincemin and Louis Cane[46]) there were the same ingredients reflecting the atmosphere of the period, and even more than elsewhere a programmatic and political rigour which were to be faithfully conveyed in their works. While their works are now often regarded as decorative items, breathing new life into the spirit of the Abstract adventure, in their day they set out to be the ascetic product of a fight against an individualist, 'neurotic and religious'[47] concept of bourgeois art, which had been turned into a fetish in private collections or museums and which should be abandoned as soon as possible for more 'neutral'[48] locations. Their works were intended to demonstrate a further step towards pictural egalitarianism, eschewing the 'hierarchical association between form and substance, resulting from the differences in value and surface area of the colour-forms'.[49] Format, like everything else, had to be denied, hence the appearance of extensible surfaces and reserves that were not put on show. Painting and sculpture were regarded as tools of self-knowledge and knowledge of the world. The artist's work should have relevance on the double front of the signifier (the material) and the signified (the ideology being conveyed). The painting should not be taken only as a subject (which would mean sinking into formalism): its history and how it worked in a more general social and political system should be thought through.

The artists in the Supports-Surfaces group – with the theoretical backing of Marcelin Pleynet, who was involved with the magazine *Tel quel* – gleaned sustenance from the social sciences, according to them, 'the most advanced: linguistics and psychoanalysis, sciences which do not place themselves outside ideology and to that extent are articulated to be cast in the mould of dialectic materialism and historical materialism, the philosophical and political weapon of the only truly revolutionary class for the whole of society: the working class'.[50] The old question of committed art reappeared, and with it the eternal contradiction that 'the working class' understood nothing of what Supports-Surfaces were doing, or what the '*avant-garde*' was doing, because it was alienated. The only possible way to be subversive was to 'prepare the theoretical and ideological

Jean-Louis Brau,
Cornucopia for Togliati's death, diptych, transfer on plasticized canvas, 1963–4.
Galerie 1900–2000 collection, Marcel Fleiss

At the 3rd Festival de la Libre Expression in Paris on 4 and 27 April 1966 at the Théâtre de la Chimère, 42 rue Fontaine (where André Breton lived), the happening '120 minutes dédiés au Divin Marquis' by Jean-Jacques Lebel was a response to the 'return to Pétainist moral order' which had already manifested itself through the case brought against the publisher of the complete works of Sade (Jean-Jacques Pauvert) and the censorship of Jacques Rivette's film *La Religieuse*, inspired by Diderot's novel. Jean-Jacques Lebel had dreamt up the plot by inviting artists like

Shirley Goldfarb, Frédérico Pardo, Philippe Hiquilly and the transsexual Cinthia to behave as they wished outside the bounds of everyday life.
A large and turbulent audience participated in the determinedly collective work described by Jean-Jacques Lebel in *Le Happening* (Denöel, 1966)
and *Poésie directe, happening et interventions* (Opus International, 1994). This happening led to Jean-Jacques Lebel being arrested and found guilty
of 'outraging public decency', a move that was immediately condemned in a written protest on 27 April 1966, signed by 100 or so public figures.

On the chessboard of commitment, the Supports-Surfaces artists were ranged beside young narrative painters; aware that narrative painting had the advantage of being comprehensible to everyone, they decreed that it was not however revolutionary to be content to reproduce an old method of production, and not to introduce a method of production of their own.[53] This 'method of production of their own' was evidence of the experimental intentions of the Supports-Surfaces group, and was also reminiscent of the materialogical tropism that is a recurring feature of Modernism. Mediums, materials and practices were renewed, revisited and diverted from their archaic meaning – this included colour, fused with the support and now used only for its materiality. Apparently at least, the Symbolist games and material effects that Abstract art had integrated were over and done with, as were 'matière' paintings, cold or hot, Futurist or 'passéist' Romanticism or heroism – the nostalgia that had been reactivated time and again in the course of the century as a solace against the advance of Modernism. Even so, Bernard Ceysson gave a reminder of the meaning of this resort to materiality: giving free rein to the repressed and unconscious which were inhibited by 'the rationalist idealism of a major part of contemporary art'.[54]

Within the logic of anonymity and often of repetition, each artist found an 'identity' for himself which was used to go through all the possibilities of the 'system of painting'. Outside or beyond their membership of Supports-Surfaces, Viallat folded and unfolded, making use of recto and verso, Arnal crushed, Dolla rolled up or made holes, Valensi and Cane cut out, stuck on or sewed, Saytour burnt, and Cane dabbed. Saytour loved printed waxed cloths, Viallat canvas awnings, sheets, polyurethane foam and pebbles, Dezeuze plastic or gauze, Valensi cardboard, canvas and carbonyl, and Dolla tarlatan, rocks or snow – for it was essential to leave the beaten tracks of the Establishment. In 1970 for example Dezeuze, Pagès, Saytour and Viallat organized twelve open-air demonstrations, 'Intérieur-Extérieur', in the south of France. As was always the case, the positions formulated by the Supports-Surfaces group overflowed its structure, which very quickly broke up. The split which began in 1970 and the violence accompanying it are implicit testimony of the internal conflicts within the art scene, and in a wider context the intellectual scene. The divergencies were all the

Daniel Buren,
Les Hommes-
Sandwichs, **1968.**
Private collection

weaponry of the intellectual middle classes',[51] and just as the eighteenth-century nobility had joined forces with the bourgeoisie, the twentieth-century bourgeoisie could join forces with the proletariat stage by stage. Meanwhile artists should not sink into 'control by the workers', putting themselves on the same level as the most alienated members of society; they should theorize, explain works which without a written explanation were inaccessible – hence the frequent appendage of 'enlightening'[52] tracts and texts.

harder to manage as the expectations had been so high. Each sect soon set about defending its own ideas against those of others while at the same time there were deep-rooted divisions: between Paris and the provinces, intellectuals and workers, Marxists and less committed Marxists, Stalinists and anti-Stalinists, one individual and another.[55] The new stance of *Tel quel,* which had been close to Supports-Surfaces, moving from Communism (the French Communist Party) to Maoism, made things no easier, while

in 1970 Cane, Devade and Dezeuze started denouncing 'all kinds of regression (spontaneist, anarchist, Trotskyist, Maoist, mechanist, etc.)'.[56]

The trap

Up to the beginning of the Seventies the art scene became increasingly radical, 1968 counting as an epic episode in a story which went well beyond the May rebellion.[57] In 1969 the 6th Paris Biennale opened in an atmosphere that was still highly charged. The premises of the Musée Galliera were sacked. Christian Boltanski, Jean Le Gac and Gina Pane mounted their 'Concession à perpétuité', taking over the ground, burying Boltanski's mannikin, and assembling and dismantling Le Gac's containers. At the same time Boltanski was still occupying the American Cultural Center (*Work in progress*) and inviting his friends to

take part. Le Gac installed *Manches à l'air du monde végétal* in the park; Gina Pane counted 1587 steps between midday and 8 p.m.; Claude Gilli threw snails at the façade (*Agressions d'escargots vivants*) photographed by Boltanski who planted and uprooted a thousand rose stakes, etc. In the manner of Robert Malaval, who had multiplied his *Cent demi-heures de dessin quotidien* (1969), as Catherine Millet observed, 'confronted with the dissolution of all rules', they all reassimilated 'elementary gestures, the archaic signposting of time and space'.[58]

At one point in the aftermath of 1968 it seemed possible to believe that artists had become masters of the situation, reaching beyond the Establishment institutions which had quite often backed the protest movements – art galleries in particular, but not only them. Museum curators and generally everybody who had to exhibit works of arts were now forced to review their practices in the light of calls for a different form of presentation, almost inevitably a 'theoretical'[59] one. They respected the artists' assumption that the place where works were presented was a separate object which the works had to relate with and confront, agreeing with it or being in tension with it, to the point of overflowing the very setting traditionally assigned to them. Before May '68 a certain number of structures had been set up to defend the interests of contemporary creativity. In 1966 Pierre Gaudibert, curator of the Musée d'Art moderne de la Ville de Paris, created the ARC (Animation, Recherche, Confrontation), an autonomous set-up within the museum where the intention was to exhibit extreme contemporary work.[60] In 1967 CNAC (Centre national d'art contemporain) was instituted with the remit of promoting living art, artists and experimenters.[61] The number of galleries of contemporary art increased rapidly, with Daniel Templon and Yvon Lambert opening their galleries in 1968. That year the monthly journal *Chroniques de l'art vivant* edited and run by Aimé Maeght first appeared. In 1969 President Pompidou decided to build a large museum of modern art in Paris. In 1971 Jacques Duhamel, Minister for Cultural Affairs, announced that he wanted to help creativity, and envisaged financial help for the first exhibition. In this seemingly favourable context the 1972 exhibition more or less stalled the reconciliation with contemporary creativity, the brainchild of the President of the Republic himself.

Exhibition of works produced in the summer of 1970 by Dezeuze, Saytour, Valensi and Viallat, Galerie Jean Fournier, 15-22 April 1971. Galerie Jean Fournier collection

The exhibition *Douze ans d'art contemporain en France, 1960–1972* sponsored by Georges Pompidou (though he played no part in selecting the artists[62]) was not only the culmination of artistic protest, it served as a psycho-drama, sending each of those playing a role off to his separate 'destiny'. Georges Pompidou who was smitten with modernity was concerned to present living art to the public at large, and possibly to restore to France the place that was then very much the preserve of the American scene;[63] but he met with violent resistance from artists, most of whom belonged to the Far Left, and was wrongfooted by their radically provocative artistic moves. In a climate of electoral tension, between the referendum on an enlarged Common Market (April 1972) and the next parliamentary elections, the exhibition soon came to be seen as the 'expo Pompidou' which had to be denounced as a project carried out by the Right wing who were in power. Up until then provocative gestures had been confined in time and space, even though artists had broken into public places not reserved for them. The *Douze ans d'art contemporain en France* exhibition[64] caused the gas canister which 1968 had only started to empty to re-explode. About twenty of the artists invited to exhibit – e.g. Filiou, Leonardo Cremonini, Jean-Robert Ipoustéguy – refused to show their work. Some removed their works (Les Malassis, Dufrêne, Villeglé, Étienne Martin and Pierre Alechinsky), Joël Kermarrec turned his upside down, and Spoerri added pieces of cheese to his exhibit as a reminder that 'the situation stinks'. The Front des artistes plasticiens entered the battle to demonstrate that Georges Pompidou was using the exhibition as an electoral ploy, which really did not make sense given the divergence between his personal artistic tastes and the habits of his electorate. Nonetheless the Front collected signatures from about thirty artists' associations on this basis.

On the day the exhibition opened a few dozen artists demonstrated in front of the Grand Palais and handed out tracts. As well as the CRS riot police traditionally stationed near the Élysée palace there were troops lining the route, followed by Queen Elizabeth, who was visiting Paris. At 4 p.m. and 6 p.m. the police intervened against the members of the Front des artistes plasticiens, giving comfort to Pierre Bourgeade who in the previous day's *Combat* had written: '25 April put paid to Pompidou's European ambi-

tions. 16 May will put paid to his claims to be a patron of the arts and a fashioner of artists .... No to money-art! No to police-art! No to the exhibition that is an alibi for politicians, profiteers and censors! We'll soon see whether M. Pompidou calls out the riot squad to deal with the artists he loves so much.'[65] In fact the most interesting aspect was the artists' feeling that the state was trying to corral them, soothe them, 'emasculate' their revolutionary aggressiveness[66] and ultimately regroup and trivialize them as belonging to a 'Pompidou-Fifth-Republic' style. This supposition was not completely invalidated by the answer given by the Minister Jacques Duhamel (drawn up by Jacques Rigaud) to Michel Poniatowski, a member of the Assemblée nationale. On 26 August Poniatowski put a written question to the Minister asking him to condemn the exhibition '*Douze ans de canulars* [practical jokes] *contemporains*',[67] and regretting that works such as *Mon urine* (1962) by Ben should be given official patronage and finance. The ministry then replied that the state had to take risks and did not regret this confrontation between contemporary art and public opinion, and that public opinion could, like the ministry, see the exhibition as a pathetic, ironic or provocative expression of the quests, disarray or even the dead ends of contemporary creativity. Moreover, the ministry said that the censor's rulings could be compared with the scathing criticisms made of Impressionism in the nineteenth century, which had become ludicrous with the passage of time. The next stage was a foregone conclusion: modern democracy French-style would give artists who enacted permanent revolution basing their innovative effects on disruption a hard time. When Maurice Druon, the Minister for Culture, speaking on 6 May 1973 stated: 'People who come to the ministry's door with a begging-bowl in one hand and a Molotov cocktail in the other will have to choose', he inevitably triggered a final scandal and nostalgia for the revolution. But history proved him at least partly right: from then on the artists' pattern-book of the violence of protest would be extremely fragmented and harnessed by the Establishment, during a new period when the Situationists had hoped for – obviously for different reasons – 'the rapid dissolution of the linear criterion of novelty' and 'a multi-dimensional inflation of trends'[64] and experiments.

In this economic situation the artists' aspirations to dou-

Claude Viallat,
Répétition, 1968,
eosin on canvas.
Galerie Jean
Fournier collection

ble up on the Establishment (art criticism, museums etc.) soon looked excessive. Fluxus had envisaged its own distribution networks and an autarchic engine of war, which was weakened by the success of some artists. All or almost all the ground lost by the Establishment was recovered: to be convinced of this we need only observe the Establishment path followed by the work produced in the Sixties. Moreover the power held by artists was transferred inexorably to Establishment bodies, which were themselves more scattered and strengthened by the artistic debate itself. For the artists, the dream of emerging from the traditional categories of art had no consequences in itself. Persuading traditional institutions that they had to take that dream seriously, and so legitimize it by entrusting it to museums, inevitably resulted in what took place. The game started by Duchamp really took shape in those years with the Establishment beginning to modernize itself, and in turn assimilate (albeit with some difficulty) the modern tempo, the acceleration in consumption and democratic and capitalist mobility. Already one of Duchamp's ready-mades had value only through the importance accorded to it by the Establishment, without which it would revert to being a simple commodity. Like Duchamp the ready-made was entirely dependent on the Establishment and its system of recognition, and the more the object was commonplace the more this link was obvious. The trend became more accentuated in the Sixties and Seventies with the increasing importance accorded to exhibition organizers. Everything became an object subject to transaction, very far removed from the permanent revolution the artists had envisaged. Therefore their goal had not been achieved, even if that was not a problem, since most of the artists who had embarked on the battle had fought, as always, less in the name of a very clear concept of the world than against a state of affairs which was perceived as intolerable, and just had to be replaced by new *situations*.

Laurence Bertrand Dorléac

1. Such as narrative figuration or critical figuration. For the period, I would refer readers to the best generalist book on the fine arts, Catherine Millet, *L'Art contemporain en France*, Paris, Flammarion, 1987, 2nd edn, 1994, and for the historical background to Michel Winock, *Chronique des années soixante*, Paris, Le Seuil, 1987.

2. Georges Belmont, 'Le mouvement "provo" gagne la France', *Arts et loisirs*, 6–12 July 1966.

3. Évelyne Sullerot, ibid.

4. For this and the following quotations, cf. *L'Internationale situationniste*, the central newsletter published by the sections of the Internationale situationniste movement, June 1958–September 1969, repub. Paris, Champ-Libre, 1975.

5. For this and the following quotations, cf. Jean Tinguely, *Für Statik*, tract of 14 March 1959, translated from German.

6. See Pierre Restany's first manifesto, *Les Nouveaux réalistes*, preface for the collective exhibition (Arman, Dufrêne, Hains, Yves le Monochrome, Tinguely, Villeglé), Milan, Apollinaire gallery, May 1960.

7. Ibid.

8. This led to him being accused (with Michel Tapié) in *L'Internationale situationniste* in 1958 of 'spontaneously running ahead of the fascist wave that is advancing in France', swelling the ranks of the 'spiritualists of all categories' who 'are in the pay of the same defence budget'. The Situationists based their comments partly on the review in *Le Monde* of 21 November 1958, alluding to Klein's 'incantatory pictural mysticism' and his way of 'engulfing himself in the captivating blue uniformity like a Buddhist in Buddha'. John Cage was also criticized for participating in 'that Californian trend of thought in which the mental weakness of the American capitalist culture has turned to Zen Buddhism': *L'Internationale situationniste*, no. 2, December 1958.

9. Yves Klein, Werner Ruhnau, 'Projet pour une architecture de l'air', *Zéro 3*, Düsseldorf, July 1961; translated from English in 1960. *Les Nouveaux Réalistes*, Paris, Musée d'Art moderne de la Ville de Paris, 1986.

10. This curious mixture of fascination with science consorting with the irrational can be illustrated by the contacts between New Realism and the magazine *Planète* on which Pierre Restany had worked; this remains true, even if not all New Realists were involved in this project.

11. The word 'kinetic' emerged in 1954.

12. This exhibition relating to movement exhibited pieces by Agam, Bury, Calder, Duchamp, Jacobsen, Soto, Tinguely and Vasarely.

13. In Germany (1957–60) Zéro drew inspiration from Fontana and Klein, transposing thoughts into visible objects 'by means of light and colour'. In Italy Enne or N (1960–64), a group of experimental designers, mixed modern and traditional materials: plastics, metals, wood, optical lenses, engines; finally the Italian, gestalt-minded Gruppo T (1959–66) produced works that triggered tactile, visual and other sensations. Three major exhibitions established the legitimacy of kinetic art: in 1964 at the Musée des Arts décoratifs in Paris; in 1965 *The Responsive Eye* at the Museum of Modern Art in New York; and finally in 1967 at the Musée d'Art moderne de la Ville de Paris

14. Title of book by Nicolas Schöffer, pub. 1970.

15. He produced his first independent cybernetic sculpture *Cysp I* in 1956.

16. Nicolas Schöffer, op. cit.

17. 'Le Groupe de recherche d'art visuel présente une journée dans la rue', programme for Tuesday 19 April 1966.

18. 'Pour un art abstrait progressiste' in *Catalogue of the Galerija Suvremene Umjetnosti*, Zagreb, 1963.

19. John Cage was emulated by some of his pupils, including Alan Kaprow, George Brecht, Al Hansen, Dick Higgins, Claes Oldenburg, Jim Dine and Yoko Ono.

20. Alan Kaprow, *Assemblages, environments and happenings*, New York, Harry N. Abrams, 1966, and 'The education of the un-artist', *Art in America*, February 1970 and May 1971.

21. Jean-Marc Poinsot, *Mail Art, communication à distance, concept*, Paris, CEDIC, 1971.

22. Mainly by Maciunas. From 1964 Dick Higgins set up the Something Else Press which published valuable works. In 1962 Ben together with Robert

Erebo published the magazine *Ben Dieu* and that same year Marcel Alocco published the magazine *Identités*.

23. Annie Baricalla, Robert Bozzi, Robert Erebo and Dany Gobert were close to it.

24. Tract by the 'Troupe d'Art total', 1963.

25. Ibid.

26. As reported by Ben in *Chroniques niçoises. Genèse d'un musée*, vol. I, 1945–72, Nice, Musée d'Art moderne et d'Art contemporain, 1991.

27. Philippe Bouvard, 'Pour faire de l'auto-stop, procurez-vous un piano à queue', *Le Figaro*, 4 June 1969.

28. See *Serge III*, exhibition catalogue, Nice, Galerie d'Art contemporain des musées de Nice, March 1988.

29. *Le Canard enchaîné*, in *Chroniques niçoises. Genèse d'un musée*, op. cit.

30. A petition was signed on 27 April 1966 protesting against 'the ban on happenings ... a clear and intolerable attack on intellectual freedom. This is a continuation of the *La Religieuse* affair and the anti-beatnik hysteria ...' Over 100 people signed, including Noël Arnaud, Philippe Audoin, Simone de Beauvoir, André Breton, Marcel Duchamp, Jean Duvignaud, Maurice Nadeau, José Pierre, Jacques Rivette, Christiane Rochefort, Éric Rohmer, Dominique de Roux, Jean-Paul Sartre and Barbet Schroeder.

31. See Jean-Jacques Lebel, *Le Happening*, Paris, Denoël, 1966.

32. Carmen Tessier, 'Sachez tout sur le happening, "art total" qui vient d'être découvert à Paris', *France-Soir*, 3 June 1964.

33. Ibid.

34. Otto Hahn, 'Qu'est-ce que le happening?', *Arts et loisirs*, 1966.

35. 'Les situationnistes et les nouvelles formes d'action contre la politique et l'art', *L'Internationale situationniste* (editor: Guy Debord), no. 11, October 1967.

36. I am repeating the slogan of the Berne exhibition in March–April 1969, 'Quand les attitudes deviennent formes', an exhibition that included Conceptual artists.

37. It was in 1969 and at the very beginning of the 1970s that 'Conceptual Art' emerged as a category, initially in the specialist press.

38. Bernar Venet, in *Chroniques niçoises. Genèse d'un musée*, op. cit.

39. Daniel Buren, 'Mise en garde', in exhibition catalogue of *Konzeption/Conception*, Städtisches Museum, 1969.

40. Ibid.

41. Daniel Buren, 'Mise en garde no. 3', *VH 101*, no. 1, spring 1970. On the opposition between visuality and non-visuality, see Michel Claura, organizer of the exhibition *Paris 18 IV 70*, who described the divisions between artists working on 'concept': 'Extrémisme et rupture', *Lettres françaises*, 26 September and 1 October 1969. See also Claude Gintz's summing up, 'L'art conceptuel, une perspective: notes sur un projet d'exposition', *L'Art conceptuel, une perspective*, Paris, Musée d'Art moderne de la Ville de Paris, 1989.

42. See Daniel Buren, *Limites critiques*, 1969.

43. Buren's action organized by Harald Szeemann was just outside the Kunsthalle in Berne (February–March).

44. *Manifestations I* and *2*, at the 18th Salon de la Jeune Peinture in January 1967, *Manifestation 3*, at the Musée des Arts décoratifs, during one evening, *Manifeste 4*, at the 5th Paris Biennale, autumn 1967. See Michel Claura, 'Actualité', *VH 101*, no. 5, spring 1971.

45. This was not unconnected with Warhol's working practices, in his series *Thirteen most wanted men* exhibited at the Sonnabend Gallery in particular. See also Benjamin Buchloh who bases his statements on the evidence of Michel Claura, 'De l'esthétique d'administration à la critique institutionnelle (Aspect de l'art conceptuel, 1962–9)', *L'Art conceptuel, une perspective*, op. cit.

46. There were other artists close to the group: Vivien Isnard, Christian Jaccard, Pierre Buraglio and Marcel Alocco; Alocco exhibited with members of the group in April–May 1969 at the École spéciale d'architecture, Paris.

47. I am repeating the expressions used on the poster of the *Supports-Surfaces* exhibition at the Théâtre de la Cité internationale, Paris, 19 April–8 May 1971.

48. From 1968 to 1973 Supports-Surfaces artists showed their works at places not on the traditional art circuit: Anfo, Cannes and Novara in 1968; Coaraze and Montpellier in 1969; Coaraze, Limoges, Montpellier and as part of *Douze expositions d'été* in 1970; Elne in Roussillon and various other places in the Camargue in 1971.

49. I am repeating the expressions used by Yves Aupetitallot in *Supports-Surfaces*, Saint-Étienne, Musée d'Art moderne de Saint-Étienne, 1991.

50. Poster for the *Supports-Surfaces* exhibition at the Théâtre de la Cité internationale, 19 April–8 May 1971.

51. Ibid.

52. The theoretical writings of members of the Supports-Surfaces group were prolific. See esp. 'Pour un programme théorique pictural', *Peinture et Cahiers théoriques*, no. 1, 1971, and later numbers, the magazine *Tel quel* and exhibition catalogues.

53. Marc Devade, 'Révolutionner la peinture ou peindre la révolution', debate held on 16 February 1972.

54. Bernard Ceysson, 'Propos à développer à propos de Supports-Surfaces, l'exposition accrochée...' in *Supports-Surfaces*, op. cit.

55. For the terms of the split, see contemporary documents: the tract of 23 September 1970 handed out at the opening of the *Supports-Surfaces* exhibition (Paris, ARC), signed Cane, Devade and Dezeuze; the tract of 14 June 1971, signed Dolla, Grand, Saytour, Valensi and Viallat; finally the tract of 15 June 1971, 'Matérialisme conséquent, et inconséquence d'une scission', signed Arnal, Bioulès, Cane, Devade, Dezeuze.

56. Tract handed out at the opening of *Supports-Surfaces* exhibition, op. cit.

57. *Mai 68 – Les mouvements étudiants en France et dans le monde*, ed. Geneviève Dreyfus, Laurent Gervereau, Paris, BDIC, 1988.

58. Catherine Millet, op. cit.

59. Bernard Ceysson, 'Propos à développer à propos de Supports-Surfaces, l'exposition accrochée...' in *Supports-Surfaces*, op. cit.

60. Suzanne Pagé took over as director in 1973.

61. Blaise Gauthier was in charge.

62. The selection committee was formed round François Mathey who had been chosen by the President of the Republic to run the exhibition; he had already organized exhibitions of the work of young artists at the Musée des Arts décoratifs. Mathey surrounded himself with specialists such as Jean Clair, M. Eschapasse, S. Lemoine, Alfred Pacquement and the collector Daniel Cordier.

63. Conversation with Georges Pompidou, *Le Monde*, 17 October 1972.

64. The exhibition opened on 16 May 1972 at the Grand Palais. Re exhibition, see Gérard Monnier, 'L'Expo *Douze ans d'art contemporain*' in *Les Affaires culturelles au temps de Jacques Duhamel, 1971–7*, report on study days held on 7 and 8 December 1993, published by the History Committee of the Ministry of Culture; David Cascaro, forthcoming, 'L'exposition *Douze ans d'art contemporain en France* au Grand Palais ou l'expo Pompidou, May 1972'.

65. Pierre Bourgeade in *Combat*, 15 May 1972.

66. Pierre Gaudibert, *Intégration et/ou subversion*, Paris, Casterman, 1972.

67. The word 'canular' would be used that same year in *Nice-Matin* when Catherine Millet's exhibition *Aspects de l'avant-garde en France* was held. *Nice-Matin*'s headline for this event was 'Avant-garde en France. Canular ou machine à (gros) sous'.

68. 'Manifeste' of 17 May 1960, *L'Internationale situationniste*, no. 4, June 1960, op. cit.

Life in the image

E ach period generates forms, some of which stand out and are exalted immediately, constituting what is seen as the 'mood of the times'. Others appear *a posteriori*, then colour the way we look at a period. Going beyond a chronology of styles and perception, the question may be asked, what generates this 'mood of the times'? What major influence can be put forward, choosing between context (political, economic, climatic, intellectual) and the singularity of each and every creative artist? It must be both, i.e. the conjunction of an artist with his or her own history and the historical moment into which he or she is plunged. So how are we to understand the Sixties, seen from the Nineties as years of nostalgia, aspirations and economic development? Which artists should be picked out? In the previous chapter Laurence Bertrand Dorléac emphasizes one crucial aspect, events as reported in the press, even the national and the more sensational tabloid press: the desire for art and life no longer to be separate, the desire to create a total art combining all the arts and merging into a transformed life and constant transformation. All the ideas and events – what the Situationists proclaimed from the late Fifties, what Fluxus and the happenings proposed, what musical spectacles (the visual, sound and sensory environments, linked with drugs and psychedelic phenomena) had to offer, what architects and designers were looking for through their desire to move 'from the work of art to the global landscape' (Stephen Bann, *L'Oeil*, November 1972), what the Provos in Holland, the hippies and counter-culture, underground, or parallel circuit movements were putting into practice – all these amounted to a material, mental, emotional, visual arts and political revolution.

That revolution raised questions about the role of art, the artist and the museum. While it set out to abolish the confines of canvas or sculpture, following the New Realists in France, it in fact ended up in the Seventies strengthening the role of museums (the only places suitable for housing 'installations') or turning plots of ground into museums ('land art'). But a different movement was developing during these years, involving a return to the image and even to imagery. While the Fifties had celebrated geometric and lyrical Abstraction at the start of the Cold War and post-war, the young generation active in the age of the robot and the pressure-cooker was surrounded by the iconography of

'cheap' culture: the *Arts et loisirs* issue of 2 March 1966 carried the headline 'Raysse, the Matisse of the Prisunics'. Through the Independent Group – Richard Hamilton and Eduardo Paolozzi in particular – the British had started to manipulate the icons of consumption in the Fifties. As early as 1953 the exhibition *Parallel of life and art* had been held at the Institute of Contemporary Arts. How did all this take shape in France? What originality was there to compare with English or American Pop art? What was the role of politics?

The return of narrative

Already in June 1962 Guy Habesque was speculating in *L'Oeil* about the return of figurative art, speaking about artists like Dado and Baj:

> In short we may fear that this new figurative art will constitute purely and simply a return to the subject and the anecdotal which, no longer daring to assume the academic appearance of pictures by Bouguereau or J-P. Laurens, will disguise itself behind the semblance of an *avant-garde* treatment (which not even Francis Bacon does).

Michel Ragon writing in *Cimaise* in 1963 felt that inspiration was emerging in London: 'The new figurative work of these young English artists is clearly linked to the spirit of comic strips'. They had been nicknamed 'Pop artists', and included Boshier, Kitaj, Blake and Peter Phillips. In its summer 1966 issue coinciding with the Venice Biennale, *Art international* officially sanctioned Pop art, emphasizing 'the choice of images: the "cliché"', and mentioning Roy Lichtenstein and Martial Raysse in the same breath. Martial Raysse was the main Pop artist on the French scene. His use of photographs and strident colours and his way of misappropriating stereotyped images of feminine beauty mark a shift of period. In this respect it is significant to compare the *Arman & Raysse* exhibition at the Schwarz gallery in Milan in April 1961 and *Martial Raysse: Mirrors and portraits 1962*, an exhibition at the Dwan Gallery in Los Angeles in January 1963. In the former, Raysse exhibited assemblages of 1960 consumer objects (*Étalage hygiène de la vision*) in the spirit of New Realism as defined by Pierre Restany; on the cover of the catalogue, Raysse and Arman are depicted rummaging through rubbish bins. In the latter Raysse exhibited

Martial Raysse,
Portrait de France,
1965, mixed media
on canvas.
Galerie Nathalie
Seroussi collection

The sixties, utopian years

Opposite page:
Peter Klasen,
Nausée, 1961,
acrylic and objects
on canvas.
Private collection

Cover of catalogue
for Bernard
Rancillac's exhibition
at the Galerie
Mathias Fels in
May 1965.
Private collection

advertising or fashion pictures misappropriated for his own purposes (*Miroir aux houpettes*). A swing from three-dimensional work towards two-dimensional work devoted to the icons of advertising had taken place.

This corresponds with an underground trend in France at the start of the Sixties, which often stemmed from artists in exile. Erró, who came from Iceland and then signed his works Ferro, introduced painted collages of industrial or domestic technology into his Surrealist-Expressionist 'populations' in 1959–60 (*Meca-Make-Up*). Peter Klasen who came to Paris from Germany in 1959 created X-rays of everyday objects (*L'Autopsie*, 1960), as Hervé Télémaque, Jacques Monory and Peter Stämpfli also did in their own manner. Several group exhibitions, resulting from a meeting between artists and the critic Gérald Gassiot-Talabot, confirmed these new focuses of interest. Thus Gassiot-Talabot played the same role for this movement as Pierre

Restany did for the New Realists, defending its practices and formulating them into a theory. In 1964 these were crystallized in the exhibition *Mythologies quotidiennes* at the Musée d'Art moderne de la Ville de Paris. Bernard misap-

propriated wallpaper for the poster. Artists of different generations were brought together. Those exhibiting included Atila, Edmund Alleyn, François Arnal, Eduardo Arroyo, René Bertholo, Antonio Berni, Gianni Bertini, Pierre Bettencourt, Éric Beynon, Mark Brusse, Samuel Buri, Dado, Oyvind Fahlström, Peter Foldes, Yannis Gaïtis, Klaus Geissler, Alberto Gironella, Léon Golub, Horst-Egon Kalinowski, Peter Klasen, Harry Kramer, Jacques Monory, Pistoletto, Bernard Rancillac, Jean-Pierre Raynaud, Martial Raysse, Antonio Recalcati, Bernard Réquichot, Niki de Saint-Phalle, Peter Saul, Hervé Télémaque and Jan Voss.

Inevitably Gassiot-Talabot referred to the New Realists, criticizing the 'paroxysm of the object', and praised Pop art, which 'has the merit of having highlighted the underlying need to reintroduce the human phenomenon into contemporary art, if only by simply designating the products of urban civilization enlarged to the dimensions of monstrous icons or publicity posters'. However he did point out one development: 'They "all" set the precious mobility of life against the static derision of American Pop art', emphasizing 'the painters' preoccupations with movement and temporality'. Then followed the instigatory exhibition of October 1965, *La Figuration narrative dans l'art contemporain,* at the Europe and Creuze galleries. 'In the beginning was narration,' Gassiot-Talabot declared in the catalogue, recalling man's prehistoric creative works. For him 'narration constitutes ... a decisive turning-point, raising questions regarding 80 years of anti-temporal dogmatism; often using new techniques and always in an unprecedented creative climate, it effects a return to deep, ancient reflexes.' He distinguished four forms: anecdotal narration, evolving figuration, narration through the juxtaposition of temporal planes, and narration through portraits or compartmentalized scenes. The influence of comic strip – a sequential narrative – could be felt, especially in the work of Rancillac who in May 1965 exhibited his series of transposed 'comics' at the Mathias Fels gallery. Gassiot-Talabot also stressed the pioneering role of the British artist Peter Foldes, living in France, who had created a picture in nine images, *Lampe électrique et papillon de nuit*, as early as 1948. He produced cartoon films and comic strips. The other trend was towards the use of triptychs, like that by Aillaud, Arroyo and Recalcati, *Une passion dans le désert*, resurrecting 'certain [formulistic]

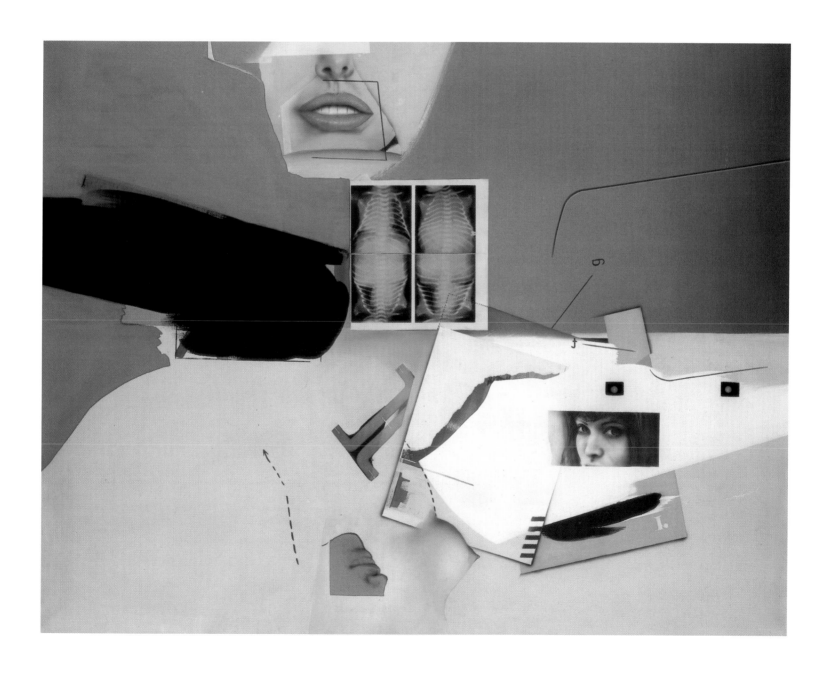

Erró, *Carscape*, 1969,
vinyl on canvas.
Private collection

Peter Stämpfli,
Tomate, 1964,
oil on canvas.
Private collection

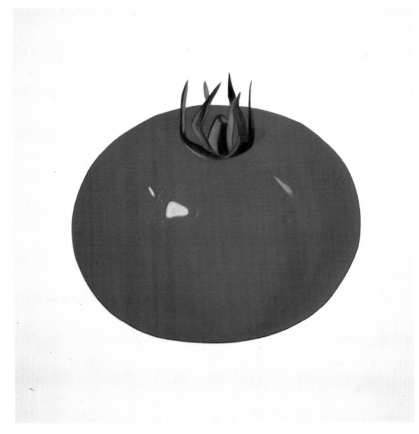

recipes' for 'figuration charged with dynamite, half-sincere and half-provocative' (Gassiot-Talabot). Niki de Saint-Phalle added a political dimension through a feminist plea (*Les Femmes*, 1964). Finally it was declared that, 'British artists have played a major role'; first and foremost was Hamilton, who exhibited, but there were also Kitaj, Peter Phillips and Peter Blake.

We are therefore witnessing a change of period. The return of narrative came in two parts: a tribute to American as well as to English Pop art (especially in view of the phenomena of the Beatles), and a rejection of New Realism. The second issue of *Opus*, honouring Jean-Luc Godard and his 'oeil vérité' in a cover by Roman Cieslewicz, expressed the previously implicit break. In a scathing article, 'À propos du nouveau réalisme', Gassiot-Talabot set forth its merits:

> By making reference to the object taken as it is and not to its representation according to an automatic reproduction of it as in Pop art (silkscreened documents, casts etc.), it appeared to put forward fundamental new choices with no ambiguity: going beyond the easel picture by defining the environment (Arman's or Christo's accumulations in a room or street) ....

But later he asserted that this use of the object had ended in a blind alley, in the repetition of the same formulas; it was necessary to change, or sink 'into humble non-art crafts-manship', for example the metamorphosis of Martial Raysse.

This argument is obviously part of the need of a new movement to distinguish itself from its predecessors, but it also shows how regression can become affirmation. For narrative figuration in fact returned to the image, even to the use of the canvas, so it differs from the use of the object or the appropriation of space. It breaks with the great post-Duchamp movement which led to Conceptual Art, in Italy to Arte Povera, to Supports-Surfaces and BMPT (Buren-Mosset-Parmentier-Toroni). Arroyo, Aillaud and Recalcati actually exhibited a collection of ironic canvases on *La Fin tragique de Marcel Duchamp* at the Galerie Creuze in 1965. Gassiot-Talabot's stance was clearly distinct from the attempts at total art then fashionable (in happenings), even more so than that of artists like Vasarely who wanted to integrate their creative works into a global conception of environments. The attempts to achieve total art were descended from Futurism, while the global conceptions were descended from De Stijl and Bauhaus environments, and Pop art from the misappropriation of industrial images and objects by Dada and Cubism. Thus in the twentieth

Poster for the instigatory exhibition *Mythologies quotidiennes*, **Musée d'Art moderne de la Ville de Paris, July 1964. Private collection**

Top left:
Hervé Télémaque,
Banania no. 3, 1965,
oil on canvas.
Private collection

Top right:
Jacques Monory,
Meurtre no. 6, 1968,
sensitized canvas.
Private collection

Below:
Jacques Monory,
Six heures du matin,
1966, oil on canvas.
Musée d'Art moderne
de la Ville de Paris
collection

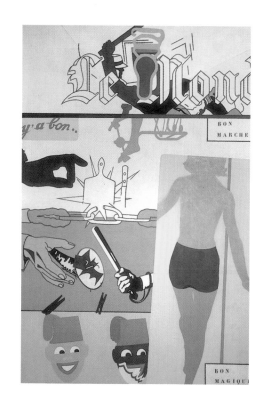

century there have been long affiliated movements which re-emerge sporadically; an accumulation of attempts, as well as knowledge about these attempts; receptivity in terms of geography (creative works from non-western sources) and time (works from the past); and a mixture between art based on a unique object and industrial dissemination. Therefore it is not surprising that a regression should be acclaimed positively as a progression. Against this background, narrative figuration set out to use the misappropriation of images found in Pop art (Hamilton, Paolozzi, Andy Warhol, Roy Lichtenstein) while introducing time and movement into them.

Desire for women, desire for somewhere else

In France this return of the narrative took place in a special context: the first issue of the magazine *Giff-Wiff* came out in July 1962. It was published by the Club des bandes dessinées, run by Francis Lacassin to study and extol the 'ninth art', bringing together journalists, academics and creative artists (Alain Resnais, Jean-Claude Romer, Rémo Forlani, Évelyne Sullerot, Pierre Couperie, Pierre Tchernia). It changed its name to CELEG (Centres d'études des littératures d'expression graphique) and was reconstructed in 1966. The way the comic strip was perceived had been transformed mainly through several protagonists and distributing bodies. In the late Fifties and early Sixties Siné and Bosc took the absurd humorous drawing of the post-war period (Saul Steinberg) and moved it on to express violent political criticism (in *L'Express* in 1958, then with *Siné-Massacre* in 1962). *Pilote*, which was launched in 1959 under the aegis of René Goscinny, one of the instigators of the wildly popular *Astérix* phenomenon, encouraged new writers and formal experiments, leaving behind its juvenile audience. *Hara-Kiri*, created in 1960 by François Cavanna and Georges Bernier, initiated an original and derisive attitude to current affairs, misappropriating the use of drawing. It gave prominence to Fred, Gébé, Cabu, Reiser, Wolinski and Topor. The appropriation of the word 'panique' by Arrabal, Topor and Jodorowsky in 1962 was part of the same attitude. The 'Panique' artists (Topor, Olivier O. Olivier and Christian Zeimert) used collage in the same way as Max Ernst and the Belgian Surrealists René Magritte and Marcel

Drawing by Roland Topor, one of the founders of the Panique group. Private collection

Postcard by Topor, Filliou and Spoerri, associated in *Fluxus, division of implosion, inc.*, 1967. Private collection

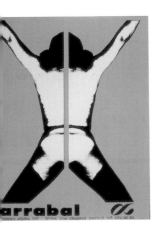

Mariën. They used an old approach to pervert the meaning of the tradition. In 1957 Roland Barthes had published his *Mythologies*, a rhetorical work where the meaning prompts the image. Every Topor drawing is a riddle; Christian Zeimert's illustrations are painted puns. In 1965 in *Pilote* Fred started the adventures of Philémon, who explores the 'letter islands' of the word 'Atlantique', and thus made different demands on the image. Narrative figuration was not just a return to figurative art, but also used it in a context in which it was perceived according to different codes.

The strip cartoon as a cultural phenomenon had been incubating since 1960, and from 1965 became important in the art scene. The audience widened and cartoons became inventive and creative. The exhibition held at the Musée des

Poster by R. Cieslewicz for Arrabal (co-founder of Panique), 1968. Private collection

Right: Poster design by Roman Cieslewicz, 1970. Private collection

Top right: Christian Zeimert, a member of Panique, *La Prise du mamelon*, 1970, oil on canvas. Private collection

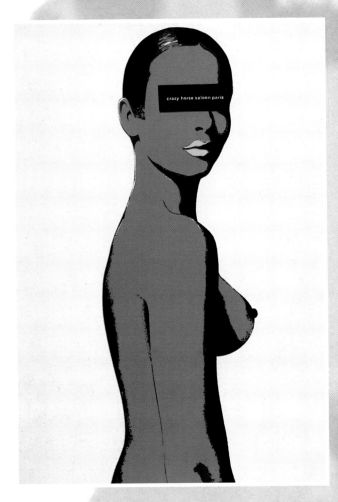

Arts décoratifs in April 1967, *Bande dessinée et figuration narrative*, tied the 'ninth art' into fine art. A history of comic strips from the nineteenth century, it linked plates by the great comic-strip creators with artists working in narrative figuration. Gassiot-Talabot was aware of the dangers of this juxtaposition: 'The potential of the narrative image ... meets its beginning and its end in realism, its birth and its death'. He asserted that this type of painting (Arroyo, Rancillac) 'raises the problem of moral and political commitment'. In a period of strict moral codes, commitment moves on to a desire for sexual freedom (for example the mini-skirt launched in Britain in 1965 by Mary Quant, then in France by Courrèges). Contraceptive pills could be bought freely after the Neuwirth law of December 1967. Figuration also emphasized the body, the female body in particular. This is clear in the case of Topor, and he, Filliou and Spoerri were joint members of *Fluxus, division of implosion, inc.* The same phenomenon drove happenings, and showed in the output of Éric Losfeld (who also published the Surrealists' work, and the magazine *L'Archibras* in 1967). The Surrealist woman, mysterious, idealized and an object of desire, haunts all these works. From spring 1962 Jean-Claude Forest published the adventures of Barbarella in a typical girlie magazine (*V Magazine*), and Éric Losfeld produced a Barbarella album in 1964 (a second edition in 1966 had a Lichtenstein-style cover); the heroine had a bra in 1968 because of censorship pressure. In 1968 Roger Vadim turned the comic strip into a film starring Jane Fonda. As in the work of Allen Jones the eroticism of popular cheap publications could be transposed.

'Cheap' sex served as a lever to arouse young people who rejected a moral order ill-adapted to their new aspirations. Guy Peellaert adopted a coloured Pop-art style to produce erotic images of stars like Sylvie Vartan or Françoise Hardy (*Les Aventures de Jodelle*, Éric Losfeld, 1966; *Pravda la survireuse*, Éric Losfeld, 1968) and play on the codes and personalities of the day, such as Gigi, Crepax

and Pichard. So comic strips were not merely a laboratory of form but a means of laughing at appearances. When Martial Raysse dribbles his fluorescent colours typical of Prisunic dolls, and even the fashion magazines take pleasure in mixing eroticism and the icons of modernity, we are in a period of confused values. In 1966 Antoine in his songs exulted in his long hair and his *Élucubrations*. The American musical *Hair* reached France in 1969, with a Californian feel, naked bodies and Julien Clerc. The rock and Pop star Johnny Hallyday succumbed to an excess of hair and 'flower power'.

Paul Muller's *Le Livre rose du hippy* (1968) celebrated free love and the female body. The whole psychedelic movement, highlighting arabesques and Modern Style plant motifs, was a hymn to female curves and eroticism, a link between drugs, the Symbolist woman, the Surrealist woman and the cheap erotic press. Brigitte Bardot expressed this ambiguity between independence and desire. The eroticization of Pop art, of objects in design or architecture and sex in music (the Beatles, the Rolling Stones, The Who, Pink Floyd, Gainsbourg etc.) crystallized hopes for change. In April 1967 *Arts et loisirs*, edited by

Cover of Jean-Claude Forest's *Barbarella* album, Éric Losfeld, 1964. Private collection

Left: Poster by Guy Peellaert with Jodelle. Private collection

The sixties, utopian years

André Parinaud, devoted its leading article to 'L'érotisme dans la presse, le cinéma, le théâtre, la littérature, l'art, pourquoi?' Kitsch, bad taste, a hotchpotch of references were given pride of place. And in 1969 a magazine like *Plexus* could publish an article like Pierre Restany's: 'L'art contemporain est le langage de la révolution sexuelle'. In 1969 Bernard Rancillac put on an exhibition entitled *Pornographie*. The singer and composer Serge Gainsbourg moved on from a relationship with Brigitte Bardot, the international mythical icon of free love (*Harley Davidson*, 1967), to an English girl, Jane Birkin. In 1969 – the 'erotic year' – he recorded a second version of *Je t'aime... moi non plus* (with Jane Birkin – the 1967 recording with Bardot had not been released) and *L'Anamour*. In 1971 the record *Melody Nelson* mixed desire and the imaginary in the British or American manner.

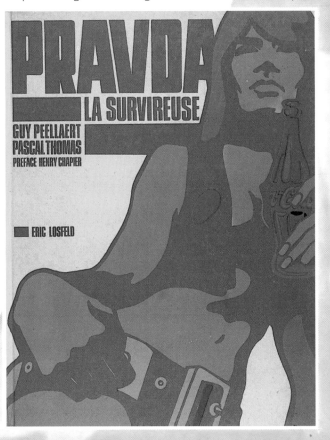

Wilhelm Reich was revered, as were the asocial person, nomadism, deviancy, madness (Antonin Artaud) and oddity (freaks or fairground peepshows).

Different values were advocated opposing consumerism. The British magazine *Oz* then the French magazine *Actuel* (first issued in 1970) emphasized freedom for the body and derangement of all the senses. An erotic festival was organized in Bordeaux in February 1968, while *Suck*, the first 'European sex paper', was published in Amsterdam in October 1969. The Australian feminist Germaine Greer was in at the start, before coming to deplore the commercial aspect: from liberation to exploitation, that was the crux of the ambiguity of hymns to the body.

The rise of desire corresponded with the aspiration towards 'somewhere else', a different life. It was expressed in emphasis on the body, the female body in particular: rooms and furniture were swathed in curves, arabesques, sensual posters and streams of images and colours. Swathing was popular, a pastime that expresses liberation and hopes, even if configuring desire in this way might be confused with the trade in eroticism. In the same way as artists involved in narrative figuration were not the authors of comic strips, and the authors of comic strips transformed narration, those who showed desire also played with kitsch. The photographer Robert Whitaker moved from the Beatles to flower women and on to Dalí, not forgetting psychedelic spectacles and LSD excesses. Eroticism was a subversion, and image and imagery became an impudent vehicle in the struggle against a separate art. Figurations composed of misappropriation, collage and a colourful, erogenous hotchpotch explode from posters, magazines and record sleeves reacting to the world of reason, work, earnestness, austerity, rules. Art and the comic strip shared a way of constructing and narrating life in which imagination and the search for pleasure were predominant.

Manipulating the image

The years 1968 and 1969 marked a turning-point in the message. A desire to bring down the established authorities was added to libertarian aspirations. Figurative works began to show direction. *Oz* in the Sixties and *Actuel* in the early Seventies reported on the manipulation of images, libertarian desires and the communal movement as well as on political battles (pacifism opposing the Vietnam War, femi-

Cover of the magazine
Plexus, edited by Louis
Pauwels, no. 6, 1967,
with a fold-out of a
work by the Surrealist
Clovis Trouille.
Private collection

Cover of *Les Chefs
d'oeuvre du kitsch*,
Planète, 1971.
Private collection

The sixties, utopian years

nist demands, opposition to racism). Herbert Marcuse who was then in the USA published *Eros and civilisation* as early as 1955 and *The one dimensional man* in 1964, denouncing stereotyped behaviour. Structuralism and psychoanalysis then contributed to a critique of the western way of life. Parallel circuits were set up. In January 1971 Louis Pauwels's magazine *Planète* talked of 'the *underground press* in the United States' and the 'fringe press in France'. Generational differences were recognized in the desire to resist the established order. While some fathers had fought the Nazi regime in their youth (clandestinely or in the army), their children listened to music radio stations like Radio Caroline – from a boat in international waters – with a fervour comparable to that of French listeners to Radio London during World War II. The children opposed conspicuous consumption, the moral order and war (in Vietnam). A myth of youth developed, with its own codes, behaviour and circuits. In the September 1966 issue of *Arts et loisirs* when Antonioni

was interviewed about his film *Blow-up* he stated: 'A whole generation of youth is already occupying a future which is beyond us'. Having set off on journeys inside their heads (in 1963 Timothy Leary advocated LSD to his students in California after trying Mexican hallucinogenic mushrooms in 1960), they also set off on the road (to India, Afghanistan). Nomadic wandering became a value, like barter, laziness and imagination.

For France 1968 is still the pivotal year. There were advance indications: the death of Che Guevara in 1967 and subsequently the dissemination of his face on posters as an icon of rebellion and a martyr for freedom, and the hardening of international opposition to American involvement in Vietnam. The Salon de la Jeune Peinture reflected the changes of 1967–8. The critic Michel Troche had been in charge of the salon since 1965, and Arroyo, Aillaud, Cueco, Recalcati, Buraglio, Parré and Tisserand were sitting on the committee. In a June 1965 poster they declared:

Eduardo Arroyo, *La colombe est étranglée*, **1963, oil on canvas in two panels. Private collection**

68

The next Salon de la Jeune Peinture will be objective and partisan ... for example the committee wants to have Chinese, Cuban, Algerian and Russian painters participating .... This would enable us to shift the debate from the aesthetic level, i.e. the links between art and art history, and put it on the only level that interests us, the links between art and history.

In January Aillaud, Alleaume, Arroyo, Artozoul, Baudin, Biras, Cueco, Dat, Fabien, Fleury, Garcia Fons, Milshtein, Parré, Peraro, Recalcati, Rosso, Saidi, Spitzer, Tisserand and Venot had paid 'hommage au vert' (homage to green) at the Musée d'Art moderne de la Ville de Paris: 'This room of painting is a boxing-hall and a *field* of battle'.

Pierre Gaudibert who had founded the ARC (Animation, Recherches, Confrontations) at the Musée d'Art moderne de la Ville de Paris in 1967 organized the exhibition *Le Monde en question* with Gérald Gassiot-Talabot. Both they and Michel Troche (involved in Young Painting) were crucial in supporting current artistic commitments. The move from *Figuration narrative* at the Musée des Arts décoratifs to *Le Monde en question* at the ARC makes 1967 a turning-point. Gassiot-Talabot explained that the organizers (Gaudibert, Arroyo and Rancillac and himself) had tried to bring together all those who were working in a spirit of 'protest'.

In 1968 it was decided that there should be a 'salle rouge', a 'red room for Vietnam' at the Salon de la Jeune Peinture. The move towards radicalism was clear cut. It was an expressly political message signed by Aillaud, Arroyo, Artozoul, Alleaume, Baratella, Bodek, Biras, Buraglio, Cane, Cueco, Darnaud, Dubigeon, Fanti, Fleury, Leroy, Olivier,

LE SURREALISME
en octobre 1967

L'archibras 2

Rieti, Parré, Peraro, Schlosser, Spadarri, Tisserand, Vilmart, Zeimert. The May uprising prevented the salon from being held, and the artists became involved in making collective posters at the École des Beaux-Arts. The exhibition actually took place at the ARC in the Musée d'Art moderne de la Ville de Paris early in 1969 with the slogan written in 1968: 'The war of the people is the only link between these pictures'. It did not have much resonance. But this sign of commitment was pivotal. From April and June 1969 the pictures were taken to the Alsthom factory at Belfort, on to the streets of Pérouges, to the exit of the Berliet factory in Bourg-en-Bresse and were subsequently used as a stage-set at Lons-le-Saunier and Besançon.

A turning-point (1967), an explosion (1968), a backlash (1968–9), the legacy and its development (1969–73): a shock enlivened the debates about what was being depicted. 'Che si' (Yes to Che) appeared on the cover of *Opus international* in 1967 with an article by Gassiot-Talabot on 'Arroyo or pictural subversion'. In the June 1968 issue with a cover by Topor the spotlight was on 'violence'. *L'Enragé* produced by the graphic artist Siné came out during the May troubles. A fiercely committed newspaper produced by graphic artists, it was published from 24 May (until 25 November). Reiser, Wolinski, Bosc, Cardon, Cabu, Gébé, Soulas and Topor were contributors. It was a precursor of *Hara-Kiri Hebdo* (first published 3 February 1969) and then *Charlie-Hebdo* (first issue, 23 November 1970). *Pilote*, the comic-strip paper that crucially experimented during these years, introduced current affairs (no. 456, 1 August 1968,

Cover of the magazine
***L'Archibras*, no. 2, Le**
Surréalisme en octobre
***1967*, Éric Losfeld.**
Private collection

The sixties, utopian years

with Fred and Gébé). That year the collective book *Art et contestation* by Cassou, Ragon, Fermigier, Lascault, Gassiot-Talabot, Moulin, Gaudibert, Micha and Jouffroy was published in Belgium with an *Intérieur américain* by Erró on the cover, dealing with questions of political commitment.

Was this purely and simply a return to Socialist Realism? The quotations by the Vietnamese in charge of the 'salle rouge' at the Salon de la Jeune Peinture, which appeared in the catalogue, in no way prevented the works from ranging widely. A series of articles in *Le Bulletin de la Jeune Peinture* in 1969 (no. 3) tackled Socialist Realism, defending commitment in Marxist terms, while also giving a differentiated vision of it. This was a characteristic of 'critical figurations', which developed from narrative figuration, but asserted meaning and commitment. However, in so doing the artists manipulated images in such a way that the unconscious and collage were used.

In 1969 the 'coopérative des Malassis' was founded, bringing together Cueco, Fleury, Latil, Parré and Tisserand. Its aim was to break the role of the artist, and to transform society. In *L'Art vivant*, a monthly run by Aimé Maeght with Jean Clair as the chief editor, the need for commitment seems to be central in 1971 and 1972. In 1972 (no. 27) Antonio del Guerico, in search of the '*avant-garde*' of the day, reviewed the 1971 Salon de la Jeune Peinture. He

mentioned *L'Appartemensonge* by the Malassis (who did not yet use this signature), *Réalité quotidienne des travailleurs de la mine* (Aillaud, Arroyo, Biras, Chambaz, Fanti, Fromanger, Le Parc, Mathelin, Merri Jolivet, Rancillac, Rieti, Rougemont, Schlosser, Spadari) and *Accidents du travail* (Ernest Pignon): they stood for 'opposition to all formalism on the one hand and a radical criticism of the realist-socialist experiment on the other'. In the same issue the Front des artistes plasticiens condemned the evaluative exhibition *Douze ans d'art contemporain, 1960–72* (May–September)

at the Grand Palais, 'intended to disguise the sad reality that France is a cultural desert'.

From 1965 Rancillac, Arroyo and the Equipo Cronica (a group from Valence consisting of R. Solbès and M. Valdès) employed Pop art techniques (use of photographs, powerful colours and acrylic paint) to produce political messages, sometimes laced with irony (Cronica, *La quantité se transforme en qualité*, or Rancillac, *Mélodie sous les palmes*). Rancillac created images that are more direct: *Les Gardes rouges défilent* (1965), or *Albanie nouvelle* (1970) and *Kennedy, Johnson, Nixon et lieutenant Calley sur le chemin de My-Lai* (1971). However, the question of creative art remained inseparable from work on the message, and this was the distinguishing characteristic of the militant crystallization initiated in 1965, which came to the boil in 1967, exploded in 1968 and occupied 1969 to 1972 by force. Jean-Paul Sartre took over the running of the Maoist *La Cause du peuple* on 27 April 1970 (to counter the ban), took part in *J'accuse* (no. 1, 15 January 1971) and edited *TOUT! Ce que nous voulons: tout* (1971). The Mouvement de libération de femmes (MLF) developed in 1970, and the Front homosexuel d'action révolutionnaire (FHAR) was founded in 1971. The programme of François Mitterand's new Socialist Party in January 1972 was entitled 'Changer la vie'. Pierre Fournier, an early opponent of nuclear power, launched the ecologist magazine *La Gueule ouverte* (with the graphic artists Reiser, Cabu, Gébé, Wolinski and Nicoulaud) in November 1972. Passions were aroused by affairs like that of Gabrielle Russier (a teacher who committed suicide in 1969 after being imprisoned for an involvement with a pupil) and the murder of Brigitte Dewevre, a miner's daughter from Bruay-en-Artois, on 5 April 1972. A strike started on 12 June 1973 at the Lip factory in Besançon where the workers wanted to take over the management. There was a festival in August 1973 on the Larzac plateau to protest

Témoins et témoignages   Actualité

Jean Cassou · Michel Ragon · André Fermigier
Gilbert Lascault · Gérald Gassiot-Talabot · Raymonde Moulin
Pierre Gaudibert · René Micha · Alain Jouffroy

Art et contestation

Cover of the collectively written book *Art et contestation* published in Brussels in 1968, illustrated with a picture by Erró, *Intérieur américain no. 5*. Private collection

against the proposed enlargement of the military camp; and the first *Guide du routard* was published.

The transformation of society cannot be separated from a transformation in the ways in which it is depicted, nor can it be equated with a simple return to realism with a message, similar to that found in Stalinist painting in the Fifties. So the artist was being torn between the quest for an '*avant-garde*' to point the way to collective liberation and liberation of form, and the desire not to stand apart from concrete struggles and strikes. This led to differentiated approaches, but again all centred on the image. The artist produced canvas and image, just as the comic-strip author used images. These images were misappropriated (Asger Jorn, who was a member of the Internationale situationniste after being part of Cobra, misappropriated old pictures or rewrote the balloons of comic strips). The psychedelic trend playfully reappropriated art, photography and images. The Beatles'

Left:
Sketch for a poster by Siné, 1967. Musée d'Histoire contemporaine collection

71

The sixties, utopian years

Henri Cueco,
L'Université, 1968,
oil on canvas.
Private collection

Erró, *Intérieur
américain no. 4*,
acrylic on canvas.
Private collection

Gérard Fromanger,
*Au printemps ou la
vie à l'endroit*, 1972,
acrylic on canvas.
Private collection

Sergeant Pepper album came out in 1967, and in 1969 John Lennon and Yoko Ono posed naked for peace (in Vietnam). In 1970 Jean-Christophe Averty with the *Dim-Dam-Dom* programme on television, Peter Knapp in magazines, and William Klein with his film and album (published by Érich Losfeld) *Mr Freedom* gave a new direction to the icons of desire and consumption. What else had Peter Klasen or Peter Stämpfli been doing since 1963? Or Jacques Monory? A whole dimension of everyday life, of the 'cheap' image, was integrated into creativity. Erró accumulated cars or juxtaposed conflicting iconographies. This period was in fact marked by a return to and reflection on the image. Art and industry were in the process of confronting one another. A movement started by British and American Pop artists developed in France in a way linked with the enormous success of the comic strip and increasing politicization.

Today the radicalization of narrative figuration (Gérard Fromanger), uniting comic strip and Socialist Realism, is seen as producing strange icons that are more deconstructions and displacements than the *illustrative* message of a structured political discourse. As in drawings in the newspapers and comic strips, this French version of 'socialist Pop art' ends up in iconoclastic marriages between the Red Guards and Coco-Cola, or Surrealism and 'surbanalisme' (Bernard Plossu). While the Nineties are full of moving images, networks, mixtures of styles and periods, mental bewilderment and confusion between the unique object and reproductions of it, the Sixties had a resonance that was strangely prophetic of the crises now occurring at the end of the millennium.

The utopias and aspirations have produced strange icons that are a reflection on artistic representation, the status of the artist and the integration of everyday life into art: life in the image; its impetuous pulse; life seized by the image; irrevocable separation; the derisory; the outline, the collision, formats, colour, physical presence; poster art; art based on juxtapositions; the unconscious at work; fixed screens; moments in time; periods full of experiment; the passage from one world to another (Philip K. Dick, Philippe Druillet). Nobody can pass through the image. Pleasure as opposed to clones of happiness. Physical love offers no way out, nor does revolution. Everything must be renewed.

Laurent Gervereau

Bernard Rancillac,
Mélodie sous les palmes,
1965, vinyl on canvas.
Galerie Krief collection

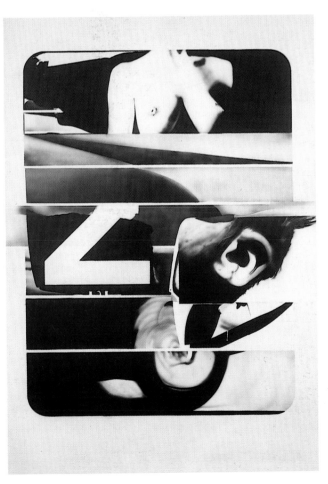

Peter Klasen,
Haute Tension, 1966,
acrylic on canvas.
Galerie Carré collection

Greer, sex and the Sixties

'Sexual intercourse began in 1963,
Which was far too late for me...'

The poet Philip Larkin was wrong; the beginning of sexual liberation in the Sixties may be dated to November 1960, when an Old Bailey jury decided, finally, that D.H. Lawrence's novel, *Lady Chatterley's lover* (1928), was not obscene. Penguin Books, who had had the temerity to publish it, sold over 200,000 copies within a few days. The judge and the defence, who asked whether the jury would wish their servants to read Lawrence's novel (focused on Constance Chatterley's liaison with her husband's gamekeeper), exemplified the rigid attitudes of a class society in confrontation with a new order.[1]

But 1963, an *annus mirabilis* for the Sixties, beginning with a winter freeze such as had been unknown since 1741, soon hotted up. On 22 March the Conservative Secretary of State for War, John Profumo, made a statement to the Commons denying any improper relationship between himself and the model Christine Keeler – icon of the new era as she was represented in Lewis Morley's classic photograph, nude, astride a curvaceous Arne Jacobsen chair; on 4 June Profumo resigned, admitting that he had lied to the Commons. It was sleaze... Harold Macmillan's government, dishonoured, entered its final phase.[2] Harold Wilson came to power in October 1964. His promises of a new era rushing to embrace the 'white heat of technology' envisioned a bright, scientific future, symbolized by the phallic, silver Post Office Tower, London's highest landmark which opened in October 1965. Women became a force in Parliament at the top level of government: Barbara Castle moved from her post as Minister of Overseas Development (1964–5) to Transport (1965–8), becoming First Secretary of State and Secretary of State for Employment and Productivity (1968–70); Jennie Lee had a seminal role to play in government policies on the arts; the 21-year-old Irish Nationalist, Bernadette Devlin, made a tempestuous maiden speech in the House of Commons in 1969.[3] Ambitious young women entered the new 'red-brick' universities as well as Oxbridge on equal terms with men. While for the majority, women's lot remained, at first, largely unchanged, it was womanpower, rather than technology's upward curve, that genuinely revolutionized the decade of the

Sixties. Sexual liberation and an evolving, feminist consciousness fundamentally changed life in England in a way incomparable to France, where the very word *'féminisme'* and the spectres it evokes are anathema, where a delayed vote for women (granted in 1944!), delayed decisions on contraception, and the conflicting demands of Marxism and psychoanalysis constituted an essentially Seventies phenomenon.[4] In England feminism gained its heroines and its 'lettres de noblesse' in the Sixties, with outrage, flamboyance and a sense of humour, despite the odds.

The contraceptive pill, invented in 1952, banned by the Roman Catholic hierarchy in England and Wales in May 1964, must take much of the credit, lifting the curse of our sex with promises of euphoric freedom. The Bishop of Woolwich declared: 'Few will now bother to ask whether the Pope is infallible. They are more concerned with whether the Pill is infallible.' (It was certainly problematic.)[5] The beautiful female pioneers, armed with this new infallibility ('You've got to excite me and you've got to be jolly marvellous to attract me.... If I want you I'll have you ...'[6]), were most likely to be a metropolitan phenomenon. London was where, suddenly, the conflation of 'high and low', the impact of mass culture across the spectrum of the arts and the interchange with the world of music and fashion involved women, crucially, as creators and consumers; poets (Sylvia Plath), novelists (Iris Murdoch, Edna O'Brien), models (Twiggy, Jean Shrimpton), singers (Sandy Shaw, Cilla Black, Dusty Springfield), groupies (Marianne Faithfull who immortalized a particular usage for Mars Bars), dancers (Babs and Pan's People on *Top of the Pops*), actresses (Vanessa Redgrave, Julie Christie, Honor Blackman clad in kinky leather in TV's *The Avengers*), girlfriends, fans – the teenagers screaming for the Beatles – all were essential for the Sixties spectacle.[7] And with these conflations of categories, class itself was to some extent dissolved and absorbed in a field of new energies, where for the first time to speak Cockney was chic; dissolved, that is, except for the very poor, who in the wake of the exposé of the Angry Young Men generation (John Osborne's play *Look back in anger*, 1956, with its 'kitchen sink' realism still described a *status quo*), began to find a voice in such works as Nell Dunn's novel *Poor cow*, dramatized for television and directed by Ken Loach. He directed its sequel, *Up the junction*,

Photograph
of Christine Keeler
by Lewis Morley,
1963. National
Portrait Gallery.
© Lewis
Morley/Akehurst
Bureau

followed by Jeremy Sandford's *Cathy come home* in 1966. Immense public concern, as a result, finally generated the Shelter campaign for the homeless in London.[8] As for the permissive society, those who were at the centre, such as Mary Quant, could proclaim: 'We are less permissive to authority .... And we are less permissive to violence .... The Beautiful People are non-violent anarchists, constructive anarchists... the young today are less materialistic and more intelligent than they have ever been.'[9]

Mary Quant epitomized the new London looks; her first mini-skirt dated back to 1958. 'Rightly or wrongly, I have been credited with the Lolita Look, the Schoolgirl Look, the Wet Weather Look, the Kinky Look, the Good Girl Look and lots of others and it is said that I was first with knickerbockers, gilt chains, shoulderstrap bags and high boots.' Gorgeous eye make-up went with the essential dark fringe. The successful woman appreciated the importance of clothes – as opposed to the 'intellectual girl' or the 'square', who neglected

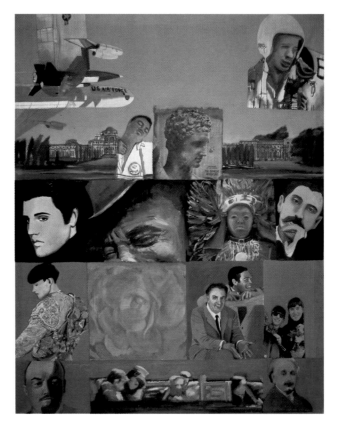

Pauline Boty, *It's a man's world I,* **1964, oil on board. Courtesy Estate of Pauline Boty.**

these issues at her peril. The first *Sunday Times* colour supplement of 1962 showed Jean Shrimpton modelling clothes by Quant, photographed by David Bailey. Quant recalled: 'I just happened to start when that "something in the air" was coming to the boil. The clothes I made happened to fit in exactly with the teenage trend, with Pop records and espresso bars, and jazz clubs, the rejuvenated *Queen* magazine, *Beyond the fringe, Private Eye*, the discothèques and *That was the week that was* were all born on the same wavelength.'[10] In contrast to the practical and dynamic Quant look, the Biba boutique, which opened in

Kensington in 1964, offered Barabara Hulannicki's neo-Pre-Raphaelitism in Art Nouveau surroundings: smudgy purple eyes, dark and dingy robes for more languorous, frizzy-haired beauties. In this period of revivalism and a Portobello Road aesthetic, Alphonse Mucha, Aubrey Beardsley and Burne-Jones reproductions vied with the psychedelic posters on many a teenage wall.

Biba wasn't just a label, it was a scene: Keith Richards and Anita Pallenberg dined in the Rainbow Room; Jean-Paul Belmondo and Diana Ross bought lampshades; Mick Jagger and Rod Stewart bought satin shirts and fake-fur jackets; Jean Shrimpton bought four of everything; David Bowie in his glam-rock phase would trawl the cosmetics counter, and Twiggy would drop by to see her best friend Barbara.[11]

England witnessed a brief and lovely feminization of the male, long-haired, clad in silks and velvets, gentle, dreamy, creative. Carnaby Street had seventeen boutiques out of which thirteen were for men:

When young men grew their hair, a great many pin-headed or coarse-featured people became suddenly finely proportioned. Being unexpectedly beautiful they found themselves able to behave unexpectedly well. Long hair and the mystique of gentleness brought the sexes together quite unconsciously, and so other developments became possible. People made better love, and more of it, than before, for which relief much thanks.[12]

As far as art was concerned – and in striking contrast to France, whose major female figure of the 1960s, Niki de

Saint-Phalle, enjoys a curiously over-determined or invisible status (she is, once again, excluded from this show) – women made their mark too on the London scene.[13] Witness the experimental poem machines, the copper light columns, the dreamy perpetual motion machines with lamps, turntables and acrylic balls by Liliane Lijn, or the early collaborative works of Joan Hills with Mark Boyle. While Jann Haworth's outrageous soft sculpture, *Snake lady* (1969–71), confronts us with a sexy Eve in snake-skin trousers who is almost throttled symbolically by her pet python, some forms of art may be seen to invite more subtle proto-feminist interpretations: David Alan Mellor has remarked upon the emergence of an art which 'might now be thought of as a form of "écriture féminine"'. The artist Gillian Ayres described her own sweeping gestural painting as 'A shape – a relationship – a body – oddness – shock – mood – cramped – isolated – acid – sweet – encroaching – pivoting – fading – bruised'. Contrast her statement with that of Bridget Riley: 'running ... early morning ... cold water ... fresh things, slightly astringent'.[14] Riley's art, with its optical zing coming out of geometrical Abstraction, had an extraordinarily distinctive psychic and sensory impact – soon copied by the fashion designers in Paris and New York. Her first solo show was held in 1962: she participated in the *New generation* show at the Whitechapel Gallery in 1964, *Painting and sculpture of a decade* at the Tate and by 1965 in the international *Responsive eye* at the Museum of Modern Art, New York.

In 1969 she won the international prize for painting at the 34th Venice Biennale.

The only English female Pop artist, Pauline Boty, opted for a figurative painting with strong geometrically-structured, coloured backgrounds which may well be compared to the work of Peter Blake, her mentor and admirer at the Royal College of Art. Indeed she posed for the photographer Lewis Morley naked on a couch save for Blake's heart-shaped tribute, *Valentine* (1962), echoed by her *Monica Vitti heart* (1963), containing her self-portrait.[15] Whereas Blake's 'fanzine' attitude in his *Girlie door* (1959), with its female pin-ups, or homage to Elvis, *Got a girl* (1960–1), is shot through with frustration and a wistful sentimentality, Boty – through her sex and authorship alone, but surely with deliberately referential irony – subverts the genre with the *Playboy*-like, boob-shot painted fragments of *It's a man's world II* (1965–6). It was not easy at first: Jane Percival, Boty's contemporary, claimed that 'Women painters like myself felt very alienated, the full feminist movement hadn't come in and we worked in isolated pools, mostly of depression.'[16] Boty, however, the 'Brigitte Bardot of the Royal College of Art', enjoyed displaying her own sexuality, if apprehensively, and performing for both the theatre and television. From 1959, with the *Daily Express* profile of Boty as secretary of the 'Anti-ugly society' (a campaign against the boom in ugly buildings), Boty combined the role of painter with that of model, actress and provocateuse. She appeared as the only female artist and in Ken Russell's television pro-

Allen Jones,
Brigitte Bardot
***T. Shirt**, 1964,*
lithograph.
Courtesy the artist

Allen Jones,
Life class, 1968,
lithograph.
Courtesy the artist

gramme, *Pop goes the easel* (1962), starring with Derek Boshier, Peter Phillips and Peter Blake. Produced by Huw Weldon for the 'Monitor' series it was broadcast on 25 March 1962 (Blake's sequence involved a dream fantasy devoted to Brigitte Bardot). Boty posed for the photographer Michael Ward in 1963, pouting suggestively in bra and suspenders in front of her paintings *Tom's dream* and *Celia with some of her heroes* (1963), and again for Lewis Morley, Roger Mayne and *Vogue*, where she was photographed by David Bailey. Besides acting herself she made costumes for a production of *The firebird* and stage designs. Her art has been rediscovered only recently.[17] The spiralling, red rose-petal square in *It's a man's world I* (1964) performs a *'mis en abîme'* of the female sex, mocking the sharp exteriority of the painted male mug-shots (sometimes viciously cropped) of astronaut, Elvis, Proust, Einstein. The same flower, dangerously hairy, is the centrepiece of the orgasmic *5,4,3,2,1* (1963), with its explicit slogan 'Oh for a fu...'; a dark eyed girl in shades with open mouth screams ecstatically at the base of the image. Boty's premature death in 1966 at the age of 28 deprived the Sixties of one of its most original female artists.

To what extent she was genuinely subversive – to what extent complicitous with the essentially phallocentric constructions of Pop art – remains the moot point essentially at the heart of the problem of women, sex and the Sixties.[18] The raw material of Pop art itself was of course the world of mass culture, for which woman herself functioned as the impotent sign. From the sublime to the ridiculous – impossibly idealized in the dream-figures of the stars (Marilyn Monroe above all, Brigitte Bardot, Elizabeth Taylor), down to the shapes and forms of new kitchen appliances – woman had to be at once unattainable, pneumatic and 'supremely, housewife, mother, cupcake' (Richard Hamilton).[19] She was treated with an almost respectful awe by Peter Blake, with a lofty intellectualized irony by Hamilton, with a 'hard-on' slickness by Allen Jones, whose horny, porny girls were painted in virulent colours with long legs and extended stilettos, or modelled on all fours as the ultimate Sixties coffee-table. (Was this liberation? Jones, of all these artists, has suffered from a feminist backlash.) The 'liberated' woman was caught in an impossible dilemma. As participant in the carnival, she enjoyed the very mascarade that signified her

own subjection, her 'desire for the fetish': she became what Germaine Greer would call a 'female eunuch'. Certainly for Greer, an exultant participant for much of the time (see her hoydenish antics in Robert Whitaker's film *Darling, do you love me?* 1967), there was at the very least a case of 'Germaine' versus 'Dr G.', made explicit in the contrast between her contributions to *Oz* magazine and *The female eunuch* (1970):

> The gynolatry of our civilisation is written large upon its face, upon hoardings, cinema screens, televisions, newspapers, magazines, tins, packets, cartons, bottles, all consecrated to the reigning deity, the female fetish. Her dominion must not be thought to entail the rule of women, for she is not a woman .... For she is a doll: weeping, pouting or smiling, running or reclining, she is a doll. She is an idol, formed of the concatenation of lines and masses, signifying the lineaments of satisfied impotence.[20]

Oz appeared in 1967, slipping in between the glossy fashion magazines, *Vogue, Harpers* and *Queen*, the intelligent man's pornography such as *Playboy* and *Penthouse*, or the satirical, newspaper-format *Private Eye*. Founded in Sydney, Australia in 1963, *Oz* was edited by Richard Neville, with photography and design input by Robert Whitaker and Martin Sharp.[21] The intellectual scene in Melbourne would emigrate in part to England, subsequent to the Beatles' tour

ber, guest-edited by Greer, 'Welcome to cuntpower *Oz*', with her article: 'The politics of female sexuality', a daring and tender paean to the female sex organ (expanded in 'Lady, love your cunt' for *Suck* magazine in 1971).[26] Yet the ironic postscript to the erupting slag-heap belied the 'cunt-power' message: 'Meet Wendy – *Oz*'s yum-yum rubber fun substitute, silent, clean, insatiable', and Judith Malina in 'The kiss of the lash' described 'the dirty jokes and dirty cartoons and the *Playboy* atmosphere' as 'the most dramatic example of female repression and female suffering', opinions ratified by the proliferating small ads for sex aids and pornography.[27] After national scandal with the notorious *Oz* trial (the police finally busted the magazine after the Schoolkid's *Oz*, no. 28, edited by minors), 'Whatever happened to the hippes?' in *Oz* no. 39 expressed the malaise which by 1971 sigalled the end of euphoria, the Sixties and *Oz* itself: 'This sagging of spirits may reflect simple depression at the endless and sickening war, at the realisation that it may be too late to do anything about ecological catastrophe, at the difficulty of finding employment even in the sterile busywork of government and the big corporations'.[28]

The year 1969 marked the 50th annivesary of female suffrage in England; Greer's *The female eunuch*, first published in 1970, was a serious and brilliant summary of the battles of the Sixties, won and lost. The *Oz* mode was abandoned for a more passionate, more intellectual discussion in which Greer situated herself within a tradition of significant precursors: Simone de Beauvoir's *The second sex* (the first English edition appeared in 1953) and Betty Friedan's *The feminine mystique* (1963), with its exposure of the fallacy of the American 'happy housewife syndrome' (the very material of Edouardo Paolozzi's 'Bunk' series of scrap-book collages) come first to mind. However, *The female eunuch* is orchestrated throughout with the great voices of liberation whose battle began in eighteenth-century England, Mary Wollenstonecraft (*A vindication of the rights of women*, 1792), William Blake (*Visions of the daughters of Albion*, 1793) and John Stuart Mill (*The subjection of women*, 1869). One may argue that the influence of such figures had led, directly, to the entry of women to Oxford and Cambridge in the late nineteenth century, creating, long before women's suffrage in 1919, the proud tradition which Dr Greer, in blue-stocking mode, inherited.[29] *The female*

eunuch, divided into sections on Body, Soul, Love, Hate, Revolution, and within these into parts (Body comprises Gender, Bones, Curves, Hair, Sex, The Wicked Womb) delightfully mixes high and 'low' culture in Sixties style, 'low' ranging from Chaucer's bawdy Wife of Bath to the contemporary Merseyside poet, Roger Macgough's 'Discretion':

> Discretion is the better part of Valerie
> though all of her is nice
> lips as warm as strawberries
> eyes as cold as ice....[30]

'So what is the beef?' Greer asks. 'Maybe I couldn't make it. Maybe I don't have a pretty smile, good teeth, nice tits, long legs, a cheeky arse, a sexy voice ....Then again, maybe I'm sick of the masquerade .... I'm sick of being a transvestite. I refuse to be a female impersonator. I am a woman, not a castrate.'[31]

Photograph by Lewis Morley of Pauline Boty, 1963. Courtesy National Portrait Gallery. © Lewis Morley/ Akehurst Bureau

The theme of the female eunuch, the woman 'castrate', is developed in another frame of reference, contemporary America, with quotations from Philip Roth's *Portnoy's complaint* and Solanas's 'SCUM manifesto': 'To be sure he's a "Man", the male must see to it that the female is clearly a "Woman", the opposite of a "Man", that is, the female must act like a faggot.'[32]

81

Transvestism itself was however a leitmotif of the 1960s: indeed, Greer takes April Ashley, the sex-change model (who married the Hon. Arthur Corbett), 'disgraced, unsexed', as 'our sister and our symbol'.[33] The art world was exploding with confessional self-representations from David Hockney's *We two boys together clinging* (1961) to Andy Warhol's self-portraits in drag, complemented by those of Michel Journiac in France or Urs Luthi in Germany. From the 1950s, the homosexual writer Genet enjoyed great popularity in the United States and England; indeed Pauline Boty created extravagant sets for a production of Genet's *The balcony* in 1964–5. Jean-Paul Sartre's preface to the translated edition of Genet's *The maids*, where he speaks of 'this perpetual challenging of masculinity by a symbolic femininity and of the latter by the secret feminity which is the truth of all masculinty', is astonishingly close to Solanas's 'Women, in other words, don't have penis envy; men have pussy envy'.[34] Only recently has the rise of Pop art in the United States been seen not merely as a figurative and popular celebration of consumer opulence, but as 'closely allied with the rise of gay identity'.[35] From Greenberg's notorious *avant-garde* and kitsch of 1939, to Susan Sontag's 'Notes on camp' of 1964 in the United States, followed by Greer's analysis of the changing London scene from 1967 to 1970, the art of the Sixties, embodied by Pop, can be seen to short circuit, precisely at the intersection of image, simulacra and masquerade, with sexual identity. Astonishingly, Sixties histories are still being written from a masculinist/formalist point of view.... [36]

Not all Sixties girls had Dr Greer's powers of analysis or sublimation, however; the Quant girls, the Biba girls, the *Oz* girls had lots of fun (as well as tears), as did many less visible, ordinary mortals. Greer's challenge to the Daughters of Albion was to replace the 'idol... signifying the lineaments of satisfied impotence' with what William Blake had called 'the lineaments of Gratified Desire'.[37] Alas! it was never easy. Greer's propositions, full of energy and hope, now seem impossibly dated: 'Ultimately, the greatest service a woman can do her community is to be happy; the degree of revolt and irresponsibility which she must manifest to acquire happiness is the only sure indication of the way things must change if there is to be any point in continuing to be a woman at all'.[38] While happiness appears as the nostalgic quest of the Sixties, from Nell Dunn's heroines to the great festivals of love and music in Hyde Park or the Isle of Wight, it was, as always, elusive – more likely to be found, Mary Quant declared, 'eating baked beans in the middle of the night' than as a Sixties super-icon.[39]

An immediate riposte to Greer came in the form of voluptuous Greek-born, Cambridge-educated Arianna Stannisopolous: *The female woman* (1973) attacked Greer and Women's Lib at its most militant (an act of both doomed competition and homage).[40] The American Kate Millet in her *Sexual politics* (1970) complemented and extended Greer's literary analyses; by the 1970s both authors had become essential reading for university literature courses.[41] All told, Greer's impact was decisive, influencing far more than her own generation. Time has turned *The female eunuch* into a rather poignant, while still exhilarating, document of its age. Greer's preface to the 21st anniversary edition of *The female eunuch* acknowledges the local emphasis of the original publication and refers to 'women of the rich world, whose oppression is seen by poor women as freedom'. Leaving the Sixties, Greer here alerts us to the predicament of poor women the world over in post-Communist consumer society, appallingly unprotected, the battle for freedom still to begin: 'Freedom from Fear, freedom from Hunger, freedom of Speech and freedom of Belief. Most of the women in the world are still afraid, still hungry, still mute and loaded by religion with all kinds of fetters, masked, muzzled, mutilated and beaten.'[42] Frenchmen may well cry 'Vive la différence!' for it is cultivated unceasingly in all aspects of life.[43] 'Plus ça change...' we may say, looking at France and England today. But with our freedoms come responsibilities: the battle continues.

Sarah Wilson

Photograph
by Robert Whitaker:
Germaine Greer in
make-up for the
filming of *Darling,
do you love me?* 1967.
Courtesy Robert
Whitaker

1. See Kenneth Tynan, 'Lady Chatterley's trial', *The Observer*, 6 November 1960 repr. in Ray Conolly, ed., *In the Sixties*, London, Pavilion Books, 1995, pp. 10–12.

2. See Clive Irving, Ron Hall, Jeremy Wallington, *Scandal 63*, London, Heinemann, 1963. Pauline Boty was comissioned to paint *Scandal '63*.

3. See Bernadette Devlin: *The price of my soul*, London, Pan, 1969.

4. See 'Dossier 1970–81. Que sont devenues ces féministes?', *Le temps de femmes*, no. 12, summer 1981; Danièle Léger, *Le Féminisme en France. 1970–80*, Paris, Editions de la Sycomore, 1982; Claire Duchen, *Feminism in France from May '68 to Mitterand*, London, Routledge and Kegan Paul, 1986.

5. By 1962, 3,536 women were taking the Pill in Britain; by 1969, 1.25 million (15%). See 'The Pill' and 'Contraception' in the indispensable Anthony D'Abreu, ed., *The Sixties* (with Christopher Booker, Tony Palmer, Roger McGough), London Sociopack Publication, 1973 (unpaginated), and Germaine Greer, 'Contraception – 1972', *Sunday Times*, 12 March 1972, and 'On population and women's right to choose', *Spare Rib*, March 1975, in *The madwoman's underclothes. Essays and Occasional Writings. 1968–85*, London, Picador Paperbacks, pp. 105–107, 192–4.

6. Mary Quant on the Pill, interviewed by Alison Adburgham, *The Guardian*, 10 October 1967, in R. Conolly, ed., *In the Sixties*, op. cit., p. 148.

7. For women's achievements in finance (Lloyds of London), industry, education, journalism, theatre and television, see Germaine Greer, *The female eunuch*, London, 1970; Flamingo, 1993, pp. 151–3.

8. Nell Dunn's *Talking to women*, London, MacGibbon and Kee, 1965 (including interviews with the artist Pauline Boty and novelist and mother Edna O'Brien), is massively preoccupied with questions of love, happiness, sex, appearances, but also guilt, fear and the emotional price of achievement and marriage. Her novel, *Poor cow*, London, MacGibbon and Kee, 1967, depicting a working-class mother in slum conditions, with criminal lovers, permanently in prison – a life of drudgery pierced by fantasies and memories of love – won paperback rights of £10,000. (Dunn was an heiress, her husband, Sandford, an Old Etonian....) For the lot of the poor see also Tony Parker's 1969 television interviews of women in prison: *Five women*.

9. See Alison Adburgham: 'Mary Quant' in Conolly, ed., *In the Sixties*, op. cit., p. 146.

10. Mary Quant: *Quant on Quant*, London, 1966; Pan, 1967, p.79, and on the 'intellectual girl' and the 'square' pp. 96–7.

11. Angela Buttolph, 'Return of the Biba babes', *Evening Standard*, 7 May 1996, p. 28.

12. Germaine Greer, 'Hippies in Asia', *Sunday Times*, 27 August 1972, in *The madwoman's underclothes*, op. cit., p. 120.

13. Despite her ferocious, angry and bloodied work of the Sixties, Niki de Saint-Phalle's work has constantly been infantilized through lack of scholarship in France; only in 1994 did her book *Mon secret* reveal the childhood abuse that generated this rage. Her film *Daddy*, with its incest theme and scenes of women masturbating or being masturbated, was shown in London at the Hammer Cinema, November 1972, and subsequently in April 1973 at the 11th New York Film Festival.

14. See 'Statement. Gillian Ayres, 1962' in David Alan Mellor, *The Sixties art scene in London*, London, Barbican Art Gallery, 1993, p. 29, and Bridget Riley quoted by Thomas Crow, *The rise of the Sixties*, London, Everyman Art Library, pp. 112–13, illustrated with a Riley copycat 'evening ensemble' from the Carpucci Winter Collection, Paris, 1965.

15. 20 out of the 54 works in *Blake, Boty, Porter, Reeve*, a group show of 1961 held by the Artists International Association, were by Boty. Christine Porter's works were apparently Abstract.

16. Boty quoted in Sabine Durrant, 'The darling of her generation: Pauline Boty was the heartbreaker of the Sixites art scene', *Independent on Sunday*, 7 March 1993, p. 14, quoted in Terry Ann Riggs, 'It's a man's world: An analysis of the life and work of Pauline Boty', MA report, Courtauld Institute of Art, University of London, 1996, p. 5, to which I am greatly indebted.

17. See *Pauline Boty, 1938–66*, London, Mayor Gallery, 1993, and Mellor, *The Sixties art scene*, op. cit. *Celia with some of her heroes*, 1963, has been acquired for the new Berardo Collection, Sintra, Portugal.

18. Boty's confusion and vulnerablility are revealed in the conversation with Nell Dunn in *Talking to women*, op. cit. For the intellectualization of the problem of 'women's desire for the fetish', see Jacqueline Rose, *Sexuality and the field of vision*, London, Verso, 1986, p. 212: 'woman is taken to desire herself but only through the term which precludes her', and Marjorie Garber on female fetishism and fetish envy in *Vested interests: Cross dressing and cultural anxiety*, New York, Routledge, 1992, pp. 126–7.

19. See Richard Hamilton's extraordinary text 'Urbane image', *Living Arts*, no. 2, June 1963, in Mellor, *The Sixties art scene*, op. cit., pp. 165–6 (conflating world capitalism, appliances, Jane Russell's Exquisite form bra, longfocus lenses, Mr Universe) and his depiction of 'feminized' cars, toasters, Braun appliances etc.

20. Germaine Greer, *The female eunuch*, op. cit., pp. 68–9.

21. See David Alan Mellor, *Underground London: The photographs of Robert Whitaker 1965–70*, Brighton Museum and Art Gallery, 1994.

22. Frank Zappa identified the 'groupie' as 'high priestess of free love and the group grope' in *Rolling Stone*, no. 27, 15 February 1961 (Greer, *The female eunuch*, op. cit., p. 297). 'A groupie's vision' is reproduced in Greer, *The madwoman's underclothes*, op. cit., pp. 11–13.

23. For recent summaries of the American feminist scene see Ellen Willis, 'Radical Feminism and Feminist Radicalism' (Ti-Grace Atkinson, Anne Koedt etc.), Rachel Bowlby, '60s feminism' and Sylvia Fererici, 'Putting feminism back on its feet' (with bibliographies), in Sohnya Sayers, Anders Stephenson, Stanley Aronwitz and Fredric Jameson, eds, *The Sixties without apology*, Minneapolis, University of Minnestoa Press, 1984, pp. 91 ff., 326–7 and 338 ff.

24. Valerie Solanas, 'SCUM (Society for cutting up men) manifesto', New York, 1968; London, The Olympia Press, 1971, with a preface by Vivian Gornick c. 1967. Having nearly killed Warhol, Solanas sets out her agenda (including the destruction of 'Great Art'): 'there remains to civic-minded, responsible, thrill-seeking females only to overthrow the government, eliminate the money system, institute complete automation and destroy the male sex', p. 3.

25. For 'The slag-heap erupts' see Greer, *The madwoman's underclothes*, op. cit., pp. 25–9.

26. For 'The politics of female sexuality' and 'Lady, love your cunt' see Greer, *The madwoman's underclothes*, op. cit., pp. 36–40 and 74–7.

27. Greer would go on to write serious articles about both pornography, 'A needle for your pornograph', *Sunday Times*, 22 July 1971, and an extensive treatment of the politics of rape: 'Seduction is a four-letter word', *Playboy*, January 1973, reproduced in *The madwoman's underclothes*, op. cit., pp. 65–7 and 152–68.

28. Alan Watts, 'Whatever happened to the hippies?', repr. from *Earth*, June 1971, in *Oz*, no. 39 (undated).

29. The founding conference of the British Women's Liberation movement took place at Ruskin College, Oxford, in 1970.

30. For this lyrical poetry of the Sixties, contemporary with the Beatles' lyrics (where love was still sentimental, polite and gentle), see Adrian Henri, Roger McGough, Brian Patten, *The Mersey sound*, Harmondsworth, Penguin Books, 1967 and reprints.

31. Greer, *The female eunuch*, op. cit., p. 70. A plethora of delightful and

learned references run the gamut from the 'high' to the 'low' of English literature and make this a worthy successor to De Beauvoir's *Second sex*. See
also Sarah Wilson, 'Femininities-Masquerades' in *Rrose ... is a Rrose ... is a
Rrose: Gender performance in photography*, New York, Solomon R.
Guuggenheim Musem, 1997, for a comprehensive account of the 'masquerade' problem.

32. Ibid., pp. 86 (Roth) and 102, quoting from Solanas, 'SCUM',
op. cit., p. 50.

33. Greer, *The female eunuch*, op. cit., pp. 70–72.

34. Jean-Paul Sartre, preface to Jean Genet, *The maids and deathwatch. Two
plays*, trans. Bernard Frechtman, New York, 1954, Appendix III, pp. 677–8,
and Solanas, 'SCUM', op. cit., pp. 6–7: 'the male, because of his obsession
to compensate for not being female combined with his inability to relate and
to feel compassion, has made of the world a shitpile...'

35. Kenneth E. Silver, 'Modes of disclosure: The construction of gay identity
and the rise of Pop Art', *Hand-painted Pop: American art in transition,
1955–62*, The Museum of Contemporary Art, Los Angeles; New York,
Rizzoli, 1993, pp. 178–203.

36. See Marco Livingstone, 'A big sensation [sic] in UK Pop', *Pop Art*,
London, Royal Academy of Arts, 1991, pp. 146–53, and notably Crow, *The
rise of the Sixties*, op. cit., 1996.

37. William Blake, 'The question answer'd': Poems from the Note-book,
1793, in *Blake: Complete Writings*, ed. Geoffrey Keynes, Oxford, OUP,
1966, p. 180.

38. Greer, *The female eunuch*, op. cit., pp. 316–17.

39. 'Now – it would seem – for a woman to be happy she must have ...
a career ... a spindryer ... diamonds ... TV ... a mink-lined mackintosh ...
a lover ... an electric toaster ... good health ... pep-up pills and sedatives ...
two cars (at least!) ... Jane Fonda's face and Simone de Beauvoir's intellect
... a working knowledge of child psychology ... a child ... a husband who
beats her every Friday.' Mary Quant, *Quant by Quant*, op. cit. pp. 143–5.

40. See Arianna Stannisopoulos, *The female woman*, London, Davis Poynter,
1973.

41. See Kate Millet, *Sexual politics*, New York, 1970; London,
Hart-Davis, 1971.

42. Greer, *The female eunuch*, op. cit., p. 11.

43. Ibid., p. 34.

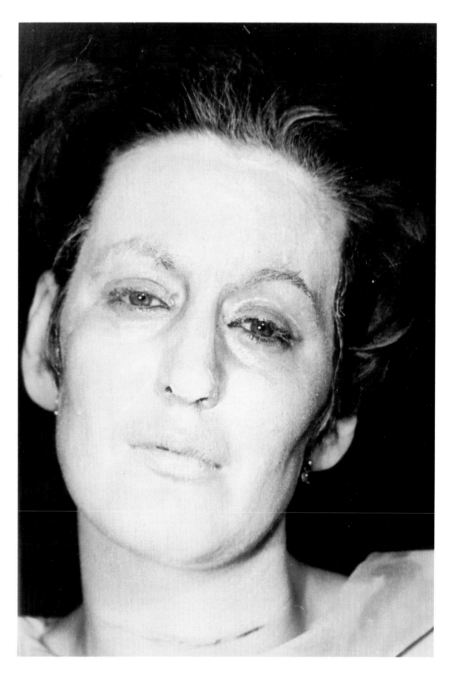

**Photograph
by Robert Whitaker:
Germaine Greer with
make-up removed
after the filming of
Darling, do you love
me? 1967. Courtesy
Robert Whitaker**

Beatlemania

Photograph by
Robert Whitaker of
Ringo Starr, USA,
1965. Private
collection

Membership card
of the Cavern Club
for 1962, the year of
the Beatles' debut.
Collection Gérard Aimé

Beatles' fan club badge.
Private collection

LES FILMS CORONIS
présentent

4 GARÇONS DANS LE VENT

AVEC WILFRID BRAMBELL

RÉALISATION RICHARD LESTER
PRODUCTION WALTER SHENSON

Les Beatles

Beatlemania

French poster for the
Beatles' first film,
Richard Lester's *Hard
day's night*, 1964. Private
collection

Figurines of the Beatles.
Private collection

Left:
'Guitar card', one
of numerous objects
made for Beatles' fans.
Private collection

The sixties, utopian years

Right:
Photograph by Robert
Whitaker, project for an
album cover, 1966.
Private collection

Photograph by Robert
Whitaker of the Lennon
family in Weybridge, 1965.
Private collection

Beatlemania

Left:

Photograph by Robert
Whitaker, project for an
album cover, 1966.
Private collection

Photograph by Robert
Whitaker of the Beatles
at Chiswick House, 1966.
Private collection

Left:

Photograph by
Robert Whitaker of
Paul McCartney and
John Lennon, 1966.
Private collection

The sixties, utopian years

Right:
Martin Sharp, project for
a Beatles' calendar, 1967.
Private collection

**Photograph by
Robert Whitaker of
George Harrison, 1966.
Private collection**

Beatlemania

The sixties, utopian years

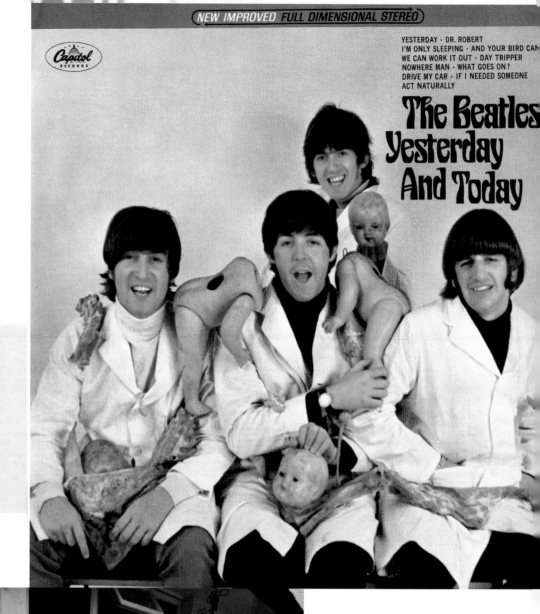

Robert Whitaker,
design for the
censored 'butchers'
cover', 1966, destroyed,
except for a few copies.
Private collection

Photograph by
Robert Whitaker of
George Harrison painting
the outside of his house
at Esher, 1966.
Private collection

Martin Sharp, *John Lennon*,
1966, painting and mixed
media on a photograph.
Private collection

Left: **Publicity photograph of
the Beatles by Robert Whitaker
for *Paperback writer*, 1966.
Private collection**

From Joe Meek to David Bowie

In the summer of 1964 The Kinks were in the studio having some problems recording their third single, the song that would go on to become the first big hit of their career. Ray Davies insisted on beginning the lyrics by singing 'Yeah, you really got me going', but this, according to Hal Carter, a music business fixer who had been advising the group on how to achieve success, needed changing – and it needed changing for a very specific and rather intriguing reason. Carter told Davies:

> You know at the beginning of the song, when you start singing? Well, I don't know whether you're singing to a girl or a bloke. I've always thought you were a bit limp-wristed and suspect, but I never imagined you singing the song to a geezer, even though I have had my suspicions about you .... So put all my doubts to rest and start the song by singing to somebody – Jane, Carol, Sue, bint, tart – even just plain 'Girl'.[1]

Davies heeded the advice, opted for 'Girl', and You really got me ended up as a Number One single. That story of its sexually ambiguous origins, taken from Davies's autobiography, may only be an anecdote but it's a telling one, illuminating the fact that British Pop music of the Sixties, on the surface the most commercially successful and culturally significant celebration of boy-meets-girl romance since the classic years of the Hollywood studio system, also held another set of meanings – unspeakable meanings, surreptitious meanings, queer meanings. The aim of this essay is to suggest some of the ways in which white male homosexuality, British Pop music's guilty secret and hidden motor, might be inferred, discerned and (speculatively) identified between the early Sixties and the early Seventies.

This is not simply a question of the contributions made to that music by gay men, indelibly significant though that was, but more to argue that the music served as one of the ways through which a marginalized and subterranean sensibility reached out to mould and inform Pop culture in general. Pop music left a profound imprint on British culture in the Sixties – for a few brief, thrilling and vertiginous years it became absolutely the core cultural form through which the nation redefined its sense of itself, and one of the most important legacies it left was the sense that sexual possibilities had widened, that the stale and unimaginative parameters of the traditional nuclear family were not the end of the story.

The starting point for any consideration of queerness and British Pop must be in a moderately sordid Fifties tale of teen idols and managerial lust. The music industry's frantic search to emulate the success of American rock-'n'-roll resulted in the selling of pretty teenage boys to less pretty teenage girls. The new idols didn't need musical gifts (that could be supplied in the studio by more experienced, much uglier session players), but they needed cheekbones, winning smiles and a passable imitation of a Presley pelvis-wiggle. Many of the managers seeking these boy wonders were homosexual, and the rumour persists, though vigorously denied, that they offered contracts only in return for certain kinds of gratification. The groundwork was being done here for the equation between gay male taste and teenage girl taste that persists in Pop to this day,[2] as evidenced by the constant deployment of camp codes in publications aimed primarily at girls, from Boyfriend in the Sixties to Smash hits in the Nineties.

The most innovative of these predatory Svengalis was not a manager but a record producer, one of the first men ever to turn that previously administrative role into something genuinely creative – Joe Meek. The word 'Svengali' here might be misplaced, since it implies a much more sexually confident persona than the one Meek actually occupied. Like most queers of his generation, he internalized heterosexual hatred and turned it into recriminatory self-loathing, finding solace only in the extraordinary hit records he produced. His two most passionate interests, beyond his love of sound itself, were spiritualism and outer space – understandably farfetched diversions from the earthbound, contemporary realities of British homophobia, and the yearning for escape is a constant thread throughout his work. John Leyton's Johnny remember me, for example, may in its lyrics be an exemplary heterosexual narrative of lost love, but Meek's production touches give it ghostly resonances that suggest more complex, less easily expressible desires. (It was, appropriately, covered in the Eighties by Bronski Beat and Marc Almond, openly gay artists who relished its camp excess but also opened the possibility of re-reading it in the AIDS era as a song about losing too soon the one you love.) Meek's most celebrated production, The Tornados' instrumental Telstar, throbs with a heartbreakingly fragile faith in the future, a belief that somewhere, elsewhere, might be a better place than the here and now. In many ways it's an absurd record, a childishly kitsch

Anita Pallenberg and Mick Jagger in Nicholas Roeg's film Performance, 1970. Courtesy British Film Institute

evocation of technological utopia, but read through the lens of sexuality its glittery textures and sweeping vistas carry other, more poignant meanings.

The instrumental hits of the early Sixties often bore titles that spoke of a wish to transcend the drab confines of Englishness – for example The Shadows' *Apache, Kon-Tiki*,

Heinz and
The Wildcats, 1962.
Private collection

Atlantis, and the most beautiful and least specific, *Wonderful land*. If now their records lack that edge of tremulous mystery that characterizes those of Meek, this is probably due to their association with Cliff Richard, whose career-long quest for pallid respectability culminated in his 1995 knighthood.

Richard's unmarried status has always prompted speculation about his sexuality, especially given his roots in the less-than-heterosexual Fifties' music business, and though his insistence on his straightness is one of the loudest and most recurring leitmotifs in British popular cultural history, it doesn't detract from the fact that his early visual image borrowed at least as much from Dirk Bogarde as it did from Elvis Presley, making him a favoured pin-up in gay circles at the time. David Hockney wittily acknowledged this via his painting *Two boys cling to Cliff all night*, suggesting that some mischievous sub-cultural listeners might have supplied an extra layer of meaning to Richard's hit *Bachelor boy*.

The importance of the Beatles for British culture is inestimably vast; for the purposes of this essay, all I would want to stress is their often-overlooked relationship to queer sensibilities and the more general widening of the sexual agenda. On an obvious level this could be seen as originating with the role of their manager, Brian Epstein (like Meek, another self-hating, music-biz queer), whose early interest in the group was not entirely musical. He was, though, enough of a businessman to tidy up the rough, leather-jacket look that so thrilled him (as, in other contexts, it was thrilling Kenneth Anger) in favour of a more marketable image. Well, more marketable with hindsight, since it is easy to forget how startling and innovative one aspect of the Beatles' look was for the early Sixties: their hair. It is no accident that 'Mop-top' became one of the most-used synonyms for the Beatles – Ian MacDonald's magisterial account of their music may be called *Revolution in the head*,[3] but their initial iconographic impact derived from a revolution on the head. (Beatles' wigs were the biggest-selling celebrity-related hair-products since the 'Chaplin moustaches' of 1915.) Their hair was floppy, shakeable, unstructured, *girlish* – never exactly effeminate, though appalled middle-aged men frequently labelled it as such, more the first step on the road to the androgyny that would flourish in Pop culture later. It was the first hairstyle deserving that word which would be festooned on every high-street salon by the end of the decade: unisex.

The Beatles' early music also displays traces of a blurring of gender boundaries. Of all the black American Fifties rock stars, the one they drew most from was the scandalously queeny Little Richard, while they covered songs originally sung by American girl groups (*Chains, Please Mr Postman*).

David Bowie album
cover, 1972, and
cover of the French
review *Maxipop*,
January 1973.
Private collection

The one single sound above all others which secured their cultural dominance was the falsetto 'oooh' in *She loves you*, not the kind of sound many British men had hitherto let past their lips. None of this detracted from their masculinity, indeed it seemed to enhance it, by casting them as the vanguard of a new kind of masculinity, one which offered their female fans a sexiness that rejected lumpen aggression in favour of sensitivity and wit, and their male fans a role model of how to avoid growing up into your dour, Brylcreemed Dad. The Beatles' unarguable place as personifications of

Marc Bolan of T. Rex on the cover of *Popmusic*, September 1972. Private collection

youth, avatars of the times to come, meant that a rejection of conventional gender identities became an integral component of what it meant to be forward looking. The degree of the rejection varied according to opportunity, inclination and circumstance, but the drive towards change of some kind was undeflectable. The 'oooh' of *She loves you* became drowned by the far louder and profounder response it provoked: the sound of audiences screaming at the Beatles was the sound of newness, the sound of unleashed female desire burying the nice-girl codes of the Fifties under wave upon wave of hormonal triumphalism. Sexual attitudes were in a state of intoxicating upheaval, and, as the influence of Women's Liberation on Gay Liberation would underline at the end of the Sixties, where women trailblaze, homosexual men are apt to follow.

ture occasionally loosened established sexual categorizations, the fey and flowing clothes of Ladbroke Grove allowed some queens to edge towards drag – but hippie music, mutating by 1970 into the sexless proficiency of progressive rock, was rarely homo music. Skinhead culture, on the other hand, asserted its identity through violent attacks on groups who failed to match up: its racism took the shape of Paki-bashing, its masculinity was forged through queer-bashing. Unlike the mid-Nineties, when a shaved head has become in some parts of Britain a virtual guarantee of homosexuality, a gay skinhead was a contradiction in terms.

Queer pop, happily, was only resting. Glam rock, the first definably Seventies movement in British music, re-established the connections between Pop, camp and ambiguity. Its initial key proponent was a reformed hippie, Marc Bolan, who ditched a moderately successful career in peddling sub-Tolkein whimsy, stole some Chuck Berry riffs, sprinkled glitter on his face and brought the teen idol back to a public starved of such things for half a decade. Bolan's semiotic strategies were never gay as such, but he shrewdly milked the proven appetite of teenage girl fans for male stars who were, well, *different*.

The next glam star, however, bypassed the stage of teasing possibilities altogether and capitalized on newly emerging social climates. David Bowie's first hit, *Space oddity* (a title, a record and a queerish use of outer-space imagery Joe Meek would have fondly admired), had been in 1969, but no successor to it was forthcoming. Deciding on a high-risk strategy, and quite possibly with at least one eye fixed on the impact of *Lola*, he began writing songs about same-sex seductions (the daringly graphic *Width of a circle*) and perverse celebrities (*Andy Warhol*), wearing dresses (telling bemused journalists, with wry cheek, that they were 'men's dresses'), and eventually saying 'I'm gay' in the pages of *Melody Maker*. The fact that he wasn't is not the issue here; what matters is that such a comment did not signal professional suicide but its complete opposite – rebirth. Thanks to Bowie's boldness (or, if you want to be moralistic, his cynically, clinically exact diagnosis of changing trends), a declaration of homosexuality, or, for the more timid, an intimation of it, secured fashionability and acclaim. The full story of glam rock lies outside the scope of this publication,[6] but it serves as a fitting end to a story that ran, at various submerged lev-

els, throughout the Sixties, in fine art, in fashion and in film, but most of all in Pop music – the story of how the British, that most erotically constrained collection of people, paradoxically found themselves in love with queerness. As long, of course, as queerness minded its manners, kept in its place and confined itself to the spheres of culture and entertainment.

Andy Medhurst

1. Ray Davies, *X-Ray: The unauthorized autobiography*, London, Viking, 1964, p. 147.
2. Sheryl Garrett, 'Teenage dreams', in Simon Frith and Andrew Goodwin, eds, *On record: Rock, Pop and the written word*, London, Routledge, 1990; and Jon Savage, 'The simple things you see are all complicated', in Hanif Kureishi and Jon Savage, eds, *The Faber book of Pop*, London, Faber, 1995.
3. Ian MacDonald, *Revolution in the head: The Beatles' records and the Sixties*, London, Fourth Estate, 1994.
4. Barbara Pym, *A very private eye: An autobiography in letters and diaries*, London, Panther, 1985, p. 347.
5. Peter Burton, *Parallel lives*, London, 1985.
6. Andy Medhurst, 'Glad to be Glam', *Gay Times*, September 1990.
7. See Burton, op. cit.

Fashion and fashion photography

Is Paris dead?

The autumn Paris collections for 1965 were the subject of a photo-essay by American photographer and film-maker William Klein, published in the London *Weekend Telegraph* magazine.[1] The clothes, which included designs by Cardin, Dior, Lanvin and Ungaro, represented the best traditions of Paris couture. Here were examples of brilliant, bravura cutting in cleanly sculpted dresses and suits and dazzling displays of skilled and labour-intensive craft, as in the literally dazzling sheath by Cardin encrusted with a swirling, kinetic decoration of sequins. Klein, who had brought a tough, incisive, satirical point of view to the subject of fashion since he was first taken up by Alexander Liberman for *Vogue* in the mid-Fifties, illustrated these collections under the title 'Is Paris dead?' The question was spelt out in Gothic script and the idea re-enforced by a cover model wreathed in flowers in a coffin and a group of models in the opening double-page spread walking alongside a horse-drawn hearse. The quality and elegance of the clothes photographed by Klein could not be faulted, and indeed the feature went on to explain: 'No! Paris is jumping!' The question, however, was not without foundation.

For although Paris couture had occupied a position of unrivalled authority over fashion through the century, and particularly since its post-war renaissance, by the mid-Sixties it was becoming increasingly evident that this authority was under threat. *Haute couture* had built its power by providing a very high-quality image of status within an elite united by wealth. As early as 1960 the young Yves Saint Laurent, head designer at the house of Dior, had introduced new notes into his designs. The spring-summer collection was praised for its youthfulness; the autumn-winter collection brought 'The beat look', described by *Vogue* as 'flamboyantly Left Bank ... pale zombie faces; leather suits and coats ... high turtle-neck collars; black endlessly'.[2] Editors picked up on the mixed messages of a mink and black crocodile jacket '... a fabulous version of the Marlon Brando windbreaker'.[3] The young and street styles derived from youth-orientated popular culture were in the process of transforming fashion's imperatives.

The clothes presented for spring-summer 1965 by André Courrèges provided the single most dramatic and dynamic statement of a new faith that the fashion world had witnessed in the Sixties. The designs were unified by the simple, crisp geometry of their lines. White predominated in a look that captured the spirit of the age of space travel. These 'clothes of the future'[4] were uncluttered, almost clinical in their simplicity, though as flawless in their proportions and execution as one would expect from a couturier who had trained under Balenciaga. Yet they swept aside the old hierarchies and conventions of couture, suggesting a new order dominated by young energy rather than old money. They proposed an alternative concept of femininity. As important as Courrèges's designs was his choice of models and the mood that they conspired to impart. He chose tanned, healthy, outdoor girls who used a new body language appropriate to the new styles. Angular, energetic gestures and poses gave an added meaning to clothes designed to liberate the limbs. Despite the paradox of couture price tags on such popular styles, Courrèges had triumphed in giving definitive form to the new direction in fashion.

The seeds of change

Fashion designers and the photographers who translated their creations into expressive images for the print media had been exploring and developing the ingredients of a fashion revolution since the turn of the decade. The battleground for this revolution was the street, and in particular certain specific streets in London. It was in the King's Road, Chelsea, and '... the narrow streets of gay clothes' shops ... off Regent Street's hallowed precincts'[5] that trends were initiated. Here the likes of Mary Quant and the partnership of Marion Foale and Sally Tuffin started to sew and sell the simply made, lively, snappy clothes that were to attract an international spotlight. The spread of street style was rapid. By 1963 *Life* magazine[6] was reporting the export of '... the Chelsea Look' to an eager American market. In a feature, 'Brash new breed of British designers', Sally Kirkland explained how: 'The same generation which has produced Britain's angry young writers has also produced a batch of nonconforming young fashion designers'. A portrait photograph of 'This giddy group' on Chelsea Embankment bore a caption that detailed their ages. All but one were in their twenties.

Study by Ronald Falloon, a photographer who had trained with John French, of house models presenting designs by André Courrèges from his autumn 1965 collection. Private collection

The image-makers

The youthful, iconoclastic tendency found full expression in the photography of a new breed of image-makers. Klein and other photographers drawn from the world of reportage, such as Frank Horvat, had since the mid-Fifties brought a new grit to fashion photography, adding a suggestion of realism to the magazine page, in contrast with traditionalists such as Henry Clarke for *Vogue* and Richard Dormer for *Harper's Bazaar*, who set women on a pedestal and whose elegant explorations of aristocratic gesture and grand style had been the dominant mode. Fashion photography in the Sixties built on these initiatives and developed a fresh approach – young, sexy, witty, bursting with energy and a sense of liberation from the old rules. New ground was broken by ambitious young 'snappers' who brought a love of women and an irreverent attitude to the task of animating fashion for a demographically shifting audience. The forum for fashion news was embracing a broader, often younger public and expanding its reach through the boom

**William Klein,
'Is Paris dead?'
with clothes by Dior,
The Weekend Telegraph,
5 September 1965.
Private collection**

In Paris the exemplary role-model for street style was ex-high fashion model Emmanuelle Khahn. She had modelled for Balenciaga and for Givenchy, but was to reject the traditions they represented when she presented her first designs in 1962, aged 24. Two years later she claimed that '*Haute couture* is dead', and declared her ambition '... to design for the street ... a socialist kind of fashion for the grand mass'.[7] In Paris, as in London, fashion polarized geographically, with couture reigning on the luxury avenues of the Rive Droite and the young *prêt-à-porter* designers drawn to the Rive Gauche. How apt that Ossie Clark and Alice Pollack should fly over in the spring of 1966 from their King's Road base to present their Quorum collection, alive with Op art stripes and metallic fabrics, against a decor of vast Union Jacks to celebrate the opening of a new nightclub on the Boulevard Saint Germain. 'From the time London arrived, the scene of the Great Couture was all agog at the girls' skirt lengths and owl sunglasses. Ironic really that London should show them how!'[8] In the same year Saint Laurent, ever sensitive to the shifting patterns of influence in the fashion market-place, launched his own *prêt-à-porter* range and christened it 'Rive Gauche'.

**Poster for William
Klein's satirical film
*Qui êtes-vous, Polly
Maggoo?*, 1966.
Private collection**

in consumer magazine publishing and, in Britain, in the increased quality of fashion reporting in the daily press.

At the start of the decade *Vogue* dominated fashion publishing in Britain and in France in terms of prestige and fashion authority. Other titles, some established, others new or revitalized, provided an approach that was less rigid and status bound, more open and experimental. In France *Jardin des Modes, Marie-Claire* and *Elle* (the latter guided by editor Hélène Gordon-Lazareff and energized by the appointment of Peter Knapp as art director in 1959) gave creative freedom and encouragement to a generation of photographers, among them Fouli Elia, Marc Hispard and Jeanloup Sieff, whose work shared a common currency of increased naturalism, a looser approach for a liberated young audience.

In Britain perhaps the most exciting fashion magazine of the early sixties was *Queen*, transformed after its acquisition in 1957 by Jocelyn Stevens and rapidly earning a reputation for the strength of its design and for the vitality of its fashion reporting. The colour magazines published by the major newspapers on the model established by *The Sunday Times* in 1962, in common with *Queen* and with *Nova* (launched in 1965), set fashion into a wider coverage of cultural and topical issues and provided a context, particularly in the second half of the decade, in which talented fashion editors and art directors used clothes as a pretext for commissioning strong picture-essays. Fashion editors Caroline Baker on *Nova*, Meriel McCooey on *The Sunday Times*, Liz Smith on *The Observer*, and Cherry Twiss on *The Telegraph*, and art directors Harry Peccinotti on *Nova* and Hans Feurer on *The Telegraph*, were among those to achieve memorable and influential results with a cross-Channel roster of photographers that included Guy Bourdin, Francis Giacobetti, Jean-François Jonvelle, Sarah Moon, Helmut Newton and Jeanloup Sieff. Both Peccinotti and Feurer also proved their talents as photographers.

Central to the fashion revolution of the early Sixties was the endeavour on the part of photographers to create a revised template of beauty and to conceive an appropriate choreography for the fashion muses of the nascent decade. In the process these photographers assumed a heightened profile. As a new mass audience became increasingly exposed to the collective impact of the commercial media, the image-makers themselves emerged as key players, high-

ly visible, integral to the mythologies that they were creating in this fluid 'ad-mass' network. Fashion photographers had to re-invent their role, turning their backs on the precious, hot-house connotations that their craft carried, plugging in to the pulse of an image-dominated culture, a two-dimensional world of hip and cool in which television, advertising, magazines and popular music fuelled a hunger for heroes and heroines. The young music scene, as consecrated in France in the pages of *Salut les copains* or in Britain on the 'mod' TV show *Ready, Steady, Go!* provided a central arena for the cross-fertilization of rhythm, fashion and image.

The voracious media demanded role-models and icons and devoured a constant flow of secular deities. Photographers were now media figures, more likely to dress and behave like the artists, designers, Pop and rock stars or louche aristocrats with whom they rubbed shoulders than in the elegant style of the discreet, suited gentlemen photographers of a previous era. David Bailey's meteoric and archetypal success in the early Sixties owed much to his intuitive recognition and exploitation of the potential of these cross-media relationships, which he was to encapsulate in his 1965 *box of pin-ups.*

Front of house still for *Blow-up*, 1966, showing the photographer hero seducing model Veruschka with his camera. Private collection

107

Fashion photography drew its energy avidly from a variety of sources. Small-format cameras gave a necessary sense of mobility, which was suggested as a potential social mobility in the fictional saga of the working-class photographer hero of Colin MacInnes's 1959 novel *Absolute Beginners*; becoming a predatory mobility in the hands of the paparazzi, whose activities were revealed to a wide audience in Federico Fellini's *La dolce vita* of 1960. From the cinema, specifically the French and Italian New Wave, came the immediacy, the informal realism of hand-held camera work.

The image-making process was scrutinized at mid-decade by Michelangelo Antonioni in his 1966 document *Blow-up*. The fashion photographer hero, a composite of characters including David Bailey, Brian Duffy, Terence Donovan and John Cowan (in whose studio much of the film was shot), reflects and compounds the popular perception of his freedom to exploit his camera, unhindered by ethical, class or sexual barriers. The image-maker is poised in a moral netherworld between realities and illusions. *Blow-up*, drawing together the cultural threads of film, fashion, art, music and drugs, reflects lifestyles at once tempting and tainted, the London scene oscillating between optimism and cynicism. In the same year William Klein completed his own, more barbed observation of the world of fashion and image-making, *Qui êtes-vous, Polly Maggoo?*, 'a film on fashion, media bullshit, movies and television'.[9]

The look

In the early Sixties the emerging look was an illusion of attainable beauty, expressed through seemingly spontaneous natural gesture, dynamic and persuasive. The most characteristic results combined a naturalism, learned from the documentary genre of Klein and Horvat, with a kinetic energy and a desire to depict models as capable of emotions with which a broad audience could relate. The kinetic theme was well explored by Norman Parkinson, who claimed: 'I was one of the first to take the scent-laden atmosphere out of photographs and the first to get girls to run, to jump, to stretch, to let air through their knees'.[10] It was central to the activity of John Cowan, who photographed model Jill Kennington swinging from a parachute, on horseback, leaping into the sky, running in the Trocadéro in Paris with children on roller skates. Ronald Traeger illustrated Op and other young fashions on girls in full movement, making images that were the frozen moments of a kinetic fashion ballet. Helmut Newton, working for numerous magazines, notably for the British and French editions of *Vogue* and for *Queen*, initiated his own experiments in the seizing of movement and started the process, which he was greatly to accelerate in the Seventies, of injecting a strong sexual content into fashion photography.

Although for Newton and others this sexual element remained for the most part discreet, the permissive attitudes which the decade boasted found expression in a readiness to depict an often complex sensuality. American photographer Bob Richardson came to Europe in 1966, settling in Paris after some months in London, and created photo-essays cast like mini-movies and laden with strong emotion and sexuality. In the late Sixties Paris-based model-turned-photographer Sarah Moon brought an intimacy, a romantic, wistful feminine eye to fashion photography. She made atmospheric images, 'Endeavouring to suggest rather than to describe ...',[11] for various magazines and commercial clients. For Biba in London she illustrated a 1969 catalogue; for Jean Cacharel in Paris she defined a mood and gave a distinct visual identity to a product line.

The most characteristic Sixties 'look' had emerged early in the decade in the person of model Jean Shrimpton, given a photographic identity by David Bailey, who cast her as the

Fashion captured in movement by John Cowan, with Jill Kennington at the Trocadéro, Paris, c. 1963–4. Private collection

Pages from the Biba
mail-order catalogue,
with photographs by
Sarah Moon, 1969.
Private collection

Photograph by
Sarah Moon for a
promotional card for
Jean Cacharel, c.1970.
Private collection

archetypal 'chick': long hair, doe eyes, young, fresh and total-ly convincing as a classless, natural beauty. Jill Kennington, with her big, darkly made-up eyes and straight blonde hair, was por-trayed by John Cowan, Helmut Newton and others as a quintessential Sixties girl. Celia Hammond's appeal was first understood by Parkinson, and she too rapidly achieved status as one of the faces that defined the era. Twiggy's adolescent frame, big eyes, expressive, highly photogenic face and authen-tic working-class origins ensured her tenure in this pantheon of beauty.

If British models made the strongest mark, the French were not without their own stars in the image-making media. Andy Warhol was swift to recognize in 1963 '... the French girls who had the new star mystiques – Jeanne Moreau, Françoise Hardy, Sylvie Vartan, Catherine Deneuve, and her tall, beautiful sister, Françoise Dorléac'.[12] Françoise Hardy, for whom Courrèges designed a white trouser suit, had the looks to match the youthful yearnings of her love songs. Pop-rock pin-up Sylvie Vartan surely had a far greater reach and influence as a fashion icon than did the sophisticated aristocratic patrons of couture, such as the Vicomtesse Jacqueline de Ribes, emblems of the old order. Vartan was enlisted as a model to give a youthful endorse-ment to the Dior collections for autumn-winter 1964.[13] A head-shot of her was featured on the cover of *Marie-Claire* with the copy line, 'Sylvie Vartan – les américains disent: "toutes les françaises lui ressemblent déjà".'[14] The cool, fine good looks of actress Catherine Deneuve exemplified the French respect for beauty combined with a certain hauteur. Her 1967 role in *Belle de jour*, elegantly dressed by Yves

Twiggy, her hair cut and styled by Leonard, photographed by Barry Lategan, 1966. Private collection

Saint Laurent, described the significant hold that the restric-tive values of the bourgeoisie still maintained in fashion, as in every area of French life. This was at once the strength and the weakness of French fashion, which found it hard to compromise on the high traditions of quality represented by the Chambre Syndicale de la Couture Parisienne. Deneuve's seduction by David Bailey was ironically symp-tomatic of the restructuring of accepted conventions.

It was their innate respect for quality that ultimately gave an edge to the French in the creation of fashions which stand out as a lasting reflection of the decade. Despite the inventiveness of British fashion, the Paris couture system served as a very effective laboratory to refine and distil into the most memorable clothes the cultural currents that shaped the Sixties. Paris couture was predicated on standards of quality and refinement which ensured lasting merit for the clothes produced within the sys-tem. Amongst the more adventurous designers was Pierre Cardin who demon-strated a highly developed sensitivity to the motifs which best captured the moods of the moment. In 1966 he designed 'target' dresses which translated a Pop iconography into sophisticated fashions and simple, func-tional tunic dresses and sculpted helmets which made ele-gant reference to the imagery of space travel. Emmanuel Ungaro cut crisp, clean-lined suits, coats and dresses in fab-rics with bold coloured stripes which implied an awareness of the 'hard edge' Abstractionists influencing the art world.

The impact of André Courrèges cannot be underesti-mated; nor can that of the individualistic Paco Rabanne. This Spanish-born designer showed his first collections in Paris in

MARIE*CLAIRE

SPÉCIAL BEAUTÉ

SYLVIE VARTAN
les américains disent:
"toutes les francaises
lui ressemblent déja"

AOÛT / N° 118 / 1,50 F
EDITION BENELUX 20 FB / SUISSE 1.80 FS
GRANDE-BRETAGNE 3/6 / ITALIE 300 LIRES
CANADA 50 CENTS / ALLEMAGNE 2 DM

Pop star Sylvie Vartan presented as an icon of fashionable beauty on the cover of *Marie-Claire*, August 1964. Private collection

1966. He achieved considerable media attention for his revolutionary idea of sculpting clothes out of a kind of chain-mail of light metal or plastic discs. These were dramatic clothes for his vision of a liberated woman, the Sixties Amazon, and were perhaps the most overtly erotic accoutrements to have emanated from the still essentially conservative bastions of *haute couture*. A celebration of Rabanne's designs by photographer Jean Clemmer was published in 1969, appropriately titled *Nues* in France and *Canned Candies* in Britain, confronting Paris couture with the heightened interest in the liberated body which had become an ingredient of fashion photography through the decade.

111

Double page spread from *Nues – Canned Candies* presenting the designs of Paco Rabanne, photographed by Jean Clemmer, 1969. Private collection

Escape into fantasy

By 1967 the character of the Sixties was in major flux. Optimism was giving ground to protest and disillusion. In fashion this became manifest in the 'hippie' styles which became ubiquitous in 1967. Exotic gypsy outfits were put together from second-hand clothes' shops and were soon being interpreted as exquisitely composed 'looks' by the top designers. Rolling Stones Keith Richards and Brian Jones and their entourage, including Tara Browne and Anita Pallenberg, gave their glamorous twist to this look, dressed up '... in exquisite clothes from various raids on Hung On You, Granny Takes a Trip and the Chelsea Antique Market'.[15] Pallenberg was featured in *Vogue*, photographed by Michael Cooper on the set of *Performance*, draped in fringed silk on a quasi-oriental litter of cushions.[16] This was fashion for the rebel rock and drug-associated counter-culture.

Yves Saint Laurent was foremost among those to translate this yearning for fantasy and escapism into sumptuous and exotic fashions. Over the following few years he was to draw inspiration from sources as diverse as Cossack garb, the harem costumes of Leon Bakst and colourful peasant outfits. In Britain Zandra Rhodes proved her flair with exotic prints and fantasy styles. Ronald Traeger's 1967 group of three models dressed as colourful fantasy Romanies against a mystical mural, all created by The Fool, the designers patronized by the Beatles, perfectly captured the fashionable tendency: '... a magician's impression of texture and colour'.[17] One of the models was Patti Boyd, a Sixties blonde from '... the old scene, the swinging London of dollies and pop stars'.[18] The others comprised an oriental girl and newly successful black model, Kelly, extending the fashion metaphor to embrace ethnic diversity.

Magazines responded to the escapist mood by sending photographers, models and fashion teams to exotic locations to bring back pictures in which extravagant clothes were set in dramatic landscapes or against the architecture of ancient or distant civilizations. None was more exotic than the team of model Veruschka and photographer Franco Rubartelli who travelled far and wide and brought back stunning picture-stories in which a highly made-up Veruschka was transformed into a painted, living sculpture. Fashion as pure fantasy. These photographic essays includ-

ed notably the features 'Veruschka and her desert bikinis', for Cherry Twiss and *The Daily Telegraph* magazine[19] and the 24-page story 'Jungle look: Une grande aventure au coeur de l'Afrique' for French *Vogue*.[20]

It was on this wave of fantasy that fashion, ever hungry for change, looked to the next decade. Clothes were being enjoyed for their decorative value; romantic, ethereal beauty such as that of model Ingrid Boulting was in vogue. The close of the Sixties meanwhile was reflecting other strands of influence which were to develop into the distinctive styles of the early Seventies. Glamour was again at a premium, evident in the attention being paid to re-vamped Thirties' Hollywood styles. Biba, the boutique which had epitomized the mid-decade look of throwaway youthful trendiness, was shifting focus and was soon to relaunch in spectacular new premises, a-glitter with mirror glass and slinky satins, evoking a Thirties liner cocktail-lounge atmo-

Still of Anita Pallenberg photographed on the set of *Performance*, 1968. Private collection

sphere; in Paris Karl Lagerfeld's Art Deco collection encouraged a reappraisal of '... these creations ... at the very source of today's design'[21] and put him at the creative epicentre of a burst of enthusiasm for highly styled glam-

Veruschka photographed
by Franco Rubartelli for
'Veruschka and her
desert bikinis', *The Daily
Telegraph Magazine*,
21 June 1969.
Private collection

114

our. Pop was already being recycled and making a brash, slick, fun contribution to the fashion scene. In London, Tommy Roberts' Mr Freedom boutique led the way; in Paris, *Vogue* published a 'Pop' issue in November 1970, linking fashion, music, art and design, and acknowledging the American influence. Photographers were to devise fresh approaches and exploit new techniques in order to capture the essence of these myriad ingredients on paper and to define the changing face of fashion in a new decade.

Philippe Garner

1. *Weekend Telegraph*, 5 September, 1965.

2. British *Vogue*, early September 1960, p. 87.

3. *Idem*.

4. *The Observer* magazine, 7 March 1965, cover and p. 23.

5. Royston Ellis, *The Big Beat scene*, London, 1961, p. 7.

6. *Life*, 18 October 1963.

7. Quoted in Joel Lobenthal, *Radical rags: Fashions of the Sixties*, New York, 1990, p. 45, original source not identified.

8. 'Paris ... London style', *London Life*, April 1966, pp. 14–15.

9. William Klein, from a public presentation on his work, Hamilton's Gallery, London, 18 February 1994.

10. Quoted in his obituary, *The Daily Telegraph*, 16 February 1990, p. 19.

11. 'Cherchant à suggérer plutôt que décrire ...', François Caillat, 'Sarah Moon', *Zoom*, no. 83, 1981.

12. Andy Warhol and Pat Hackett, *Popism – The Warhol '60s*, 1980; UK edn 1981, p. 40.

13. 'Collections: Sylvie Vartan chez Dior', *Jours de France*, 5 September 1964.

14. *Marie-Claire, Special Beauté*, August 1964, no. 118.

15. Marianne Faithfull, *Faithfull*, London, 1994, p. 78.

16. British *Vogue*, December 1968, p. 110.

17. British *Vogue*, January 1968, p. 55.

18. Marianne Faithfull, *à propos* Chrissie Shrimpton, *Faithfull*, London, 1994, p. 87.

19. *The Daily Telegraph Magazine*, 21 June 1969.

20. French *Vogue*, July–August 1968.

21. '...ces créations ... à la source même du design actuel', 'Un styliste d'aujourd'hui aux sources du design', *L'Oeil*, October 1969, p. 53.

Clothes and backdrop designed by The Fool, photographed by Ronald Traeger for British *Vogue*, January 1968, p. 55. Private collection

Architecture and design

Economic and industrial prosperity in the west soared in the Sixties. These were years when models of architectural modernism spread rapidly, and architects' professional practice, faced on all sides by great social demands, tended to prevail over the debate and ideological confrontation which in the preceding period had made the meetings of CIAM (Congrès internationaux d'architecture moderne) events with a worldwide resonance. For design, however, the late Fifties and the Sixties established the configuration, doctrines and structures of the profession. From 1956 conferences brought together those practising industrial design; new bodies, in touch with the needs of industry, stimulated product design, and the first specialist agencies (Technès, 1953) were set up in France.

While Britain and France were emerging after the post-war period to growth and from hardship to consumption, architecture and design were based on quite distinct cultural and social realities. In France, where reconstruction was not altogether complete and compromises, particularly with regionalism, had been the rule in the formal treatment of the urban environment, pre-war Modernism set the terms of reference. As in Scandinavia the generation of architects who had made their names before the war were still there, more or less. Those who had illuminated the 1930s were still very much influencing the present. The worldwide stir created by Le Corbusier's late works (the Unité d'habitation in Marseilles, the chapel at Ronchamp, the Notre-Dame-de-la-Tourette friary, Chandigarh) contrasts with his relative isolation in France: their lyricism, their sculptural originality and their status as works of art opened an attractive path for the renewal of architectural Modernism. British architects and critics were very receptive to that message, and it was they who explored this field of research most fruitfully: James Stirling and James Gowan, for example, in the housing estate at Ham Common (London, 1956), and Denys Lasdun, formerly a partner in the Tecton group, in the National Theatre (London, 1963–7). In 1966 Nikolaus Pevsner (*Pioneers of modern design*, 1936), criticized the move towards 'Expresssionism' and a 'personality cult', identifying it with a 'post-Modern style'. But others took the opposite view, encouraging this move towards New Brutalism (Reyner Banham), the critical Constructivism advocated by young architects like Alison and Peter Smithson who were close to artists of the Independent Group, which was at the roots of Pop art.

The work of Auguste Perret and his pupils (the rebuilding of Le Havre) provided points of reference mainly for French architects, like Jean Prouvé, Paul Nelson and Pingusson, whose projects were still the exception. The contribution to the aesthetics of domestic architecture made by Perret and his followers had a wider impact. Along with Charlotte Perriand and members of the UAM (Union des architectes modernes), they set the tone for the domestic interior with a freshness and elegant simplicity very much in tune with the optimism of the day. At the end of the Fifties design found a basis for development in new industrial products. It was then that the standardization of architectural and residential forms got under way, while town planning pushed housing towards huge industrial buildings, commissioned by technocrats and banks. Architecture and town planning at the start of the Fifth Republic stagnated before new efforts were initiated after 1965 aimed at controlling urban growth using new towns and redevelopment.

The situation in Britain was different; in the 1950s a new generation of architects was interpreting both the international culture and the tremendous demand for modernity from a population largely composed of town dwellers. The British had long since assimilated the effects of industrial output on everyday life, and were much more familiar with the mass media and modern forms of advertising than their continental counterparts; television and the telephone had become established in the daily life of all social strata more quickly there. In England, in Greater London in particular, rebuilding and the Labour government of the immediate post-war period had instigated an early debate about town planning and the modern town, more than twenty years before they were considered by the French government: the concept of new towns was embedded in the New Town Act of 1946. We have to bear in mind the impact of the Welfare State and educational reforms on the production of social facilities, and especially on the teaching of architecture at schools and universities. All through the Sixties public bodies with responsibility for building, like the London County Council's Architecture Department which designed the Festival of Britain buildings for London in 1951, acted as a laboratory for Modernism.

Photograph of the La Tourette friary designed by Le Corbusier. Private collection

One of the best illustrations of these differences can be found in car design. As in all engineering industries, which in Great Britain were given a temporary extra stimulus by the war, for a long time tried and trusted technologies went hand in hand with forms that were often outmoded, as an indigenous means of resisting the Americanization of design. Where sports cars were concerned, important in the export market, Austin-Healey, Jaguar and Lotus created outstanding classic models with elegant, dynamic lines in the Fifties and Sixties, but popular British car design for a long time remained stuck, with insipid, borrowed traditional styles. A conspicuous novelty was the appearance of the Austin Mini, developed and designed by Alex Issigonis, which went into production in 1959. Its structural innovations (the transverse engine block and gearbox and its compact hydroelastic suspension) gave an amazing amount of internal space in view of its minimal external dimensions. With its compact shape

The Maison de la Radio designed by Henry Bernard in 1961. Private collection

– in no way a cut-down version of larger cars (unlike the pretentious Austin A40) – this radically new design laid down an enduring formula on which the French Twingo is still closely dependent. Through its careless disregard for the distinguished conventions which at that time underlay the imaginary ideal of the car (opulent chrome bumpers and a large boot, suggestive of long journeys) and the irony of its details – the projecting strap hinges on the doors, the huge glove box etc. – the Mini was very much a contemporary of British Pop art culture. This was in complete contrast with the successive French updates of the popular car: the 2CV Citroën and the Renault R4, which by the Sixties were being sold in a market no longer characterized by hardship, were products both of very rational mechanical thinking (resulting in technical innovations – far from negligible in the case of Citroën – in the engine, transmission and suspension) and of the fact that their intended market was still that of rural France, as indicated by the capacity to carry heavy loads in the back, to drive over all types of ground, great toughness, etc. As we know, the 2CV which was perfected in the immediate post-war period when times were still hard was aggressively stripped of all the expected features which were signs of luxury; the flat sides made of sheet metal or canvas covering volumes formed by utilitarian pressings, and the way they were assembled, with the joints visible, are remote from any reference to the art of body-building. The R4 was designed for a promising market at the beginning of the Sixties, and the infelicities in the design of the front, the flat windscreen and the neglected details (door hinges, visible screwed joints), reveal an intention to differentiate the product in a downward direction, on a scale where elegance of form was becoming generally accepted (Dauphine, Caravelle). The fact that their durability turned out to be very convincing – and the way they were used ultimately diverted the meaning of these rustic contraptions (because people were fond of them) – in no way alters their formal status: this 'hard design', French-style, attracted no imitators.

In contrast, the comparison between France and Britain in the higher categories is transposed. British middle and top-range cars were conformist in design and typical of the stagnation in the engineering industries in the Sixties; but the design of the Citroën DS19 was a success. After producing the popular but outmoded front-wheel drive for twenty

shape of the modernization of French industrial infrastructure, opening up the way for product design in French companies. Téléavia televisions (designed in 1963 by Robert Tallon) and the seats designed by Pierre Paulin (for Artifort) and Olivier Mourgue (for Airborne) were to reintroduce something of these organic, flowing forms, so different from functionalism, into the domestic sector. But these achievements were not indicative of the state of design in France, which was still very protected from imports, Many industrialists paid scant attention to the appearance of their goods, and for the same reasons treated problems of quality in a similar way, i.e. not agreeing to adequate investment.

The differences in the way in which architecture was practised in France and Great Britain are just as big, but this

years, the end result of perfecting the body design that went on until 1966, Citroën came up with the DS19, which became a model for the appeal strategy of all industrial products. Stimulating the phantasm of the machine as part of the living world and reinventing the formal codes of good adaptation to movement, the allusive organic forms spelt out the principles of modern car design: a new art of body-building and a unitary garb possessing corporeality and complexity that are simultaneously concealed and revealed by the gaping vents and the wide joints (as Roland Barthes was percipient enough to recognize). While Peugeot cars, more the 'happy medium' than ever, turned to the safe values of Italian design, the adventurous DS19 was well in advance of consumers' tastes. Along with the famous Caravelle manufactured by Sud-Aviation, it represents the bold, symbolic

The sixties, utopian years

Barbie doll living-room
furniture, 1970s.
Écomusée de Saint-
Quentin-en-Yvelines
collection

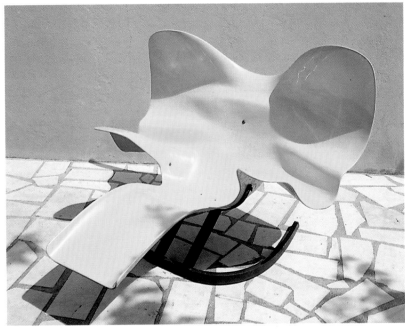

Fauteuil éléphant by
Bernard Rancillac, 1966.
Artist's collection

Right:
Oeuf garden chair by Peter
Ghyczy, 1968. Écomusée
de Saint-Quentin-en-
Yvelines collection

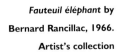

Cup.
Écomusée de Saint-
Quentin-en-Yvelines
collection

time Britain comes off best. Social demand that was more open minded towards modernization met a generation of designers who were entrusted with major commissions at an earlier age than in France, ever since the start of post-war reconstruction. The rebuilding of Coventry city centre was entrusted to the young Donald Gibson, and the cathedral was rebuilt after a competition won by Basil Spence at the age of 43. No such opportunities existed in France.

From the late Fifties the public authorities in Britain were dynamic in leading in the construction of large buildings. The building of university facilities provides an illuminating comparison between the two countries. In Britain ambitious plans started to be built ten years before the disastrous French university campuses, and most of them were entrusted to young architects. For the University of Sussex near Brighton Basil Spence combined concrete and brick, his aesthetic sense betraying the influence of recent buildings by Le Corbusier. The Engineering Building at the University of Leicester (1959–63), with its contrasting volumetry typical of an industrial building, designed by James Stirling and James Gowan, renewed the typology of university architecture. In the same spirit of renewing Modernism through contact with current technological advances, James Stirling subsequently worked for the universities of Cambridge (Faculty of History library, 1964–7) and St Andrews in Scotland (student residences, 1964–8) and Queen's College, Oxford (the Florey building, 1966–71). For the University of East Anglia in Norwich (1962–8) Denys Lasdun used the design principles of 'proliferating' continuity, applying them to tiered volumes, in a typological recomposition of the students' residence, modelled on urban continuity. Employing very different methods,

Stirling and Lasdun were able to use these university projects, which lent themselves to a powerful and original approach, as the launching-pad for highly successful careers.

The university buildings constructed in France over the same period, on the other hand, even when they were interesting, did not arrest the attention of contemporaries. For example, the Jussieu university complex built in Paris in 1965 by Édouard Albert and associates, with the boldness of its tubular structure, successfully answered the new problems posed by a university institution. The University of Lyons II campus built at Bron in 1970–72 (architect R. Dottelongue), close to the University of East Anglia in the way it applied urban continuity but nearly ten years later, used an industrialized metal construction to create an original composition in clusters. The volumes of the Fondation

Diabolo chair and
stool by Philippe
Barbier, 1969–70.
Écomusée de Saint-
Quentin-en-Yvelines
collection

Avicenne, the former 'maison de l'Iran', built 1966–8 at the Cité internationale universitaire in Paris by Claude Parent and associates, are suspended from spectacular, visible welded-steel structures. These three buildings, using a steel construction, show that French architects were attracted by experiment and a technology-based approach. But the fire at the metal-constructed Collège Édouard-Pailleron in Paris in 1973, and the effects of the oil crisis, combined to suspend research into metal in building for a long time.

By way of contrast this technology-based approach, used for the programme of industrial buildings, was the point of

121

departure for a positive development in Great Britain. From 1967 Norman Foster (b. 1935) and Richard Rogers (b. 1933) broke with convention for the Reliance Controls factory at Swindon (Wiltshire), affirming their belief in welded-steel structures. They turned away from public architecture, and at the start of a real boom in industrial building were ready to produce sophisticated prestige architecture for the manufacturing sites of the new leading-edge industries. Some brilliant solutions were developed in this field in Britain after 1970; the press gave the not very subtle label 'hi-tech' to this new 'art of building'. But it was in France, the historic home of building rationalism, that this innovative approach was recognized for what it was when the daring design by Renzo Piano and Richard Rogers won the competition for the Centre Georges-Pompidou in 1971.

The renewal of the typology of urban residential estates provided another common purpose. When the most demanding architects in both France and the UK were confronted by the upheaval caused by renovation

Optic fibre lamp. Écomusée de Saint-Quentin-en-Yvelines collection

projects of a fairly brutal nature in old centres and the inadequacies of residential estates where social life had been completely disrupted, the need to invent a new typology for building towns resulted in several new approaches on both sides of the Channel. Of interest here are those that asserted the continuity of the built line and the density of the town centre instead of devising monolithic blocks and towers. The creation of a continuous urban centre at Cumbernauld in Scotland was the start in about 1960, before projects for Toulouse-Le-Mirail (from 1962) by the team led by Candilis and for La Villeneuve de Grenoble (from 1968) by the AUA. Common features are groups of buildings in 'proliferating'

clusters, and the separation of traffic in three-dimensional space. This new typology, which was taken up by Moshe Safdie in Montreal at Habitat 67 and elsewhere, is an important Sixties'contributions and was further developed by Jean Renaudie in France and Arthur Erickson in British Columbia.

From the concrete proposals of 'proliferating' architecture to the vision of a town supported by 'megastructures', France and Great Britain led the way in devising the passionate utopias that brightened the period, which coincided with the move from pre-industrial architecture to mass production. In France Paul Maymont ('the vertical city') and Yona Friedman, who was author of the *Manifeste de la ville spatiale*, were at the heart of a nexus involving Nicolas Schöffer ('the cybernetic town') and Claude Parent ('oblique architecture'). In London the magazine *Archigram*, published from 1961 to 1970, provided a powerful platform for the group of young architects led by Peter Cook and Ron Herron who put all their enthusiasm and technical skill into drawing up urban spaces that reconciled the *avant-garde*, Pop culture and the resources of technology.

In concluding this quick review, the advances made in the history of architecture in Britain over this period are significant; just before the industrial fabric of the country was transformed in the Sixties, the history of British industrial architecture was discovered. In enhancing the sites, developing museology and restoring an unparalleled technological heritage, as at Iron Bridge for example, British architectural historians were justifiably restoring earlier architectural sources to the hi-tech vogue.

Gérard Monnier

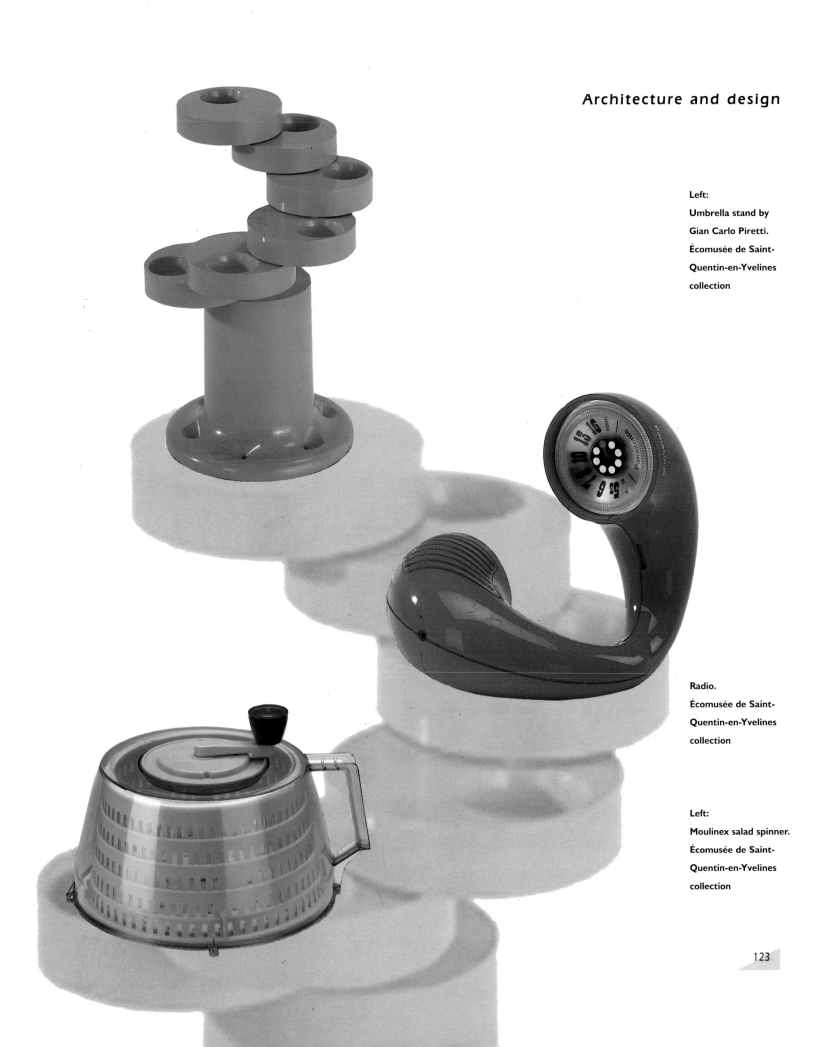

Left:
Umbrella stand by
Gian Carlo Piretti.
Écomusée de Saint-
Quentin-en-Yvelines
collection

Radio.
Écomusée de Saint-
Quentin-en-Yvelines
collection

Left:
Moulinex salad spinner.
Écomusée de Saint-
Quentin-en-Yvelines
collection

Young British architects

People may be creative at all times and in all places, but it is a quality they generally take for granted. In Britain in the Fifties and increasingly in the Sixties a new generation of architects and designers made a cult of creativity. If the urban world was to be transformed it would be through an effort of the imagination. For this effort to be successful the past had to be overthrown, for it had set in place those systems that inhibited imagination. In his introduction to *this is tomorrow*, the seminal exhibition of 1956 at the Whitechapel Art Gallery in London, the critic Lawrence Alloway wrote: 'Purity of media, golden proportions, unambiguous iconologies, have been so powerful that we have contracted art and architecture, a many channelled activity, as factual and as far from ideal standards as the street outside'. Alloway's manifesto held good through most of the Sixties. Its themes were reiterated, even if the exhibition itself was scarcely ever mentioned again.[1]

Section 6 of *this is tomorrow* featured Alison and Peter Smithson, the best known vanguard architects of the decade. In the catalogue they appear in a group portrait with the sculptor Eduardo Paolozzi and the photographer Nigel Henderson. The Smithsons believed in the role of the artist as seer. In 1967 in *Urban structuring* they credited the insight of artists in the Fifties: 'It was necessary in the early 1950s to look to the works of painter Pollock and sculptor Paolozzi for a complete image system, for an order with a structure and certain tension, where every piece was correspondingly new in a new system of relationship.'[2] In 1970 in *New lives, New landscapes*, they recalled coming on the paintings of Jackson Pollock at Peggy Guggenheim's palazzo in Venice: 'In a roomful of academic abstract painting Pollock seemed too good to be true: the ghost of the twenties had at last been laid and the way was clear'.[3]

The Smithsons' respect for the insight of artists survived into the Sixties, but with a difference. The new generation of young architects, whose spokesman was Peter Cook, the editor of *Archigram*, believed that liberation still had some way to go. In his editorial for *Archigram* no. 4, from the spring-summer of 1964, 'ZOOM', Cook disparaged 'the conventional closed architect/aesthete situation' as he recommended imagery produced outside that situation – 'the SPACE COMIC/SCIENCE FICTION BIT'. In 1970 in *Experimental architecture*, a summing up of the attitudes of the Sixties, Cook outlined his misgivings about the New Brutalism, with which the Smithsons were closely associated: 'It seems alien to the gregariousness and to implicit plurality of current architecture'.[4]

Despite their rejection, on elitist grounds, by a new generation, the Smithsons claimed priority. In a statement and manifesto of 1973, 'Without rhetoric', they explained just how much the vernacular and unco-opted 'art' of the 1950s meant to them. They recalled images 'whose technical virtuosity was almost magical so that one page must have involved as much effort as the building of a coffee-bar. This transient thing was making a bigger contribution to our visual climate than any of the fine arts'.[5] The Smithsons never passed up an opportunity to explain, and it was this didactic tendency which probably separated them from their successors who preferred to think in terms of a more equal relationship between those involved in the contemporary process. Cook wrote of 'conversations', as if the cultural world amounted to a prolonged seminar, in which issues were never quite resolved.[6]

The new generation around *Archigram* was ungrateful. The Smithsons had struggled, often ineffectually, against tradition and against the massed ranks of British inertia. With their contest with archaic Britain unresolved they found themselves despised by self-declared representatives of a millenarian future. In *Experimental architecture*, for example, Cook applauded the technology and building skills of the space industry in the USA: 'By comparison, architecture is a peasant technology riddled with imprecisions and with a value system made up of hocum'.[7] The Smithsons, of course, were devotees of peasant technology and aesthetics (in Japan and the Mediterranean especially)[8] and wrote and taught always in terms of ethics. The new generation could hardly declare itself hostile to ethics, but believed that creativity was an overriding value, and benign in the end.

The new generation of architects as announced in May 1961 by *Archigram* relished ambiguity. It would be new, but at the same time not new; its break with the past would be absolute, but at the same time only apparent. Its exponents would be outspoken, but not really dogmatic, because dogma would foreclose on 'conversation': 'A new generation of architecture must arise with forms and spaces which seem to reject the precepts of "Modern" yet in fact retain

Archigram, 'Living city', design for *Living Arts* magazine, no. 2, 1963. Private collection

those precepts. WE HAVE CHOSEN TO BY-PASS THE DECAYING BAUHAUS IMAGE WHICH IS AN INSULT TO FUNCTIONALISM.'[9] In the third issue of *Archigram* in the autumn of 1963 the editor promised, in capitals, not to bulldoze Westminster Abbey.

The new generation was entranced by techno-utopian visions of the future. Reyner Banham's influential *Theory and design in the first machine age* had been published in 1960, bringing the Futurists to public prominence as never before; and in 1963 Contads and Sperlich's *Fantastic architecture* came out in English with news of the dreams and disappointments of the early moderns.[10] Young architects may have taken heart from the tradition, but little else, for the earlier utopians often thought institutionally and coercively. Prescriptive imagining in the Sixties was never an option because, as the young architects understood it, the shape of the future was already implicit in the present situation. What, then, was required was an attentive, unclouded reading of the present, which would somehow facilitate the arrival of a future, which would arrive anyway.

Although British Futurism of the Sixties has its major monument, in the shape of the Piano-Rogers Centre Pompidou of 1977, it was never meant to result in a style. Nor was it meant to produce architect-builders in any traditional sense, for the architect of old was no better than a tyrant. An ideal operative under the new terms simply mediated among social forces which were too powerful to be denied – and which were, at the same time, benign and reasonable. Credit could be given for innovation, but guardedly, on the grounds that it was the *zeitgeist* which really mattered. For example, the editorial matter in *Archigram* 4 begins airily with 'A respectful salute in the general direction of Roy Lichtenstein and we're off...'[11]

The problem, in retrospect, was that the Techno-Futurists, with their faith in pre-fabrication and 'plug-in' building, overestimated both the power and the reasonableness of the collective imagination.[12] The future as anticipated took place but in a blighted form. They imagined world-wide broadcasting, but not the dissemination of debased sporting events and re-cycled entertainment. They looked forward to spectacular new structures housing whole communities, but the innovative industrial world in which they invested such high hopes volunteered oil-extraction

Archigram, 'Living city', design for Living Arts magazine, no. 2, 1963. Private collection

platforms. Cities, which were meant to respond to treatment, continued to choke themselves to death. Having declared themselves for the future as it would inevitably disclose itself, their reputations stood or fell on the strength and accuracy of their projections. Thus, as the future failed, they could be dismissed as utopians, victims of wishful thinking. *Archigram* suffered principally because of its reliance on the spoken word, or because of its belief in 'conversation', for conversation – despite its democratizing ethos – ruled out

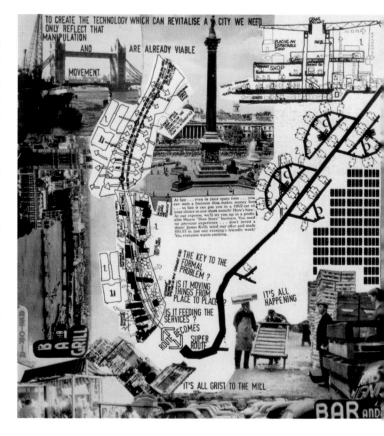

the kind of thoroughness which would have taken economic tendencies into account.

Despite subscribing to an idea of technological inevitability, the young architects were ideologues in so far as they believed in, and even took for granted, the possibility of personal choice. They projected an energetic, creative society which had somehow fought free of impersonal economic determinants, in which individuals would henceforth decide for themselves on the kind of matters that had previously been decided for them by the authorities – of whatever sort. This doctrine of free choice lay behind their preoccupations with indeterminacy in building; for if every citizen was forever at liberty to make up his or her mind then there could be no determinate solution to any building problem. Indeterminacy was what Cook had in mind when he outlined a proposal for a Fun Palace in Monte Carlo in *Experimental architecture* in 1970: '...basic props with which the public can make its own circumstances...'[13]

Archigram's credo was libertarian, even anarchic,

although in the early Sixties it was also hospitable to *dirigistes* on the Left. Its tone, though, was usually nearer to the following: 'does a planning ideal, and administrative theory, an advertiser's merchandising policy, a technocrat's computer, or an architect's ego, justify trammeling an individual into a pattern against his will?'[14]

Just why the libertarian attitude should become widespread and meaningful in the Sixties is a more complex question. In the Fifties Alison and Peter Smithson admitted that choice was a priority in their programmes for housing:

'We should say that the form of the house groups should be such that an individual can choose his degree of contact...or protection...and thereby pleasure...in the machine-served society.'[15] The Smithsons' view on choice, as the extract indicates, was that it should be exercised in the face of an overbearing culture at large. They believed always in an architecture which would compensate for the ills of the social moment.[16] For their successors by contrast the ability to make choices was the hallmark of the new epoch – about to be revealed.

It seems, on the evidence, that the Smithsons and their more extremist successors reacted sharply to conformism, endemic in British architectural culture and in the culture at large. Looking back, the Smithsons attributed the development of their own indeterminacy to the too-rigid conception of the post-war English New Towns.[17] Prudent polemicists, the Smithsons were reformists rather than revolutionaries. Their successors, by contrast, were disgusted by what they had inherited: 'The *Archigram* group came about through a succession of reactions to the boredom and obviousness of post-war English office blocks and local authority housing.'[18] It was less that the building was bad, according to a new set of values, than that it was boring. Nowhere else was the present so threatened by tradition, and by a degenerate public, even if it was a public of straw men: 'In England it is not easy for architecture to survive without the assent of the (mythical) man in the street.'[19] Much of Cook's *Experimental architecture* – one of the key texts of the decade – reads as if it had been contrived in a court of cultural and architectural law, in which the case against the new had been brought again and again from all the angles imaginable. Cook warns, for example, against the epithet 'experimental' for it can so easily be substituted by the pejorative 'utopian',[20] just as he warns against the meretricious vanguardism of festivals and fairs, which reduce the genuinely new to gimmickry.[21] The Smithsons too regretted that 'the English only think in terms of words', by which they meant that the title New Brutalism had been applied unfairly to their architecture of the 1950s.[22] There was something deadening in the culture which elicited hysterical responses.[23]

If an effort could be made, tradition would be exploded (a favourite term of the time)[24] and boredom would be no more. Cook *et al.* thought of themselves as inhabiting a transitional phase leading to a bright new era. History would be pushed forward less by underlying changes in the economic base than by the energy and intelligence of liberated people. In 1970 Cook wrote, perhaps in terms of the new atomic vocabulary of critical mass, of 'an increasingly well-informed mass which is prepared to take the initiative without heeding the established institutions'.[25] Will-power and intelligence by themselves would do the trick. In the same text Cook invoked another on-going conversation, in which the dread of boredom is a determinant:

Boutique decoration by BEV, London, 1967. Private collection

The idea is that in some relatively isolated and under-privileged provincial towns of England and America there exists a potential intelligence and culture which could be boosted by their linking or 'networking'. This process could be stimulated by the visit of a travelling circus of such sophistication and catalytic effect (as it honed-in on such towns) that a progressively developing inter-town organism would be created.[26]

The image of 'isolated...provincial towns' had been boredom's emblem since the onset of the industrial age at least. Why should it have begun to count for so much in the 1960s in Britain? There was a new confidence in answers to problems. If the problem could be identified and analysed it could be solved, but in order to reach solutions it was first necessary to sweep away archaic, provincial modes of thought. It was less perhaps that the problem was an affront in itself, than that its *remaining* a problem was an affront to the self-esteem of a new generation. Young architects of the *Archigram* generation recognized that they had the answers to problems that were not yet widely acknowledged as such, and that unless they worked as publicists the situation would remain the same.[27]

They took encouragement from a theory of threshold moments, among which they numbered their own. According to this assumption, which Cook shared with the Smithsons, qualitative change occurred when enabling conditions had sufficiently accumulated. There had, for example, been enough emergency situations over the preceding half century to 'force the development of a rational design for survival'.[28] Texts of the time referred to architect-inventors who had devised solutions: Frei Otto (suspended roofs and inflated elastic structures), Jean Prouvé (prefabrication), Konrad Wachsmann (modular co-ordination).[29] Even the problem had been identified – as summarized by John McHale in a book of 1962 on the career of Buckminster Fuller: 'The central theme of this third-of-a-century pioneer's explorations has been one of dedication to the idea of a world-wide "architectural" or "shelter" facility as part of the scientifically designed investment of total world resources in the service of all humanity.'[30] Where the Smithsons, for example, had thought of practical answers to finite difficulties, their successors cited 'humanity' and 'the metropolis'. With respect to such large-scale motifs there

could be neither success nor failure, in material terms at least. What was at issue, though, was rather the mobilization of the imagination, which could not be secured by investment in the kind of relatively local issues that preoccupied the Smithsons. Housing projects and other local matters inevitably entailed specialisms, which in turn foreclosed on 'conversation' and on the play of creativity so valued by *Archigram*.

If Otto, Prouvé and Wachsmann allowed the young architects of the Sixties to envisage a millenarian future of 'plug-in' cities, it was Buckminster Fuller who supplied their intellectual procedures. Cook, looking back in 1970, referred to an increasing feeling of dissatisfaction with the 'formal mythology' of architecture, and with its 'decrepit technologies propped up by an elitist aesthetic language'.[31] Fuller proposed how this despised language could be circumvented, and had done so at least since the original publication of *Nine chains to the moon* in 1938. His procedure was to use synonyms as radically as possible, so that the situation in architecture and design could be seen afresh. In his respect for words and for what they might teach Fuller was an early modern, from the generation of Ezra Pound and Heidegger even. His audience was to learn from the word HOUSE': 'it is etymologically connected with hut-hide-hoard-hood and hat, and among its various synonyms are residence, lodging, booth (bothy) and shelter'.[32] He persisted etymologically for as long as practicable, and when that approach failed he turned for insight to active/passive analyses designed to disrupt present complacency: 'In archi-

tecture "form" is a noun; in industry, "form" is a verb. Industry is concerned with DOING, whereas architecture has been engrossed with making replicas of end results of what people have industrially demonstrated in the past'.[33] Fuller's loyalties were to activities spontaneously carried out in answer to current predicaments. For Fuller tradition meant a deadening stasis: 'At the outset, certain new words must be introduced, among which are *vitalistics* to replace the dead word *statistics*, and *mobilata* to supersede *data*'.[34]

Although Fuller's handling of syllogisms was always challenging it was at the same time liberating: 'The triangle, through the ages, has been the symbol of the architecture of motion, first in tents, then in the rigging of sailing ships,

**'Pneu world',
cover of *Architectural
Design*, 1968.
Private collection**

**Photograph by
Robert Whitaker of
Michael English
decorating the Indica
Bookshop, 1966.
Private collection**

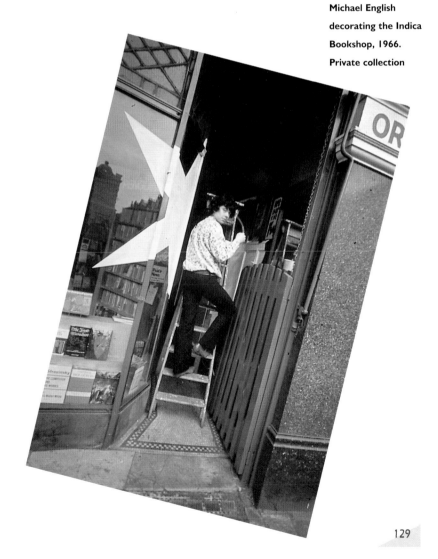

thereafter in trestles, and most recently in airplane wings and radio masts'.[35] *Archigram*, firmly committed to the present, eschewed the elemental and originative which so appealed to Fuller's generation. Instead, Cook found a vocabulary of enlightenment in contemporary commerce, as in this editorial of autumn 1963:

> Our collective mental blockage occurs between the land of the small-scale consumer-products, and the objects which make up our environment. Perhaps it will not be until such things as housing, amenity-place and workplace become recognised as consumer products that can be 'bought off the peg' – with all this implies in terms of expendability (foremost), industrialisation, up-to-dateness, consumer choice, and basic product design – that we can begin to make an environment that is really part of the developing human culture.[36]

There was to be 'throwaway' architecture, which was to be sold, like any new commercial product, in terms of its 'features'.[37] Much of it would have originated as 'spinoff' from space technology, and it would be ultimately assembled in a 'Plug-In City'. The architecture business, once so carefully controlled, would become a shop, or even a garage; for not only would the new architect be what Cook called an 'opportunist', a term commonly associated with sharp practice, but would be an expert in the use of 'tuning elements', or parts that could 'be added to an existing structure, temporary and exchangeable, perhaps derived from a different heritage'.[38] Cook's irreverent citing of topical commercial terms meant giddiness to the Smithsons, especially when the words became forms: '...we are right to worry about buildings in which plumbing vents are made

to look like ship air-intakes, and towns like oil-refineries, where our emotions are engaged by reminders of previous or other technologies'.[39]

Although *Archigram* never chose to explain its place in any wider conspectus, its terms of reference were phenomenological. Cook was opposed to root-and-branch explanations of the sort that claimed to know exactly what society was and how its requirements might be satisfied. This was why 'housing' could never interest the new generation, for 'housing implied access to a total picture of social needs. Instead Cook wrote and taught as if understanding was sufficient, and alone justifiable. To understand meant to accept the situation as it was, and the situation was constituted of individuals subject to circumstance, liable to change without good cause. If the new generation was acted on by 'some of the poetry of countdown, orbital helmets' then it was foolish to deny it.[40] And if life was increasingly time-bound, or 'part of a process',[41] that too had to be allowed for: 'We can see (again in the more privileged sections) that the student, the bachelor, the old person or the family which is able to have two locations (dependent upon the weather or the part of the week) are making quite different demands upon the standard day and night cycle and standard services of the dwelling'.[42] The meaning of all this, of course, was that if this ceaselessly varying surface of life was to be properly taken into account the architect had somehow to insist on remaining involved. There was to be no possibility at all of falling back on the basics of explanation, for that was the way to stasis, to the dreadful culture of old answers to new problems.

Ian Jeffrey

25. Op. cit., p. 153.

26. Op cit., p. 122.

27. *Archigram* continued to publish statements by young architects, like this from Nick Grimshaw, taken from his thesis study at the Architectural Association, 1964–5: 'We will be designing the instruments and writing the score for perhaps only one performance. Perhaps a script for a day, a month, a year – and all the time we must be prepared to scrap, to adapt, to add to our environment with all the means at our disposal.' Grimshaw was the designer, in the Nineties, for the spectacular Trans-Marche train shed at Waterloo Station.

28. Cook, op. cit., p. 116.

29. *Archigram* cited all three, and their influence can be detected in the later building of Warren Chalk (the Imagination design in Store Street, London) and Nick Grimshaw (Waterloo).

30. John McHale, *Richard Buckminster Fuller*, London, 1962, pp. 9–10. McHale, a writer and Constructivist-collagist, exhibited in the 2nd space in *this is tomorrow* (1956) with Richard Hamilton.

31. Cook, op. cit., p. 7.

32. *Nine chains to the moon*, 1938; repub. 1963, London, p. 33. The title came from the idea that humanity in line would stretch nine times to the moon.

33. Ibid., pp. 42–3.

34. Ibid., p. 49.

35. Ibid., p. 129.

36. *Archigram* no. 3.

37. For an account of 'features' see Cook, op. cit., p. 131.

38. For 'opportunism' and 'tuning' see Cook, op. cit., pp. 26–7.

39. Smithson, 'Without rhetoric', op. cit., p. 66.

40. From the opening statement in *Archigram* no. 1, May 1961: 'The love is gone. The poetry in bricks is lost. We want to drag into building some of the poetry of countdown, orbital helmets. Discord of mechanical body transportation methods and legwalking. LOVE GONE.'

41. Peter Cook, *Architecture: Action and plan*, London, 1967, p. 74.

42. Cook, *Experimental architecture*, op. cit., p. 128.

1. *this is tomorrow* ... london ... the whitechapel art gallery ... august 9–september 9...1956.

2. Alison and Peter Smithson, *Urban structuring*, London, 1967, p. 34.

3. Alison and Peter Smithson, *New lives, New landscapes*, London, 1970, p. 86.

4. Peter Cook, *Experimental architecture*, London, 1970, p. 43.

5. Alison and Peter Smithson, 'Without rhetoric', London, 1973, p. 6.

6. Cook, op. cit., p. 122.

7. Cook, op. cit., p. 112.

8. Smithson, 'Without rhetoric', idem.

9. *Archigram* was published about once a year throughout the Sixties; in the beginning it amounted to little more than a series of illustrated sheets either folded or stapled.

10. *Fantastic architecture*, originally brought out in German in 1960, was specifically recommended by *Archigram*, along with *Paris Match* and *Galaxy Science Fiction*.

11. Issue no. 4 of *Archigram*, from spring-summer 1964. 'ZOOM' took its cue mainly from science fiction illustrations.

12. For an early use of the term 'plug-in', see *Archigram* no. 3, autumn 1963, under 'Projects': 'Caravan web: These are being promoted in U.S. van circles and are in fact the manifestation of something that has been spreading as an architectural idea: PLUG-IN HOUSING, albeit from an unexpected direction'.

13. Cook, op. cit., p. 142.

14. *Archigram* no. 2. In its early issues the magazine published statements by recently graduated architects; this was contributed by Timothy Tinker, at the Architectural Association, London, 1955–60.

15. Smithson, 'Without rhetoric', op. cit., p. 14.

16. For their beliefs on this question, see 'Without rhetoric', idem.

17. Smithson, *Urban structuring*, op. cit., p. 29.

18. Cook, op. cit., p. 90.

19. Idem.

20. Op. cit., p. 28.

21. Op. cit., pp. 17 and 119.

22. Smithson, 'Without rhetoric', op. cit., p. 4.

23. Cook in particular insisted on the need to react: 'yet there is the broad and horrific mainstream of recent architecture which must be recognised', Cook, op. cit., p. 7.

24. For example for Cook throw-away architecture 'keeps exploding the notion that architecture is buildings', Cook, op. cit., p. 67.

Archigram, 'Living city' design for *Living Arts* magazine, no. 2, 1963. Private collection

Omtentacle designs on The Flying Dragon restaurant, from 'Negozi a Londra', *Domus* magazine, 1969. Private collection

Comic strip and newspaper cartoons

Comic strip is a particularly successful art form in France which reaches a wide and varied public of adults as well as children and adolescents. This is a direct legacy of the remarkable creative effervescence of the Sixties. *Pilote*, a weekly magazine first published in 1959, dominated the genre and has always been and is the most important French comic-strip magazine; and it brought about a positive cultural revolution in the world of 'comics'.

Tintin, Spirou, Vaillant and the others

Since the appearance of *La Famille Fenouillard* by Christophe in 1889 in Armand Colin's *Le Petit Français illustré,* comic strips had evolved in books and newspapers but stayed firmly as children's literature. They were always regarded as a rather bastardized, vulgar branch of the traditional picture book. To indicate what is now called *bande dessinée* (or BD) – a term that was not used until the Sixties – people generally referred to '*illustrés*', an aptly suggestive word.

Within these confines the Belgian tradition dominated the French market, and even the European one, thanks to two great rival weekly magazines: *Tintin* (published in Brussels) and *Spirou* (published by Dupuis, based at Marcinelle near Charleroi). *Spirou* was founded in 1938, but did not really take off until just after the war. Gradually it assembled the talents of Joseph Gillain, known as Jijé (creator of *Blondin et Cirage, Valhardi, Jerry Spring*), André Franquin (for a long time he did the drawings for *Spirou et Fantasio* before creating *Gaston Lagaffe*), Morris (*Lucky Luke*), Victor Hubinon (*Buck Danny*), Will (*Tif et Tondu*), Peyo (*Johan et Pirlouit*, then *Les Schtroumpfs* – or Smurfs) and Maurice Tillieux (*Gil Jourdan*). Imagination, modernity, dynamism and humour were the distinguishing features of this peerless team.

Tintin was more serious, with adventures, suspense and fantasy being given pride of place. The original team formed round Hergé in 1946 consisted of Jacques Laudy (*Hassan et Kaddour*), Paul Cuvelier (*Corentin Feldoë*) and of course Edgar P. Jacobs, originator of the legendary *Blake et Mortimer*. *Alix l'intrépide, Michel Vaillant, Chevalier Ardent, Dan Cooper* and *Ric Hochet* were subsequently added to the great heroes of *Tintin*.

In France two great illustrated papers emerged from the Resistance, *Coq Hardi* and *Vaillant*. The first, with Marijac,

failed to outlive the Fifties. *Vaillant*, an offshoot of the Communist press, was longer lived thanks to excellent adventure series which, paradoxically, were inspired by classic American strip cartoons. All genres were covered: science fiction with *Les Pionniers de l'espérance*, historical epic with *Yves le Loup*, aviation with *Bob Mallard*, detective stories with *Jacques Flash*, Westerns with *Sam Billie Bill*, etc. There were also Catholic publications for children, the two leaders being *Coeurs vaillants* published by Fleurus and *Bayard* from the Bonne Presse. Many other titles were available to young people, often survivors of pre-war publications (*L'Intrépide, Tarzan, Pierrot*, etc.). *Le Journal de Mickey* contained mainly foreign comic strips, but the excellent saga *Mickey à travers les siècles* was the work of the talented Frenchman Pierre Nicolas.

Without appealing to a different public or departing from the rules of the law of 16 July 1949 regulating publications for young people, these illustrated publications did evolve during the Sixties. *Tintin* in particular developed new subject areas under Greg, its chief editor from 1965 to 1974. For instance, a few female figures appeared in a world which until then had been very macho, with only racing drivers, airmen, reporters and other detectives having right of entry. Moreover, children's publications were the first to publish authors who later became stars of adult comic strip. For example Claire Bretécher worked for *Spirou* on *Les Gnan-Gnan* and (with Raoul Cauvin as scriptwriter) on *Les Naufragés*, while Gotlib and Nikita Mandryka won their spurs on *Vaillant*. This journal was the first in France to publish *Corto Maltese* by the Italian cartoonist Hugo Pratt. But by then (1970) *Vaillant*, rechristened *Pif gadget*, had already started on an irreversible decline.

Pilote was launched on 29 October 1959 with support from Radio Luxembourg, and at first seemed to be traditional, drawing on Belgian models (*Tintin, Spirou* and *La Libre junior*) as well as British (*Eagle*) and French (*Record*) ones. The first issue saw the start of three series destined to have a brilliant future: *Tanguy et Laverdure, Barbe-Rouge* and above all *Astérix le Gaulois*.

Jean-Michel Charlier, a prolific scriptwriter and a master of hectic adventure, already wrote the scripts of *Buck Danny, La Patrouille des castors* and *Marc Dacier* for *Spirou*. As a former pilot, in *Tanguy et Laverdure* he indulged his passion for

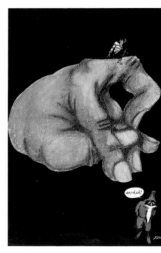

Drawing by Fred,
Philémon et le
***Manu-Manu*, for**
the cover of the
19 August 1971
issue of *Pilote*.
Private collection

flying. Albert Uderzo illustrated the first adventures of these two French Air Force aces, so proving that he was at home in both serious and humorous genres. *Tanguy et Laverdure* inspired a television series *Chevaliers du ciel* from 1967 (a rare feat for a strip cartoon). Jacques Santi played Michel Tanguy, the 'competent professional', with Christian Marin as Ernest Laverdure, the 'likable stooge'.

The cartoonist Victor Hubinon was an old collaborator of Jean-Michel Charlier's; they had worked together on *Buck Danny* and on the life of the pirate Surcouf. Returning to the sea, for *Pilote* they created the story of the pirate *Barbe-Rouge*, 'the demon of the Caribbean'. This blood-thirsty character mends his ways under the influence of his adopted son, Éric, and enters the service of the king of France. René Goscinny and Uderzo later took pleasure in parodying the *Barbe-Rouge* characters in any episode where *Astérix* took to the sea.

Astérix meets Hara-Kiri

In March 1960 Georges Dargaud, the publisher of the French edition of the Belgian weekly *Tintin* since 1948, bought *Pilote*, which was in financial difficulties. He tried to find a successful formula, for some time adopting the fashion for Pop. Comic strips were given primacy from 1963 when Dargaud put Goscinny, the scriptwriter of *Astérix*, in charge. Unconventional new heroes like *Blueberry*, *Achille Talon* and *Le Grand Duduche* were brought in to strengthen the paper, and started to give comic strip a new impetus. But it was very much the *Astérix* series that attracted general attention to the merits of 'la nouvelle bande dessinée'. Goscinny's humour which could be understood at several levels attracted read-ers of all ages. The series became a cult from 1965 and the paper profited from its phenomenal success. By devoting its cover to the little Gaul on 19 September 1966 the maga-zine *L'Express* formally sealed his incredible popularity.

Goscinny had collaborated with the cartoonist Uderzo since 1951, bringing to life first *Jehan Pistolet*, then *Luc Junior* and finally *Oumpah-Pah*, a Red Indian adventurer from *Tintin*. He was also the scriptwriter of *Lucky Luke,* with drawings by Morris, and of the *Le Petit Nicolas* stories illustrated by Sempé. Later he created the *Dingodossiers* with Gotlib and *Isnogoud* with Jean Tabary. When *Pilote* was launched in 1959

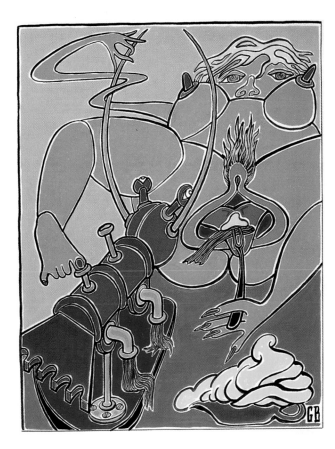

Drawings by
Gébé for *Hara-Kiri*,
early 1960s.
Private collection

the two associates had to produce a new idea in a hurry. They thought of 'our ancestors the Gauls'. The subject was new, appealing and full of possibilities. The Romans would be the natural enemies, and the inspired plot was of a small village, still and perpetually, holding out against the invader thanks to a magic potion made by its Druid (in 1959 Charles de Gaulle, symbol of the Resistance, had just returned to power). Caesar's ill-fated opponent Vercingetorix inspired the idea of names ending in '-ix', while Astérix, Obélix, Abraracourcix and all the others were to embody the supposed virtues and failings of the French: generous, quarrelsome, greedy, insubordinate, touchy, chauvinistic ... and fearing just one thing: that the sky would fall on their heads!

Astérix was a turning-point in cartoon humour. Its ingredients were: the free and irreverent use of historical facts, the saucy caricature of national characteristics, the Latin quotations and other cultural references, the use of anachronisms for satire, the effectiveness of characters that are both anti-conformist and archetypal, the sense of burlesque. Created by improvisation, it established a real mythology and came up with successful new ideas until Goscinny's premature death in 1977.

As the years went by, Goscinny reassembled his own cast of characters in *Pilote*: *Lucky Luke* (from *Spirou*) and *Isnogoud* (a defector from *Record*) joined *Astérix*. These series, along with *Norbert et Kari* by Christian Godard and *Achille Talon* by Greg, brilliantly ensured the continuity of the Franco-Belgian tradition. In parallel, *Pilote* gradually adopted satire, current affairs, nonsense and baroque science fiction,

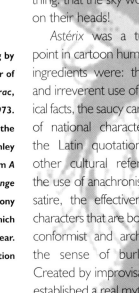

Original drawing by Gotlib for the cover of *La Rubrique-à-Brac*, vol. IV, 1973. He is parodying the poster for Stanley Kubrick's film *A clockwork orange* (based on Anthony Burgess's book), which came out that year. Artist's collection

featuring signed comic strips which appealed to students and young adults. The arrival of new cartoonists from *Hara-Kiri* and *Charlie-Hebdo* – first Fred, then Cabu, Jean-Marc Reiser and Gébé – hastened these developments.

Hara-Kiri had started as a modest cultural magazine sold on street corners in the Latin Quarter; it was founded in September 1960 on the initiative of François Cavanna, a mason who became a newspaper cartoonist, and Georges Bernier who had fought in Indo-China and was later to be famous as 'Professeur Choron'. Soon taken over by the Éditions du Square, making wider circulation possible, it revolutionized the satirical press, thanks to a team of young cartoonists called Fred, Topor, Reiser, Cabu, Gébé and Georges Wolinski. In the tradition of French humorous drawing, these cartoonists invented a humour that was 'stupid and naughty', drawing equally on Americans – Steinberg and Charles Addams – and the satire of the team on the newspaper *Mad*. Misappropriating advertising material, using photographic montage and absurd and macabre humour, resorting to unrelenting anarchism and provocative vulgarity, *Hara-Kiri* was soon at odds with the censorship of the Gaullist regime. Banned in 1961 and again in 1966 (when some of the team transferred to *Pilote*), taken to court again and again, the magazine nonetheless continued to attract a considerable following, especially among students and young people.

In 1967 Delfeil de Ton and Willem joined the team for the newspaper's golden age. In May '68 this group of cartoonists were at the forefront of protest. Wolinski did drawings for *Action* and created *L'Enragé* together with Siné. In 1969 in rapid succession the Éditions du Square launched *Charlie Mensuel*, a comic-strip magazine, which will be discussed below, and *Hara-Kiri Hebdo,* banned after its famous lead story, 'Bal tragique à Colombey – un mort', its way of hailing General de Gaulle's death on 16 November 1970. Publication resumed under the name *Charlie-Hebdo*.

Introducing ecology (the Éditions du Square launched the ecological monthly *La Gueule ouverte* in November

The story of *Hara-Kiri* and *Charlie-Hebdo* cannot on its own sum up the development of humorous drawing and newspaper cartoons in the Sixties. Such established cartoonists as Effel, Bosc, Mose or Tim (Tim had appeared in *L'Express* since 1958) were still hard at work. Although André François abandoned drawing for painting and sculpture and Chaval committed suicide in January 1968, in the Sixties such talents as Topor (co-founder of the Panique group in 1962), Siné (the most virulent graphic talent in the anti-Gaullist camp) and Sempé appeared, while

Part of a block by Gotlib relating to the first steps on the moon, published in *Pilote* in 1969. Artist's collection

1972), using drawings for reporting (Cabu) and describing the revolutionary utopia (*L'An 01* by Gébé), the *Hara-Kiri* cartoonists who saw themselves primarily as journalists gave comic strip a new political, satirical, denunciatory role. Significantly, in the ecumenical pages of *Pilote* the Left-wing chorus appears alongside reactionary writers like Serge de Beketch, Greg, Loro, Guy Mouminoux or even Mic Dilinx, several of whom a few years later appeared in the pages of newspapers associated with the Far Right.

Desclozeaux started work to immediate acclaim in 1965. Sempé worked with Goscinny in 1960 on *Le Petit Nicolas*, and his first album, *Rien n'est simple,* was published by Denoël two years later. Current affairs publications also timidly opened their doors to comic strip. Copi produced motionless sketches and ones with dialogue for *Le Nouvel Observateur* from 1965 under the title *La Femme assise*, before the joint work of Bretécher and Reiser for the same weekly.

Right:
Cover of *Scarlett Dream*
album, script by Claude
Moliterni and drawings
by Robert Gigi,
Éric Losfeld, 1967.
Private collection

Block by Nicolas Devil
for the *Saga de Xam*
album, Éric Losfeld, 1967.
This collective album
(the youthful Philippe
Druillet contributed to it,
for example) still marks
a decisive stage in
transforming the way
comic strips are
structured.
Private collection

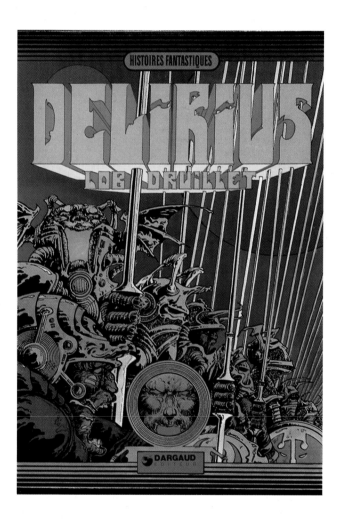

Block by Philippe Druillet,
Yragaël ou la fin des temps,
published in *Pilote* **in 1973.**
Artist's collection

Cover of *Délirius* **album**
by Philippe Druillet,
vol. II of the adventures
of Lone Sloane,
Dargaud, 1973.
Private collection

Pilote's finest hours

Between 1969 and 1972 *Pilote* succeeded brilliantly. A large part of it was devoted to current affairs pages where the cartoonists who met every Monday as an editorial committee offered their dislocated view of the major and minor events in the world. This team work (famously described as '*gros tas de chouettes copain*', a 'great load of smashing pals') enabled *Pilote* to establish points or characters of reference shared by all its writers: for instance *Hal*, the super-computer in Kubrick's film *Space Odyssey 2001*, and *Molyneux*, the traveller who finds himself on a station platform in his dressing-gown. In another ploy to connive with its readers, the cartoonists depicted each other. Goscinny and Charlier are featured in *Achille Talon*, the character who hangs around the editorial office of *Pilote* magazine, while Goscinny (again), Fred and Gébé are depicted by Gotlib in *Les Enquêtes du commissaire Bougret*. The spirit of May '68 blew over *Pilote*. Antimilitarism appeared in the excellent *Sergent Laterreur* by Touïs and Frydman. The

'Astérix and Obélix paper' had turned into a 'paper that gets fun out of thinking'. Bretécher worked alternately on *Salades de saison* (forerunner of the famous *Frustrés* comic strip of the Seventies) and *Cellulite*, a mediaeval princess not blessed with good looks and the first 'anti-heroine' of French comic strip.

Gotlib and Fred cultivated other forms of humour, one resorting to the absurd and the other to the strange and wonderful. In no. 300 (1965), the silhouette of a teenager wearing a striped polo shirt first appeared: this was

Philémon. The brainchild of Fred, this appealing dreamer travels with his donkey Anatole and M. Barthélemy, a sinker of wells, in a parallel world, one made of the letters that form the word 'Atlantique', islands in the middle of the ocean. In this Lewis Carroll world Philémon meets many curious characters. On his return he invariably encounters the incredulity of his father. Fred's humour and poetry are also in the scripts he wrote for other cartoonists, particularly in the *Time is money* series with drawings by Alexis.

Gotlib, who drew a weekly *Gai-Luron* story in *Le Journal de Pif,* came to *Pilote* in 1965, first illustrating the *Dingodossiers'* strip with Goscinny as scriptwriter, then creating his famous *Rubrique-à-brac* in 1968. Gotlib's subjects are mainly animals, fairy tales and cinema, parodies of the television series *Les cinq dernières minutes*, and he features himself as a megalomaniac artist. *Rubrique-à-brac* has no hero, but there are recurring characters – Isaac Newton, Professor Burp and of course the ladybird. Expressive drawing serving an 'icy, sophisticated' humour that recognized no boundaries made Gotlib a star, and later he became the spiritual mentor of a new generation of humorists (François Boucq, Daniel Goossens, Édika and others).

A renewal of science fiction was initiated by Jean-Claude Forest. Barbarella, the first 'liberated' heroine, started life in *V Magazine* in 1962, and was officially recognized in Roger Vadim's 1968 film with Jane Fonda in the title role. *Les Naufragés du temps* scripted by Jean-Claude Forest for Paul Gillon, first appeared in *Chouchou* in 1964. Forest, who later

Top left:
Block by Wolinski.
Musée d'Histoire
contemporaine
collection

Cover of the fanzine
Zinc by Nicoulaud,
June 1973.
Private collection

Bottom left:
Cover of *Pilote* by Alexis,
2 September 1971.
Private collection

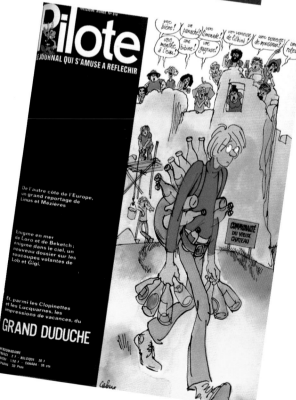

Drawing by Cabu
showing 'le Grand
Duduche' in a commune,
cover of *Pilote*,
26 August 1971.
Private collection

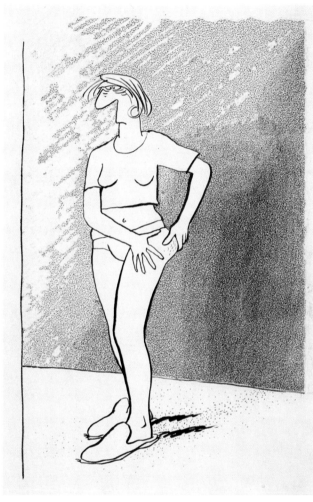

Comic-strip authors tended to hide behind their characters. *Pilote* was the first illustrated magazine to give its cartoonists star status. Their portraits, drawn by Alexis, graced the tops of the pages they illustrated. This treatment was adopted in the albums published in increasing numbers by Éditions Dargaud. At its height *Pilote* attracted all the new talents of French comic strip. Philippe Druillet, Alexis, F'Murr, Jean Solé, Jean-Pierre Dionnet, Jacques Tardi, Enki Bilal, Régis Franc, Gérard Lauzier and René Pétillon were introduced in its pages, while the caricaturists Mulatier, Morschoisne and Ricord achieved fame through *Grandes Gueules*, a saucy gallery of famous personalities at the end of the magazine.

Drawing by
Claire Bretécher.
Artist's collection

Claire Bretécher,
original design for
album cover, 1972.
Artist's collection

tried television and photostories, did not join *Pilote* until 1972, with the wild adventures of *Hypocrite*. Science fiction appeared in *Pilote* in 1967 with *Valérian, agent spatio-temporel*. With virtuoso drawings by Jean-Claude Mézières, Valérian roamed the galaxy, allowing scope for imaginative architecture and technology as well as extra-terrestrial flora and fauna. Pierre Christin's scripts are notable for their political dimension, humour and Laureline, Valérian's delightful girlfriend who often proves to be smarter than he is. The first blocks by Philippe Druillet appeared in *Pilote* in 1970. The grandiose, baroque saga of his hero Lone Sloane, the space fighter, expanded French science fiction, which was soon enriched by the contributions of Moebius and Enki Bilal, and found its true home in *Métal Hurlant*.

journal plein | d'humour et de bandes dessinées | juil. 69/3 francs

From Chouchou to Charlie Mensuel

Adults who liked strip cartoons could also find them in the daily newspapers, most of which carried not very original series supplied by agencies, but papers like *L'Humanité* or *France-Soir* (edited by Pierre Lazareff) had a proper creative policy. Heroines found a natural home here. For example the love life of Françoise Morel, the heroine of *13, rue de l'Espoir* (with drawings by Gillon), made young women's hearts beat faster, and Jean Ache depicted the tumultuous adventures of Arabelle, the 'last siren'.

In the specialist comic-strip press two other titles were innovatory. *Chouchou* was short-lived, but *Charlie Mensuel* lasted some time. *Chouchou,* launched on 12 November 1964, took its name from the hairy mascot of the radio programme *Salut les copains!* Edited by Jean-Claude Forest and Remo Forlani for the publisher Filipacchi, *Chouchou,* with a

Cover of *Charlie Mensuel* by Georges Wolinski (who also edited the magazine). Private collection

Cover of album by Jean-Marc Reiser, Éditions du Square, 1970. Private collection

large format (56 x 40 cm) and full colour, contained strips that were diverse in both nature and provenance.

Forest himself came up with *Bébé Cyanure*, very Surrealist in tone, while at the same time writing the script for Gillon's *Les Naufragés du temps*, a science-fiction series later in *France-Soir* and then in *Métal Hurlant*. Jacques Lob and George Pichard collaborated for the first time on *Ténébrax*, a fantastic, humorous series set in the Paris Métro. American comic strips (Chester Gould's *Dick Tracy* and Charles M. Schulz's *Peanuts*) made early appearances in the French press in *Chouchou*, and Hugo Pratt arrived with the Western *Billy James*. Such variety, although common in the following decade, disconcerted readers, and despite the publisher's perseverance and changes, sales remained limited and *Chouchou* closed in May 1965 with its fourteenth issue.

Charlie Mensuel, subtitled a 'paper full of humour and

strip cartoons' and directly inspired by the Italian monthly *Linus*, was launched in February 1969 by the Éditions du Square. The arrival of Wolinski as chief editor provided inspiration. While scriptwriting the adventures of the curvaceous Paulette with drawings by Pichard, Wolinski opened *Charlie Mensuel* to more international comic strips. Besides *Peanuts*, a remarkable range of American work was introduced: *Krazy Kat*, a classic from the Twenties illustrated by Georges Herriman and the truculent *Popeye* invented by E.C. Segar. Wolinski also honoured Fifties cartoonists like Jules Feiffer with his political slant, and Harvey Kurtzman, the creator of *Mad*. The Italian Guido Buzzelli published several stories where his deep pessimism was expressed in Expressionist black and white; the adventures of *Valentina* showed the cerebral eroticism of Guido Crepax; and Benito Jacovitti regularly produced delirious sketches stuffed with salami and fishbones.

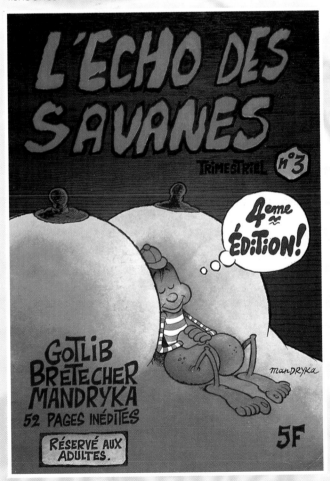

For many readers the discovery of the masterly Alberto Breccia from South America was a shock. From the *Coeur Révélateur* to *L'Éternaute*, he completely revived the treatment of fantasy and science fiction. Other important series included the adventures of the New York detective *Alack Sinner* by José Antonio Muñoz and Carlos Sampayo, and the stories by the Dutchman Joost Swarte, founder of the neo-Hergéan 'light line' school, later to become very fashionable in France. But this takes us into the Seventies, a decade during which *Charlie Mensuel* also uncovered the talents of French authors like the Varenne brothers, Alex Barbier and Francis Masse.

Éric Losfeld, often a victim of censorship, was a book publisher for the Surrealists and of erotic novels, including the famous *Emmanuelle*. In 1964 he brought out very successfully the first collected adventures of *Barbarella*. He then added other adult albums to his list, such as *Jodelle* and *Pravda la survireuse* by Guy Peellaert, influenced by Pop music, and the first *Lone Sloane* album by Druillet. Using a story by Jean Van Hamme, then a novice scriptwriter, Paul Cuvelier, a regular contributor to the weekly *Tintin*, deployed all the sensuality of his graphic art in *Époxy*, and Nicolas Devil put his name to *Saga de Xam*. This monumental erotic and aesthetic journey through the history of the art is so richly detailed that the original edition included a magnifying glass! Éric Losfeld was the first to give comic-strip authors the opportunity to express themselves at length and for the first time in books.

An art seeking legitimacy

The emergence of 'la nouvelle bande dessinée' brought a positive reassessment of this means of expression. Comic-strip authors became more ambitious because their work gained cultural status. In the Sixties a militant following for the comic strip developed, and this had a powerful impact on the perception of what would soon be called the 'ninth art'. This movement had its origins in the desire of some *aficionados* to recover from oblivion the heroes of their childhood. The Club des bandes dessinées was formed in 1962 (later pompously rechristened the Centre d'étude des littératures d'expression graphique, or CELEG) and SOCERLID (Société d'études et de recherches des lit-

Cover by Mandryka for *L'Écho des Savanes* (founded by Gotlib, Mandryka and Bretécher in 1972), 1973. Private collection

The sixties, utopian years

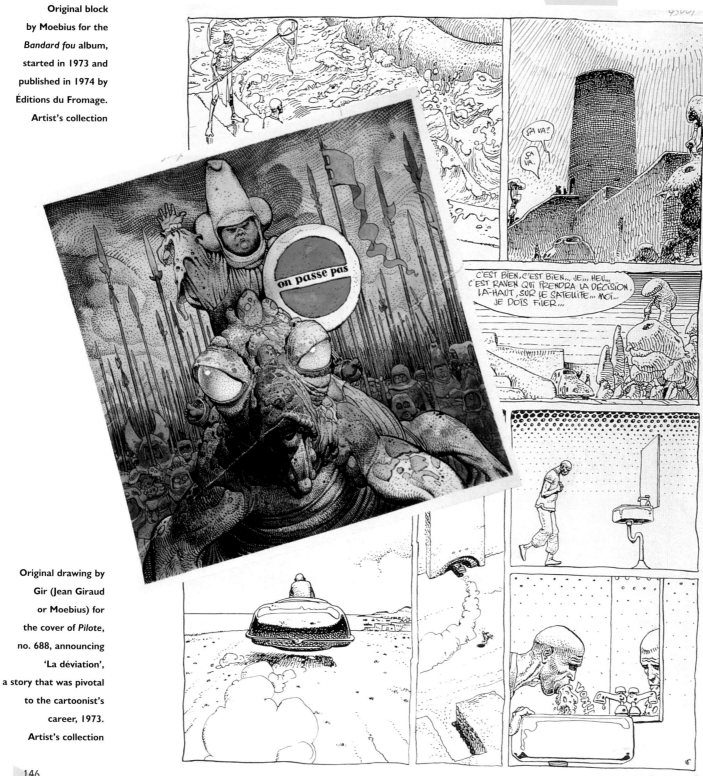

Original block
by Moebius for the
Bandard fou album,
started in 1973 and
published in 1974 by
Éditions du Fromage.
Artist's collection

Original drawing by
Gir (Jean Giraud
or Moebius) for
the cover of *Pilote*,
no. 688, announcing
'La déviation',
a story that was pivotal
to the cartoonist's
career, 1973.
Artist's collection

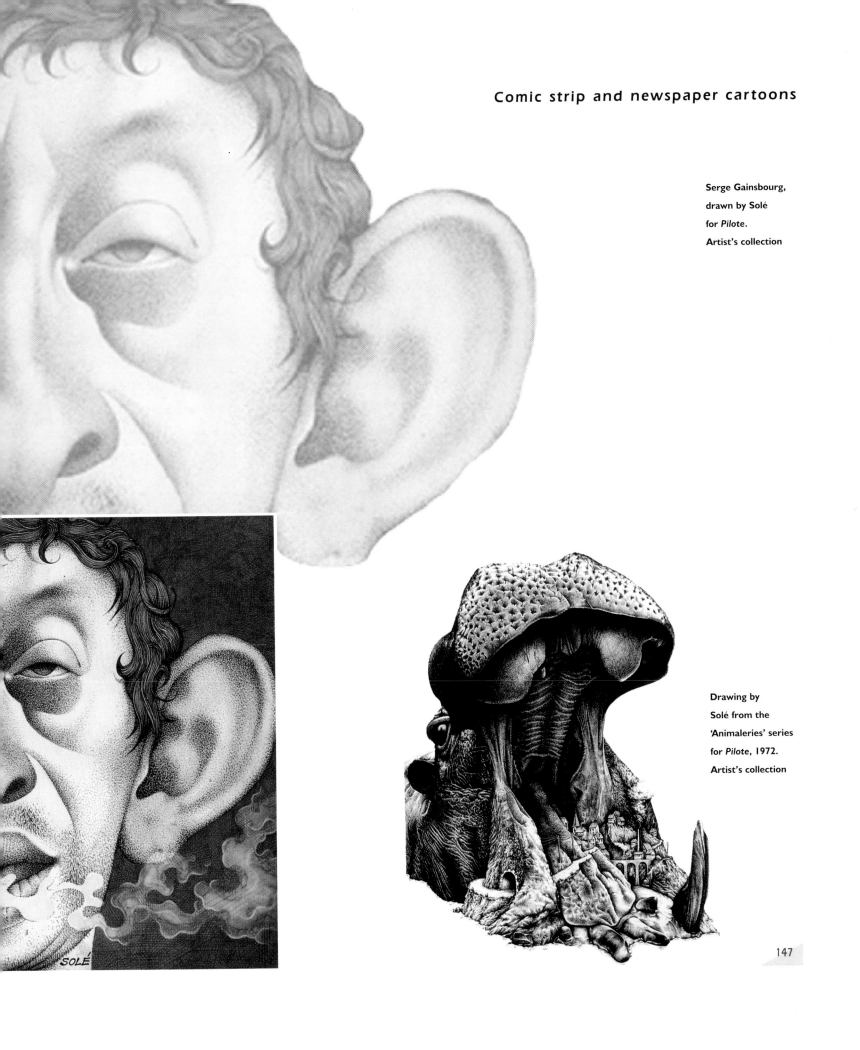

Serge Gainsbourg,
drawn by Solé
for *Pilote*.
Artist's collection

Drawing by
Solé from the
'Animaleries' series
for *Pilote*, 1972.
Artist's collection

tératures dessinées) in 1964. Both associations published journals (*Giff-Wiff* and *Phénix* respectively), republished pre-war (mainly American) classics and participated in organizing the first comic-strip festivals. Among these early militants were some well-known names, such as Alain Resnais, Pierre Lazareff, Remo Forlani and Francis Lacassin.

Before 1960 there were only three books in existence devoted to comic strips (to *Tintin*, *Christophe* and *Pif le chien*). The publication in 1966 of the slim *BD et culture* by the sociologist Évelyne Sullerot was an important milestone. The following year the ORTF (French radio and television) devoted its first programmes to comic strip, and an anthology of comic-strip masterpieces was published by Planète. In 1967 SOCERLID organized the first major exhibition of comic strips at the Musée des Arts décoratifs. Although it was very successful with the press and as a curiosity, the exhibition showed only photographic enlargements.

Nearly 30 years on, comic strip has still achieved only semi-legitimacy as a cultural phenomenon. It has been admitted to museums and is sold on the art market. Its greatest exponents are very much in demand for films, advertising, newspapers, journals and books, but the media and universities still talk very little, badly or condescendingly about comic strip. No longer does anyone ask if comic strip has become an adult art: most readers are now aged between 25 and 40, and most of the output is directed at them.

Thierry Groensteen
assisted by Jean-Pierre Mercier

Musical chronicle by Solé and Lesueur in *Pilote*, 1973. Artist's collection

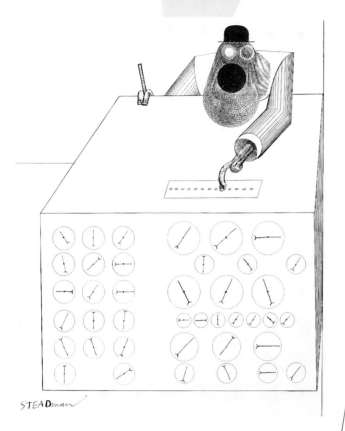

SI C'EST BIEN, JE PARLERAI DE VOUS POUR L'EXPO POMPIDOU...

Drawing by Ralph Steadman, *Office work*. Artist's collection

Block by Cabu for the *Les Aventures de madame Pompidou* album, Éditions du Square, 1972. Musée d'Histoire contemporaine collection

Jean-Claude Forest, cover of *Giff-Wiff* magazine, Jean-Jacques Pauvert. Created in 1962 and redesigned in 1966, this magazine studied comic strip, acting as a pioneer in highlighting it as the 'ninth art'. Private collection

giff.wiff

REVUE DE LA BANDE DESSINEE

trimestriel.decembre 1966 . n° 22 . 9 francs

Jean-Jacques Pauvert Editeur

NON, IL NE FAUT PAS M'AIMER...

or the power of the ephemeral

The New Wave

The New Wave, or 'la Nouvelle Vague', corresponded to the state of French society as the Fifties gave way to the Sixties: the eruption of a new generation of young people, aged between 20 and 30, with all their preoccupations, ways of life, words and culture. Their arrival did cause problems, in particular to the preceding generation, which had suffered during the war, fought, sometimes resisted, at least survived, and had come through the experience with increased stature, or alternatively with a feeling of guilt; they had then rebuilt their country, which had often involved sacrifices and hard toil, but had been sustained by a sense of collective usefulness and cultural mission, sometimes inspired by the enthusiasm engendered by that task. This generation had been marked by history, had lived through it sitting in the front row. What about those who followed?

In an anti-youth pamphlet, *Les Chiens à fouetter*, François Nourissier recognized the spectre of a loss of fighting will, a loss of brain capacity and of futility.[1] This is a portrait of the new generations whose shortcomings in 1960 were purportedly due to a lack of suffering: 'Here we see emerging the huge, well-fed, politically unmotivated cohort of French youngsters under 20 years of age, affluent realists who have experienced no drama and are ignorant of history.'[2]

The expression 'Nouvelle Vague' was forged to describe that alarming vacuum, and to shed light on the collective profile of the enigmatic young: to describe that profile, to illuminate it, but above all to give it meaning, a sociological, cultural and commercial meaning. *L'Express*, a magazine dependent on the 'cohort' of new readers, very quickly (from 1958) adopted the subtitle 'l'hebdomadaire de la Nouvelle Vague'. The term had first appeared in its columns, as a symptom and an answer to that symptom. On 3 October 1957 *L'Express* had used 'Nouvelle Vague' as the heading for the *Rapport sur la jeunesse* with comments by its main feature writer, Françoise Giroud. A few months later, in June 1958, she put together her impressions on the phenomenon, along with personal accounts sent in to the letters page in a successful book published by Gallimard, *La Nouvelle Vague, portrait de la jeunesse*. Then the term applied mainly to a social debate, which, however, soon adopted a cultural hue. The question quickly became: what culture is the younger generation forging for itself, and hence giving to the country? It was certainly a culture based on rebellion, but the elements still seemed to be generally unformulated or dispersed at the time when the expression 'Nouvelle Vague' was coined.

The English example influenced the questions being asked about a new culture, because traditional England had been shaken for some years past by the phenomenon of the Angry Young Men. At the beginning of 1958 *Les jeunes gens en colère vous parlent* (*Protest* in English), an anthology expressing the views of the leading figures from the youthful artistic and literary scene in Britain, had just been very successfully translated and published in France. While the book[3] certainly included a contribution from Lindsay Anderson, who had founded the magazine *Sequence*, directed several documentary shorts and was the leader of the 'Free Cinema' movement, he was not the star of the anthology. That was John Osborne, the dramatist who had invented the expression (his play *Look back in anger* appeared in 1957[4]); he was already known in France and his work would be staged at the TNP by Georges Wilson in 1964. Thus in Britain the cultural rebellion of the young seemed to have chosen the theatre as its vehicle. In France the medium was different, as Françoise Giroud seemed well aware when she launched another major enquiry among her readers in *L'Express* at the end of 1958: the aim was to find a match for the favourite term 'renewal' by asking for 'all sorts of ideas for making a film about youth'.

So fairly soon the expression 'Nouvelle Vague' was applied to the hopes vested in the cinema. However, the French cinema of the Fifties could almost be described as anti-youth, its two major heroes, one rough and burly (Jean Gabin), the other stiff and proper (Pierre Fresnay), very much overshadowing the theatrical appearances of 'young' Gérard Philippe. Not until Brigitte Bardot burst into prominence in the autumn of 1956 could a body be seen on the screen that was truly contemporary with those of the young audience watching it. That novelty caused a sensation (*Et Dieu créa la femme*), but it did not completely disrupt an expensive system of cinema traditionally based on the importance of its scripts, the contribution of its major stars, the professional dedication of its senior directors and all the studio apparatus – subtle *chiaroscuro* lighting, imposing sets, camera movements measured in millimetres etc. That tra-

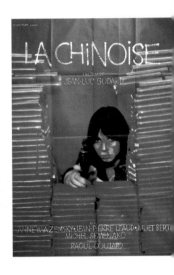

Poster for *La Chinoise* by Jean-Luc Godard (1967) describing the May '68 protest before it took place. Godard was to direct *One plus one* with the Rolling Stones in 1969. Musée d'Histoire contemporaine collection

Cover of *Cahiers du cinéma*, March 1961. Private collection

Poster of Jacques Tati's film *Play time* in which he lampooned the affluent society, 1967. Musée d'Histoire contemporaine collection

dition was dubbed the 'tradition of quality'. However, some time previously a new generation of film directors (making shorts) and film critics (using the *Cahiers du cinéma*, a small monthly magazine,[5] and the weekly magazine *Arts*) had emerged; they were aged between 25 and 35 in 1958, and strongly critical of 'the cinema of the past'. This theoretical protest became the 'Nouvelle Vague' when all these young people – Claude Chabrol, Jacques Rivette, Alain Resnais, François Truffaut, Jean-Luc Godard and Éric Rohmer in turn – moved on to direct their first full-length films between the autumn of 1957 and the summer of 1959. More specifically the term 'Nouvelle Vague', which had come from the fashionable social sciences, was applied to the cinema in February 1958 when the critic Pierre Billard first used the label to describe the group of still budding young film-makers associated with *Cahiers*.[6]

The public date of birth of the 'Nouvelle Vague' phenomenon can also be pinpointed: the 1959 Cannes Film Festival in the first fortnight of May. As soon as the French selection and the films to be shown that year were announced, a breath of youthful air swept through the French cinema: those chosen included *Orfeu negro*, Marcel Camus's second film shot in Brazil using unknown black actors, *Hiroshima mon amour*, Alain Resnais's first feature film with a script by Marguerite Duras, and *Les quatre cents coups*, the first film by a young director, François Truffaut – aged 26, unknown to the general public but already famous in cinematographic circles because of his stinging pen and unceasing attacks on the most officially accepted French films of the Fifties. The Cannes selection committee had given its support to youthful directors. Jean-Luc Godard, who was

Poster for Jacques Rivette's film *La Religieuse*, banned by the censors, 1966. Musée d'Histoire contemporaine collection

Poster for Nelly Kaplan's film *La Fiancée du pirate* presenting Bernadette Lafont as a free woman, 1969. Musée d'Histoire contemporaine collection

Poster used for
the French release
of Michelangelo
Antonioni's film
Blow-up, 1967.
Musée d'Histoire
contemporaine
collection

determined that he too would move on to directing films, had this peremptory message for members of the Academy who were guardians of 'French quality':

> All we have to say to you is this. Your pan shots are ugly because your subjects are poor, your actors act badly because your dialogue is lousy; to sum up, you cannot shoot films because you do not know what cinema is. Today we have won the day. It is our films that will prove at Cannes that France looks good, cinematographically speaking. And next year it will be the same. Let there be no doubt about that! Fifteen new brave, sincere, lucid, beautiful films will again stand in the way of conventional productions. We may have won a battle, but the war is not yet over.[7]

That 'we' effectively confirmed their victory when the prizes were announced: *Orfeu negro* received the Palme d'Or, and *Les quatre cents coups* and *Hiroshima mon amour* won awards. It is understating the case to say that the screening of François Truffaut's film created a stir. *Paris Match* devoted four full pages of its 9 May 1959 issue to a detailed account of the discovery. For some time this public, critical and financial enthusiasm bore the young film-makers along: in 30 months 97 first films were shot in France, financed by producers on the look-out for talent, a totally unprecedented occurrence in the history of world cinema.[8]

Thus the New Wave, which had been initiated in the social sphere and been set in motion by the revelation of a young generation of film directors, finished up as a full-blown, major cultural fashion. For several months from the summer of 1959, work was started on a hundred or so films branded 'Nouvelle Vague', dozens of young actors found work, and a few major successes illustrated the phenomenon (Truffaut's *Les quatre cents coup*, Chabrol's *Les Cousins* and Godard's *À bout de souffle* each attracted an audience of 500,000). But stars (Brigitte Bardot, Jean-Paul Belmondo and soon Alain Delon) were also born, and a generation of writers collaborating on the scripts in progress (Sagan, Duras, Robbe-Grillet), marked by a tone and manner that were very 'Nouvelle Vague', made their presence felt. The pages of the newspapers, parties at Saint-Tropez and 30 or 40 films were all suddenly full of certain mannerisms, clothes, a look, a way of talking. Most of the films would be quickly forgotten, but this should not disguise the identification that took place between a sector of youth and a moment of cinema: for the first time in France a new and crucial way of living with, in and through the cinema had emerged.[9]

The 'Nouvelle Vague', beyond or rather within the social phenomenon, included several circles of film-makers. The new directors making their first full-length films between 1957 and 1962 compose the largest circle, i.e. a good 100 directors and nearly 200 films (some directors were able to shoot several films in rapid succession). Most of these young film-makers would not make a name for themselves – their careers were carried with the wave, and ebbed with it towards different horizons. Nonetheless twenty or so directors who emerged from the New Wave did continue making films, often in a very personal manner. A restricted but sufficient audience then grew up in France and abroad, enabling the film-makers who had emerged to work independently. Among them certain tendencies can be distinguished. First there was the group from the *Cahiers du cinéma*, critics who became directors like Chabrol, Truffaut, Godard, Rivette and Rohmer, the real centre of the New Wave. Then there were the 'Left Bank' directors, more intellectual and literary, working with writers involved in the 'nouveau roman' and showing political commitment: Alain Resnais, Jacques Doniol-Valcroze, Pierre Kast, Chris Marker, Jacques Demy and Agnès Varda. Then there were those who could be grouped (somewhat artificially) as adventurers with a camera, skilled in experimenting with light, hand-held cameras and direct cinema, filming live, close to documentary film-making, such directors as Jean Rouch, François Reichenbach, Pierre Shoendorffer or even, in a different genre, Jean-Pierre Mocky and Jacques Rozier. Finally, another group, more fragmented, included young directors from the commercial cinema (they had been directors' assistants in the Fifties) who were carried along by the wave to the point of identifying with it, people like Louis Malle, Édouard Molinaro, Claude Sautet and Philippe de Broca.

However, this typology of directors is unsatisfactory, as it gives no idea of the real impact of the New Wave. It is more appropriate to see what changes occurred in the French cinema within a few months. During 1960 the New

Wave came under severe attack, and in a letter dated 26 September 1960 Truffaut gave a very pessimistic assessment of its state, talking of a movement 'insulted every week on radio and television and in the newspapers'. He went on:

> it is becoming clear that films by the young, immediately they deviate even slightly from the norm, are at present being met by a barrage from promoters and the press. It has to be said that this year there is a very large number of big old-style French films which will occupy cinema screens for a long time. It smacks of revenge by the Old Wave.[10]

These attacks focused on the drop in the number of people who had gone to the cinema at the start of the Sixties. Many journalists and people in the trade ascribed this development to the New Wave, which became a scapegoat and accused of having turned away the crowds from a cinema perceived as 'intellectual' or 'boring'. Truffaut pinpointed the start of these large-scale attacks to the autumn of 1960: 'The turning-point, the shift from praise to systematic denigration, came with the film *Rue des prairies* by La Patellière and Michel Audiard which was promoted in advertising as an anti-New-Wave film: "Jean Gabin settles his score with the New Wave".'[11]

In the course of a few months several of the major names writing in the national press in fact turned against the new French cinema. In an article published in *Arts* the scriptwriter Michel Audiard accused the new film-makers of

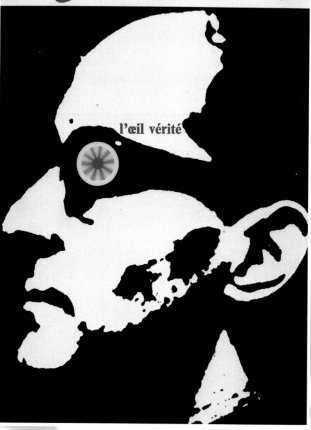

Cover by Roman Cieslewicz for the magazine Opus international, no. 2, July 1967. Private collection

causing revulsion among the cinema-going public at large, so serving the cause of television:

> Monsieur Truffaut would like to convince the customers at Fouquet's that he is to be feared, that he's a dangerous character. It makes those in the know laugh, but it impresses poor Éric Rohmer. At one time people who had nothing to say met round a teapot, but now they meet in front of a screen. Truffaut applauds Rohmer who the week before applauded Pollet who will next week applaud Godard or Chabrol. This cosy family pat one another on the back. That's the game that's been being played in the French cinema for over a year. The practical outcome: 1960 ends with successes by Delannoy, Grangier, La Patellière and Verneuil, those baldpates, those frightful people, those professionals. Pah! That's where they've got to, or rather where they were. For it would be pointless to go on talking about them in the present tense. The 'Nouvelle Vague' is dead. And now we can see that it was much more 'vague' than 'new'.[12]

Henri Jeanson, another fashionable scriptwriter, attacked the young 'tricheurs-en-scène' (play of words on *metteurs-en-scène*, i.e. directors, and the New Wave film *Les Tricheurs*) in *Cinémonde*, *La Croix* and *Le Journal du dimanche*, while in *Arts* Jacques Lanzmann asked quite seriously: 'Does the young French cinema have its future behind it?' On France Inter Jean Nocher denounced 'cinéma-cafard' (cinema based on boredom). A complete issue of *Positif* in 1960 inveighed against the New Wave, and *Télérama* was equal-

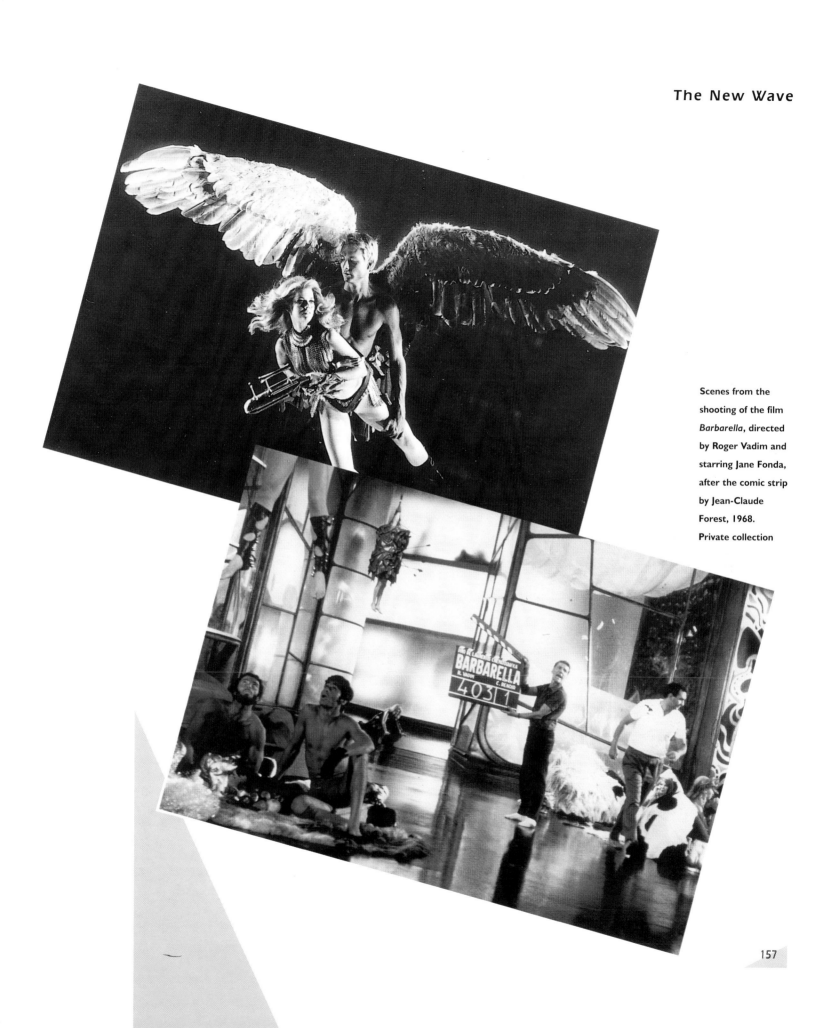

Scenes from the
shooting of the film
Barbarella, directed
by Roger Vadim and
starring Jane Fonda,
after the comic strip
by Jean-Claude
Forest, 1968.
Private collection

ly sceptical in a 'Survey into the film tastes of the French'. In a very caustic conversation published in *Cinéma 62* Jean Aurenche virulently castigated the 'fashionable pseudo-talents', while Jean Cau, formerly Jean-Paul Sartre's secretary at *Temps modernes*, went on behalf of *L'Express* to view 'some new French films'. He gave his reactions in February 1960, coming out with some crude, harsh opinions on the way:

> I say that these 'youngsters' have been more or less trumpeting at us for the past ten years, 'Oh, if only you would give us a camera!'.... In the end we took them at their word. We gave them one. What do they say? What a shock, nothing! What do they have in their heads and hearts? Surprise, surprise, a tinkle. And in their hearts? Horror of horrors, water!

Poster by Siné for the magazine *Positif*. Musée d'Histoire contemporaine collection

I admit that I am dumbfounded with amazement and sadness .... We realize that the young film directors have virtually nothing to say.

Thus confronted, the leaders of the New Wave reacted, sometimes adopting a pedagogic approach, François Truffaut in particular: it was a question of explaining the New Wave's ambitions, what was special about it. Through this attempt at self-definition, the young directors tried to explain what were the real upsets in the aesthetic and economic system of the French cinema ushered in by the New Wave. Truffaut explained:

> When the attacks started to become demagogic, i.e. when the journalists who had launched the movement two years earlier turned violently against it, we had to change our attitude. Before that, in interviews, Godard, Resnais, Malle, Chabrol, I myself and others would say: 'The New Wave doesn't exist, it's meaningless.' After that I did claim to belong to the movement. Then we had to be proud of being part of the New Wave, as of being a Jew during the Occupation.[13]

So Truffaut insisted that there was a 'New Wave spirit', in spite of the diversity of its exponents, and that this 'spirit' had to do with praising quick, economical, light shooting, establishing a 'cinema of personal expression' and a certain truth that was conferred on things and people recorded in real-life situations. At the time a New Wave film cost five to ten times less than a film produced according to the normal standards of the French 'quality' cinema. The lightness of the equipment, the lack of a star, the sensitivity of the film to natural light which made it possible to do most of the shooting out-of-doors; these were all elements that are crucial to the changes brought about by the young film directors' movement in the French cinema.

Truffaut was aware of the state of the traditional French cinema, having understood the depth of the crisis it faced in his articles for *Arts*. He had expressed a wish for a profound renewal of its subject matter, actors and production and shooting methods. Above all, he had constantly sung the praises of the independent 'auteur', acting as writer and director, unencumbered by studios, recognized the influence of professional scriptwriters and the constraints imposed by the star system, seeing himself as descended

Poster by Georges Wolinski for Gérard Pirès's film *Erotissimo*, 1968. Musée d'Histoire contemporaine collection

mon, a number of rejections: rejection of figuration, rejection of a theatrical plot, rejection of lavish sets, rejection of explanatory scenes; they are often films with three or four characters and very little action. Unfortunately the linear aspect of these films has cut across a literary genre which annoys the critics and the select public greatly at present, a genre that could be described as Saganism: a sports car, bottles of whisky, quick love affairs, etc. The intentional lightness of these films is taken – sometimes wrongly, and sometimes rightly – for frivolity. So this is where the confusion arises: the qualities of this new cinema – grace, lightness, modesty, elegance, speed – lie in the same direction as its defects – frivolity, lack of awareness, naivety. And the result? All these films, whether good or bad, detract from one another! The paradoxical thing is that this

Poster by Reiser for a play by Claude Confortès, which like the cinema participated in the post-'68 spirit. Musée d'Histoire contemporaine collection

from a few lone European masters (Jean Renoir, Roberto Rossellini, Max Ophuls), or the freedom and formal inventiveness of Hollywood directors. This was the main strand forming a crucial link between criticism and directing. Truffaut himself put this method of quick, economical shooting into practice when he made *Les Mistons*, training his own technicians, writing his own stories and dialogue, choosing new actors. He then agreed to defend the New Wave openly in a long conversation with Louis Marcorelles published in *Le Nouvel Observateur* on 19 October 1961. It was no longer the creator of *Les quatre cents coup* or *Tirez sur le pianiste* speaking, but the leader of a movement, the public figure, the former critic. Truffaut explained the New Wave and its difficulties.

> I recognize that there is a sense of unease, a difficult time to get through and solutions to be found. I attribute this unease to the following paradox: the main effort of the 'new cinema' has related to its emancipation from the cinema industry. Films had become impersonal because of the constraints on them. We felt that everything had to be simplified so that we could work freely and make modest films about simple subjects, hence the many New Wave films with only one thing in com-

Bande Sonore Originale
MUSIQUE DE GATO BARBIERI

UNE PRODUCTION ALBERTO GRIMALDI

Marlon Brando

Le Dernier Tango à Paris

(Last Tango in Paris)

STEREO UAS 29440-U

Sleeve for the tape of the original soundtrack for Bernardo Bertolucci's scandal-provoking film starring Marlon Brando and Maria Schneider, 1972. Private collection

Music by Pink Floyd for the legendary film on drugs shot in Ibiza by Barbet Schroeder, 1969. Private collection

Chinoise he managed to prolong and radicalize the New Wave spirit. But he was completely isolated. Chabrol worked to commission, Truffaut had gone into exile in England, Resnais, Rohmer and Rivette worked only intermittently. The 'enemy' films, French-style comedies (*La Grande Vadrouille* was the major success of the decade), films with a message, films with stars and literary adaptations, renewed their grip on the French cinema. And it was not until the 1970s that the main New Wave 'auteurs' re-emerged and gradually achieved recognition, with Truffaut, Rohmer, Resnais and Chabrol gradually picking up the threads of their personal careers. At the same time the New Wave produced its first direct descendants, Jean Eustache, Philippe Garrel and André Téchiné, a generation of progeny who were both inspired and overwhelmed – they would win public recognition only by very slow stages. But the myth remains. The strength of the New Wave lies in the fact that it imposed a sense of the imaginary, a mythology, a universe of gestures, appearances, bodies and objects, a universe that can be quickly conjured up by nostalgia: Jean-Paul Belmondo and Jean Seberg walking along the Champs-Élysées, Jean-Pierre Léaud running away from his delinquent adolescence to a beach in Normandy. Here we have images, *exempla*, that have left their mark on a

praiseworthy attempt to achieve lightness is bearing fruit three years too late, i.e. at a time when the cinema-going public is very disenchanted, at a time when an organized beating down of audiences is taking place with offers of the grandest and most spectacular films ever made. There used to be one super-production a year, a Bible story or something else. Now there is one a month, all trailing *Ben-Hur*. These films are aimed at countering television and against them our small-scale, touching or jokey films, shot any old how, don't stand a chance.

So the New Wave had been outlawed by the survival instinct of the traditional French cinema. Caricatured, badly copied and soon decried, it was no more than a passing experiment. By 1962 the reflex action of the traditional cinema had become overwhelming, and paradoxically the French cinema of that decade was amazingly staid, almost kindly and very traditional, except for Jean-Luc Godard – with such films as *Le Mépris*, *Pierrot le fou*, *Weekend* or *La*

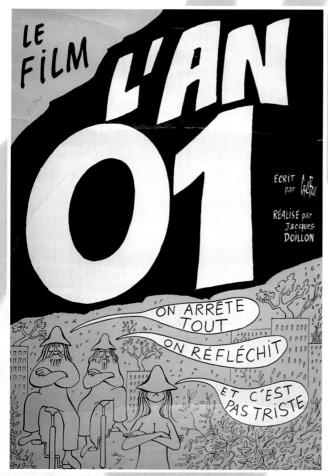

Alain Tanner, Martin Scorsese and many others are the children of the New Wave. This letter was written to François Truffaut by a young American producer in September 1962, when the movement finally became bogged down in France, and it shows the hopes aroused throughout the world by the eruption of the New Wave.

It is an ideal moment for a brilliant young French director to come and shoot a low-budget (in our terms) film in the United States. I really know how the cinema works over here, and the outlook is very grim for the traditional studios. More than anything else this industry currently needs your example: producing truly personal and artistic films at a reasonable cost. That could be a decisive factor leading to an upturn. I think that the American system would gain a lot from following the example set by the New Wave, because 'super spectacles' costing millions of dollars will not be able to remedy the situation. I would like to persuade financial backers here to produce this kind of New Wave film. Throughout America there are young, talented directors who are just waiting for that to happen. And I think a film by Jean-Luc Godard or you along these lines could launch an important revolution.[14]

Antoine de Baecque

Poster for Jacques Doillon's film *L'An 01*, after Gébé, 1972. Private collection

generation and can still be found on book covers, in visual quotations, on posters in the bedrooms of the children and grandchildren of the New Wave.

But if the New Wave had any real success it was on the international scene. During the Sixties the movement's aesthetic and economic model bore fruit throughout Europe, sometimes even on the other side of the Atlantic. The Italian, Polish, British, Hungarian, Yugoslav and Czech cinemas as well as the Japanese, Brazilian and even independent American cinemas drew much of their inspiration from French films with their technical and financial suppleness. For many young film-makers throughout the world the New Wave meant a new freedom to shoot completely personal subjects thanks to ludicrously cheap filming costs. It was a revelation, and the large number of festivals created at the time welcomed its fruits. Young national cinemas were reborn with unparalleled vitality during the Sixties. Bernardo Bertolucci, Jerzy Skolimowsky, Nagisa Oshima, Karel Reisz,

1. François Nourissier, *Les chiens à fouetter, sur quelques maux de la société et sur les jeunes gens qui s'apprêtent à souffrir*, Paris, Julliard, 1957.
2. *Les Nouvelles littéraires*, 24 June 1963.
3. *Les jeunes gens en colère vous parlent*, Paris, Pierre Horay, 1958.
4. John Osborne, *Look back in anger*, published in French in 1962 by Gallimard as *Jeune homme en colère*.
5. Antoine de Baecque, *Les Cahiers du cinéma. Histoire d'une revue*, 2 vols, Paris, Éditions de l'Étoile, 1991.
6. This article was published in the magazine *Cinéma 58*, February 1958.
7. *Arts*, 22 April 1959.
8. Cf. 'Dictionnaire des nouveaux cinéastes' published in a special *Nouvelle Vague* issue of *Cahiers du cinéma*, December 1962.
9. Antoine de Baecque, *La Nouvelle Vague*, forthcoming, Paris, Flammarion, 1997 (in 'Mouvements, Modes et Manières' collection).
10. These documents come from François Truffaut's personal archives held by Films du Carrosse. I would like to thank Madeleine Morgenstern for allowing me free access to all of these files. This is from file CH 60 (2). My trawl through these records has led to a biography, to which readers are referred for more detailed information: Antoine de Baecque, Serge Toubiana, *François Truffaut*, Paris, Gallimard, 1996.
11. *Cahiers du cinéma*, May 1967.
12. *Arts*, 16 December 1960.
13. *Le Nouvel Observateur*, 19 October 1961.
14. Archives of Films du Carrosse, file CH 62 (2).

British cinema in the Sixties

'Everywhere the "Carnaby-tion" army marches on
Each one a dedicated follower of fashion.'

Ray Davies, 1964

Fashion is the continuation of class by other means, according to orthodox accounts of British cinema in the Sixties. Such accounts tend to divide the films into two groups. First (chronologically speaking), they identify a wave of 'northern' realist films such as *This sporting life* (1963) which gave the British working-class donkey jacket the same credibility as Marlon Brando had given the pea-jacket in Elia Kazan's *On the waterfront* (1954); and second a cluster of London-centred 'bohemian-middle class films' such as *Darling* (1965) and *Blow-up* (1966) which, revelling in the latest designs of Mary Quant and focusing on the fashion scene (the model Veruschka appears in *Blow-up*), confirm that London was the capital of the Swinging Sixties.[1] Fixated on questions of class, such arguments simply reveal a blindness about how the most interesting Sixties movies exploiting fashion do so not to confirm class clichés but to rethink questions of national, and particularly English identity – and do so in a most playful manner. And this is true of the most unlikely movies.

Take a sequence from Richard Lester's *A hard day's night* (1964), that Dick Whittington-tale of the Liverpool lads on their way to London. Relaxing after a recording session of *And I love her*, in the film John, Ringo, Paul and George find themselves surrounded by a troop of actors dressed in Duke of Wellington army uniforms. John poses in a fake beard, while Paul recites Shakespeare ('O that this too too solid flesh should melt...'). Wigs and make-up are tossed around the changing room as Ringo sits quietly under a hair-dryer, reading a copy of *Queen*. 'He wants to be in the Guards,' teases Lennon, as he preens Ringo's black fur hat. 'It's my considered opinion,' shouts the old grandad (Wilfred Bramble as Paul's grandfather), 'that you're a bunch of cissies'.

This period dressing up – this rifling through the dressing-up box of English history (from Shakespeare to Wellington and the Guards) – is indicative of a whole strand of Sixties British cinema that revelled in play-acting, in trying on English clothes, and that one might even loosely call Brechtian (the touchstone for radical virtue at the time). After all, even the *A hard day's night* sequence unsettles the

past since it suggests that the past is something that can be performed and staged, something that can be made or unmade. It also confirms how much Englishness, masculinity and the military were seen to be closely affiliated, even in that decade of peace and love.

While the most obvious example of Sixties dressing-up cinema is perhaps Richard Attenborough's adaptation of the Theatre Workshop's production of *Oh! What a lovely war* (1969), itself indebted to the theatrical idiom of Brecht's Berliner Ensemble, it is far from being the most interesting one. Take *The charge of the Light Brigade* (1968) directed by Tony Richardson, a director at the Royal Court where Brecht was introduced into mainstream British theatre. That film begins with a Brechtian prolegomenon in the form of a cartoon sequence by the animator Richard Williams. But the innovative way that the film unsettles the past is by the appearance of the protagonist, played by David Hemmings. His look, the braided and brass-buttoned jacket and red trousers of the 'cherry-picker' uniform, is so close to the image of the dandy that is being paraded in contemporary London that he might even be the boy on the street or one of the Beatles on the cover of *Sergeant Pepper*; there is no attempt made to rob him of his contemporary look; the film revels in it.

But Hemmings is hardly the only military boy in the Sixties. After all, from *The charge of the Light Brigade* through *Zulu* (1963) to *Far from the madding crowd* (1967), some of the most memorable images in Sixties film are of the beautiful boys in costume: blond-haired Michael Caine (in *Zulu*), Terence Stamp in his brief but scarlet appearance as Sergeant Troy in *Far from the madding crowd,* and Peter O'Toole in flowing mufti robes in *Lawrence of Arabia* (1962). Bound up with this Sixties cinematic appropriation of the military is an awareness that the uniform no longer has a function in Sixties post-Suez Britain, that its utility is being emptied out, and that it can now be used as a complex sign of past Englishness and masculinity (note Wilfred Bramble's accusation in *A hard day's night* that the boys are 'a bunch of cissies'). In the Sixties the uniform belonged to entertainment and the street, not to the battleground. These young dandies in uniform seem both to mock and subvert the uniform's purpose, and yet at the same time, by so dressing, summon up a nostalgia for an Old England, manliness and patriotism.[2]

Robert Whitaker photograph of a street scene in London, 1967. Private collection

To be understood in fashion terms these films need to be placed within two contexts. The first is historical: they were made in a nation-state in which a great deal of swooning over the military has taken place over a long historical period. This is 'a culture that is used to fighting and [which] has largely defined itself through fighting', claims the historian Linda Colley, whose work *Britons: Forging the nation, 1707–1837* shows not only how war has helped to make and remake the nation but how central the military uniform

dam busters (1954).[4] Certainly in the light of Professor Colley's argument it is possible to revisit key British films, such as *The four feathers* and *Lawrence of Arabia,* and note how they turn upon a moment when a military man sheds both his uniform and his English manhood and dresses in 'foreign' garb.[5]

The second context for the 'dressing-up' movies is more immediate and entails the Sixties' attempt to re-situate the decade in relation to World War II and the culture it gen-

has been to forging notions of Englishness and Britishness, all the way from the 'impractically gorgeous' fashions of the eighteenth-century armed forces to the sombre uniforms of the man of action of the later period.[3] Such swooning over the military has of course found its way into the arts in Britain, not least in the twentieth century, with Kipling's *Barrack room ballads* and Housman's *A Shropshire lad* as well as innumerable films from *The four feathers* (1939) to *The*

erated. In this regard, three influences on these films can be briefly conjugated, the first being the Fifties' radio programmes of the Goons. They were clearly an important source in, for example, those films of the Beatles which featured the image of the soldier; not only in *A hard day's night* and *Help!* but also in John Lennon's character in *How I won the war* (1967) and Victor Spinetti's goonish and nonsensical colonel in *Magical mystery tour* (1967). But there was

ished in 1960) was in the shops including the famous I Was Lord Kitchener's Valet and Lord John where they found their uniforms. This street fashion army descended on the theatrical and army surplus stores in Carnaby Street and the Portobello Road.

Paradoxically the generation whose slogans were 'peace' and 'love', incorporated symbols of war and imperialism into its visual identity. The same band who produced the song *All you need is love*, also appeared in psychedelic uniform on the cover of *Sergeant Pepper*. And in Richard Lester's *Help!* (1965) the Beatles perform love songs in the middle of a battlefield. Juxtaposing images of peace and love with Englishness and the military, the boys, dressed in a jumbled mixture of military uniforms (from both world wars), perform *I need you* on English hills against an absurdist backdrop of rolling tanks, cannons, clay-pigeons and Stonehenge.

While the films of the Beatles flirt with military symbols, a more sophisticated process goes on within the fully-fledged 'dressing-up' films of the period. In these films, stars already associated with the dandy or 'swinging' figure are dressed for war and moved from London into pastoral England. Nowhere is this clearer than in the case of Terence Stamp, as Troy the soldier in *Far from the madding crowd* (1967). Before he was cast as the soldier, with his brilliant red military jacket and whiskers, he had played London *flâneur* Willie Garvin in Joseph Losey's *Modesty Blaise* (1966). His move from Blaise satin shirts and black-dyed hair to the pomp and restraint of military uniform solidified the association between period costume and the swinging

Robert Whitaker photograph of Ringo Starr and John Lennon wearing kimonos, Tokyo, 1966. Private collection

one critical difference between the Beatles and the Goons: whilst the Goons had themselves participated in the war, beginning their performance careers in the army, the Beatles were more distanced. The uniform was a theatrical device – the boys were clearly still Pop scene heart-throbs.

The second influence was the British Pop scene and the Pop artists of the Fifties' Independent Group. For instance the artist Nigel Henderson was absorbed in that icon of the British army, Lord Kitchener, who would become an omnipresent student poster-image in the Sixties; but like that of the Goons, Henderson's fascination derived from family connections with the army.[6] Influenced by Pop Art and out of the same art school culture, Sixties' British Pop music demonstrated an interest in the military and the dandy. The fascination extended beyond the Beatles to those satirists of Englishness, The Kinks. Dave Davies even completed his dandified musketeer-look with a sharp and effective sword.

The third, and perhaps the most important, influence was the emergence of a second-hand shopping culture, not for economy but for style. As Angela McRobbie has argued, the clothes were acquired in part for their 'shock value' to an older generation who knew the shame of being forced to wear second-hand.[7] In dressing up in uniform the young emphasized the gulf between the Forties' man who had fought in uniform and the Sixties' boy who posed in it. The nearest such boys came to war (National Service was abol-

Still by Robert Whitaker from *Help!*: the British army guards the Beatles on Salisbury Plain, 1965. Private collection

The sixties, utopian years

scene. The theatricality of Losey's film (in its psychedelic sets and references to the Peter O'Donnell cartoon) is carried over into *Far from the madding crowd*, where both Stamp and his co-star Julie Christie were found 'too modern' to be convincing.[8] To the critics they appeared too much like contemporary London boys and girls dressed up. But that is precisely the point, as it is with David Hemmings as he passes from photographer-as-*flâneur* in Antonioni's *Blow-up* to whiskered cavalry officer in *The charge of the Light Brigade*. The film's casting two year later of Vanessa Redgrave opposite Hemmings (a mirror image of the casting in *Blow-up*) simply confirms that Richardson never wants the audience to forget that Hemmings, fine limbed and delicate (and no match for Redgrave), is only a small boy in fancy dress and that the historical drama is just a charade. Inside its Crimean costume the film is resolutely contemporary, dealing with the state of British manhood in a decade of sexual liberation and military decline.

1. On 'northernness' see Philip Dodd, 'Lowryscapes: Recent writing about "the North"', *Critical Quarterly*, pp. 17–28.
2. The best of the *Carry on ...* films, *Carry on ... up the Khyber*, 1968, is of course equally involved with dressing up, Englishness and militaria. See Andy Medhurst, 'Carry on camp', in *Sight and Sound*, August 1992, pp. 16–20.
3. Linda Colley, *Britons: Forging the nation, 1707–1837*, London and New Haven, 1992, p. 9.
4. The writing on Englishness is extensive: see Tom Nairn, *The break-up of Britain*, London, Verso; Robert Colls and Philip Dodd, *Englishness: Politics and culture, 1880–1920*, London, Croom Helm, 1986; Alison Light, *Forever England: Femininity, literature and conservatism between the wars*, London, Routledge, 1991; Philip Dodd, *The battle over Britain*, London, Demos, 1995.
5. For an analysis of the crisis in masculinity in the late 1920s and 1930s see Kathryn Dodd, 'Engineering the nation: Documentary film, 1930–39' in Andrew Higson, ed., *Dissolving views: Key writing on British cinema*, London, Cassel, 1996, pp. 38–50.
6. For a photograph of a Lord Kitchener image in Eduardo Paolozzi's studio see David Robbins, ed., *The Independent Group: Postwar Britain and the aesthetics of plenty*, London, Institute of Contemporary Arts and Cambridge, Mass., MIT Press, 1990, p. 228. Henderson's familial relationship with the army is confirmed by a conversation with Henderson's friend Eduardo Paolozzi, March 1966.
7. Angela McRobbie, 'Second-hand dresses and the ragmarket' in Angela McRobbie, ed., *Zoot suits and second-hand dresses: An anthology of fashion and music*, London, Macmillan, 1989, p. 34.
8. Robert Murphy, *Sixties British cinema*, London, British Film Institute, 1992. For a review see James Price, 'Far from the madding crowd', *Sight and Sound*, winter 1967–8, p. 39.

Of course these films are not the only Sixties' ones absorbed in renegotiating English masculinity. Consider *If...* (1968), with its climax where Malcolm McDowell fantasizes machine gunning a church service full of people dressed in military uniform; or *Performance* (1970), with its dialectic between the dandy and the traditional tough-boy British male. However it is only in dressing-up movies that the full weight of the relationship between masculinity and national identity can be taken. Such films turn the uniform into an item of aesthetic pleasure and allow it to retain some of its traditional meaning as a signifier of 'imperial greatness'; they pose an extravagent, peacock-like dress against the dullness of post-war khaki Britain; they fill out a signifier of traditional masculine Englishness with the androgynous ('cissy') qualities of the Sixties' dandy; and allow the boys of love and peace to wrap themselves in the robes of war. Through fashion these films worked to ask questions of the nation. To rephrase James Joyce, for them English history was a military parade from which they were trying to awake.

Philip Dodd and Vicky Allan

Robert Whitaker photograph of the Lord John boutique decorated by BEV, 1967. Private collection

Robert Whitaker
photograph of the
interior of Gear
boutique, selling posters
and flags, 1967.
Private collection

Robert Whitaker
photograph of the frontage
of I Was Lord Kitchener's
Valet boutique, 1967.
Private collection

The television revolution in Britain in the Sixties

The home-centred society

Between 1955 and 1960 television was transformed into the dominant communications medium and fastest-growing leisure activity in the Britain; the proportion of the population with a television set in their homes increased from 40% to 80%, with the great majority able to receive both the British Broadcasting Corporation (BBC) channel and the new, advertising-funded (but still highly regulated) Independent Television (ITV). Television became the defining feature of a new 'home-centred society'. Following the final disappearance of post-war rationing in 1954, people in the late Fifties saw clearly the spread of an 'age of affluence', the 'never-had-it-so good' consumer paradise proclaimed in 1957 by the new Prime Minister, Harold Macmillan. Underpinned by full employment and by low inflation, the new 'consumer durables' – washing-machines, vacuum cleaners, refrigerators, record-players, telephones and cars – gave irrefutable, tangible and solid evidence of a world of continuous progress; for many at last the fruits of the hard-won victory of World War II seemed to be at hand.

Television was at the heart of it in three respects. First the television set itself was a desired physical object – an expensive, and therefore status-giving, investment whose presence in the family living-room forced the living space to be redesigned, with the set (rather than, as traditionally, the hearth) providing the focal point around which the new furniture, bought on hire purchase, was arranged. Secondly, both through the rapid spread of advertising on ITV from its beginnings in 1955 and the typical dramatic settings of much situation comedy and popular drama, television became the main channel for spreading the ideal image of the home-centred society and the nuclear family which dwelt within it. Finally, watching 'the telly' was itself the core evening leisure activity of the home-centred society – undermining the attractions of going out to the public house and the cinema alike.

Yet the medium itself was, in many respects, still primitive: substantially transmitted live (with video technology still in its infancy), black and white with intermittently poor defi-nition, restricted in its hours of transmission and subject to considerable criticism concerning its unknown (and unknowable) social effects. The speed of its advance had made both planning and control difficult as the numbers of new staff and programme ideas required grew rapidly in a situation for which there was no precedent. In both the spheres of responding to the market (with low-cost 'popular' programmes) and of radical experimentation (stemmimg from the many recent Oxford and Cambridge graduate recruits at the BBC), the inherited conceptions of 'public service' (to which both BBC and ITV were required to conform) came under considerable strain. Television in 1960 had yet to find a comfortable place in the cultural map of Britain.

Staying British

Throughout the Sixties the structure and content of British television programming were determined by a number of guidelines and rules. 'Balance' was essential between serious and popular programming, national and regional output, majority and minority interest and in the treatment of national politics. On ITV advertising was highly regulated, with direct sponsorship of programmes and shopping magazine slots forbidden (the rules were tightened in 1962 following the highly critical Pilkington Report which attacked many aspects of the commercial practice of ITV). The number and kind of cinema films able to be shown were strictly limited as the cinema industry tried, increasingly in vain, to protect its audience – and there were clear rules about the permitted proportion (around 14%) of non British-originated programmes. The latter constraint reflected a concern prevalent in British governmental and cultural institutions since the 1920s, the fear of Americanization. Without strong restrictive controls, the argument went, it would be impossible to prevent the cheap dumping of filmed American series (crime, Westerns, variety, situation comedy) available at marginal cost, which would then only reproduce in television production the devastating effects which Hollywood had had on the continually struggling British film industry. Despite these restrictions (while also proving their necessity) a number of American drama series (notably spy thrillers) figured among the most popular programmes of the decade.

A British family watching television. Courtesy Hulton-Getty

The arrival of television as a genuinely mass-audience medium in Britain coincided with a specific transitional moment in the country's sense of its own identity. In the years immediately after the 1914–18 war a key argument for setting up the BBC as a public service organization (modelled in part on the Imperial Civil Service) had been the need to serve, preserve and protect the British Empire.

In the period 1957–63, as television established its key position in national life, this Empire effectively ended, as in Africa, the Caribbean and in smaller states over the globe independence was granted to many former colonies. Britain's failure to gain entry to the EEC in 1963 confirmed that, in the words of the American diplomat Dean Acheson, 'Britain has lost an Empire, but not yet found a role'.

It is then not wholly surprising that much of the most innovative British television of the early and mid-Sixties was insular and self-regarding – taking stock of a post-imperial, post-war society that was attempting to graft a new form of capitalist social democracy on to a range of inherited and traditional practices. This mood of self-reflection was especially evident in the new forms of drama, serious and popular, which emerged.

Forms of drama

The single most successful and popular programme of the Sixties was *Coronation Street*, running nationally twice weekly from March 1961 in a prime-time, half-hour evening slot. At its peak audiences were in excess of 20 million. This transplanting of the successful radio continuous serial or 'soap opera' format had almost accidental origins in the requirement for the Manchester-based ITV Granada company to produce a specified amount of regional programming. *Coronation Street* took a defining stereotype of the industrial north – the local 'urban village' of the working-class districts of the northern cities, with its own micro-institutions of pub, shop and small business – and played on the viewers' sense of nostalgia for a world that they had lost (or in most cases had never had). The gossip, characters and local community of *Coronation Street* then replaced all that which (so much contemporary social commentary claimed) the coming of television and the privatized, home-centred society was itself helping to destroy. In 'The Street' the charac-

ters rarely, if ever, were to be found watching television and much of the wider world passed them by; yet the truth of *Coronation Street* was guaranteed to viewers by the northern accents, the mundane ordinariness of the settings and the trivial nature of much of the incident.

The success of *Coronation Street* provoked both the BBC and other regional ITV companies to seek similar formulae, typically with more obviously contemporary forms of community. However such BBC ventures as *Compact* (1962–5, set in a women's magazine office), *United* (1965–7, about a professional football team) and *The newcomers* (1965–9, life on a new housing estate) proved short lived. ITV's *Crossroads* (from 1964), set in a motel near Birmingham, the most central city in England, and combining a set of regular characters with a continuous variety of motel guests, survived through the decade, despite achieving great notoriety for its low production values caused by a chronic lack of rehearsal time for its four episodes a week.

These failed attempts to emulate the popularity of *Coronation Street* indicated that it was not so much its continuous series format as the selection of a plausible, or desired, national self-image which made it a success. Specifically the project of investigating how the traditional (pre-war) working-class community was faring in affluent Britain was a key cultural theme of the early Sixties – in cinema, fiction and theatre – as well as television. The BBC weekly police drama *Z cars* (from 1962) drew on this subject and the success of *Coronation Street* in presenting a more challenging view of communities in transition in a more mobile society. Of course, in a series dealing with crime and police work, language was stronger, relationships more aggressive and social problems more prominent than in *Coronation Street* but, above all, these elements were presented by combining a wider range of technical resources (film and video inserts, the use of back-projection with the police Z car on rollers, speedy cutting between cameras and scenes) to bring what was still initially live, studio-based transmission a sense of pace and pressure. It was *Z cars* (to 1965, with derivative successor series through the rest of the decade) that created the expectation (still present) within British television that it is to the police series that the viewer looks for a mirror of the changing values and pressure points within British society.

The sixties, utopian years

Both the series and the continuous serial were well adapted to the needs of television for routine and regular dramatic production; as such they necessarily had limitations, notably that each episode had to end in a way that implied a degree of continuity. However shocking the action on *Z cars* might be, some element of reassurance was always present – the police and the familiar characters would be back next week. Single play drama had no such requirement for continuity, and it was here (particularly when the new mixed genre of drama-documentary was involved) that many of the most challenging and disruptive images of the reality beneath the surface of the new affluent Britain were presented. As the Fifties idea that the television play was simply a species of 'armchair theatre' was dispelled so the genre came of age in its own right, most strikingly through the BBC's 'Wednesday play' series from 1963. This formed an umbrel-

la title for a wide range of experimental and innovatory work throughout the decade. The drama-documentary format of Ken Loach and Tony Garnett – as in *Up the junction* (1965), dealing with illegal abortion, and *Cathy come home* (1966), dramatizing the plight of the young homeless – was one strand, but equally challenging, for example, were the eight

plays of Dennis Potter's screened between 1965 and 1969, very consciously and extravagantly dramatic in a specifically televisual way. Potter was perhaps the first genuinely major television dramatist (as opposed to those who saw either theatre or film as their preferred medium), arguing strongly for its democratic potential and using it to launch vigorous critiques of politics (as in the two Nigel Barton plays of 1965) and aspects of organized religion (*Son of man*, 1969). By the late Sixties in Britain there could be little dispute that the television play had replaced the cinema film as the form that offered simultaneously the most popular and the most penetrating fictional commentary on contemporary British life.

To inform and entertain

Through such drama, and through some documentaries, television offered critiques of dominant assumptions about the new affluence. However, for such attacks to be effective, there had to be an already strong consensual position worthy of criticism, and increasingly television was also the medium through which the information and evidence passed to sustain this consensus. Necessarily as television viewing became widespread so did the importance of its news and current affairs in providing the basic information (political, economic, sporting, about lifestyle) on which a mass democratic and consumer society must be based. Newspapers, radio news and cinema newsreels all had to adapt or perish as television news viewers increased (in 1960, for example, the BBC shifted its long-standing 9 p.m. main radio evening news to a later slot, admitting that most listeners now watched peak-time television at that time).

The key values within television news were balance and the obligation to offer no editorial opinion (this only encouraged popular tabloid newspapers to distinguish themselves from television by offering increasingly biased and opinionated 'news'); the point of balance was inevitably struck around some unacknowledged assumptions about British common sense and fair play. It was especially easy in a peri-

od of very strong two-party politics to reflect this by the televisual construction of politics as a straight fight between two contenders, with the broadcaster as a neutral and unbiased referee. In the first thoroughly planned television General Election (1964) it was soon clear that the Labour Party under the more youthful and technocratic northerner, Harold Wilson, understood the rules of the contest much better than a faltering and apparently anachronistic Conservative Party led by the almost cadaverous aristocrat Sir Alec Douglas-Home.

The opposition between these two was described on the BBC cabaret-style satirical programme *That was the week that was* (commonly known as 'TW3' and screened during 1962–3) as a choice between 'Dull Alec and Smart Alec'. The directness and degree of invective of TW3's political

Sir Alec Douglas-Home, the Prime Minister, watching himself on a TV monitor, 1964. Courtesy Hulton-Getty

commentary caused much comment, both adverse and strongly supportive; the programme made considerable use of the new alliance between television and the political process by simultaneously satirizing the politicians themselves and the televisual forms through which they were presented. The sharpness of TW3's criticisms and concerns about the difficulty of institutional control (it was transmitted live late on a Saturday evening) led to its early closure well ahead of the 1964 election, and various successor programmes later in the decade proved less effective; however the precedent of imitating and mocking leading politicians on television was firmly established and gradually became a staple of mainstream television entertainment.

As in all western countries, the dominant use of television in the Sixties in Britain was for evening relaxation and entertainment. In the middle of the decade (1966) the most popular of the programmes alongside *Coronation Street* were the American spy thriller series, *The man from U.N.C.L.E.*, the game shows *Take your pick* and *Double your money* and the variety shows *Sunday night at the London Palladium* and *The black and white minstrel show*. Such programmes were the dominant recipe for securing and retaining the 'family audience' in a decade when the single-set household was very much the norm; necessarily this presumed a lot as to the common tastes of the various family members, particularly those of different ages. Television scheduling was structured to try and take some account of this; day-time viewing was limited and mostly confined to programmes for pre-school children who were presumed to see *Watch with mother*,

The team of resident satirists on the BBC TV programme *That was the week that was*, 1963. Courtesy Hulton-Getty

5–6 p.m. was for school children's leisure viewing (of which a significant element had an 'improving' or informational character), 6–9 p.m. was for 'family' viewing (led by adult tastes but suitable for children) and post–9 p.m. was after the 'watershed' and available for adult viewing (although not, so many argued, for anything that the viewer would not wish to encounter in his or her own living-room).

One social group remained somewhat excluded from this neat arrangement, precisely the group that had newly emerged on to the social stage and the leisure market in a highly visible way – teenagers. Teenagers posed a particular problem for television programme planners, for of all social groups they were most likely to resist the idea of incorporation into family domestic leisure within the home-centred society. In this context any proposed specialist (typically one that was music-based) teenage programme ran the risk of either being too banal to appeal to its target audience or, alternatively, necessarily, of offending the adult family members by its reflection of youth culture's deliberately transgressive styles of music, language, dress and movement. A number of early evening programmes – *Juke-box jury* (1959 onwards, which solved the problem by dramatizing and ritualizing the inter-generational cultural conflict), *Top of the Pops* (from 1964) and *Ready, Steady, Go!* (1963) – found a way of resolving this dilemma, but in general the newer manifestations of youth culture found only a marginal and occasional place in the schedules, except as exemplars of social problems in need of a solution.

A less explicit, but equally significant case of strain on the concept of the unitary family audience was that of another

Preparations for the
BBC TV broadcast of
the 1966 election.
Courtesy Hulton-Getty

Transmission of *Juke-box
jury*, BBC TV, c. 1965.
Courtesy Hulton-Getty

major area of leisure viewing – spectator sport, which held a favoured place in the schedules. Live sport (horse racing, motor sport, rugby, wrestling) dominated Saturday afternoons on both channels, and throughout the year a series of already traditional television occasions marked out an annual calendar – the Grand National, the Boat Race, the FA Cup Final, the Derby, the Test Matches, the two weeks of Wimbledon, the Five Nations Rugby internationals. More occasional events became landmarks in television history – as for example the World Cup Final of 1966 watched by 27 million viewers. During the decade the seeds were sown for a future in which the fate and structure of all professional sports were to become increasingly determined by their televisual possibilities. Yet, with the possible exception of tennis, professional sport remained the most gender-bound of all leisure activities and men formed the substantial core of the viewers. At the same time, televised sport both reinforced traditional gender divisions within the family and, in doing so, fuelled the experience which would lead to their coming under challenge.

By the late Sixties the habit of regular and universal television viewing no longer seemed new or remarkable – and as production flexibility increased (video recording and editing becoming the norm, more portable and flexible film

Mods dancing during a TV Pop programme, 1964. Courtesy Hulton-Getty

equipment), and under pressure of world events, British television more fully took on an international perspective. Although transatlantic satellite communication was available from the early Sixties (Eurovision links, symbolized by the annual *Eurovision song contest*, had been in place since the Fifties) the costs of satellite transmission to the broadcasting companies, even when the new Early Bird satellite became available in the mid-Sixties, were prohibitive. This began to change rapidly in the late Sixties, celebrated by the BBC when it orchestrated *Our world* programme in June 1967, linking five continents live in a musical celebration, culminating in the Beatles making a live recording of *All you need is love* – a maxim categorically disproved when, from 1968, both BBC and ITV news carried graphic film of Vietnam demonstrations in America and Britain, the May events in Paris, the Soviet invasion of Czechoslovakia, Biafra, Vietnam itself and the beginnings of the Troubles in Ulster. Meanwhile, from above, television's crowning moment came with the live transmission of the moon landings in July 1969.

Advances in production techniques began to be matched by developments in the quality of reception. The third channel, BBC2, launched in 1964, could only be received on 625-line sets (as against the existing inferior 405-line sets); the need to purchase a new TV held up the expansion of its audience but was seen as a necessary step towards the introduction of colour programmes, which began on BBC2 in 1967 and on the two main channels in November 1969. As definition improved and more production came to be in colour so British television production took more seriously the possibility of communication through visual impact; the major BBC2 productions *The Forsyte saga* (period drama based on the novels of Galsworthy) and *Civilisation* (Sir Kenneth Clark's history of man's cultural achievements) took high production values as one of their main features. By 1970, as all viewers began to review their domestic budgets to enable them to purchase colour sets, the first signs began to emerge of the multi-set households of the Eighties, which were finally to erode the concept of the unitary family audience.

Indeed if the fates of television and the family were intertwined during the Sixties, by 1970 it was almost as though their positions had become reversed. The liberal legislation of the late Sixties on abortion, divorce and homosexuality, together with increasing geographical and social mobility and the growing impact of the women's movement, made the existence of the family as a stable entity increasingly difficult to visualize. Television by contrast had come of age, moving from alien intruder in the living-room to become the focal point of the culture for politics, sport, news, entertainment and national celebration (whether World Cup victory or the investiture of the Prince of Wales in July 1969). Its progress throughout the decade is neatly exemplified by the career of one of its leading figures, David Frost, the man who 'rose without trace'; Frost, a Cambridge graduate, first came to prominence as the compère and linkman of TW3, the 'enfant terrible' of the television satire movement. In the mid-Sixties he moved on to head both his own comedy show (*The Frost report*), which included some mild social commentary, and a series of talk shows (*The Frost programme*), which included regular serious interviews (and sometimes exposures) of public figures. In 1968 he was one of a number of television 'personalities' to head a consortium which successfully bid for the ITV London weekend franchise and in the following year was among the ITV team which reported live on the landing on the moon. Like David Frost, British television in the Sixties moved increasingly from the margins into the centre of the culture – a position from which it has yet to be displaced.

Stuart Laing

French television

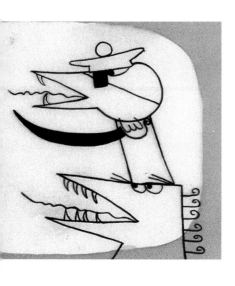

French television and the Sixties: images, memories, embroidered or incomplete, which form beads and come back to the mind, hallowed by time. These fugitive, funny memories, sometimes moving, refer back to a reality that was in fact more orderly. The decree of 4 February 1959 gave French radio and television a statute. From then on the public body with its industrial and commercial aspects, a state monopoly, came under the authority of the Minister for Information, and was run by a Director General. Part of the same organization, radio and television followed different, though intersecting paths. Television, a new consumer commodity, was seen as a recent technique for sending pictures over a distance. The young organization, already unwieldy in the way it functioned, conceived, made and broadcast programmes of unfolding and diverse genres.

Winning over the public

The wide-ranging moves aimed at creating programmes undertaken by Jean d'Arcy, director of programming from 1952 to 1959, were bearing fruit. By engaging the interest and support of the critics and depending on programme-makers as a professional group whose ideas and talents were developing, Jean d'Arcy contributed to the process of making French television visible as an institution and gaining recognition for it. Winning over the public was an evolving rational exercise based on a cultural plan with a pedagogic dimension and democratic aims.[1] Claude Santelli writes:

> We dreamt of this very special communication directed at each individual in isolation yet intended for the whole nation. A popular art had still to come ... It was a party, really shared by the viewer who approved, laughed with us, became passionate, made discoveries. About what? Everything or almost everything. A motley assortment, art, theatre, circus, science, life and first of all himself, the Frenchman, the citizen to whom we tried to hold up a mirror.[2]

Thus the arts were given documentary treatment in *Les Journaux de voyage* by Jean-Marie Drot.[3] Villages and provinces were filmed by Hubert Knapp and Jean-Claude Bringuier. Their *Croquis* provided an opportunity to collect traditions, memories and thoughts, generally recounted by unknown people to attractive celebrities.[4]

However, most broadcasts were live, especially plays. About a hundred works drawn from the repertory were created each year. Historical programmes like *La caméra explore*

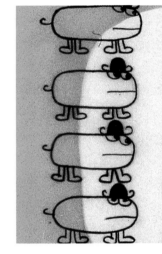

Original drawings by Jacques Rouxel for the *Shadoks*, 1968. Artist's collection

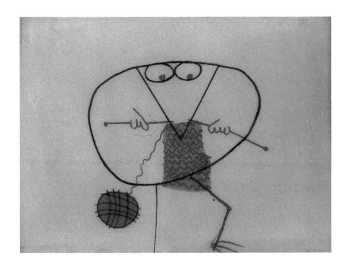

le temps, police stories in *Les cinq dernières minutes* and great trials re-enacted in *En votre âme et conscience* provoked curiosity and became programming regulars.[5] Televised news contributed to this visibility. Founded by Pierre Sabbagh in 1949, television news introduced new forms of participation and information, gradually inventing special equipment, particularly during the election and on the evening following the referendum of 28 September 1958. Politicians discovered television as a tool, and its power to amplify, which they could either use or tone down. Thus television news was established as the vehicle for General de Gaulle's policy during the Algerian War. As a new means of providing information to the French people, contributing to political life, it was the object of double concern, from the press – which highlighted its limits and the constraints resulting from the way it

Original drawings by Jacques Rouxel for the *Shadoks*, 1968. Artist's collection

was controlled – and from the political sector.

News and other programmes were governed by quite distinct rhythms and logics, but an identical concept of the purpose of television united them. Jean d'Arcy declared: 'I believe that television really is a remarkable instrument for homogeneity within a country, and it seems to me that this should even constitute a rule, a law in what we do.'[6] The idea of cohesion and national unity permeated everything. The Sixties, which brought social and political transformations, tested and shifted that idea. Growth was at hand.

Apprenticeship for growth

Between 1960 and 1970 there was a rapid advance in the number of households with televisions. While 13% had

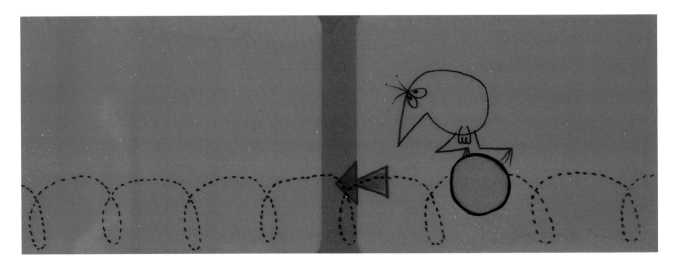

a television set in 1960, 66% had acquired one by 1970.[7] During that period the installation of transmitters throughout the country was completed, enabling the one and only television channel to be received, while at the same time the means were developed whereby a second channel would be available from 1964. Television in the Sixties was faced with years of change in response to conflicting choices and logics. Growth had to be managed and the new methods of organizing and producing programmes had to be integrated, while preserving creativity and the dissemination of cultural values, both pedagogical and civic, in keeping with its role as a public service, which was itself changing. Television did become firmly established as a new communication tool, but the Sixties also confirmed its position as witness and actor in the history of the present.

The development of television was accompanied by the arrival of the specialist magazines *Télérama* and *Télé 7 jours*, devoted mainly to programmes on the small screen. Television reviews were accorded space in the national and regional dailies as well as in the weeklies, and found their own rhythm.[8] Such writers as François Mauriac and

Emmanuel Berl watched television and made it the subject of their pictorial chronicle. Assessments and demands abounded, and anger and enthusiasm mingled.

Between 1959 and 1964 under the directorship of Albert Olivier the great cultural principles and guidelines were upheld: *Lecture pour tous*,[9] presented by Pierre Desgraupes, Pierre Dumayet and Max-Pol Fouchet, skilfully brought together writers, their works and the public. But the forms of fiction were changing. Live programmes lost ground to prerecorded ones. Exteriors, natural decors and landscapes formed the new sets. *Le Mariage de Figaro* directed by Marcel Bluwal in 1961 illustrates that change, foreshadowing his *Don Juan*,[10] in which trees lining a brightly lit path reflected the character's darkness and destiny.

Serials about ways of life – with short episodes inspired by everyday life – made their successful debut. In 1961 *Le Temps des copains* by Robert Guez, then *Janique Aimée* by Jean-Pierre Desagnat in 1963, marked the arrival of young people – the fifteen-to-twenty age group – as a source of programming, a subject for thought and an audience. In 1960 magazine programmes for young people were introduced, pioneered by Françoise Dumayet, who devised and made *L'Avenir est à vous* with Jean-Pierre Chartier.[11] Working life, the choice of a career, years of apprenticeship as well as starting

181

a family, marriage, the psychological aspect of adolescence and parent-child relationships became the main themes. Young people in these reports were not presented as a homogeneous social category. Apprentices and young wage-earning workers did not appear on the same programmes with students, whose wide-ranging backgrounds were underlined. But they were all bonded together, over and above their differences, by the qualities recognized and promoted: seriousness, dynamism and a sense of responsibility.[12]

Youth was also present in variety programmes – e.g. *Âge tendre et tête de bois* by Albert Raisner, made at the Golf Drouot – and was embodied by idols who confided in Denise Glaser in *Discorama* or revealed themselves, like Johnny Hallyday, in answer to abrasive questioning from Pierre Desgraupes in *Cinq colonnes à la une*.[13]

Scene from the serial ***The prisoner***, with Patrick McGoohan; the first episode was screened on 29 September 1967 on BBC and on 18 February 1968 on French Channel 2. Courtesy British Film Institute

However, television as entertainment, variety and game shows – such as *Intervilles* presented by Guy Lux – were the subject of controversy and debate tinged with anxiety at the sidelining of the pedagogical, civic and cultural mission of television. The argument then under way specifically reflected the tensions arising from growth on the eve of the launch of a second channel in April 1964.

Programme innovations and unease

Between 1964 and 1968 expansion favoured innovations in programming and promoted deepening dissatisfaction. Competition, not complementarity between the two

channels became more acute, heightened by the abolition of the production monopoly.[14] Growing unease within television was composed of contradictions and weaknesses. Even so, it was accompanied by inventiveness in the forms of programmes and their technical equipment, and was typified by an expansion in the range of subjects treated.

The straitjacket keeping television as an adjunct of the state and the strict supervision exercised on information fed growing criticisms within the press and from opposition politicians. In giving television a new statute in 1964, when the ORTF (Office de radiodiffusion et télévision française) was set up, Alain Peyrefitte, Minister for Information from 1962 to 1966, tried to provide guarantees on a relaxation of government control by placing the ORTF under the trusteeship of the Minister rather than under his authority. The 1965 presidential elections sharpened the debate and influenced the government's attitude. The candidates campaigned, and General de Gaulle failed to win outright in the first round. He reacted by appearing in televised conversations with Michel Droit. These elections were important in helping to create greater freedom of information, a slow process which was as yet precarious and far from complete, with television news still the centre of tensions.

However, there was a cautious softening of attitude. The first *Face à face* debate by Jean Farran and Igor Barrère went out on 24 January 1966, and from then on the programmes were broadcast live on Monday evenings featuring a well-known political figure (Guy Mollet, Valéry Giscard d'Estaing, Waldeck-Rochet, François Mitterand etc.) answering questions from journalists, some from newspapers and magazines. Current affairs magazines were created, and the development of programmes on Channel 2, entrusted to Jacques Thibau, deputy director of television, was very much based on the opening up of information.

'I remember the Harris and Sédouy programme *Seize millions de jeunes*,' Georges Pérec writes. And the first programme, shown when Channel 2 started up in April 1964, put the spotlight on marriage and the living conditions of students who were already parents. It reintroduced the question of contraception to television after the silence that had followed *Faire face* by Igor Barrère and Étienne Lalou in 1960, an outstanding debate on birth control, and a report on *Cinq colonnes à la une* devoted to the opening of the

Family Planning centre in Grenoble in November 1961. *Seize millions de jeunes* analysed the social and cultural malaise of the young every week on Channel 2.[15] This new magazine programme, which reached only a fairly limited audience, became a laboratory for experiment where intuition was allowed full play. Their abrasive inquiries changed the way the young were regarded: apart from their material difficulties and worries about work, their private and love lives were sometimes probed. Personal stories were given an airing, showing the confusion of values among girls whose first affair, although no longer a prelude to marriage, was still an important consideration. And there was discussion of fears about the personal choices that had to be made by those whose life was still in suspense.

The previous generation, in families that had already formed, did not escape the shift in moral values either. The futures of mothers and daughters would not be the same, and television took note of this. *Les Femmes aussi*, a documentary series produced by Éliane Victor from 1964, provides evidence of these attitudes.[16] The women portrayed in the programme showed signs of a shift, openly revealing the principles behind their daily and domestic behaviour, and their aspirations towards individual development.

With greater seeming nonchalance *Dim, Dam, Dom*, invented in March 1965 by Daisy de Galard, provided freshness and humour every month in a magazine programme that mixed genres and topics, fashion and literature, beauty and artistic talent. Concepts and equipment were developing, as Jean-Christophe Averty showed: 'He treats space and the screen like an empty page, although he plays with black and white, dreams up Surrealist and provocative transitions and uses electronic keying and special effects,' wrote Christian Bosséno.[17] Averty's shows (*Les Raisins verts*, *Happy new Yves*, *Johnny Hallyday et Sylvie Vartan*) were bold and jarring.[18] He produced multiple images of faces, dancing bodies, motifs and panels. In 1967 he planned the evening scheduling on Channel 2 and introduced the first colour.

Television gradually became more open to social questions. Current affairs magazines (*Panorama*, *Tel quel*, *Caméra III*, *Séance tenante*, *Zoom*), with some subterfuge, contributed towards this.[19] However within the organization the situation became more fraught, aggravated in 1967 by the debate over the introduction of advertising, which the

ORTF unions opposed. Outside, the argument about freedom of information became wider. On 23 April 1968 the opposition put down a motion of censure on 'the government's anti-democratic policy in the field of information, and in particular its misuse of the audiovisual media made available to the state by the nation'.[20] The report by the Senate's controlling committee, undertaken in 1967 and handed in on 13 April 1968, expressed grave reserves about the way the ORTF operated.[21] In a communiqué dated 11 May journal-

ists and producers working on the major magazine programmes condemned 'the scandalous way in which television news had shirked its responsibilities during the recent events'. Staff were mobilized and voted in favour of a general strike on 17 May 1968, which continued until 23 June. Journalists followed suit a little later on 25 May, continuing their action until 13 July. Freedom of information was central to the conflict, marking a turning-point in the severing of the links between the authorities and television. However, the sanctions then imposed on the journalists were severe. Some were sacked and some programmes were dropped when work resumed. The return to work in September was a gloomy affair. Then progress restarted, but there were still some clashes.

Scene from the serial *The prisoner*. Courtesy British Film Institute

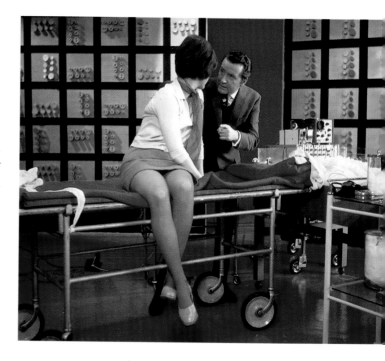

The search for new forms of expression

The years 1969 and 1972 are the two poles of a period of conciliation and experiment in liberalizing the flow of information, inspired by the Prime Minister, Jacques Chaban-Delmas. Two autonomous news services were created, the Channel 2 service being entrusted to Jacqueline Beaudrier, while Pierre Desgraupes took on Channel 1. He recruited young journalists from newspapers or radio and launched new programmes. 'There were more and more platforms, debates and factual reports in 1970, one of the most prolific years for information,' Noël Nel observed.[22] Every month political duels were broadcast live.

During this pivotal period, social change, the women's movement's claims for a job and a fair wage for women, the extension of the Neuwirth law on contraception and the sharing of household tasks figured in these debates (*Hexagone*[23]). However, the contentious implications of the women's movement for the family were glossed over. The lowering of the age of majority and sexual education for young people were also discussed (*Procès*[24]). The young continued to be an object of debate. 'Youth as a problem' in the public sector also became a factor in private life. Adolescence and generational conflicts were examined in detail. People turned to psychology to explain family relationships. The quest for independence by family members became pronounced. Relationships were established as a subject for investigation.

These themes were also taken up by fiction. Michel Polac, with *Un fils unique*, screened in 1970, came up with a new form of film-writing to depict the quiet boredom of a middle-class teenager, stifling underneath his parents' silences or stereotyped conversations. Unprecedented ways of apprehending the lives of individuals were sketched through documentary images or fictional stories set in a convincing translation of reality. For example, Bernard Gesbert plunged into *Grigny-la-Grande-Borne: L'enfer du décor*, and in *De la belle ouvrage* Maurice Failevic followed the broken life of a skilled worker when he was superseded by a higher-capacity machine.[25] Nevertheless, such programmes did not represent the everyday reality of programming, expanded by longer air time and the opening of a third channel on 31 December 1972, but they are indicative of a renewed awareness – both in subject matter and form – of social change.

The programme *À armes égales* became the emblem of a more expansive platform for political discussion, demonstrating a relaxation of the links between the state and television.[26] But it also revealed the gaps between principle and practice. In December 1971 the word 'aversion' in an original commentary presented by Maurice Clavel was censored by those in charge of the programme: 'At a time when the President of the Republic talks to a major American newspaper about the aversion and annoyance the French Resistance inspires in him...'. The writer, who was a journalist and television critic with *Le Nouvel Observateur*, left the platform in outrage, applauded by some of the audience. This caused a scandal, strong emotions, and consternation among the journalists and to Jean Royer, the mayor of Tours, who saw his opponent leaving the platform. 'Freedom is indivisible', a headline in *Le Monde* above an article by Pierre Viansson-Ponté reminded readers.[27] The limits of independence were visible, highlighting the apprenticeship and appropriation of this new means of disseminating information and communication, at a time of expansion and redefinition of its rules and principles.

The zenith had been reached. Pierre Desgraupes was considered too bold or not bold enough. After the departure of Jacques Chaban-Delmas in July 1972 it was Desgraupes's turn to go. This marked the end of a period. At his press conference on 21 September 1972 President Pompidou reminded his audience: 'Whether we wish it or not, television is regarded as the voice of France, both by the French and abroad'. The relatively bright period marked by the

'Desgraupes years' did nonetheless put the emphasis on new forms of television participation in political life.

The organization was battered by different criticisms. The impoverishment of programming was deplored. It seemed impossible to manage and control such a business. Scandal over covert advertising weakened the ORTF still further. The debate sparked off by the law of July 1972 even questioned the very concept of the monopoly which had been safeguarded. It was the final stage where the ORTF was concerned.

French television in the Sixties grew amid clashes. But most striking during those years was the organization's ability to produce and screen programmes which – in their diverse forms, their inadequacies, their normative aspect and their innovative or forward-looking dimension – con-

tributed to social and political shifts. It is the interplay of these contradictions that paradoxically constitutes their strength.

Marie-Françoise Lévy

1. Jean-Louis Missika, Dominique Wolton, *La Folle du logis. La Télévision française dans les sociétés démocratiques*, Paris, Gallimard, 1983.
2. Jacqueline Beaulieu, *La Télévision des réalisateurs*, foreword by Claude Santelli, Paris, INA-La Documentation française, 1984.
3. *Les Journaux de voyage* started in 1956, ending in 1979 with 13 films.
4. *Les Croquis* by Jean-Claude Bringuier and Hubert Knapp consisted of a series of films made between 1957 (*Les Croquis lyonnais*) and 1967 (*Les Croquis en Périgord*).
5. *La caméra explore le temps* by Alain Decaux, André Castelot and Stellio Lorenzi (1957–65) originally went out under the title *Les Énigmes de l'histoire* (May 1956–September 1957). *Les cinq dernières minutes* by Claude Loursais (January 1958–1972) was a series of 56 films with Raymond Souplex playing

the role of Inspector Bourret. After Raymond Souplex's death the programme continued until the 1990s and there were also repeats. Cf. Jacques Baudou and Jean-Jacques Schléret, *Meurtres en séries. Les Séries policières de la télévision française*. Paris, Huitième Art, 1990. *En votre âme et conscience* by Pierre Desgraupes and Pierre Dumayet (28 February 1956–13 December 1969).
6. François Cazenave (ed. and collater), *Jean d'Arcy parle*, foreword by Henri Pigeat, pp. 63, 64.
7. J. Beaulieu, op. cit., pp. 145-66.
8. Michèle de Bussière, Caroline Mauriat, 'Les débuts de la critique de télévision 1953–60' in *Les Années cinquante à la radio et à la télévision* (report on the study day held on 9 February 1990), Paris, CHR-CHTV-GEHRA, November 1991, and 'La critique de télévision', *Dossiers de l'audiovisuel*, no. 47, January–February 1993, Paris, INA-La Documentation française.
9. *Lecture pour tous* by Pierre Desgraupes, Pierre Dumayet and Max-Pol Fouchet, 1953–68.
10. *Don Juan*, Channel 1, 6 November 1965.
11. *L'Avenir est à vous* or *Le Journal des jeunes* by Françoise Dumayet and Jean-Pierre Chartier with the collaboration of Georges Paumier. Fortnightly magazine, Channel 1, 18 February 1960–18 May 1968.
12. Marie-Françoise Lévy, 'Les Représentations sociales de la jeunesse à la télévision française. Les années soixante', *Hermès*, nos 13 & 14, Paris 1994.
13. *Âge tendre et tête de bois* by Albert Raiser, 30 May 1961–10 November 1964; *Discorama* by Denise Glaser, 24 January 1959–22 December 1974; *Cinq colonnes à la une*, programme broadcast on 8 September 1961.
14. Jérôme Bourdon, *Histoire de la télévision sous de Gaulle*, Paris, Anthropos-INA, 1990.
15. *Seize millions de jeunes* by André Harris and Alain de Sédouy, April 1964–May 1968.
16. *Les Femmes aussi* by Éliane Victor is comprised of 76 documentary programmes screened on Channel 1 and made between 1964 and 1973.
17. Christian Bosseno, *Deux cents téléastes français*, Cinémaction-Corlet-Télérama, 1989.
18. *Les Raisins verts* by Jean-Christophe Averty, Channel 1; *Happy new Yves*, *Johnny Hallyday et Sylvie Vartan*, Channel 2, 1965.
19. *Panorama* by Jean-Louis Guillaud, Claude Désiré, Gilbert Larriaga, Channel 1, 9 April 1965–1 September 1969. From September 1969 to June 1970 the programme was entrusted to Olivier Todd. *Tel quel* by Pierre Charpy and Henri Marque, Channel 2, 21 April 1967–12 May 1968. *Caméra III* by Henri de Turenne and Philippe Labro, Channel 2, November 1966–7 May 1968. *Zoom* by André Harris and Alain de Sédouy, Channel 2, 23 December 1965–14 May 1968. *Séance tenante* by Jean-Louis Guillaud and Éliane Victor, 18 April 1957–23 August 1968.
20. Jérôme Bourdon, op. cit., p. 249.
21. Jean-Pierre Filiu, *La Crise de l'ORTF en mai-juin 1968*, thesis for the Institut d'Études Politiques de Paris, 1984.
22. Noël Nel, *À fleurets mouchetés. Vingt-cinq ans de débats télévisés*, Paris, INA-La Documentation française, 1988, p. 32.
23. *Hexagone* by Enrique Martinez, Igor Barrère, Pierre Charpy and Henri Marque, 7 April 1970–19 September 1971.
24. *Procès* by Éliane Victor, 24 November 1970–26 September 1972.
25. *Grigny-la-Grande-Borne* by Bernard Gesbert was screened in 1973 as part of the programme *La Vie ensemble* by Jacques Frémontier; *De la belle ouvrage*, drama by Maurice Failevic, was screened in 1970.
26. *À armes égales*, programme produced by Jean-Pierre Alessandri, André Campana, Michel Bassi and Alain Duhamel, directed by Igor Barrère, 17 February 1970–15 April 1973.
27. 'La liberté ne se divise pas', Pierre-Viansson-Ponté, *Le Monde*, 15 December 1971.

Linda Thorson playing Mrs Peel in *Chapeau melon et bottes de cuir*, 1968. Courtesy British Film Institute

British interior design, 1960–73

The Sixties have presented problems of periodization for historians of British culture. For some, the modes of consumerism, liberalization and libidinization which have come to characterize that decade emerged in the mid-Fifties; for others the Sixties only became recognizable in 1963 with the new Labour government, the Beatles and other manifestations of Swinging London. There is, however, a strong measure of agreement that the various forms of protest which found ways of expression at the end of the decade were signs of ideological commentary, economically endorsed by the oil crisis of 1973, on the long post-war boom.

In Britain the Sixties have become a rich source of images and meanings – an episode of innocence and enterprise, but also, and especially for the political Right, a period of devaluation. Interior design, like everything else in that decade, was a terrain on which many innovative skirmishes were fought. Perhaps the most significant issue for designers, journalists and consumers of 'interiors' was that in a relatively brief period, bricolage, fashion and fantasy seemed to triumph over a long-standing tradition of sensible functionalism.

As in every other aspect of this period, there was an extraordinary variety of proposals and solutions. The Sixties were both radical and fantastic. The arts of that period are characterized by an intensive realism as well as an exploration of every kind of imaginative excess. With the decline of urban ideals there was a new focus on 'environments', both personal and natural. The living 'space' acquired a new kind of autonomy. Prompted by the awesome technological self sufficiency of astronauts, and the ecological awareness of tribal cultures, the architectural *avant-garde* sought a new kind of autonomy for the 'living unit'. The availability of television and new communications media and access to a 'global village' of ethnic variations on 'lifestyle', promised a revolution of the concept of home.

In the drive to de-programme and free up assumptions, many traditional notions of comfort, harmony, formality were challenged. The home became less a refuge from work than an expression of leisure and desire. There was a marked shift in interest by the *avant-garde* away from megastructural solutions to subliminal and psychotropic ones. For the average consumer of domestic goods, however, this theorizing had limited impact. But it would have been difficult for any one to avoid the injunctions to take up pleasure, autonomy and authenticity which were encoded in so many products. There are many ways of thinking about interior design and its relation to the ideas circulating in any period. There is always an *avant-garde*, there are institutions, there is a popular realm of marketing and advice and there is what people make of it all.

In the Sixties, perhaps more than in any period since the years of 'heroic Modernism', the home was put in question. The nuclear family was challenged in the interests of communality, but also as a violation of the pure autonomy of the nomadic, foetal individual. Reyner Banham, a spokesman for some of the most radical formulations of the time, wrote a manifesto in 1965 entitled: 'A House is not a Home', in which he suggested that the supporting services, hardware and software were the most significant components of the house and that its furnishings and its sheltering and insulating properties could take extraordinary forms. Various technological and vernacular solutions were proposed, challenging all conventional thinking, and radical renegotiations of Modernism were quite widely disseminated in the press and even by department stores. The iconoclastic *Archigram* group exhibited at Heals and at Oscar Woolands and presented their ideas on national television. Maples provided exhibition space for Mex Macintyre's 'Trip Box' and Roger Dean's 'escape pod'. Most consumers would have experienced these ideas within a generalized anticipation of futurity which was shaped by the space race and incorporated robotics and 'push-button' homes and which was composed around 'services', often modularized, mass produced and mobile. On the other hand, various modest other components of the *avant-garde* vision were marketed and found their way into the home as inflatables, disposables and in the peripheries of entertainment.

There were attempts to propagate 'good design'. The two chief versions were those sponsored on the one hand by the Council of Industrial Design, the Design Centre (which opened in the Haymarket in 1957), the Duke of Edinburgh's award scheme and the journal *Design* and on the other by the Consumer's Association (also founded in 1957) and its journal *Which*. The former group was in the main concerned with propagating what it saw as virtues which were chiefly formal – a reasonable British

Vernon Panton,
Living tower, 1968.
Private collection

The sixties, utopian years

Modernism, which respected the values of Georgian taste and the Arts and Crafts Movement and was opposed to the 'Detroit Jazz' of American design and what Paul Reilly, writing in *Design* in 1957, called: 'the perky chatter of contemporary clichés'.[1] The Consumer's Association was pragmatic; it was concerned with performance and price. The increased attention devoted to design at the end of the Fifties was symptomatic of a situation in which the con-

sumption of objects was no longer motivated simply by need. Increasingly, after a decade of relative affluence, low inflation and wage increases of 25% to 35% between 1955 and 1960, the goods that people consumed were charged with meaning and the capacity to define their owners.

The defenders of 'good design' were forced to make some concessions because of the impact of youth, new notions of leisure, new materials and processes and, most important of all, new ideas. Young designers and theorists of the Independent Group suggested that symbolism was as important as functionalism in the design economy of the post-war years. The phenomenon of 'Carnaby Street' – its marketing of lifestyle and of shopping as fun – had a considerable influence on the mediation of design. Furniture could no longer be regarded as a sensible investment to be handed on to the next generation. Traditional genres and uses were put in question; subdivisions of the house, which

had been inert rooms, were now expected to 'communicate'. Nevertheless, good design persisted – designers like Robin Heritage and Hille continued to represent it for *Design* magazine – and contract furnishing and spectacular instances of British ensemble design, such as the ocean liner the *QE2*, were offered as exemplars.

Until the blooming of Carnaby Street, design journalists seemed unsure of the characteristics of British design. One typical article cited Sheraton and Hepplewhite, before conceding that the English are 'better at absorption, adaptation and neat regurgitation'[2] than at producing distinct styles. Exemplary British interiors usually contained important foreign components: were based on an American ranch house, had 'continental-style beds' often made by 'local carpenters' and relied on 'lamps from Casa Pupo'. The point was frequently made that central heating, which began to be more

188

commonplace in the Sixties, made lighter fabrics and colours more appropriate and played a part in a general 'continentalization'. The arrival of the phonomenon that was entitled Swinging London helped to resolve this problem. Shel Silverstein, the American journalist who first gave it that name in an article in *Time* magazine, identified the genius of the place as a synthetic one – a combination of Old England, American drive and continental flair. A similar dynamic seems to account for the remarkable success of British design consultancies, many of which originated in the Sixties.

One identifiable British element was 'Pop'. In the Fifties, British artists had taken a particular interest in the American home environment – a cargo of cultish enthusiasm for what Henri Lefebvre has described as 'the domesticated sublime'. Although the advertising sections of popular 'home' magazines were full of 'dream' solutions, the characteristic fantasy of the Sixties was not the kitchen of tomorrow' but Habitat's 'action kitchen', efficient, modular but receptive to the accumulated wisdom of continental culinary skills. Pop, as it affected interior design, induced a mood that favoured bright colours, nostalgic allusion, games with scale and icons. For furniture the main influence was the sculptural boldness of Italian design. The work of such British designers as Roger Dean (Sea urchin chair, 1967), John Monk of Datum (ply stacking stools, 1968) and Max Clendenning (Mediscus range for Aerofoam) was all regarded as manifestations of a Pop spirit. Terence Conran was the entrepreneur who codified and integrated products in a way

Four-poster by Heals
Chair by Interior
Warm-air central
heating by
Electricaire

Electricaire is warm-air central heating by electricity. Many modern homes have it now, and many more will have it. It's extremely efficient, surprisingly flexible and accommodating, quiet, and cheap to install and run. One compact thermal storage unit is the core of it. Ducts deliver the warmth to each room through discreet grilles. No pipes, fumes, flues, radiators, fuel stores or trouble. Simple programming controls it. And, being electric, Electricaire is the cleanest central-heating system there is.
Electricaire is specially designed to run on the off-peak tariff. That's why it's so cheap, because it runs on half-price electricity. Ask your builder or architect about Electricaire; your local Electricity Board or an approved installer. The best homes deserve the very best central heating, don't they?

Better things are electric

Electricaire
warm-air
central heating
runs on half-price
electricity

Advertisement for Electricaire, 1968. Private collection

that was essentially British, and of its time. He provided the means for a participation in continental domestic styles only enjoyed by the upper middle class in previous decades, while maintaining close contact with modern design. Habitat introduced an eclectic range of objects into, and reconciled them with, everyday British design: French cooking utensils; furniture by Magistretti, Eames and Colombo; contract furnishings; oriental fabrics and a reprise of 'classics' from nineteenth-century England: Chesterfield sofas, bentwood chairs and the contents of the Victorian toy cupboard.

The design journals of the Sixties reveal and celebrate a dynamic mixture of ideas and styles. It is difficult to account for the impact of these on average consumers and their interiors. Although it would have been hard to remain unaffected by the abundance of new products and the sense that making a home was now an expressive and eclectic activity, there were severe constraints of availability, money and the cultural capital necessary to this process of 'freeing up'. One survey undertaken at the end of the decade indicated that the British spent little on new furniture (on a per capita basis, slightly less than a quarter as compared with the average German and less than half compared with the French); this may have been partly a result of a more ambivalent attitude on the part of the British to 'newness' and a corresponding willingness to incorporate second-hand or antique items.

One significant shift in the general awareness of design was attributable to the coming of age of the post-war baby

189

The sixties, utopian years

Right:
Peter Murdoch,
child's paper
chair, 1966.
Private collection

boomers. Teenagers had been discovered in the Fifties as new and volatile consumers, particularly in the realms of fashion and entertainment. By 1967, the fifteen to nineteen age group accounted for 50% of all sales of clothes, and from the beginning of the decade there was evidence that they were having an impact on the sale of household goods. Perhaps not surprisingly fashion became an issue in designing interiors. The needs of youth were widely explored. One significant area in which young people were served by designers was in the expansion of higher education. In the new universities and in the new accommodation built to serve the expansion of the existing ones, £160 was allocated to the provision of fixtures and fittings for each study bedroom, an influential example of 'unit' living.

In the Sixties, many new household items appeared for the first time and the mass of new products was often dramatized at the point of sale. The market share of chain and multiple stores increased from 28% to 37%, a considerably higher proportion than elsewhere in Europe. More signifi-

Roger Dean,
Sea urchin chair.
Private collection

cant than just economic dominance was the assimilation of the research and development work so visibly evident in the highly individual and creative culture of the boutiques of Soho, Chelsea and Kensington. In 1964 Terence Conran's first Habitat shop combined the informality of the boutique with the abundance of a warehouse. Interior design was becoming less the concern of the expert practitioner or salesman, and no longer a matter of purchasing the correct items and arranging them in a sensible way; it was conceived as a way of accessing different lifestyles, of manipulating space and light in a manner that testified to individually creative solutions.

Increasingly, guidance was supplied by a range of magazines. Notably influential were the new colour supplements of Sunday newspapers, particularly the 'Design for living' section of the *Sunday Times*, which consistently favoured individual and irreverent solutions to interior design problems. There was also a change in the relationship to the installation of new purchases – they were less likely to be ordered or delivered. Flat packs and the principle of self-assembly, for which the 'Do it yourself' vogue of the Fifties had prepared consumers, meant that carpets, curtains and furniture were more likely to be taken home and put in place immediately. Choosing between 'styles' and 'looks', understanding the uses of new utensils and incorporating new activity-orientated furniture were tasks which demanded intelligent consumption.

In the Fifties and the earlier years of the Sixties the advice offered by such influential journals as *Homes and Gardens* characteristically assumed that clients had limited means for changing the appearance of their interiors and that existing items of furniture would need to be taken into consideration. Priority was put on simplicity and the harmonizing of new pieces with old. Clutter was the enemy – Eero Saarinen described his own designs as an attempt to clear 'the slum of legs', and all signs of the past which could not be refocused as 'features' were to be eliminated. The solutions offered were often architectural, in the interests of providing unity and an uninterrupted continuity of space. Ilumination was to be co-ordinated and wires and bases discarded in favour of wall or track lighting; colour was to be used boldly and concentrated, and storage was to be localized. A 1963 article in *Homes and Gardens* asked: 'Could the cutlery drawer and drinks cupboard be incorporated into a wall of storage, coping with books, records, space for sewing and even a television set?'[3] Firms like G-Plan and Remploy advertised unit furniture, emphasizing the flexibility and choice it provided. One G-Plan advertisement of 1960 offered 200 possible permutations with one range of 'low line' furniture.

The theme of the creative potentialities of the individual consumer was even more prominent in the continued interest in 'Do it yourself', which had been a significant innovation in the previous decade. In the Sixties manufacturers increasingly met the consumer half way by supplying furniture in kit form. Customization took an even more extreme form when young designers like Max Clendenning offered the Maxima range of 'transformation furniture', which consisted of 25 parts but was capable of composing more than 330 separate pieces of furniture. Inflatables and paper and plywood kits suggested a domestic space subject to perpetual reformulation, adaptive to social circumstances and needs, more like a theatrical set than the traditional idea of home.

A preoccupation with storage indicated a necessary response to the growth of personal possessions, and increasingly there was an acknowledgment that provision

might be essential for collections of idiosyncratic heirlooms or amusing junk, with the implication that ordinary people might have begun to accumulate the inspirational repertoire that had previously been the stock-in-trade of designers. The concept of 'storage' also served the notion that only a proportion of furnishings might be in use at any one time. Furniture itself came in forms that folded, could be stacked or hung on walls. Interestingly, the exotica, plant forms and toys – the decor of the earlier years of the decade – became the models for furniture designs of the later Sixties. Although interior design journals had always acknowledged the value of antiques to set against the hard lines of Modernism, the category expanded in the Sixties to include outmoded objects like signs, clay figures, tins and furniture which could be adapted by stencilling collaging or painting. Stripping 'back to the original' became a popular and lasting way of reconciling the past to the present.

What then of the brief Sixties, which have become enshrined in a period style, of 'youth quake', psychedelia, unisex, camp and revolutions? The impact of youth culture was significant in interior design, but only as part of a more complex shift in values. From the mid-Fifties the sense of a growing informality is apparent in writing about design. The

David Goodship, prototype double rocker chair in lacquered plywood. Private collection

young architects of what was described as the 'third wave' (of Modernism)[4] were assimilating a diversity of influences ranging from high technology to 'architecture without architects' and the 'symbol-rich environment' of consumer capitalism. Perhaps the most common theme in deliberations on the future of design was the 'death' of architects and designers and the birth of the consumer/user. The need to design for the real world, the possibility of a manufactured world which would need only a basic infrastructure of services, the exploration of 'counter-design' and the selective technology of the Whole Earth catalogue all pointed to a discontent with traditional roles and assumptions.

Coinciding with and partly dependent on a radicalized youth market was the availability of new materials and various technology transfers from space exploration and weapons development. Some materials which troubled the domestic conventions of upholstery and jointed wood were rediscoveries – like cane and bentwood – others, such as particle board, vinyls, acrylic, polyurethane foam and treated paper, were relatively new. Peter Murdoch's laminated paper chairs, which sold in flat sheets for 30 shillings (£1.50), were much celebrated, as was Bernard Holloway's TomTom range of furniture based on cardboard tubes. Design magazine commented: 'now even hardy provincial buyers are sold on gay expendable items'.[5]

For some time furniture had been proclaiming its modernity by being made lower. The greening of the consumer led to new notions of comfort and intimacy. Furniture became more symbiotic than ergonomic, a resting-place for increasingly informal and libidinized bodies. The fusion of chairs, tables and storage into a total environment provided metaphors for domestic space that would have been quite alien to a previous decade: rafts, wombs, pits, eggs and landscapes were some of the more extreme examples of descriptions that seemed to induce a mood which was intent on naturalizing the hitherto culturalized interior.

For most consumers this lowering of the centre of gravity and the free fall of the body may only have resulted in the purchase of studio cushions, bean bags and sculpted foam. One design critic suggested that the availability of washable, stimulating, brightly coloured interiors was the inevitable consequence of the coming of age of a generation, whose members had been accustomed to such rational features in their

nurseries. Certainly, one of the characteristics of the decade was a belief that regression offered better options than did the alert posture of super-egotistical Modernism.

Another feature of the Sixties, which was enshrined as high theory in Venturi's seminal Complexity and contradiction in Architecture (1966), was the refusal to countenance consistency or a single focus. In an irony-rich atmosphere, the technological future could happily co-exist with a rediscovery of the wisdom of the past. Lifestyle became an exercise in recognizing affinities with a range of assimilated ancestors and pasts. Key exhibitions and publications helped in this excavation of a deployable past – Alphonse Mucha (1963) and Aubrey Beardsley (1966) at the Victoria and Albert Museum and Les Annes Vingt Cinq (1966) in Paris. In a review of a new book on Art Nouveau in Design, the author traced the portents of what he called 'kinky-classics' – the boot handle on the new Jaguar, the sets for Half a sixpence and wallpaper designs and rising prices in the Portobello Road.[6] Before the entropy and disillusion of 1973, it was possible to explore the past without being aware of the potentially atavistic consequences of its gravitational pull.

In 1973 a range of avant-garde Italian design was exhibited at the Museum of Modern Art in New York – I have borrowed its title, The New Domestic Landscape, to express what I take to be the dominant project of the Sixties' interior – to reconceive the domestic environment as a 'natural' setting for the drama of life and possessions and to explore the interface between private leisure and the exciting new world of stimuli which seemed to be opening up. The micro environments and software on show in New York at the end of the period were in many ways prophetic – the exhibition responded to the impact of robotics, global media and environmental control on living spaces. However, it failed to account for the power of tradition and the mysteries and mundanities of 'home' and 'property' – the repressed of the Sixties have been returning ever since.

Barry Curtis

1. Paul Reilly, Design, April 1957.

2. Homes and Gardens, October 1967.

3. Homes and Gardens, January 1963.

4. See The third generation, London, Philip Drew, 1972.

5. Design, June 1968.

6. Anthony D. Hippisley Coxe, Design, November 1964.

Ian Ballantine, *Sleeping
environment*, 1968.
Private collection

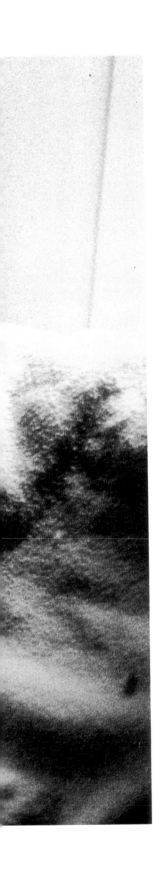

Psychedelic living

Photograph by Robert Whitaker: Richard Neville, editor of the magazine *Oz*, waking himself up by reading the rival magazine *Private Eye*, 1967. Private collection

The sixties, utopian years

Above:
Photograph by Robert
Whitaker: Fiona Milner,
Martin Sharp and Abigail
Maria Margarita McColl
smoking in the back of a
London taxi, 1967.
Private collection

Left:
Photograph by Robert Whitaker of the Phaesantry Studio, Chelsea, 1968. Private collection

Photograph by Robert Whitaker of an Op art shop window in Paris. Private collection

Left:
Martin Sharp and Robert Whitaker, *Plant a flower child*, pull-out poster from the magazine *Oz*, July 1967. Private collection

The sixties, utopian years

Right:
Martin Sharp, *Blowing*
in the mind, **1967,**
silkscreen poster with
Bob Dylan.
Private collection

Martin Sharp and
Robert Whitaker,
record sleeve for
Disraeli gears **by the**
Cream, 1967.
Private collection

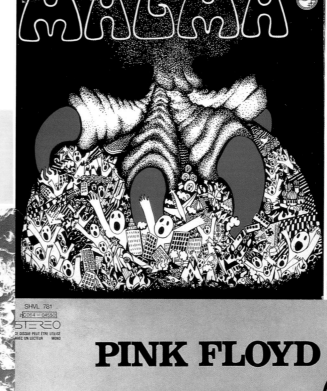

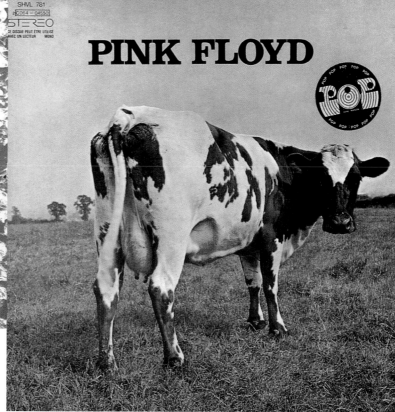

Record sleeve for the French group Magma. Philippe Bone collection – Ressources et Réseaux

Left: Record sleeve with relief vision of changing scenes from the Rolling Stones, *Their Satanic Majesties request*, 1967. Philippe Bone collection – Ressources et Réseaux

Record sleeve for Pink Floyd album *Atom heart mother*, 1970. Private collection

The sixties, utopian years

Right:
Record sleeve of *Magic*
bus **by The Who, 1968.**
Private collection

Photograph by Robert
Whitaker: *Psychedelic*
Bentley, **1967.**
Private collection

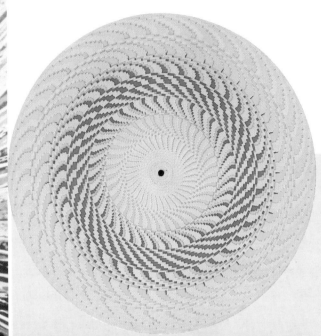

Peter Sedgley,
videodisk, 1968.
Private collection

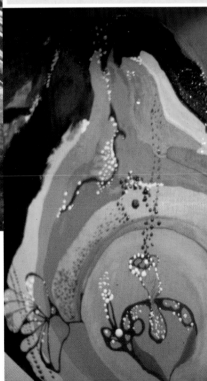

Top left:
Photograph by Robert
Whitaker: painting by
Martin Sharp, 1967.
Private collection

Photograph by Robert
Whitaker: psychedelic
painting by Paul
McCartney, 1966.
Private collection

The sixties, utopian years

**Painted photograph
by Martin Sharp of
Robert Whitaker and
Fiona Milner.
Private collection**

**Left:
Photograph by
Robert Whitaker of
Jenny Roth, 1967.
Private collection**

The sixties, utopian years

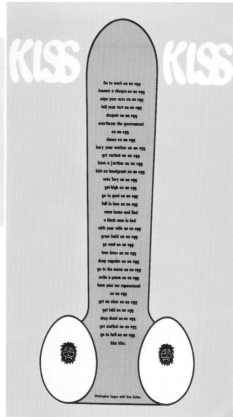

The year 1965 was marked by two events which symbolize the apparent contrast between Great Britain and France: the death of Winston Churchill in Britain, where Labour had won the election the previous year; and in France, the success of General de Gaulle in the first election for a President of the Republic under universal suffrage. The French, who were subject to Gaullist power imbued with public morality, carefully controlling the television that could now be received in homes rapidly being equipped with sets and making optimum use of the machinery of a centralized technocracy, were amazed at the news from the other side of the Channel where the 'permissive society' was breaching the old canons of the Victorian era. Innovation was henceforth a British preserve. Whereas the Gaullist administration was enthusiastic about perfecting its atomic bomb – the first French atomic explosion had taken place in the Sahara in 1959 – Britain experienced the large-scale Campaign for Nuclear Disarmament which mobilized wide swathes of young people in a far-reaching moral crusade. Mods, rockers, hippies, skinheads were all collective demonstrations of youth with which old England astounded the Continent. And right to the fore came the Beatles, conquering the entire planet with concerts which attracted crowds of ecstatic adolescents and records that beat sales records everywhere. The Union Jack became fashionable on the Continent to the point where department store plastic bags sported its colours on the street. While France was trying to regain its place at the top table by means of the grandiose policies of General de Gaulle, tirelessly campaigning for the independence of nation states and standing out against the hegemony of the super powers, Great Britain, losing its power, was busy asserting its cultural pre-eminence – one that no longer came from the creativity of an elite, but which heralded mass culture.

The political differences between the two countries seemed so great that De Gaulle refused to allow the British to join Europe. In his eyes they were too close to the Americans and would therefore impede the construction of an independent Europe. The British for their part had only recently started to aspire towards being part of Europe, and did so for purely economic reasons: they had noted the dynamics of the Common Market, and were rightly concerned that it might prosper to the detriment of their own economy, the relative decline of which had become obvious. They were hardly stirred by any feeling of belonging to Europe. It would be tempting to pursue the comparison right up to the social and cultural explosion that shook France in May 1968. Where Britain achieved its change in its traditional manner, without major public disturbances, French society, lagging behind, seemed incapable of making any shift without tearing up the cobble stones, quoting the authority of Trotsky or Che and provoking police repression, all as a tangible and seemingly necessary sign of change. Nonetheless, the period is now sufficiently remote for a careful examination to show that, if we look carefully, the resemblances – the parallelism of the developments in the two countries and the concurrences between so many factors on both sides of the Channel – seem more important than the divergences. By simplifying the picture it is possible to characterize the Sixties both in France and in Britain by six phenomena which affected both nations.

The end of imperial power

Prior to World War I Britain and France had created the two most extensive colonial empires, managing to preserve and even expand them after 1918. World War II shook those empires profoundly. For both countries, embarking on the Suez expedition to preserve their control over the Suez Canal which Colonel Nasser had just nationalized, the year 1956 had signalled their decline: called on by the Americans and the Russians to withdraw, French and British troops had to return home, sick at heart. Neither Britain nor France could any longer claim to be a great power. The Algerian War, which had already started, triggered the end of the process of decolonialization whereby, after Indo-China, France had to concede independence to Tunisia, Morocco, its territories in equatorial Africa, and finally Algeria itself in 1962. Certainly Britain, which had started down the road of emancipation earlier, still preserved special links with the Commonwealth, and De Gaulle restored France's prestige in the world through the boldness of his foreign policy, but nonetheless it had to be accepted as a reality that both countries had become middle-ranging powers after for so long dominating the fate of the world, even through their very rivalry.

London hippies: Richard Neville (author of *Playpower*) and 'Frisco' baiting an Anglican vicar, photograph by Robert Whitaker, 1967. Private collection

The affluent society

It was in the Sixties that what the British called the 'affluent society' and the French the 'société de consommation' became established. Until the beginning of the Fifties both countries had suffered hardship; rationing had continued in the United Kingdom until 1954 – the same year as France had experienced a terrible housing crisis which brought Abbé Pierre to prominence. By the Sixties the effects of growth were visible: a higher standard of living, full employment, households equipped with domestic appliances, a boom in car ownership, longer schooling, the birth of a 'leisure culture', a growing number of super-

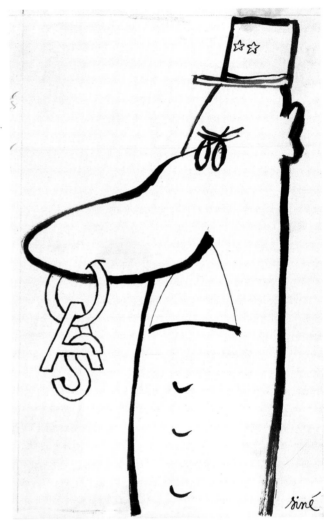

markets, the apotheosis of advertising, etc. Admittedly, increasing global prosperity left some shadowy areas – people bypassed by growth and glaring inequalities. The rapid rise in living standards itself led to frustrations, with everyone thinking he or she was less well rewarded for his or her work than others. These years of wealth were also accompanied by claims and strikes, sometimes violent. Nonetheless, like other western countries, France and Britain were transformed during the Sixties as never before. The affluent society prompted intellectual, moral and spiritual criticism, but the decade was not perceived as a causal moment in history: both countries had embarked on mass production and consumption and the prospects seemed limitless. The cup was overflowing, and people had discounted the idea of depression.

The triumph of mass culture

With the affluent society went the strong development of mass culture in the context of an urban society. Even more than the progress of traditional culture, imparted through schools, and the 'democratization of education', the distinguishing characteristic of the Sixties must be the arrival of cultural forms no longer originating from the elite and affecting all strata of society. This mass culture had existed for a long time through popular newspapers, sports matches, cinema and radio, but the tone was still set by people from the world of learning – teachers, intellectuals and critics in the major newspapers. The Sixties saw a profound change, resulting from the general availability of records, transistor radios and television. Television sets were installed rapidly in homes. Millions of citizens enjoyed the same serial or the same game show at the same time, and it became a topic of conversation the following day. New channels were also created during this period, with Britain commissioning the first commercial channel. The new 'household fairy' had its detractors, with professional people being the last to buy television sets. No doubt society was as yet unaware of all the profound disruptions which the triumph of television would cause: the unification of the national language but competition with reading, the imparting of knowledge but also of accepted ideas, the wider dissemination of major works of

art, literature and music but the loss of local cultures, deep influences on our morals, styles and ways of living... A balance sheet has still to be drawn up on the impact of television. In a parallel development the Sixties saw the supreme triumph of the 45 rpm record, with record-players now available to all. Records and transistor radios together were major factors in establishing the new mass culture, which cannot be separated from the arrival on the market place of a new generation, the generation produced by the post-war baby boom.

Poster by Michel Bongrand for the 1967 parliamentary election campaign. Musée d'Histoire contemporaine collection

The Prime Minister Harold Wilson depicted by Martin Sharp as Mr Toad, a character from *The wind in the willows*, on a calendar issued by the magazine Oz, March 1967. Private collection

Drawing by Ralph Steadman, *X my arse*. During the 1970 election campaign some people thought Harold Wilson and Edward Heath didn't care about the electors. Private collection

turning the Beatles, Mick Jagger and Bob Dylan into worldwide stars, in the wake of Elvis Presley. The music also expressed sexual liberation from the canons of puritan morality. The liberalization of sexual morals was under way. The new social class resulted in 'mass beauty' – nothing illustrates this better than the spread of the mini-skirt and of T-shirts: Parisian couturiers had to tailor fashion to teenagers. Old lycée photographs showed that until the Fifties the boys who would later take their baccalauréat wore the same clothes as their teachers and looked ten years older than they were, while the girls all wore identical overalls. From now on imagination and attractiveness were allowed into lycées and factories. More than that, youth gradually made its standards, fashions and ways of talking prevail. The example was no longer set from above – adults tended to copy teenagers.

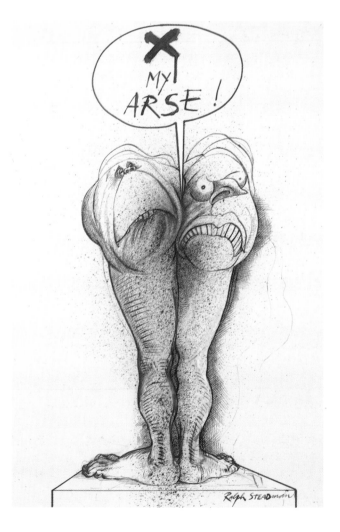

The rise of youth

Margaret Mead defined that new generation at a lecture she gave in London in 1968 in the following terms:

Changes have taken place at such a rapid pace in the past 25 years that adults cannot assimilate them .... Children are growing up in a world that was unknown to their parents. They are brought up by television. They do not form part of any religious, national or ethical structure that their parents knew. They belong to the whole world.

The new youth culture had no frontiers. How could it be recognized? Trendy clothes (jeans for everyone, no tie, basket-ball boots, etc.); hair grown to a length that was the despair of heads of families; fervent, gregarious following of rock and Pop music, made easier by the tuning of amplifiers,

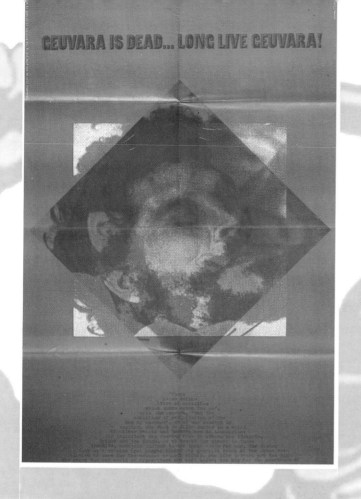

GUEVARA IS DEAD... LONG LIVE GUEVARA!

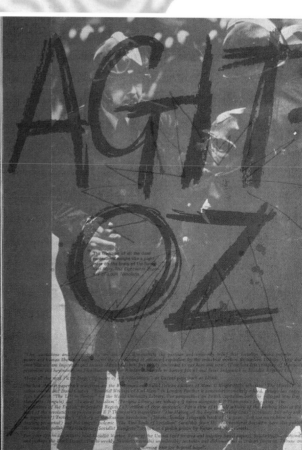

Staying young, looking young, acting young, became a leit-motif in magazines and a new obsession for the mature.

Not only did this large generation make its presence felt as a model of the affluent society, it also had political importance. The Angry Young Men movement had already been seen in England at the end of the Fifties, opposing the prevailing conformism, while in France protest had emerged in opposition to the war in Algeria. At the beginning of the following decade, in France after the end of the Algerian War in particular, it looked as if there was a general loss of interest in politics. The tone was set by the Pop stars of the day – Johnny Hallyday, Françoise Hardy, Richard Antony, Sylvie Vartan – who made a lot of noise but their words were meaningless. But in fact the success of these 'idols' did not detract from the renewal of a specifically youthful form of

Posters backing Georges Pompidou in the 1969 presidential election. Musée d'Histoire contemporaine collection

commitment. Outside the major parties and unions young people throughout the world marched for peace in Vietnam. Pacifism did not preclude new revolutionary hopes, but the young looked to Fidel Castro or Mao rather than the Soviet Union. The underground protest culture, more prevalent in Britain and America, expressed the desire to transform the world here and now. Although it had local variations the youth culture of the Sixties had become international. Frank Musgrove summed up its characteristics:

Absence of interest in power and deference for authority, rejection of frontiers and labels, an absolute desire for authenticity, a wish for free, non-possessive sexuality, a liking for art, music and ecstatic trances, a sense of community and sharing, a passion for leisure and freedom, the rejection of any form of appropriation...[1]

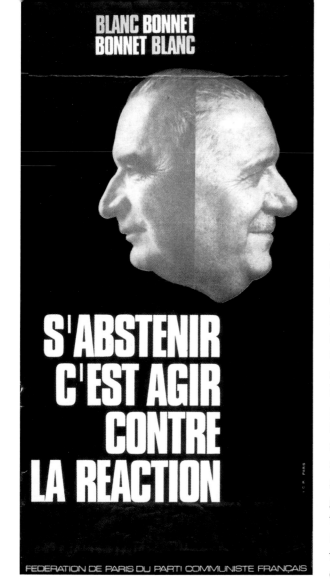

BLANC BONNET
BONNET BLANC

S'ABSTENIR
C'EST AGIR
CONTRE
LA REACTION

FÉDÉRATION DE PARIS DU PARTI COMMUNISTE FRANÇAIS

Accelerated secularization

In both Britain and France, society saw the process of secularization which had started in the nineteenth century accelerate rapidly in the Sixties. It had already made a strong impact on Protestant communities in Britain, but now the Catholic church too encountered a rising tide of indifference: too few recruits for the priesthood, fewer conversions and a sharp decline in those practising their faith. The French Catholic church was also affected, even seeing the number of baptisms drop from 92% in 1958 to 85% in 1970. God had been segregated. While for centuries religion had deeply penetrated the Establishment, social practices and morals, henceforth it tended to be more of a personal matter. The affluent society favoured disaffection towards the churches and their standards; its inherent hedonism turned believers away from religion's secular rigours. Belief in science also gained ground as a substitute for religion at a period when technological progress of all kinds was accompanied by economic growth. When religious feeling was manifested, it tended to be towards something other than the traditional establishments: new Messianic, eastern tropistic or syncretic movements and sects. Katmandu took the place of Rome.

Communist Party poster for the second round of the 1969 presidential election depicting Georges Pompidou and Alain Poher. Musée d'Histoire contemporaine collection

Jacket worn by a young hitchhiker setting off for Afghanistan and India. Gérard Aimé collection

Women's expectations and a falling birth rate

France and Britain both experienced a drop in the birth rate in the mid-Sixties, and this would become even more marked in the Seventies. The decline in child-bearing in both countries could also be observed in all expanding industrial societies at the same period, Catholic and Protestant alike. This phenomenon was correlated with the individualistic morality of the affluent society which made it possible to hope for social advancement, as well as the trend towards secularization, depriving the religious authorities of their former influence, and the developing mass communications which made it easier to teach people about contraception. The drop in the birth-rate was compensated by the arrival of a growing number of foreign or immigrant workers from the former colonies. Both countries received a massive influx of immigrants. The decline in child-bearing must also be linked with the movement for female emancipation. Women had become a large-scale presence in the tertiary industries, filling the majority of office jobs. In both countries they rejected the traditional image of the mother in the home. Many were now studying and continued working even after the birth of their children. A new female outlook developed, one with ambitions for every woman to achieve financial independence so that she would no longer have to be dependent on the protection of her marriage partner. At the end of the decade the extremely rad-

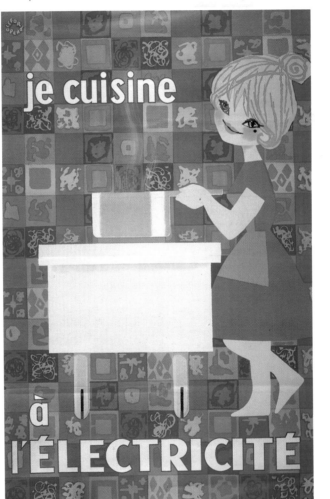

Poster by Lefor and Openo promoting household electrical appliances. Musée d'Histoire contemporaine collection

ical feminist protest movements would emerge: MLF in France and Women's Lib in Britain.

Ultimately the observer is struck by the convergences between George Pompidou's France and Harold Wilson's Britain, two countries that had for so long been separated by vast mutual incomprehension, constant rivalry and an often contemptuous stand-offishness. The question of Britain's insularity again surfaced during the Sixties, particularly in her application to join the Common Market. French pride, in spite of the return to power of a nationalist soldier, had to back down: greatness no longer went with modestly proportioned countries. However, both societies adapted to the new challenges of modernity less through government dictate than in response to pressure from young people wanting a decisive break with the past. Nonetheless Britain and France adhered to their own methods of change – the former gently and quietly, give or take a few scandals, indignant outbursts and the nostalgia of the old guard; the latter violently, with a predilection for ideology and passionate drama. But in the last analysis, Britain without the May tumult and France with it, both converged in their own ways towards a new society which witnessed the advent of the masses, a new revolution in the media and the demand for collective happiness.

Michel Winock

1. François Bédarida, *La Société anglaise du milieu du XIXe siècle à nos jours*, Paris, Le Seuil, 'Points-Histoire' collection, pp. 368, 369.

oui à l'avenir

In the Sixties, Pop music – an abbreviation for 'popular music' – had not yet become the pale version of rock dedicated to the hit parade and easy success, which was to typify the subsequent decade. Quite the opposite: it was rock shedding its image of music for adolescents and renouncing innocence, gaily crossing the boundaries between the genres and introducing into the two-time beat the sounds of jazz, folk, oriental and classical music. It was Bob Dylan crossed with the Beatles, opening up to the world and crossing the threshold into adulthood.[1]

It was not until 1966–7 that Pop music became the accepted form of rock-'n'-roll. The emergence of the hippie movement in the United States and the release of *Sergeant Pepper* (the Beatles) marked a turning-point. Five years later the dream was over. Flirting with virtuosity and getting mixed up with jazz or classical music, Pop music ended up forgetting rock along the way. All that was left were turgid records, weighted down with pride and pretension, and an industry devoid of any fighting spirit. Moreover there had been too many deaths in a very short space of time (Brian Jones, Jimi Hendrix, Janis Joplin, Jim Morrison) for music still to believe in the Sixties. The start of 1971 marked the end of an epoch – a chronology which had nothing to do with what was happening in France. Pop music there had such great difficulty in establishing itself in the face of the hostility of the public authorities, the resistance of variety-hall music and the onslaughts of Left-wing politics that in the end it tended to be imported, reflecting a utopia that could not sustain the rebellions of the young.

Yet the decade had got off to a good start in France. The post-war baby boom generation had reached adolescence, LPs and transistors were in every home, standards of living were rising: the ingredients for rock were there, as were the adolescent stars. In 1963 'La nuit de la Nation' brought together hundreds of thousands of fans to applaud the idols of the day – Johnny Hallyday, Sylvie Vartan and others – and should have been an apotheosis, but it turned out to be no more than the premature epilogue of a truncated adventure. The teenage Pop-fan period, ushered in at the Nation, was to be a period marked by renunciations. Instead of Beatlemania the France of the baby-boom generation came up with Sheila and Claude François. There were solo stars who lacked the impact of a group, silly adolescent love songs,

sanitized adaptations of English or American rock and a cruel absence of talent. A look at the record sleeves tells the story: close-up shots of smooth, smiling faces, a candid gaze turned towards the camera lens, well-groomed hairstyles and ties, all far removed from David Bailey's photographs on the first albums by the Rolling Stones – aggressive adolescents with over-long hair and evasive eyes. France under De Gaulle opted for reassuring idols, happily accepted by adults. Johnny Stark was the leading impresario. The lyricists were Charles Aznavour or Pierre Delanoë (Delanoë 'adapted' Bob Dylan for Hugues Aufray). And Antoine or Jacques Dutronc embodied Pop music French-style.

So the revolution brought about by Beatlemania did not happen in France – its first tremors were not felt until 1966 when groups like the Variations were formed, performing a kind of blues-rock, but heavy and devoid of genius. But a start had been made. British and American records started selling in the original versions, and with the 'concept album'[2] adaptation became a risky business. There were more concerts, at Olympia or the American Cultural Center in the Boulevard Raspail; on radio José Artur launched his *Pop Club* on France Inter; and the first issue of *Rock & Folk* which was derived from the magazine *Jazz Hot* appeared. But the change-over was cautious. In 1968 the traditional French repertory still accounted for 90% of the turnover of record outlets in mainland France. Rock was still short of halls and clubs as venues, and needed a revolution in the music industry. Beside enthusiastic reports from New York and San Francisco, *Rock & Folk* still found space for variety, sometimes of the very worst kind, and politics were barely featured.

To be honest, at that time protest and Pop music coexisted side by side totally ignoring one another. Music distrusted politics, and protest attached little value to rock. The Revolutionary committee for cultural action (CRAC) was concerned with poetry and theatre, but had nothing to say when it came to music. When the Sorbonne was occupied people can remember hearing only Bobby Lapointe's pianist and the Haricots Rouges playing New Orleans jazz in the courtyard. Radio broadcast the same throbbing refrains which had managed to come out just before the record factories went on strike: *Rain and tears* by Aphrodite's Child, or Julien Clerc's *La Cavalerie* – not exactly Pop. When the proletarian Left chose a hymn (*Nous sommes les nouveaux partisans*

Photograph by
Robert Whitaker:
Mick Jagger starring in
Tony Richardson's film
about the Australian
outlaw *Ned Kelly*, 1970.
Private collection

The sixties, utopian years

francs-tireurs de la guerre des classes – We are the new partisan guerrillas of the class war), they turned to Dominique Grange for it, a former teenage idol who had switched her focus towards politically committed songs. Even the leaders seemed to have no liking for the two-time beat and electrical instruments. Those who were interested in music preferred jazz – Michel Le Bris for example, the former chief editor of *Jazz Hot* who later took over *La Cause du peuple*.

However the May '68 protest did have an impact. The old restraints of French society were beginning to break down and Pop music turned that to its advantage. First of all there were new groups: Alan Jack Civilization, Triangle, Martin Circus followed by Zoo, Ame Son, Gong, Dynastie Crisis, and this time they were coherent formations capable of conveying a style which was more than just plagiarized British and American rock – but most of them had no commitment to protest. Concerts were organized throughout 1969 in Paris, Blois, Le Bourges and in Amougies in Belgium. Tours by the Maisons des Jeunes provided a rudimentary infrastructure for French rock music, and it conquered bastions that had been regarded as impregnable: the Communist party and the Fête de l'Humanité, or the Théâtre des Champs-Élysées. Radio stations opened their doors with programmes like *Campus* by Michel Lancelot who went over the themes of the counter-culture on Europe I, or Jean-Bernard Hébey on RTL. Some attempts were made to launch independent labels. Byg put out records of contemporary music, free jazz and French Pop, while Futura specialized in more radical music. And there were new magazines: *Best* and *Pop Music* stuck to music, while *Le Parapluie*, *Le Pop* and *Actuel* were inspired by British and American underground newspapers like *IT* and *Oz*, with music, protest and counter-culture. The first two had a fairly short, chaotic existence, but *Actuel* was a success: 50,000 copies by 1971.

In *Actuel* the spirit of May '68 did to some extent meet up with music. Jean-François Bizot who set it up inherited a fortune made in textiles; he loved jazz, and initially followed the classic path of protest, belonging to the Vietnam committees and then to the PSU (Parti socialiste unifié). But he had a dilettante approach to militancy, and was not really convinced by what was being said around him. In the summer of 1969 he travelled back and forth across the United States, visiting everywhere that counted on the underground scene.

It was a revelation. Now thoroughly convinced and enthusiastic, he returned to France and decided to found a counter-culture newspaper. He met Bernard Kouchner, Jean-Paul Ribes and Michel-Antoine Burnier, veterans of the 1968 student revolt who had already tried their hand at newspaper publishing. They gave him a cautious welcome. The counter-culture, drugs and Pop music were exotic themes for these tried and tested militants. Even so, they met again. Eventually Jean-François Bizot took over *Actuel* with Michel-Antoine Burnier's support, relaunching a title which was then in the doldrums. He needed tenacity; the counter-culture had such a precarious foothold in France that it took a long hard search to find anything to report. But Bizot, carrying the banner for new sounds, unearthing experiments, keeping an eye on life on the fringes of society and pleading the cause of the American underground, 'made believe' there was.

He was not alone. In the musical press the rebellion of youth against the old world was an inexhaustible theme, and mental revolution and physical liberation were advocated. The affluent society and its misdeeds, police repression and the Vietnam War were denounced. There was a desire to break down the family and invent different forms of human relationships. There were attempts to create communes free of materialism and money. From London to New York the counter-culture sang the same song: dislodge the old world by undermining it from the margins. But there was an echo here of 1968. What was being written about Pop music was directly descended from May '68, a juvenile, playful version, a rebellious May rather than a revolutionary one, a May rebelling against all forms of authority, claiming an opportunity for all to develop in full.

Initially the Far Left was oblivious of what was going on. It totally disregarded the concert at Le Bourget in March 1969, 'that harmless get-together of party-goers'.[3] But Pop music did progress and the public turned up, the great majority of them young. So the festivals were chosen as a mission ground. This was too good an opportunity for the public authorities to miss. France under Georges Pompidou was none too fond of long-haired young people, and deployed an impressive arsenal against the Pop world's 'drug addicts' and 'Left-wingers', firmly supported by public opinion. Not a single festival or Pop concert failed to arouse the wrath of the powers that be, first being reported, then cancelled. As early as the

CHARIOT
PETULA CLARK
DANS LE TRAIN DE NUIT - DARLING CHERI
CLAQUEZ VOS DOIGTS, Snap your fingers

EPL. 8000

SOUVENIRS, SOUVENIRS
JOHNNY HALLYDAY Vol. 2
POURQUOI CET AMOUR
JE CHERCHE UNE FILLE
J'SUIS MORDU

EPL 7 755

LES PLAY BOYS
SUR UNE NAPPE DE RESTAURANT
•
ON NOUS CACHE TOUT, ON NOUS DIT RIEN
•
LA FILLE DU PERE NOEL

Jacques Dutronc

FRANCOISE HARDY

autumn of 1969 the 'Actuel' Festival bringing together all the groups that made up French Pop music was to be held at Les Halles in Paris; in the end it took place in the cold at Amougies in Belgium, after roaming from Saint-Cloud to Reuilly and from Puteaux to Courtrai. During the summer of 1970 the festival of Aix-en-Provence was banned barely ten days before it was due to start. It finally was held, after the organizers had

The audiences failed to turn up (around 15,000 when the organizers were hoping for a Woodstock), American and British stars swore they would not be caught out a second time, Soft Machine refused to play at Biot as the 4000 tickets sold were not enough to cover the group's fee. At the end of August the battle moved to Britain. A thousand young French people entered the Isle of Wight Festival by force to shouts of 'Festival free, festival police'. After marches, negotiations and slogans they were given permission to take up a position on a hill overlooking the festival perimeter, but the demonstrations continued. The British response, from the authorities and the young offspring of the counter-culture alike, was glacial. After the protesters had returned to France, there were renewed battles, at the Rolling Stones' concert at the end of 1970, the concert of the École des travaux publics held at the Palais des Sports in Paris in January 1971 and others as well. These confrontations were like a 'bloody parody of an earlier spring'.[4]

It is hard to say with any certainty who was behind it. It would seem that the Isle of Wight was masterminded by Jean-Jacques Lebel, a pioneer of happenings in France who

agreed to turn it into no more than an 'extended concert'.

It was in fact at Aix-en-Provence that the Far Left embarked on its campaign against Pop and its associations with 'money and the middle classes'. At every festival (Aix-en-Provence, Biot, Valbonne) the scenario was the same: people refusing to pay, breaking their way in, taking over the microphone on stage, concerts disrupted by intemperate slogans and if necessary the destruction of equipment. Every time the balance was disastrous, financially and artistically.

had organized Festivals de la Libre Expression at the American Cultural Center in 1964–5. He claimed descent from Marcel Duchamp and the Surrealists, summing up his credo as: 'We no longer paint battles, we fight them.'[5] Rock was to provide him with an excellent training ground, with the help of a few newly converted festival-goers delighted to benefit from such a godsend. In France the 'Maoists'[6] intervened at Aix-en-Provence and Biot before making way for FLIP (Force de libération et d'intervention du Pop), a faction created at the end of 1970. FLIP was an odd sort of set-up, made up of 'Vive la révolution!' militants, the proletarian Left, Trotskyists, anarchists and musicians from the

most politically committed and radical tendency in French rock. There were Maajun, Red Noise – founded by Patrick Vian, the son of Boris Vian – and Komintern: experimental music, a purely political discourse, the reading of tracts against an electrical acoustic background, rounding up with 'Free Le Bris, free Le Dantec'.[7]

The call went unheeded, but at least Left-wing beliefs had given rock an opportunity to ponder about its links with protest. The question asked was, what carries revolution? Sounds, discourse, structures? The protest power of music, going beyond the divisions between the genres and capable of overthrowing the mental structures of those hearing it,

found a few defenders. They maintained that such disruptive Pop music, rejecting stage and harmonic conventions, could and must make 'the middle classes tremble, and frighten them'.[8] This was the underlying cause of the very early defence by the radicals of a return to the purest form of Pop (spearheaded by Velvet Underground, then MC5 and the Stooges). But as a rule they expected nothing from music: it was the music of the whites, American to boot, and sustained an industry – enough for it to be accused of serving American imperialism and bourgeois interests. It then became important to redirect the way it was used and its message, ridding it of its capitalist excesses and turning it against the middle classes. Léonard Cohen's fee at Aix-en-Provence and Bob Dylan's on the Isle of Wight in 1969 were held up as evidence of their betrayal. Led Zeppelin was too professional to be honest. And Creedence Clearwater Revival were 'no more than a huge deviationist money-making machine'.[9] To smash the logic underlying the industry, non-paying entry had to be imposed, the 'supreme negation of the bourgeois public performance',[10] the relationship between performer and spectator had to be redefined, and getting a return for your money had to come to an end, along with festivals that were 'repressive and hostile to the people, profiting and benefiting the middle classes'.[11] No, festivals had to be opened up to the people, 'or the people will close them down'.[12] To those who pointed out that groups did not play for nothing and that it was necessary 'as things were' to stick to the logic of audiences paying to attend public performances, the advocates of radicalism replied by making reference to protest against bourgeois society and the alienation inherent in it, its laws and its 'guard dogs'. Pop had to go out to the people, to the places where they were, to people's homes, factories and high schools. 'We will choose the times and the places. We ourselves will create the situations'.[13]

Record sleeve featuring Antoine; with his *Élucubrations* and his long hair he represented the hippie, French style, 1966.
Philippe Bone collection – Ressources et Réseaux

225

ly demanded violence and tended to sneer at Buddhism, Zen and all the eastern claptrap that invaded the world of rock. But those in the Left-wing movement hardly benefited from this. In their irreverence, which was at odds with the high-minded sector of the hippie movement, they wanted to have no truck with 'political priests and their sinister catechisms'.[16] Political infantilism, petty-bourgeois, pseudo-revolutionary, vulgar, sterile, cheat, school kid, were among the hail of compliments exchanged during the battle of the festivals. The true revolution had to turn its back on the absolute happiness that was being promised for tomorrow by splinter groups, and battle against the concept of the radiant future. 'We wanted to break the political Left-wing movement, an archaism which was placing a strait-jacket on people's minds.'[17] Something of the stprit of May 1968 had survived. This time around that spirit very quickly took up an

In the United Kingdom and the United States, especially with the 'yippie' movement (a cross between Left-wing beliefs and hippie flower people), radicalism erupted into music. But it had no history or political tradition on which to lean. In France, on the other hand, it was the counter-culture which did not take root, as if there were something in its credo that was irrevocably alien to French protest. Drugs, for example, were never really accepted, being seen as deadening consciousness rather than as setting it free. Pop in France always managed without amphetamines and LSD. 'We don't need hallucinogenic substances for our revolution. The creative spontaneity of socialism is enough for us',[14] a 1968 tract proclaimed. Pacifism and non-violence were regularly mocked as a 'bleating ideology',[15] fit only to appeal to stars going through a crisis of conscience (John Lennon, Joan Baez), seen as an appeasing semblance of quiescence serving the interests of the 'system'. Protest open-

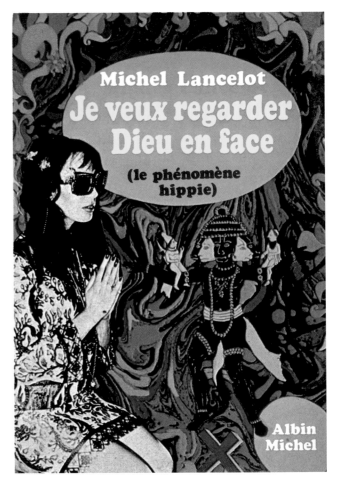

anti-totalitarian stance ('If it were possible for a Chinese Dylan to exist, his songs would be anti-Mao'[18]), not very far removed from the Pop revolution, as personified by someone like Jerry Rubin,[19] but without the drugs and more vehement and impatient, more libertarian and less playful, determined to fight here and now without waiting for the counter-culture to undermine the old world's resistance: an idea that survived obstinately and angrily in a simplified form, crossed with the two-time beat but still alive:

> It's hard for an old humanist to stand by silent and watch the brains of credulous souls being washed, a prelude to their bodies being massacred. What we need is a festival organized by Daniel Cohn-Bendit and filmed by Jean-Luc Godard.[20]

At the start of the 1970s, who really wanted a musical rerun of May '68? Politicians trying to mobilize the masses, critics seeking to give themselves legitimacy (being to rock-'n'-roll what the magazine *Cahiers* was to the cinema), while the public at large just stuck to the music. In Aix-en-Provence, Biot or Paris the revolutionary diatribes were met with laughter, cat-

calls or polite indifference. 'Our seizure of the hall remained highly symbolic,'[21] FLIP conceded after a concert by the Rolling Stones. Pop groups with a revolutionary message had only a very limited audience, while those that formed the second wave of French rock[22] never mentioned politics.

It is paradoxical that France produced the most virulent critics and the most neutral music. No one wrote a single hymn to compare with *Revolution* by the Beatles, *Street fighting man* by the Rolling Stones or even *Won't get fooled again* by The Who. And hardly any impact had been made on the structures of the music industry either. The old impresarios were still there. They had simply:

> moved on from tours by Lucky Blondo or Sheila to tours by Peter Brown and Martin Circus. And more or less everywhere, schools, village fairs, universities and commercial fairs booked a group where two years ago they would have booked Brel at best, or Mireille Mathieu.[23]

Rock-music magazines grew in number, but their combined

Left:
Original record sleeve of Serge Gainsbourg's song, *Je t'aime... moi non plus* with Jane Birkin (banned on radio), 1969. Philippe Bone collection – Ressources et Réseaux

Libretto of Serge Gainsbourg's concept record *Melody Nelson* with Jane Birkin, published by Éric Losfeld in 1971. Philippe Bone collection – Ressources et Réseaux

The sixties, utopian years

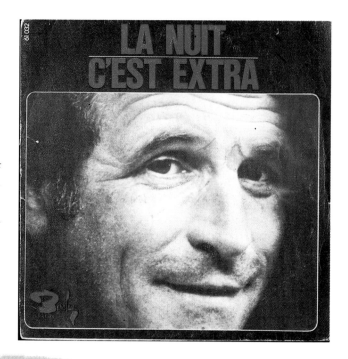

sales in 1970 were 150,000 copies – *Salut les copains* had a circulation of 900,000.

Whether Pop music was involved in protest or not, there was still a question-mark over its credibility. The sales of albums were insignificant: in 1969, 17,000 copies of *Tommy* by The Who, 45,000 of *Let it bleed*, 200,000 for *Abbey Road*, to ignore the French groups. Concerts were a minor cultural activity: in 1974, 92% of French people said they had never attended a Pop or jazz concert. In Britain Pop music replaced protest, and *Street fighting man* by the Rolling Stones summarizes it nicely: 'But what can a poor boy do, except to sing in a rock-'n'-roll band, 'cause in sleepy London town, there's no place for a street fighting man'. In America the two went together. In France protest and Left-wing intervention blocked the music. The violence reinforced the authorities in their attitude: distrust, surveillance, bans. Concert promoters finally gave up: in July 1971, after incidents at a Santana concert, the Olympia theatre closed its doors to rock. Pop music had nowhere to go. There was no network of clubs, theatres and music-halls monopolized variety shows, and records and equipment were costly.

But there was another factor. The prophets of protest in popular music were tried and trusted singers like Jacques Brel, Georges Brassens or Léo Ferré who succeeded tolerably well in making a synthesis between music and an

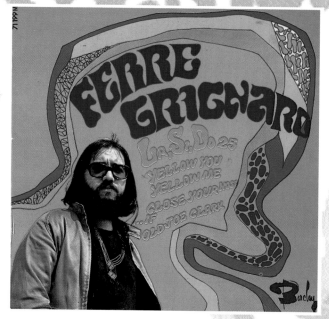

anarchic style of protest in the French tradition. At the end of the Sixties, a new generation joined them: Colette Magny, Graeme Allwright, Catherine Ribeiro and (in his fashion) Serge Gainsbourg. They too adhered to the variety-hall framework: solo artists, three-minute format, discreet guitars and classic harmonies. Thus the song with a message was the 'monocultural block' raised like a 'decisive, impassable obstacle'[24] across the path of rock.

In fact France in the Sixties did not like crossbreeds, it did not recognize bastards, and that brings us back to the foundations of rock: young whites appropriating black music. Nor did it like individual liberation as opposed to collective ventures. In a country where the revolutionary tradition was still alive and kicking, any change taking place through culture and the individual smacked of alienation and a move away from the class struggle. The revolution wanted to change life, not make do with working on its fringes (the world of the imagination, partying, the road), or accept a parenthesis coinciding with youth. It wanted a rational discourse anchored in social reality, asking clear questions about power, while Pop music was derived from play, masks and a certain kind of disenchantment.[25] That gave rise to a failure of understanding that ran right through the Sixties. Only after the political sphere had experienced its crisis and disappointments were music and its giddiness consecrated. By the time that happened at the start of the Eighties Pop music had ceased to exist. All that remained then was rock-'n'-roll which had eventually been taken over as protest: unless the French really ended up liking it.

Marianne Amar

1. Between 1966 and 1972 what is called today 'rock' is commonly called 'Pop music' by the French, following the model of 'Pop art', 'Pop revolution' etc. Generally in Britain 'Pop music', or 'popular music' corresponds more or less, during 1962-6, to what is known in France as 'yé-yé'.

2. Until then albums had been compilations of the songs on 45 rpm issued in the preceding months. With Pop they became coherent works on their own.

3. Hervé Hamon and Patrick Rotman, *Génération. Récit*, Paris, Le Seuil, 1988, vol. II, p. 163.

4. Philippe Paringaux, *Rock & Folk*, March 1971.

5. Interview published in the American magazine *Boss* in 1967, quoted in *Rock & Folk*, May 1968.

6. In particular see the testimony of Jean-François Bizot, founder of *Actuel*, in Hamon and Rotman, op. cit., vol. II, p. 262.

7. The chief editor and the director of the (Maoist) *La Cause du peuple*, sentenced to eight months and one year in prison respectively.

8. Paul Alessandrini, *Rock & Folk*, February 1970.

9. Jacques Chabiron, *Rock & Folk*, June 1970.

10. Georges Haessig, 'Une expérience de détournement, le FLIP', *Musique en jeu*, no. 2, March 1971.

11. *Tout!*, 23 September 1970.

12. *Tout!*, op. cit.

13. Manifesto of FLIP, *Musique en jeu*, op. cit.

14. Tract by Comité d'action révolutionnaire, 10 June 1968, in Schnapp and Vidal-Naquet, *Journal de la Commune étudiante*, Paris, Le Seuil, 1969, p. 460.

15. *Tout!*, 23 September 1970.

16. Philippe Paringaux, *Rock & Folk*, September 1970.

17. Jean-François Bizot in Hamon and Rotman, op. cit., p. 266.

18. Philippe Paringaux, *Rock & Folk*, September 1970.

19. Apostle of the 'yippie' revolution in the United States.

20. Philippe Paringaux, *Rock & Folk*, September 1970.

21. *Tout!*, 8 October 1970.

22. The first at the beginning of the decade was headed by Johnny Hallyday, the Chaussettes noires and the Chats sauvages.

23. Philippe Constantin, 'Pop et profit, le changement dans la continuité', *Musique en jeu*, op. cit.

24. Paul Yonnet, *Jeux, modes et masses*, Paris, Gallimard, 1985, p. 193.

25. Paul Yonnet, 'L'esthétique rock', *Le Débat*, no. 40, 1986.

Left:

Martin Circus was the best-known French Pop group at the beginning of the 1970s, along with Tringle, Magma and Ange.

Private collection

Cover of a French Pop music magazine (1972) which proved to be short-lived, unlike *Rock & Folk* or *Best*.

Private collection

Youth culture and subcultural style

'Wonderful world, Beautiful people'

The Sixties stand as a decisive decade in the history of British youth culture. Seldom has the pace of change within youth style been so rapid, nor the social impact of youth culture so resonant. More specifically, youth culture became a critical terrain on which the period's wider social upheavals and political struggles were played out. However, the saliency of youth as a cultural category in Sixties Britain cannot be grasped without first appreciating its context within a wider set of social, economic and political changes occurring after World War II.

In 1945 the Labour Party's landslide general election victory heralded an era of political consensus. Throughout the Fifties and Sixties British governments of all political hues operated within a framework of shared key assumptions that embraced the maintenance of high levels of employment and a commitment to the Welfare State and a mixed economy. This new political landscape, moreover, seemed to be part of a more wholesale social transformation. Full employment and a demand for labour sustained rises in real earnings and incomes, laying the basis for a steady growth in consumer spending and a rise in living standards. In retrospect much of this prosperity can be seen as transient. Sixties' affluence depended on a level of growth that the British economy was simply not in a position to maintain, and by the end of the decade the scale of this problem had become apparent. In the early Sixties, however, it seemed as though a new dawn was breaking. The pace of economic growth seemed to be steadily ameliorating social divisions, ushering in a new epoch of classless 'post-capitalism'. This, of course, was a myth. The British class structure did not, in any sense, disappear. Nonetheless, with the enhancement of workers' incomes and the redevelopment of traditional working-class neighbourhoods, Britain certainly gave the appearance of being on a trajectory leading towards classless prosperity. And it was the lifestyles and culture of British youngsters which, more than anything else, seemed emblematic of these changes.

Conceptions of 'youth' and chronological age invariably figure in attempts to make sense of social change, these concepts becoming powerfully extended at moments of profound transformation. This was particularly true during the 1960s, when young people were an important 'ideological vehicle' for the discussion of wider shifts in British social relations and cultural life. Beginning in the mid-Fifties, a wealth of official research increasingly presented youth as a category integral to wider social change, often featuring the young in a favourable, almost celebratory light. The media could also present youngsters in glowing terms. Newspapers and magazines, especially, helped to popularize notions of 'youth' as an excitingly new social force, a vigorous and uplifting contrast to the tired, old, traditional order. Particularly striking was the deployment of images of youth as a shorthand signifier for unbridled pleasure in what appeared to be a new age of hedonistic consumption. Young people seemed to embody all that the consumer dream stood for, advertisers habitually using representations of them to associate their own products with dynamic modernity and 'swinging' enjoyment.

The equation of youth with consumption was exemplified, above all, by the addition of the term 'teenager' to everyday vocabulary. First coined by American market researchers during the mid-Forties, the word was imported into Britain late in that decade and was integrated into popular discourse during the Fifties and Sixties. In the image of the teenager, mythologies of classless affluence found their purest manifestation. Taken as the quintessence of social transformation, teenagers were perceived as being at the sharp end of the new consumer culture, distinguished not simply by their youth but by a particular style of conspicuous, leisure-orientated consumption. As Peter Laurie contended in his anatomy of what was happening, *The teenage revolution* (1965), 'The distinctive fact about teenagers' behaviour is economic: they spend a lot of money on clothes, records, concerts, make-up, magazines: all things that give immediate pleasure and little lasting use'.[1]

The teenager, then, was an ideological terrain upon which a particular definition of social change was constructed. Central to notions of the teenager was the idea that traditional class boundaries were being eroded by the fashions and lifestyles of newly affluent young consumers. Teenagers were presented as a class in themselves, what Laurie termed a 'solidly integrated social bloc',[2] whose vibrant, pleasure-orientated culture seemed to represent a symbolic foretaste of good times waiting around the corner for everyone. Of course, the idea of teenage affluence and a

Publicity graphic design for *A clockwork orange*, 1971. Private collection

The sixties, utopian years

new 'culture of youth' misrepresented the true nature of change in the lives of British youngsters. Social class did not disappear but continued, as it still continues, to mediate young people's cultural practices and experiences. Indeed, for many youngsters during the Sixties, economic hardship and poverty remained a grim reality. Nevertheless, with their labour in high demand, the earnings of working youngsters generally rose, laying the basis for an unprecedented expansion of the commercial youth market.

During the Sixties the range of products geared to this market seemed to be boundless, consumer industries interacting with and re-enforcing one another in their efforts to cash in on youth spending. The importance of this market registered especially in the field of popular music. During the 1950s the initial wave of American rock-'n'-roll stars had been matched by comparatively pallid British imitations such as Tommy Steele, Billy Fury and Marty Wilde. In the 1960s, however, the British Pop industry came into its own. Beat music and rhythm and blues flourished, and British groups like the Animals, The Who and of course the Beatles and the Rolling Stones began to lead the field in the international world of Pop. Official British radio broadcasters, in contrast, were slow to associate themselves with changes in youth culture. During the early Sixties the field was left to offshore pirate stations like Radio Caroline, the BBC only beginning to target a specifically young audience with the launch of Radio 1 in 1967.

Compared to radio, the younger medium of television responded relatively swiftly to the developing youth scene. Programmes addressing young people had begun to appear in the Fifties, though shows like *Six-five special* (1957) and *Oh Boy!* (1958) were always tempered by their attempts to embrace a more heterogeneous family audience.[3] During the early Sixties these gestures towards a general appeal diminished. Programmes such as *Ready, Steady, Go!* (1963) made few concessions to an adult audience, revelling in a preoccupation with the music, fashions and the tastes of the young, especially the developing 'mod' subculture of the early Sixties. Indeed, the importance of television in promoting and propagating subcultural style has often been overlooked. Coverage by television, and the media more generally, gave subcultures such as that of the mods not only national exposure but also a degree of uniformity and definition unknown in their predecessors.

'Dedicated followers of fashion'

During the Fifties the subcultural styles of British young-sters had been dominated by American influences and images. The teddy boy's drape jacket and 'duck's arse' hairstyle for example were inspired by the iconography of the Mississippi gambler and the zoot-suit styles imported with the arrival of GIs during the war. By the early Sixties these American influences were being surpassed by styles derived from Europe. Italian design aesthetics, in particular, bewitched the consciousness of British style. Popularized by films such as *Roman holiday* (1953) and *La dolce vita* (1960), the chic, smoothly tailored lines of Italian fashion were first sported in Britain in about 1958 by the 'modernists', the fashion-obsessed youngsters who frequented the clubs and back streets of west London. Immortalized in Colin MacInnes's novel *Absolute Beginners* (1959), the modernists cultivated a sharp line in sartorial flair with a preference for light, expensive yet understated suits with short, bum-freez-er jackets and tapered trousers that set a pace for subcultural style at the beginning of the Sixties.

Though their 'look' quickly diffused into the provinces, the subculture of the original mods was centred on London. Their quest for exquisitely cut clothes took them to Soho tailors and shops like John Stephen on Carnaby Street, itself transformed from a fairly mundane London back street into the centre of the mod universe and, subsequently, into a bazaar of fashion and style and the hub of Swinging London. Other centres of mod culture included such London clubs as the Scene and the Flamingo, where young, white mods came into contact with black, American soul music. Mod musical preferences also embraced black American rhythm and blues (emulated by mod groups like The Who and the Small Faces) and Afro-Caribbean ska and bluebeat. Indeed, this exchange between mod and Afro-Caribbean style marked a crucial stage in the developing intersec-tion between black and white popular culture, and became a central feature to British youth subcultures throughout the Sixties. Additionally, mod's fairly ambiguous construction of gender made it more accessible to women than many comparable subcul-tural milieux, the average mod as often being a young woman as a young man.

The mods, many of whom came from the housing estates of east and south London, were emblematic of a working class in transi-tion. The mods' neat image of cool sophistication reflected the upwardly mobile character of post-war working-class life and contrasted sharply with the more class-bound qualities of their contemporary adver-saries, the rockers. The media played an important role in consolidating the mod/rocker polarity, but the distinction was not pure invention. Tending to have lower paid, less skilled occupations, the rockers represented an affirmation of 'tra-ditional' working-class lifestyles. With their motorbikes, leather jackets, jeans and boots the rockers rejected the effeminacy of conspicuous consumption and cultivated an

Front page of the Brighton *Evening Argus*, 18 May 1964, describing mods and rockers rioting, Brighton. Private collection

233

image of sturdy masculinity. The mods, on the other hand, were often employed in lower white-collar jobs, and their scooters and pristine dress made them the standard-bearers of the working class in the age of affluence.

Superficially clean-cut and well-dressed, the mods in appearance were amenable to co-option within notions of post-war dynamism and modernity. They were treated as the trend-setters of Sixties' stylishness and mobility, the media eagerly charting changes in the minutiae of their dress and music. However, British media reaction to post-war youth has always been characterized by a Janus-like quality.[4] Almost simultaneously, youth has been both celebrated

as the exciting precursor to a prosperous future and vilified as a deplorable feature of a more general cultural bankruptcy and social decline. Hence, while the mods were fêted as classless consumers *par excellence* they were also reviled as representing a neurosis of the affluent society. This negative response was shown, above all, in the moral panic that surrounded the mod 'invasions' of several seaside towns in 1964. Working-class youngsters had traditionally visited seaside resorts at holiday times, but Easter 1964 was cold and wet and facilities for young people in such places were limited. In Clacton scuffles broke out between local youths and

visiting Londoners, a few beach huts were vandalized and the odd window was broken. These small-scale acts of vandalism, however, were given front-page prominence by an outraged national press which wrote of a 'day of terror' in which a whole town had been overrun by a marauding mob 'hell-bent on destruction'. During the rest of the year sensational press coverage trumpeted about bank holiday 'disturbances', the moral panic continuing sporadically throughout the remainder of the Sixties.[5]

'Skinhead Moonstomp'

The mods' flamboyant style of conspicuous consumption meant they could be easily incorporated within the mythology of classless affluence. In the late Sixties, however, no such co-option was possible with the skinheads, whose self-conscious invocation of a traditional working-class heritage was irreconcilable with notions of disappearing social divisions in the culture of British youth.

The skinhead style first began to be noticed within British youth culture in the mid-Sixties. Debate surrounds the specific location of the skinheads' roots. Some commentators cite Glasgow or the north-east of England as the origin of the classic skinhead 'uniform' of steel, toe-capped work boots, rolled-up jeans, braces and convict-style cropped hair, while others point to the East End of London as the skinheads' birthplace. Irrespective of its exact geographical origin, it seems certain that the skinhead 'look' first developed as a harder branch of the Sixties mod scene. The actual term 'skinhead' came into general circulation in 1969 through its usage by the popular press, but it is impossible to pinpoint changes in British youth culture with any degree of temporal precision; one subcultural style always

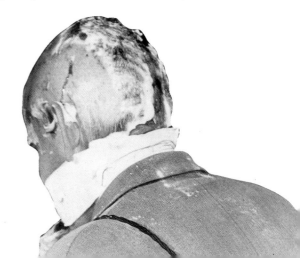

Mods fighting in Brighton, 1964. Private collection

Right: Still of the shaven-headed chauffeur in *Performance*, 1971. Courtesy British Film Institute

merges seamlessly into another. In fact, youngsters wearing boots and sporting closely cropped hairstyles could be found within mod circles as early as 1964, though by the later Sixties the skinheads had evolved into an identifiably distinct cultural group.

Important elements of continuity linked the skinheads to the mods, particularly with regard to music. Like the mods before them, skinheads favoured American soul and Jamaican ska. Jamaican artists such as Desmond Dekker and Prince Buster were particular skinhead favourites, and record companies like Island, Trojan and Pama sprang up in Britain to meet the growing demand for ska and reggae which came not just from the West Indian community but also from an increasing number of white youngsters. Like the mods, skinheads also drew on elements of black culture as a source of fashion and style. A crucial cultural reference point was set up by the Jamaican rude boys, the hustlers and small-time gangsters of the slums of West Kingston, whose 'street cool' apparel of two-tone 'tonic' suits, 'pork pie' hats and wrap-around dark glasses found echoes in both mod and skinhead styles. In other respects, though, skinhead subculture differed markedly from that of mod, especially in the way that the football ground became a key cultural locus.

Aggressively partisan behaviour was not unique to post-war British football. Since the modern game's inception in the late nineteenth century there has been a long and connected history of fights between players, violence between supporters and attacks on game officials. Only in the Sixties, however, did disturbances at football matches begin to become more specifically associated with younger sections of the crowd. The national press first made regular references to hooligan gangs operating in relation to football during the 1966/7 season, a period in which segregation by age was becoming more pronounced in league football grounds. Groups of young men increasingly began to stake out the football terraces as their own territory, acting in ways that either deliberately or inadvertently discouraged the presence of older spectators. These phenomena were closely associated with the rise of the skinhead and his liking for 'aggro' and 'bovva'. Strident support of a local football side was congruent with the skinheads' assertion of a stylized proletarian aesthetic and their celebration of tradi-

tional loyalties and aggressive masculinity. Attending football games *en masse,* groups of skinheads laid claim to grounds in a manner unknown to previous generations, adopting the names of the terraces – the Chelsea 'Shed', Arsenal's 'North

Bank' or 'the Loft' at Queens Park Rangers – and there developed an extensive network of violent rivalries between the various football 'ends', with shared memories of past victories and defeats and complex cycles of retribution.

Towards the end of the Sixties, then, notions of British youth as a homogeneous and economically prosperous cultural group proved increasingly difficult to sustain. In their place social researchers began to pay greater attention to dimensions of class and conflict in youngsters' lives. Instead of dismissing youth subcultures as simple fads or fashions, commentators also began to understand these stylistic assemblies as important purveyors of social meaning, intrinsically linked to wider patterns of cultural change. Such a perspective was especially associated with the work of members of the Centre for Contemporary Cultural Studies (CCCS) at Birmingham University.[6] Drawing on a rich blend of cultural theory and semiotics, the CCCS group argued that subcultural style was a symbolic or ritualistic expression

**Still:
a 'performer' gets
a good hiding in
Performance, 1971.
Courtesy British
Film Institute**

of social experience. Youth subcultures were interpreted as forms of cultural insubordination, expressions of defiance and rebelliousness as working-class youngsters appropriated articles, artefacts and icons and symbolically re-worked them to take on new, threatening and subversive meanings. The effect of this approach was to turn subcultural styles into texts, various semiotic techniques being employed to 'read' the subversive meanings implicit in the mod's elaborately customized scooter or the skinhead's boots and braces.

The CCCS authors' restoration of class as a factor central to young people's life experiences was an important contribution. Yet, in their eagerness to present youth subcultures as meaningful strategies of 'opposition', the CCCS group probably over-romanticized their subjects, many of whom were aggressively sexist and racist in their attitudes (the skinheads, for example were infamous for their assaults on immigrants). Their fixation with the deviant and the spectacular was also problematic. It should not be forgotten that the vast majority of British youngsters have always been fairly 'mundane' in their apparel and behaviour; nor should the importance of the media and commercial industries in giving subcultures cohesion and definition be overlooked. Certainly, young people themselves were involved in stylistic inception, but this dimension of self-creation should not be exaggerated. Media and commercial interests, for example, were intrinsic even to a group as apparently 'authentic' as the skinheads, whose 'movement' simply would not have coalesced into a recognizable form without intervention from entrepreneurs and retailers and would have quickly disappeared had it not been galvanized through exposure in newspapers, on television and in pulp fiction, such as Richard Allen's series of skinhead novels.

The dynamic quality to these subcultural styles is also often overlooked. All too frequently subcultural forms are discussed as though they were immutably fixed and static phenomena. Nothing could be further from the truth. Constant change and flux have been endemic to the universe of youth subcultures. The skinhead style, for example, quickly developed and mutated. By the end of the Sixties the emergence of the suedehead marked a sublime variation on the skinhead theme, a less severe, crew-cut hairstyle being coupled with a more fastidious fashion sense, including a preference for city gents' Crombie overcoats,

accessorized with a black umbrella. Bowler hats even made an appearance after they had been sported by the futuristic hooligans featured in Stanley Kubrick's film *A clockwork orange* (1971). The suedehead style itself quickly metamorphosed, giving way to the smooth styles of long hair, flared trousers and sleeveless tank-top pullovers that became a hallmark of British youth fashion during the early Seventies.

'All you need is love'

At the beginning of the Sixties the British youth 'spectacle' was primarily a working-class experience. Middle-class youngsters' participation was circumscribed by their tendency to remain at school for longer than their working-class peers, so limiting their disposable income and constraining their social freedom. Nevertheless, the young of the middle class were not completely excluded. The generic term 'beat' or 'beatnik' was applied to a collection of nonconformist and unconventional middle-class young people that appeared in Britain from the mid-Fifties.

The origins of beatnik culture lay in the *avant-garde* literary and artistic cliques that emerged in post-war Paris. Their creed of existentialism and individual expression provided a set of reference points and images subsequently drawn upon by disaffected youngsters around the world. In America the work of beat writers like Allen Ginsberg, Neal Cassidy, William Burroughs and Jack Kerouac pioneered and eulogized the beats' 'on the road' ethos and lifestyle. Published in Britain in the late Fifties, these writings helped consolidate the developing beatnik culture. Creativity and introspection were focal concerns in the British beatnik scene, beat culture encompassing a quixotic mix of jazz, poetry, literature, eastern mysticism and drugs. British beats saw themselves as imaginative dissidents and cultivated an image of the pauperized intellectual, thread-bare jackets and fishermen's jerseys being set off by goatee beards and horn-rimmed spectacles in a montage of studied dishevelment. The beatniks certainly enjoyed a high social profile, but it was not until the mid-Sixties that a larger, more significant counter-cultural formation began to emerge.

The massive expansion of British universities in the mid-Sixties was intended to lay the basis for a more accessible system of higher education, yet it was the middle classes who

Covers for the
skinhead epics of
Richard Allen: *Skinhead*
(1970), *Skinhead girls*
(1972) and *Skinhead
escapes* (1972).
Private collection

most successfully exploited the new educational opportunities. Compared to working youngsters this group possessed relatively little disposable income, yet higher education had its compensations – offering middle-class students significant leisure time, coupled with the independence of living away from the parental home. It was this growing experience of 'studenthood', then, that provided a crucial foundation for the growth of a diverse range of loosely affiliated anti-Establishment and bohemian youth groups in Britain during the late Sixties.

In the late Sixties' counter-culture the beatnik's *avant-garde* pretensions were fused with the exotic and psychedelic fashions peddled in the growing legion of London boutiques. Cheesecloth shirts, beads and flared denims were complemented by 'ethnic' kaftans and Afghan coats in a pot-pourri of patchwork and tie-dye. Attempting to generate an aesthetic lifestyle that stretched the boundaries of respectable society to breaking point, the British counter-culture also took many cues from the American west coast. In both countries counter-cultural strategies encompassed a wide-ranging engagement with media forms and images. In Britain this was especially evident in the prodigious output of the underground press, the lead being taken by *International Times* (or *IT*, launched in 1966) and *Oz* (launched in 1967). More than simple information sheets, the alternative press explored through its very form the imagery of dissent by the use of fantastic visuals and striking symbolism. The same strategies could also be found in a range of cultural initiatives, including 'alternative' posters, films and the various experimental projects of the Arts Lab movement. Music, of course, also figured prominently. In 1966 venues such as the Roundhouse and UFO became centres to the burgeoning London underground while the rise of 'art rock' – in the form of Cream, Soft Machine, Pink Floyd and later albums by the Rolling Stones and the Beatles – aspired to an anti-commercial creativity. Loosely organized 'be-ins' and 'happenings' of various kinds were also important: festivals, concerts and other gatherings helping to generate and maintain commitment to alternative lifestyles. In January 1967 Pink Floyd topped the bill at the 'Giant Freakout' at the Roundhouse followed, in April, by 'The 14-Hour Technicolour Dream' held at Alexandra Palace and, in August, by the three-day 'Festival of the Flower Children' at Woburn Abbey. In the late Sixties there were enormous

free concerts in Hyde Park, Pink Floyd in 1968 and Blind Faith and the Rolling Stones in 1969.

Generalizing about the history and development of youth cultures is always difficult, especially so in the case of the counter-culture, which was always a disparate collection of factions rather than a coherent formation. Nevertheless, a broad shift in the British counter-culture can be detected, the rhetoric of 'peace' and 'flower power' being displaced by that of street-fighting and political protest as the 1967 'summer of love' gave way to 1968, the year of revolts. Though not on the scale of the events in Paris in May 1968, Britain went through its own episodes of student militancy and radical protest. Opposition to the war in Vietnam became a passionate cause, several massive demonstrations taking place outside the US Embassy in Grosvenor Square. Student politics also developed a more radical complexion, with a series of fierce confrontations between student groups and the administrations of a number of universities and colleges, most notably at the London School of Economics and Hornsey College of Art.

For many, the outlandish activities of the counter-culture and the turmoil of the 'street-fighting years' held the promise of a new, revolutionary youth movement with the potential to transform society according to more progressive ideals. Such views, however, were rose tinted to say the least. The radical movements of the Sixties never attracted more than a minority of the young, most youngsters staying firmly committed to more mainstream values and attitudes. Based around 'art' and 'individualism', the counter-culture's strategies of 'opposition' also tended to evade rather than confront the structural sources of inequality. More fundamentally, the counter-culture's radicalism often proved to be a thin veneer. Despite its egalitarian sloganeering, sexual inequality remained pronounced. Traditional sexual divisions of labour were largely reproduced and the sexual revolution often amounted to little more than an intensification of the sexual exploitation of women. Furthermore, notwithstanding its scorn for 'breadheads' and capitalist materialism, the Sixties' counter-culture was a resounding market success. From its inception the counter-culture had been 'a nice little earner' for a network of 'hip capitalists' who marketed everything from illicit drugs to psychedelic posters. Indeed, in some instances these enterprises proved phenomenally lucrative, Richard Branson's 'alternative' record business becoming the launching pad for his Virgin empire.

In these terms, rather than being a movement *against* dominant ideologies, the counter-culture was a movement *within* the dominant culture. Though superficially incompatible with the dominant order, the counter-culture's libertarian ethos of 'doing your own thing' was actually rooted in the soil of classical liberalism and *petit bourgeois* individualism. Just as the subcultures of the mods and the skinheads sprang from working-class lifestyles in a state of transition, the counter-culture issued from a bourgeois culture struggling to adapt itself to the new contours of the post-war environment. The traditional middle-class world that had emerged during the eighteenth and nineteenth centuries – with its emphasis on the work ethic, moderation and decorum – was increasingly out of step with a capitalist economy that now prioritized consumption and immediate gratification. The counter-culture, then, fulfilled an adaptive role, initiating and experimenting with new cultural forms and lifestyles, which ultimately gave the dominant order greater flexibility.[7]

Here, a link can be established with what Pierre Bourdieu has identified as the rise of a new *petit bourgeois* 'habitus'.[8] Contemporary western society, Bourdieu contends, has seen the rise of 'cultural intermediaries', a new bourgeoisie formed from those whose occupations deal with the production and dissemination of symbolic goods and services. This emergent group stands apart from traditional class structures in its preoccupation with the attributes of style, distinction and refinement – its narcissistic obsession with lifestyle and self-expression making the members 'natural' consumers. Though a characteristic feature of the Eighties and Nineties, this formation traces its roots to the Sixties' counter-culture. For not only do the ideologies of expressivity and personal 'liberation' derive from these movements, but many of today's cultural intermediaries were themselves the 'beautiful people' of the Sixties.

'You've lost that lovin' feelin''

Although the counter-culture was a by-product of transformations taking place within the dominant normative order, this should not obscure the dimensions of meaningful opposition in some areas of the movement. The symbolic disaffiliation of the counter-culture led, in some instances, to a sharper and more intense form of political protest. Indeed, as the political consensus of the early Sixties steadily disintegrated and social and economic conflict became increasingly pronounced, the counter-culture's political expressions were subject to mounting hostility and repression: the 1968 demonstrations against the Vietnam War were subject to intimidatory policing; in 1970 punitive prison sentences were passed on six protesters objecting to a visit by Greek military leaders; in the same year the editors of *Oz* were imprisoned after their prosecution for obscenity; and in 1971 sentences of ten and fifteen years were passed on five members of the Angry Brigade, a Situationist group responsible for a series of bomb attacks the previous year. Like the subcultures of working-class youngsters then, the counter-culture began to figure in an imagery of societal deterioration and breakdown. However, whereas mods and skinheads were presented as *symptoms* of decline, the counter-culture was cast as actively *causing* a collapse of law and order and social stability.

By the end of the Sixties, therefore, images of youth had become central within a generalized move towards more disciplinarian and repressive forms of social regulation. These more abrasive and authoritarian forms of control, moreover, were set to be extended to many more areas of social, economic and political life during the following decades.

Bill Osgerby

Robert Whitaker's photograph of Birgitte Bjerke in Indian make-up. Private collection

1. *The teenage revolution*, London, Anthony Blond, 1965, p.9.
2. Ibid., p. 11.
3. See John Hill, 'Television and Pop: The case of the 1950s' in John Corner, ed., *Popular television in Britain: Studies in cultural histoiy*, London, BFI, 1991.
4. See Dick Hebdige, 'Hiding in the light: Youth surveillance and display' in Dick Hebdige, *Hiding in the light*, London, Routledge, 1988.
5. See Stanley Cohen, *Folk devils and moral panics: The creation of the mods and rockers*, St Albans, Paladin, 1972.
6. See Stuart Hall and Tony Jefferson, eds, *Resistance through rituals: Youth subcultures in post-war Britain*, London, Hutchinson, 1976; Paul Willis, *Profane culture*, London, Routledge and Kegan Paul, 1978; Dick Hebdige, *Subculture: The meaning of style*, London, Methuen, 1978.
7. See John Clarke, Stuart Hall, Tony Jefferson and Brian Roberts, 'Subcultures, cultures and class: A theoretical overview', in Stuart Hall and Tony Jefferson, eds, op. cit.
8. Pierre Bourdieu, *Distinction*, London, Routledge and Kegan Paul, 1984.

Forms of photographic expression

Since the end of World War I photography had consistently advanced as an essential and reliable means of information and communication. A large number of photographic agencies were set up in the Twenties in the United States, France (eighteen were listed in the 1929 Press Yearbook) and elsewhere in western Europe, confirming the great need for images, a need that grew as the subjective power of the images themselves grew. The photograph was a means of informing and attracting, but primarily a vehicle for myths and dreams; it took possession of our lives to the point of disguising one part of them, reality.

In the Sixties new photographic equipment emerged, sophisticated yet simple, which attracted the professional as well as the consumer. The cameras came directly from the United States where the first Polaroid, producing photographs which could be developed more or less instantaneously, was marketed in 1960. In 1963 Kodak, who were already pioneers of both images and equipment, launched the Instamatic, a small, easy-to-handle camera with very simple optics, to succeed its legendary Brownie black box with its two viewfinders, as well as colour films with good definition that could be used by anyone. The age of rapid consumption had arrived. Photography was given new opportunities, for everything could be done by everybody. The multiplicity of equipment resulted in a very considerable extension and diversity in the use of photography. However, to examine the concept of photography in the Sixties, I have decided to concentrate on three forms of visual expression that were important, with technological developments undoubtedly being their common factor: stars, fashion and photography by 'authors'; I have deliberately excluded photo-journalism whose main role is to narrate stories and events developing under our eyes, quickly and on a day-to-day basis. The photographer had then to be a sort of interpreter who worked through the press (Pop, fashion) and books or exhibitions (the 'author' photographers).

Post-war photography was involved in the concept of renewal, movement, the desire to 'express oneself differently', but it was not totally revolutionary. In spite of the flare-up in May '68, the Sixties in France and Germany have been described as an 'abandonment of the field of photography'; at best a case for photography might be put in terms of exploration and attempts. Not until the Seventies was the idea of photography reborn and it is finally possible to talk of French photography taking off. Nearly all the great trends of this period were derived from American ideas reaching France via Britain. Thus in his own special way each photographer tried to define and make his mark, outlining what he was seeking to do. Finally there emerged in France at the end of the Seventies of a new line of research, 'photographie plasticienne' (fine-art photography) relating photography – or blatantly opposing it – to the work of the painter, engraver or even the sculptor. That movement went beyond simply describing the subject to make photography a pure creative act. Coming from Holland and West Germany (Berlin in particular), fine art photography once and for all abandoned 'humanist photography',[1] which nevertheless continued to be very fertile then, as it still is today.

Photographers of the stars (reading SLC)

It was already a few weeks old, and our anticipation was heightened by ever increasing eagerness. Our ears were glued to our transistors switched to Europe no. 1 every evening at 5.30 as the magic jingle to the tune of Big Ben rhythmically announced: 'SLC. Salut les copains'. It was a multi-faceted radio programme that had a huge impact, made in association with the fashion journal *Marie-Claire*. Teenagers in search of an ideal – far removed from the extremes of existentialism which had virtually nothing to do with them, from the jazz music of Saint-Germain-des-Prés which affected them only moderately or from an excessively earnest literature which attracted them hardly at all – needed something new: their own novelty, belonging to their own generation – though it undoubtedly reflected English and American culture.

Frank Ténot and Daniel Filipacchi, the presenters of this innovative programme, were musical journalists (they already presented the late-night programme *Pour ceux qui aiment le jazz*) who sensed teenagers' desire to know everything about the lives of the stars through pictures. Following the radio programme they launched a magazine which set out to be completely different and fresh, telling readers everything, absolutely everything, about the lives of their idols. It was not a new plan but thanks to the concept and the advertising the idea took off: marketing geared towards young people was under way.

Photograph by
Bernard Plossu
from *Voyage*
mexicain, 1965–6.
Private collection

Right and below:
Autographed
photographs of Sheila
and Claude François.
Private collection

A lot of magazines were already being published for young people, and large-circulation magazines like *Ciné monde* or others with a more limited readership like *Disco-revue* aimed at a specialist public, *Music-Hall* and *Jeunesse cinéma* (to name but a few) were full of photographs. Pictures of established stars, with their families, in recording studios, on tour or giving a concert, were already featured with the intention of catching as wide an audience as possible. There were centre pages that could be pulled out or stickers to put on satchels or exercise books. In spite of all that, the covers were still dull and relatively unappealing. So the exertions of the two journalists would set a new tone, and the new publication could not fail to fire the enthusiasm of young people, the 'copains' (pals): it was an immediate success.

The first long-awaited issue came out in July 1962, using the same title as the radio programme, *Salut les copains* (publication ceased in 1976). It was a monthly magazine and the price was FF 1.50. The young editorial team spoke the same language as their readers. The advertising had not lied, the new magazine was what we had been looking for, a true, live reflection of our youth. The cover, very much of the Pop world and using glossy paper, finally showed us the true face of the idol of idols, the sacred monster of the moment, as it had never been shown before: Johnny (Hallyday), young and smiling, a head-and-shoulders portrait, just right for the page,

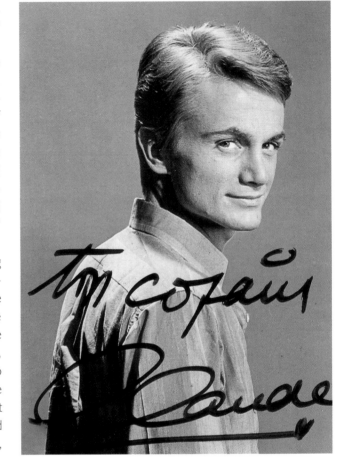

Sylvie Vartan,
the future model for
the comic strip
Les Aventures de Jodelle
by Peellaert (1966),
who like all the
Pop stars of the period
was confirmed as
a star by the magazine
Salut les copains
(created in 1962).
Collection Sousse
Ohana

spilling out of it, with flattering colours, and above the brand new title a star-shaped spot with names and all the announcements listing the contents of that issue. Care had been taken over the magazine's lay-out. We would be able to learn everything about our idol, his life, his aspirations and even the aspirations of 'Sylvie in colour!!!' (the singer Sylvie Vartan later became the media-hyped wife of Johnny Hallyday. *SLC* got exclusive rights to the pictures of their wedding). But above all we were going to SEE.

The photographic credits below the list of contents were highly significant: the part played by photography was large, and right from the start it was given pride of place. It was in fact the vehicle for the narrative context; the writing was adapted to the pictures, as photographs spoke volumes to the teenagers who very quickly identified with their idols. The idols were shown with false simplicity, leaving room for dreams. The stars, most of them singers, were very young

– a youthful face is easy to photograph, and wide use was made of scarcely necessary artifices by talented make-up artists and hairdressers. The natural look – albeit fallacious – was the order of the day. The celebrity's love life was very important: the more conquests he or she had, or the more reasons for happiness, the better the magazine would sell (the spirit of the old photostory was still alive and well). For the picture to pay off photographers had to be resourceful, setting out to achieve an original composition and framing that set off the subject to advantage. To get a satisfactory result they usually proceeded stage by stage: first they would arrange an appointment with the star, suggesting where the photographs should be shot, outside (natural light offering a constantly changing quality of lighting), in the studio (importance of the lighting, longer working time, possible retakes) or on a television studio set ('instants stolen by chance'). Stars were also tracked down to fashionable places like the Golf Drouot in Paris, the Mecca of the Pop world, on to the sets of television programmes like Albert Raisner's *Âge tendre et tête de bois* or Daisy de Galard's *Dim, Dam, Dom*. Photographers would be there whatever the circumstances, accompanying the first steps of a hypothetical future celebrity. The star's doings, family life, hobbies, secrets, everything had to be depicted, even if it entailed setting up original situations: these could captivate readers and help the magazine sell. One photograph followed another (film came cheap) so as to get a picture that would be just right, flattering the subject and promoting publicity. Interest was almost inevitable. Shots varied according to the 'clients': the themes of their songs, the newspaper or medium for which the photograph was intended.

Photographers found work as best they could and there were a great many hopefuls. Large organizations provided sophisticated equipment, well-kitted studios and, above all, far from negligible financial rewards, but of course there were fewer photographers so rewarded. Results depended on 'talent', but also on luck and opportunity. Photographers generally used two cameras, one for black and white and the one for colour. To get good quality Ektachrome transparencies[2] a special large-format camera known as a 'chambre'[3] had to be used; though transportable it was heavy and very cumbersome. German optics were still favoured. Leica, Rolleiflex or Tecnika Linhof were widely used. Before long, for obvious reasons of convenience, these very heavy cameras would be replaced by small, light, manageable camera cases accommodating 24 x 36 mm negatives. Japanese equipment, already in existence in 1959 in the form of the 35 mm Nikon reflex[4] camera with a single viewfinder, gradually broke into the market. The photographs in themselves were not really more 'beautiful' than before, but colour and optical precision helped to lend an attractive impression of novelty. Framing and lights showed no great innovative originality.

It was mainly the ways in which photographs were used that changed. For example the image underwent all sorts of transformations, starting with reframing or photomontage to provide an attractive lay-out in magazines. Then photographs were used for various purposes: autographed

Posed photograph typical of the early Sixties. Private collection

243

postcards for the fan-clubs which were starting up all over the place because of an idol's popularity, record shop prospectuses for parties or promotions of some sort, record

Photomontage for the magazine *Elle* by Roman Cieslewicz – along with Hubert Knapp, Helmut Newton and William Klein, he revolutionized fashion photography, 1964.

Private collection

Right:

Double page by Roman Cieslewicz for *Vogue*, a magazine that together with *Elle* and *Marie-Claire* defended the new aesthetic approach.

Private collection

244

sleeves, small and large posters, giant ones even to be exhibited on street hoardings, enlargements for television programmes, all sorts of advertising, and double centre-page spreads to be used as posters and stuck up on the walls of teenagers' bedrooms. Special care was lavished on record sleeves – the picture of the star had to be as flattering as possible: the aim was to sell, and the extremely rich record shops encouraged these promotions. The square shape of the 45 rpm sleeve was particularly popular with the public. Some photographers who were already adept at composition showed great talent in portraying these new, still young and inexperienced faces.

From being the craftsman who manufactured dreams, the photographer could himself become a star. The case of Jean-Marie Périer, *SLC*'s pet photographer, still provides the best example, a case of the biter bitten! Some Pop stars who were more photogenic than others were photographed for fashion magazines. Françoise Hardy, for instance, with a thin physique resembling that of Twiggy or Jean Shrimpton, was specially well suited to modelling work. Other very young girls

were shown in suggestive poses, almost offered, along with coveted or consumer objects, on the front page of magazines.

The cover of a book published in 1987 describing *Les Années de chrome*[5] shows a superb saloon car stopped on the Champs-Élysées with Johnny (Hallyday) at the wheel. The picture is distinguished by the angle from which it was taken, skilfully studied to highlight the object – the car – and its user – the idol. The diagonal effect with the vanishing trace receding towards the Place de l'Étoile shifts the photograph into the realms of imagination and yearning. The use of an already old photographic technique, with low-angle or high-angle shots, or inverting the vanishing trace, magnifies this symbol of wealth and affluence, yet of plaintiveness too, a symbol characterizing that generation of consumers of images. Those images had to reflect fashion, youth and a generation that was on the move. Of course that photograph was taken for promotional purposes, but viewed from this distance in time it becomes invaluable sociological testimony.

The fashion photographer (maker of images, manufacturer of dreams)

Fashion photography was the aspect of photography that immediately benefited most from the technological advances of these years, because there was potentially more money in it. If the late Fifties marked the beginning of a social downgrading and demystification of fashion, with the development of off-the-peg clothes, they were also the beginning of major

transformations which would allow photographers to work with great freedom of manoeuvre. The possibility of immediately controlling light, colour, framing and the image, thanks to Polaroids – still very expensive – was still the preserve of professionals. This made it possible to select images before 'tackling' them definitively. The new Balkar electronic flashes which could recharge in under half a second, replacing the excessively slow Strob flashes, or the rapid motor-driven Bolex Paillard 16 mm cameras gave photographers greater freedom. Shots could be taken in rapid succession, like the splutter of machine-gun fire, while zooms made it possible to move very quickly into and out from a detail. All this highly sophisticated equipment, obtainiable virtually without restriction, resulted in superb quality and made possible, *ad infinitum* by allowing all sorts of fine feats, even the creation of 'live fashion'.

Initially magazines would not accept 24 x 36 mm negatives, which they regarded as too small, and they seldom accepted 6 x 6 Ektachromes, preferring 13 x 18 or even 24 x 30 and bigger, which did not make the photographer's job any easier. This work still meant using large-format cameras but gradually, with preferences varying, Leica, Rolleiflex and Hasselblad came to be highly prized. Photographers worked in studios, often in teams, following a specific commission – while this placed restrictions on their imagination it was also exciting. Besides the photographer the team or staff consisted of hairdressers, make-up artists and assistants (electricians, camera operators, film editors etc.). The role of hairdressers and make-up artists (good ones were few and far between – they had to be hunted down all over the world) was important for photographers who snapped up

female models, transforming them into consumer goodies rather than into all too fleeting images. The presence, warmth and competence of the model was crucial to the correct correlation between desire and the final object. These young women had to 'give themselves' and use their bodies like instruments. Peter Knapp said that good models tended to be girls who had previously studied at art school, and therefore understood the end purpose of an image. So success depended on the bipolar relationship between photographer and model.

Fashion photographers were a fairly small group working together for the same magazines and agencies, and they soon achieved celebrity status. By the end of the Sixties the public would easily recognize the authors of photographs, the 'dream merchants' whose images jostled the world of the imagination, creating phantasms to whet consumers' appetites. The use of colour, appealing and just a mite 'tarty', would provide a still wider creative field than black and white through a varied chromatic palette, but it was not necessarily richer when it came to creative inventiveness.

Fashion photography had always been a prestige symbol, hallowed like everything closely or even remotely associated with *haute couture*. It had already been taken out on to the street by Richard Avedon, and would display itself there extravagantly, thus becoming a coveted object. The photographer became the messenger of our dreams: in our homes; through lavishly illustrated fashion magazines he offered all women the chance to be as beautiful as the models. This presentation sold clothes by showing them to their best advantage: business coupled with the imaginary.

Double page by Roman Cieslewicz for *Vogue*. Private collection

245

The sixties, utopian years

Like music and the emergence of Pop idols, fashion photography, with its rather soft emphasis and adulterated naturalness, reached France from the United States, and great photographers worked more or less for American-based magazines which had subsidiaries in Paris, like *Vogue* or *Harper's Bazar*. Inheriting the legacy of the American-made advertising culture as well as the work of their predecessors in the Thirties and Forties, like Edward Steichen or George Hoyningen-Huene, the number of such craftsmen, pastors of fashion, was relatively low. Heirs also to Willy Maywald or the Seeberger brothers (photography was a Seeberger family tradition) who dominated fashion photography in France in the Fifties, followed by the great humanist photographers, Robert Doisneau, Brassaï or Henri Cartier-Bresson, Sixties' photographers profited from the irresistible evolution of morals and customs reflected in their images, catching the reader's eye, using black and white images or colour ones, depending on what the photographer was seeking to achieve.

European fashion had for some time been overshadowed by the war, with the focus shifting to the United States, but in the early Sixties it was about to make a comeback, reasserting its claim to distinction and regaining full strength. Thus the magazine *Elle*, the leader among women's magazines, set about demonstrating the renaissance of high fashion, using every trick in the book: as well as appeal, it also showed imagination, mixing sometimes provocative boldness with an aesthetic sense. The role of such magazines was to become very important, and they were the real promoters of photography, often assigning it considerable budgets.

qu'est-ce que c'est ? une laine nouvelle la pure laine vierge contrôlée

Great names became established. Often these photographers had first worked as painters or in design. This generation of 'women's men' (very few photographers were female), French or foreign, with their bountifully fertile imaginations, would permanently and pleasurably fix extravagant images of luxury in our minds. For example there is a picture created in 1962 by William Klein for the magazine *Vogue*, showing two models in an absurdist setting at the Musée Grévin (waxworks and illusions), simultaneously hallowing and demystifying the waxwork figures. Mickey and Antonia mingle gracefully with characters who seem to belong to another age. Their dresses stand out amidst motionless silhouettes suggesting absence. Great actors, writers and film-makers are there in wax: Ingmar Bergman, Anthony Perkins, Georges Simenon, Louise de Vilmorin, Françoise Sagan, Jean Cocteau, Pablo Picasso and René Clair; the flesh-and-blood models move inside this static scene, bursting forth from it. Klein, who was a great fashion reporter and photographer, wanted to be a photographer at the centre of the action, putting himself at the very heart of what he depicted. When he had just been voted the best photographer in the history of photography at Fotokina 1963 in Cologne, Klein said of his work: 'I photograph what I see in front of me. I go up close to see better and usually use a wide angle to fill the frame to the maximum.' In 1965 he (temporarily) abandoned still photography for the cinema.

Though Klein would always be provocative, Guy Bourdin who worked for *Vogue* and *Elle* was just as controversial, with his choices of framing often showing just part of a body (the foot, hand or back ...) to present the consumer object. The attitudes of his models and his extremely unconventional settings show that he was someone who seemed not to want to let himself be trapped by formalism or the commonplace. Working in an open-minded way he chose to show women as beautiful and sophisticated in an original manner.

Like Richard Avedon, Frank Horvat, who constantly magnifies women, takes us outside the studio, magnanimously setting his subjects amidst everyday life. He gets his models moving in the very heart of society, in the street, in bars or restaurants, at the races, in department stores or other public places. His taste for doing so touched on the antagonism between the photographic subject – the object of desire – and commonplace or magnified reality. The lights were skilfully studied since they would be taken to be real, and the angle of the shot verged on the anodyne, in a flirtation with reality. The illusion is there and the model seems all the grander. The sought-after effect of exaggerated realism is achieved.

A possible descendant of Irving Penn or Erwin Blumenfeld, from the early Sixties Peter Knapp was seen as the paragon of fashion photography, an authority, and and his work a benchmark. Originally Swiss, he had studied at the Bauhaus (a mediator between art and industry) and started his career in graphic art, advertising and painting. He very quickly became the artistic director of *Elle* magazine and with the total agreement of its editor Hélène Gordon-Lazareff he set about redefining its brand image. This operation involved photography and Peter Knapp decided to produce his pictures himself. Like his British counterpart David Bailey, Knapp played on the close relationship between the photographer and his model, on the connivance or complicity between them or the reciprocal trust they gave one another. He put himself in the role of a man desiring and seducing a woman in order to make his pictures more alive. He constructed his photographs round the model and the clothes, coaxingly using colour, glamour, lightness of touch and charm, exploiting all the new technical possibilities with talent. In the end his most splendid photographs are those allying space, the void and black and white geometry. He worked in the subtlety of dislocation, full lines intersecting and hitting one another, following the geometric creations of André Courrèges or Paco Rabanne. His contributions to the television programme *Dim, Dam, Dom* take us into geometric delights which have been compared to the rigidity of the rigorous and systematic approach of a sector of the German *avant-garde*. His colour presentations of shoes from the top makers give an unusual vision of women: a truncated body viewed from above leaving only the long legs, sometimes adorned with stockings or tights, in an extremely sober yet descriptive high-angle shot. Peter Knapp worked in a lavishly equipped studio and seems to be dancing attendance on these women, thus enabling him to 'play' with the images and reveal his own phantasms so as – perhaps! – to share them.

Finally there was Sarah Moon, the only woman fashion photographer in this early Sixties period, a former model who worked a lot with the couturier Cacharel. Her trademarks are her intimist pastel colours hesitating between the pictorialism of the Twenties, a subtle subjectivity, a sophisti-

Mafia bag by Roman Cieslewicz, 1970.
Private collection

247

The sixties, utopian years

Photographs by
Bernard Plossu of life
on the road, *Le Voyage
mexicain*, 1965–6.
Private collection

Photographs by
Bernard Plossu on
hippies and freaks,
Le Voyage mexicain,
1965–6.
Private collection

cation which speaks to our unconscious through the sense of strangeness emanating from the images, and an immense tenderness conveyed by the opaqueness of the filters and the cameo-like nature of the tones.

The 'author'-photographer ('Sous les clichés, la plage' – Beneath the snaps, the beach)

Humanist photography had not yet been sacrificed to fashions from elsewhere, and the pillars of those images of everyday life were still very much present, whereas on the other side of the Atlantic the craziest trends were fomenting new ideas. The actual photographic equipment was less important in this field than for photographs of fashion or the stars, and obviously the leading figures showed a strong preference for Rolleiflex or Leica cameras. Henri Cartier-Bresson, Robert Doisneau, Willy Ronis, Édouard Boubat, Pierre Jahan and a great many others (male) were still the undisputed masters and were imitated by the younger generation: the picture as witness of the everyday, the commonplace or the comical was very much in evidence. And the humorous and indignant photographs of René Maltête, completely forgotten today, were published in album form,[6] exuberantly recounted unimportant, burlesque details of the period. Amongst these photographers of everyday life J.-P. Charbonnier, a precursor of what lay ahead, produced disturbing photographs of something else that has now become familiar, the world of mental hospitals in 1954. These arresting images show a new approach already going beyond simple reportage, and are the first indicators of contemporary thought.

During the Sixties Lucien Clergue explored the naked female body tossed by the ocean waves. From 1963 John Batho started his study of colour and composition. A few women stand out in this solidly male fraternity: Sabine Weiss (for a time Willy Maywald's assistant), Agnès Varda (who worked in Avignon in the theatre), Janine Niépce (a powerful, dynamic and militant feminist), Thérèse Le Prat (with her well-known mask-faces) and Martine Franck (who collaborated with the actors in Ariane Mnouchkine's Théâtre du Soleil company). Yet it was becoming important, perhaps even urgent, for the reporter to change his shoulder-height lens in order to capture the isolated reality of a fraction of a second, the 'likeness', and express it 'differently'.

It was really from the Sixties that the idea of photography started to change. With the opening of galleries, more frequent exhibitions and the publishing of art books, it could take its place in a field that had previously been the preserve of 'artists'. Photographers wanted photography to be recognized as an art, and then they themselves wanted to be regarded as artists. Very quickly a large number of exhibition areas opened up in Paris and the provinces (Limoges, Grenoble, Châlons-sur-Marne, Bièvres, Foix, Épinal, Toulouse ...). In 1972 Paris was full of photographic exhibition spaces, with galleries such as Daniel-Templon, Zabriskie, La Demeure, Montalembert, FNAC, Rencontre, Multitude, Nikon, 2C-2A (rue Saint-Sulpice), Du quai des Fleurs, Des Quatre-Vents, Camille-Renaud etc. At the same period Claude Nori, an advertising and fashion photographer, opened his publishing firm Contrejour, which succeeded or served as a counterpart to the classic publications of the Fifties produced by Robert Delpire. Nori enabled a large number of photographers from the same generation to get their work appreciated.

The photographer's point of reference would continue to be all his thoughts about life. Thus photographers would set out to be chroniclers of the social scene in which only its inner truth was important. When working as reporters attached to agencies or journals, their work consisted of providing as much information as possible about a given subject so that it could be exploited quickly and lucratively, with no recognition other than the payment made by the client. The excessive disparity between the reporter, the photo-club amateur and the photographic artist caused the reporter to become more demanding in what he did, and towards the end of the Sixties – after the May '68 troubles to be more specific – several photographers banded together with the ideal of 'describing the same thing' with different images as their stated common aim. They wanted reportage to be included in aesthetic photography – while retaining a separate identity – or to integrate their universe, their personal reality, into social behaviour. This was the origin of the Viva agency founded in 1972; its founder members, Claude-Raymond Dityvon (the group's moving spirit), Hervé Gloaguen, François Hers, Martine Franck, Jean Lattès, Guy Le Querrec, Alain Dagueberre and Richard Kalvar, were in search of a truth and worked on elaborating it. They

Cover of the first
issue of the
magazine *Photo*,
June 1967

very soon parted company: the communal experiment was not entirely successful. Their vision seemed too alike, with people even speaking of 'Viva photos'. Later they all followed their own 'anchorite' path or moved to other already established organizations.

While photographing stars and fashion and photography derived from idealist associations are based on team work, the author-photographer's work is a solitary creative act: interior, intimist photography engaging in a dialogue with a ritual that defies periods and fashions. Claude Batho said: 'My photographs are filled with the passage of time over children, people and things. I set out to make very simple moments perceptible, to preserve their silences...' In 1972 François-Xavier Bouchart, the first French photographer to work with the panoramic technique, embarked on an extraordinary adventure, which would last until 1977, between the world of Marcel Proust and his own inner world. His vision, full of delicate touches, leads us into an extremely personal and sensitive dreamlike atmosphere. The image of a long silent bedroom, bathed in serene light and simply decorated, plunges us into that Proustian universe and one almost has to be silent to take in all that is there (*La Chambre de tante Léonie, Illiers-Combray*). From 1967 Pierre Bérenger, Gilles Ehrmann's assistant, went regularly to the Grande Galerie of the Muséum d'Histoire naturelle in Paris (closed to the public), which is full of stuffed wild animals and where a heavy dusty ambience prevails, on the outer edge of reality, to carry out a black and white study of these huge, silent, Surrealist beasts. Roger Vulliez produced bitingly humorous self-portraits. In the post-'68 period these 'hunters of images'[7], more alone than ever, set out on great journeys through the world, seeking to conquer an 'elsewhere' that would be different and perhaps better. It was a complex period and never before had there been such a profusion and effervescence of creative ideas in photography. Thus hippie-style *Easy rider* (a legendary US film of the Seventies) journeys, made easier by the expansion of the means of communication and transport, allowed these 'heralds' of modern times to satisfy their ideals. Bernard Plossu, a young hitchhiker who undertook an initiatory journey to Mexico between 1965 and 1966, describes his travels:

I travelled with a little camera with no express desire to be an important person in society. All I wanted was to describe the journey, the road, the friends, the freedom, to hover over them. I had been nurtured on images from films and my 'masters' and reference points were Bresson or Dreyer, and at the time I had no knowledge of photography. I learnt with the camera.[8]

He worked in colour using a wide-angle lens, selling his pictures to geographical magazines like *Atlas*. He later destroyed all his colour negatives, feeling that his personal field of research was defined by black and white, using an ordinary lens. The black and white pictures of his travels in Mexico, with no commentary, are confirmation of his view: social reportage (provided it includes an intention to report) can indeed be creative photography. Jean-Claude Gautrand, a historian of photography, very soon gave his regular and enthusiastic support to all these young 'researchers into photography'.

Following these new ways of looking an even more individual school was formed, centring its ideas on photography as an art and medium. The Seventies saw the start of photography considered as a fine art, like the searches carried out in the context of modernity in the Twenties (Man Ray, Marcel Duchamp). The old quarrel, photography versus painting versus art versus documentary, was aggravated still further, and was expressed through photographic works which dabbled in the great artistic trends of the day: Pop art, land art, performance art or happenings, in all their ecstasy. The debate is still in progress. Artists like Ben, Christian Boltanski or Yves Klein (d. 1962) made noted forays into the photographic field, telling a story with snaps of commonplace everyday life to which they added a text clarifying how to interpret them, though it did not take the form of captions. The example of Boltanski, an *avant-garde* painter 'who does not use a paintbrush', a photographer and a freelance artist, is also fairly representative of the late Sixties. At that time intellectual rather than intuitive examination of the past, of childhood – reconstituting other people's – seemed to be his main preoccupation, the distinguishing mark of his 'work'. His pictures with a commentary relating to simple objects from the everyday life of the past (unmade bed, child's pyjamas ...) take us back to reflecting about the ego and the interest of the stuff of art. Like Ben he put photography by photography-lovers on the level of contemporary art. A major exhibition of photographs at the Musée d'Art moderne de la Ville de Paris in 1970 sanctioned the relevance of his work. In the view of Michel Frizot, a historian of photography: 'Photography has "entered art", not by adopting the objectives or the appearance of painting, but by substituting the photographic medium for the canvas and stretcher rejected by a number of artists.' This profusion of ideas arising in the aftermath of '68 still influences our current lines of research.

With the entry of all these images, from the worlds of variety and fashion or from author-photographers, into museum collections or major galleries, the concept of photographic creativity was finally accepted. From 1950 to the end of the Seventies the Bibliothèque nationale was the only place where photographers were acknowledged; it regularly showed them at an annual national Salon. It was also the first French establishment to set up a real photographic collection, on a par with its collections of prints, engravings or manuscripts. It now has a rich assembly of material from the Sixties, proving that the photographic act as a creative act exists on the same basis as that of the acts of the artist or writer. The controversy and argument are far from over.

Thérèse Blondet-Bisch

1. Marie de Thézy, ed., *La Photographie humaniste, 1930–60. Histoire d'un mouvement*, Paris, Contrejour, 1992.

2. Ektachrome: a positive colour transparency of varying dimensions (24 x 36 to 18 x 24 mm and over) giving very precise image definition.

3. Chambre: a usually large-format bellows camera the lens of which forms the image directly on to the glass plate or the single negative.

4. Reflex: camera with a mirror that reflects the image in the lens on to a glass viewfinder. The first Rolleiflex reflex camera dates from 1929.

5. Jean-Marc Thévenet, *1960: Les Années de chrome*, Paris, Du May, 1987.

6. René Maltête, *Au petit bonheur la France*, Paris, Hachette, 1964.

7. An expression borrowed from the photographer François Tuefferd who uses it humorously to define his work.

8. Conversation with Bernard Plossu, 25 October 1995.

References (*Magazines, television programmes, shows*)

1960: There were eleven magazines devoted to photography (often coupled with cinema) for amateur enthusiasts, professionals or academics (cf. *Le Répertoire de la presse française*, H. Raux, Paris, La Documentation française), including *Photo-ciné-revue* created in 1888 at the same time as the first Kodak camera was created by George Eastman. The Swiss magazine *Caméra* was very successful. Its chief editor, Roméo Marinez, was an important figure in the world of photography.

1960: *Art roman du soleil* exhibition by Jean Dieuzaide in Toulouse, then in

1962 at the Pavillon de Marsan in the Louvre, Paris.

1962: *Retina revue*, intended for a limited, technical readership; ed. M. Cordier.

1962–5: The writer Michel Tournier directed a television programme on photography, *Chambre noire*, with the participation of Jean Dieuzaide.

1963: The 'Libre Expression' group founded by Jean-Claude Gautrand and Jean Dieuzaide.

1963: *Photographie nouvelle*, free independent magazine created by Henri Calba.

1964: *Terre d'images*, fortnightly publication.

1965–7: Peter Knapp with Daisy de Galard directs the television programme *Dim, Dam, Dom*, with Jean-François Jonvelle contributing his note of freshness.

1965: *Photographies et Paris* exhibition, Musée des Arts décoratifs, Paris.

1966: *Bandes à part*, magazine created by François Jouffa to supplant *SLC*.

1967: *Photo* first published in June with a dishevelled Catherine Deneuve on the cover holding several sophisticated cameras in her hands, under the heading 'The professionals helping the amateurs'. Daniel Filipacchi was its founder and editor.

1970: The first Rencontres internationales de la photographie (RIP) are held in Arles, giving official sanction to the actual idea of photographic creativity.

1970: First publication of the magazine *Zoom*.

1970: Major photographic exhibition at the Musée d'Art moderne de la Ville de Paris.

1973: *Le Nouveau Photo-Cinéma*, a monthly magazine, ed. Pierre and Roger Montel, Paris (taking over from *Photo-cinéma*).

1973: A photography course is set up at the ENSBA (École nationale supérieure des beaux-arts, Paris).

The two associations Gens d'images and 30/40 (a real breeding ground for the exchange of ideas in the Seventies) continued their long-established activities.

Bibliography

Michel and Michèle Auer, *Encyclopédie internationale des photographes de 1839 à nos jours*, Hermance, Camera Obscura, 1985

'De l'instant à l'imaginaire. 1939–70', *Histoire de voir*, no. 42, Photopoche, Paris, Centre national de la photographie, 1989

Michel Frizot, ed., *Nouvelle Histoire de la photographie*, Paris, Bordas and Adam Biro, 1994

Bernard Plossu, foreword by Sergio Leone, *Le Surbanalisme, séquences photographiques*, Paris, Le Chêne, 1972

Bernard Plossu, foreword by Denis Roche, *Le Voyage mexicain, 1965–6. Carnet de voyage*, Paris, Contrejour, 1979, reissued 1992

Naomi Rosenblum, foreword by Anne Cartier-Bresson, *Une Histoire mondiale de la photographie*, Paris, Abbeville Press, 1992 (trans. of the work originally pub. 1984)

Vanités, Paris. Centre national de la photographie, 1993

Sigma: London counter-culture

W riting in 1971 Peter Stansill and David Mairowitz observed that the nature of subcultural (or counter-cultural) underground activity had identifiably changed in 1965:

the gloomy earnestness of the 'protest' mentality is displaced by a new 'tough' frivolity and creative lunacy ... the debate is no longer between Right wing/Left wing, but rather between the oppressions of the external world and the desire for internal liberation, between activist commitment to the continuing social struggle and dropping out of a cultural milieu that won't allow it.[1]

The groundwork for this shifting position had largely been carried out by the writer, sculptor and cultural activist Alexander Trocchi in the decade before 1965. In Paris, New York, Mexico and London he forged a project whereby the alienated individual might triumph and take part in an 'Invisible insurrection of a million minds'.

At the 1962 Edinburgh Festival, Trocchi declared that 'Modern art begins with the destruction of the object. All vital creation is at the other side of nihilism. It begins after Nietzsche and after Dada'.[2] Speed, violence, engagement and the negation of any artistic or other categorization provided the leitmotif for a generation that enacted a retreat from the word as much as from the object and the past; a creation of new time and new space.

Twice, during the 1967 congress 'The dialectics of liberation: towards a demystification of violence', speakers told the story of how, during the Paris Commune the Communards shot at all the clocks in Paris and broke them, putting an end to the time of their rulers, and inventing their own time.[3] Just as the Communards held time in contempt, in the Sixties John Latham accused words of constricting freedom of thought and as a result chewed them up or burnt them down, while William Burroughs saw words as agents of systems of control that had to be cut up, dislocated, subverted. Similarly, Regis Debray[4] wrote at the same time of liberation as a freeing of the present from the past. To both Trocchi and Burroughs time had given way to the demands of space. The demands of being a 'Cosmonaut of Inner Space'[5] forged a new grammar and language that was in Trocchi's terms meta-categorical and avowedly non-Aristotelian; 'to free themselves from the conventional object and thus pass freely beyond non-categories, the twentieth century artist finally destroyed the object'.[6] Present Time became a place without defining objects, a space in which intersections could be mapped and where new horizons could be sought; a space in which an alienated state of being could be deconstructed and so provide a platform for the subversion of social and cultural norms.

For William Burroughs, points of intersection were mapped by his use of the cut-up and fold-in techniques, discovered in October 1959 by Brion Gysin.[7] Their potential for laying out a fragmented time of experience on the space of the printed page, akin to browsing through a newspaper from column to column, was recognized by Burroughs, and between 1964 and 1966 he utilized this column format for his regular cut-up contributions for Jeff Nuttall's mimeographed magazine *My own mag,* variously entitled 'The Burrough' or 'The Moving Times'. In 1962 Burroughs had claimed that through the cut-up: 'I am acting as a map maker, an explorer of psychic areas .... And I see no point in exploring areas that have already been thoroughly surveyed.'[8] He believed that these random juxtapositions of words pointed to another consciousness for which the technique became the medium for prophecy. Instead of telling stories, re-combined words now held the space of future time: 'Tomorrow's news today'.[9]

The cut-up decisively announced a dematerialization of narrative in which words charted experience and where the authorial voice was questioned. In the words of Hassan I Sabbah, 'Nothing is true, everything is permitted'.[10] This renunciation of narrative threatened traditional comprehension and brought about a new relationship between the author and reader that prefigures Jacques Derrida's later recognition of a complex web of textuality wherein, 'nothing remains but an immense web of reading and writing, folding, unfolding and refolding indefinitely. The reading of it is no longer external to the writing.'[11]

The charting of intersection points was, for Trocchi, as for Burroughs, characterized by a fissuring of the wordscape. In Edinburgh he had explained how he aimed to continue 'writing, stumbling across tundras of unmeaning, planting words like bloody flags in my wake. Loose ends, things unrelated, shifts, night journeys, cities arrived at and left, meetings, desertions, betrayals, all manner of unions, triumphs, defeats'.[12] This listing of his subject matter clarifies

Photograph by Robert Whitaker of Allen Ginsberg in Hyde Park, London, 1967

the nature of his alienation from the norms of society that he intended to subvert as 'a member of a new underground'.[13] From 1963 he identified this underground with Project Sigma in providing the motivation and means for a 'meta-categorical revolution', for the 'Invisible insurrection of a million minds'; a 'coup du monde'.

Between 1952 and 1955 Trocchi had been the editor of *Merlin*. Published in Paris, it quickly positioned itself at the leading-edge of the *avant-garde*, printing Ionesco, Beckett, Sartre, Genet, Brassaï, Corneille, Hayter and Austryn Wainhouse's study of Sade. At this early date Trocchi saw his fight as being against political, social and aesthetic absolutism,[14] and his departure from Scotland and arrival in Paris is unsurprising, being the result of the 'very unsophisticated attitude towards the notion of engagement on the part of my contemporaries in London'.[15] This was no narrow political engagement but suggested that the outsider should be *engagé* by a form of *dégagement* from the prevailing notions of reality. To be *engagé* in such a situation was to go beyond politics, beyond categories and categorization, beyond tradition and beyond traditional manifestations of language. His use of drugs, and especially heroin from 1954, played a part in this, while his meeting, in 1954, with Guy Debord, and subsequent involvement with the Lettriste Internationale (LI), offered another frame through which cultural revolution could be lived and realized.[16] Although Trocchi left for America in 1956 and did not return to London until 1961,

Alexander Trocchi, 'The Moving Times'. Private collection

Debord still counted him an ally, making him a founder-member (in his absence) of the Situationniste Internationale (SI). When, in September 1960, he was arrested for contravening American drug laws the SI took up his case during their 4th congress, published 'Hands off Alexander Trocchi' in October 1960 and agitated for his release.

On his escape to London, and certainly by June 1962, Trocchi was back in regular contact with Debord.[17] This, coupled with the encouragement he gained from his first meeting with Burroughs in Edinburgh in August, pushed him into developing his own position, and this was made clear with the publication in the January 1963 edition of *Internationale Situationniste* of his essay 'Technique du coup du monde', the founding and defining manifesto of what became Project Sigma. Although Debord had encouraged him to write this text and had been supportive of its thesis,[18] by the time Trocchi had launched Project Sigma in 1964 a break with SI was inevitable.[19]

The first three items that initiated the *Sigma Portfolio*, 'The Moving Times' broadsheet poster, 'Invisible insurrection of a million minds' (the English version of 'Technique du coup du monde'), and 'Sigma: A tactical blueprint', were assembled in 1963-4 and give an indication of its elusive aims and its fluidly contingent identity. Project Sigma's publications were ephemeral, low-cost and flexible and echoed the LI's *Potlatch* in form and intention; a gift of ideas which might spark an exchange and response. This was at one with Trocchi's Situationist[20] belief that any progress or evolution lay in embracing the notion of the meta-category, where specialization breaks down: 'It is no doubt because conventional classifications become part of prevailing economic structure that all real revolt is hastily fixed like a bright butterfly on a classificatory pin ... question the noun; the present participles of the verb will look after themselves'.[21] To define Sigma would destroy its potential for achieving spontaneous revolution, and 'it would be misleading ... to differentiate between its communicative and research aspects, since there was no question of there being some (static) informations to be communicated, but rather a way of life (a creative posture) to be adopted and lived infectiously'.[22] To these ends, Trocchi admitted that Project Sigma may seem to be 'imperfect, fragmentary and inarticulate ... it is now in the process of becoming conscious of itself'.[23]

Such a programme of ill-defined action called for an absolute and urgent engagement with the flow of life (at the core of Trocchi's thought was the idea of a 'Spontaneous University'), and this he signalled by adopting Artaud's uncompromising words: 'We must believe in a sense of life in which man fearlessly makes himself master of what does not yet exist, and brings it into being ... Furthermore, when we speak the word "life" [we refer] ... to that fragile, fluctuating centre which forms never reach. And if there is still one hellish, truly accursed thing in our time, it is our artistic dallying with forms, instead of being like victims burnt at the stake, signalling through the flames.'[24]

Project Sigma was born into a time of alienation when the world seemed 'at the edge of extinction',[25] and Trocchi

HANDS OFF ALEXANDER TROCCHI

For several months the British writer Alexander Trocchi has been kept in prison in New York.

He is the former director of the revue "Merlin", and now he participates in experimental art research in collaboration with artists from several countries, who were regrouped on September 28th in London in the Institute of Contemporary Arts (17, Dover Street). On that occasion they unanimously expressed in public their solidarity with Alexander Trocchi, and their absolute certainty of the value of his comportment.

Alexander Trocchi, whose case is due to be tried in October, is, in effect, accused of having experimented in drugs.

Quite apart from any attitude on the use of drugs and its repression on the scale of society, we recall that it is notorious that a very great many doctors, psychologists and also artists have studied the effects of drugs without anyone thinking of imprisoning them. The poet Henri Michaux has hardly been spoken of in recent years except on the successive publications of his books announced everywhere as written under the influence of mescaline.

Indeed we consider that the British intellectuals and artists should be the first to join with us in denouncing this menacing lack of culture on the part of the American police, and to demand the liberation and immediate repatriation of Alexander Trocchi.

Since it is generally recognized that the work of a scientist or an artist implies certain small rights, even in the U.S.A., the main question is to bear witness to the fact that Alexander Trocchi is effectively an artist of the first order. This could be basely contested *for the sole reason that he is a new type of artist*, pioneer of a new culture and a new comportment (the question of drugs being in his own eyes minor and negligable).

All the artists and intellectuals who knew Alexander Trocchi in Paris or London ought to bear witness without fail to his authentic artistic status, to enable the authorities in Great Britain to take the necessary steps in the U.S.A. in favour of a British subject. Those who would refuse to do this now will be judged guilty themselves when the judgment of the history of ideas will no longer allow one to question the importance of the artistic innovation of which Trocchi has been to a great extent responsible.

We ask everyone of good faith whom this appeal reaches, to sign it, and to make it known as widely as possible.

October 7th, 1960

Guy DEBORD, Jacqueline de JONG, Asger JORN.

Address : 32, rue de la Montagne-Sainte-Geneviève, Paris-5e

chose the title 'Sigma' as a neutral term to indicate the necessity of beginning 'with the fact of being alone: the one ultimate: consciousness presupposes it .... Now, consciously, spontaneously, to live with others: tentatively ...'.[26] Trocchi felt that it was necessary to reject the whole political and social structure that contributed to alienation; the cultural revolution was to be 'the necessary underpinning, the passionate substructure of a new order of things'.[27] Artaud had called for the death of the object and for the beginning of a new experiential language of theatre that was not representation but life and would live. Artaud, as Trocchi here, was not contemplating a 'symbol of an absent void' but went beyond a nihilist stance to offer a positive affirmation of a new cultural and social way of living that attacked mimesis and the effect of categorization whether in Theatre or Politics. Trocchi liked to play on words and suggested that he was not calling for revolution but evolution; a '(r)evolt' that was characterized as 'a transition of necessity more complex, more diffuse than the [*coup d'état*], and so more gradual, less spectacular .... What is to be seized is ourselves'.[28]

The 'Poets of the world/Poets of our time' event, organized in part by Project Sigma, at the Albert Hall on 11 June 1965 offered an example of the Spontaneous University in action as much as of the emergent underground whose sprawling nature Project Sigma so well encapsulated.[29] Similarly the creation of the *sTigma* environment four months earlier in February 1965 in the basement of Better

Broadside: 'Hands off Alexander Trocchi'. Private collection

257

The sixties, utopian years

Books, by a number of artists, such as Bruce Lacey and Criton Tomazos, who were grouped around Nuttall and Latham, showed artists trying to project ideals of social and political engagement and achieve change by altering the actual contexts within which the work of art might operate. Recalling this work, Nuttall stressed that, 'We were eaten up by repressed violence and we were soured by the constant terror of inconceivable violence being committed on ourselves and the rest of man'.[30] The environment reflected a feeling for sickness and suggested what Gustav Metzger, who the following year would organize the 'Destruction In Art Symposium', termed the 'aesthetic of revulsion'.[31] Trocchi had already realized the closeness of art to language,[32] now art could be seen to be moving closer to the conditions of life.

Trocchi's suggestion – 'Art can have no existential significance for a civilization which draws a line between life and art...; we envisage a situation in which life is continually renewed by art, a situation imaginatively and passionately constructed to inspire each individual to respond creative-

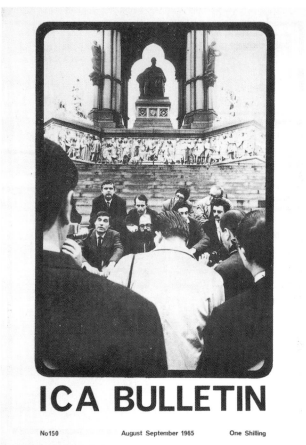

ICA BULLETIN

No 150   August September 1965   One Shilling

ly'[33] – was being realized. He also intended Project Sigma to be a catalyst in the cultural debate around perceptions of external oppression and expression as well as the desire for internal liberation. One means of achieving this aim was in the place Trocchi gave to drugs, where the fragmented

word had been forged out of a sustained use of heroin. In *Cain's book*, Trocchi had described a heroin fix in terms of both a dislocation of traditional language and the creation of a heightened language of an individual, alienated, yet total, experience. Categorization becomes irrelevant.

> The mind under heroin evades perception as it does ordinarily; one is aware only of contents .... The perceiving turns inward, the eyelids droop, the blood is aware of itself .... The ritual itself, the powder in the spoon, the little ball of cotton, the matches applied, the bubbling liquid drawn up through the cotton filter into the eye-dropper, the tie round the arm to make the vein stand out, the fix often slow because a man will stand there with the needle in the vein and allow the level in the eye-dropper to waver up and down, up and down, until there is more blood than heroin in the dropper – all this is not for nothing, it is born of a respect for the whole chemistry of alienation.[34]

In June 1964 he wrote to Burroughs with the news that 'we've connected with some off-beat psychiatrists who will collaborate in our drugs and the mind laboratory (one of the aspects of the spontaneous U) .... I am meeting them ... to talk about a large premises for Sigma'.[35] These anti-psychiatrists, R.D. Laing, Aaron Esterson, David Cooper, Leon Redler and, later, Joe Berke, had founded The Philadelphia Foundation, and the curative ambience of its Center for Treatment and Research, in making little distinction between analyst and analysand in the treatment of schizophrenics, was recognized by Trocchi to be close, in the removal of

Braziers Park John Latham had constructed and ritually burnt his first *Skoob Tower* (a tower made from discarded books that would then be destroyed by fire) and in September he travelled, with Trocchi, to the Edinburgh Festival where he burnt copies of *Cain's book*. Latham's act, as in the case of his 1966 *Skoob Towers*, called for an immaterial sculpture founded on change as one means of opposing a rigidly deterministic culture.

While in New York, R.D. Laing had introduced Sigma to the psychiatrist Joe Berke, who immediately wrote to Trocchi telling him that it 'reiterates and develops ideas

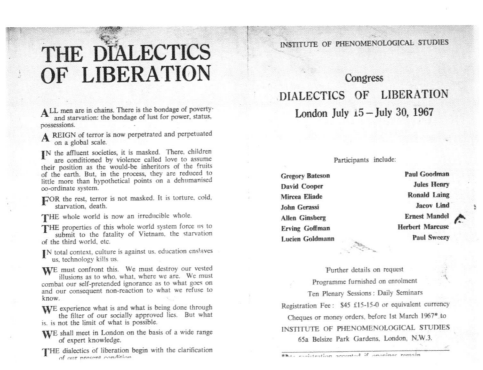

THE DIALECTICS OF LIBERATION

ALL men are in chains. There is the bondage of poverty and starvation: the bondage of lust for power, status, possessions.

A REIGN of terror is now perpetrated and perpetuated on a global scale.

IN the affluent societies, it is masked. There, children are conditioned by violence called love to assume their position as the would-be inheritors of the fruits of the earth. But, in the process, they are reduced to little more than hypothetical points on a dehumanised co-ordinate system.

FOR the rest, terror is not masked. It is torture, cold, starvation, death.

THE whole world is now an irreducible whole.

THE properties of this whole world system force us to submit to the fatality of Vietnam, the starvation of the third world, etc.

IN total context, culture is against us, education enslaves us, technology kills us.

WE must confront this. We must destroy our vested illusions as to who, what, where we are. We must combat our self-pretended ignorance as to what goes on and our consequent non-reaction to what we refuse to know.

WE experience what is and what is being done through the filter of our socially approved lies. But what is, is not the limit of what is possible.

WE shall meet in London on the basis of a wide range of expert knowledge.

THE dialectics of liberation begin with the clarification of our present condition.

INSTITUTE OF PHENOMENOLOGICAL STUDIES

Congress
DIALECTICS OF LIBERATION
London July 15 – July 30, 1967

Participants include:

Gregory Bateson   Paul Goodman
David Cooper   Jules Henry
Mircea Eliade   Ronald Laing
John Gerassi   Jacov Lind
Allen Ginsberg   Ernest Mandel
Erving Goffman   Herbert Marcuse
Lucien Goldmann   Paul Sweezy

Further details on request
Programme furnished on enrolment
Ten Plenary Sessions : Daily Seminars
Registration Fee : $45 £15-15-0 or equivalent currency
Cheques or money orders, before 1st March 1967* to
INSTITUTE OF PHENOMENOLOGICAL STUDIES
65a Belsize Park Gardens, London, N.W.3.

*Late registration accepted if openings remain

Flyer for the 'Dialectics of Liberation' congress, July 1967. Private collection

fixed boundaries, to the creative meta-categorical ambience of '(r)evolt' found in Sigma's Spontaneous University.

As a result Trocchi organized a meeting during the weekend of 2–5 July 1964 at a Quaker commune, Braziers Park, near Reading, to explore mutual action between Project Sigma and the Philadelphia Foundation's anti-psychiatrists.[36] Trocchi's deep-seated Situationist fear of the 'passive spectator' meant that the meeting was unable to formulate a coherent framework of action or definition of Project Sigma. Nevertheless an impetus had been created. At

which I and others here have been on to for some time'.[37] Berke became Sigma's most assiduous propagandist in New York and, with Allen Krebs, founded the Free University of New York in 1965 based on Trocchi's Spontaneous University and encouraged Trocchi to found a similar establishment in London.[38]

In September 1965 Berke left America for London and on his arrival became immediately involved in John Hopkins's attempt to start a Free School in Notting Hill Gate and in research at Kingsley Hall. Trocchi's alienated drug

addict, journeying through inner space towards the formation of a new society, was a corollary of the position of the mad in institutional culture, banished to the margins. The study of madness – and specifically of the schizophrenic – was a central image for a cultural revolution in which there were only participants and no spectators. Just as Project Sigma was described as an 'interpersonal log book', Laing studied schizophrenia by mapping a field of interaction, or 'inter-experience', which eventually led to his reappraisal of the relationship between analyst and analysand. The resemblance to Trocchi's 'Invisible insurrection' is no coincidence, and a speech by Laing (later included in the *Politics of experience*) was distributed as item 6 of the *Sigma Portfolio*. The Anti-University, founded without Trocchi (although he did 'teach' there) but on his principles, was initiated in London in 1968 by the Philadelphia Foundation's Institute of Phenomenological Studies (which had earlier organized the 'Dialectics of Liberation'). It lasted under a year and aimed to 'unify disparate perspectives .... We must do away with artificial splits and divisions between disciplines and art forms and between theory and action'.[39]

Martin Sharp,
cover design for
***Oz*, no. 10, 1968.**
Private collection

By then Project Sigma had all but ceased except on a personal level (reflected in Trocchi's distribution among friends of drafts of his never-finished work *The long book*). The list of contributors to the *Sigma Portfolio,* and the hundreds of people that made up the 'interpersonal log', map the underground, both in London and internationally. The failure by 1968 to define and communicate the aims of Project Sigma characterized most underground activities and its brief re-appearance in 1969, in collaboration with Burroughs, as Pool Cosmonaut hardly changed anything. Counteracting the 'basic modern aggression ... against the individual's right to have his own inner space',[40] again Trocchi claimed the non-existence of Sigma, except on the inter-personal level, and item 37 of the *Sigma Portfolio*, 'My own business' by Burroughs, characterized the 'Invisible insurrection' as an internalized libertarian stance ranged against the forces of state and other interference. Disengagement was complete. And yet even if, faced by the demands of the Vietnam War and the events of May 1968, such a stance failed to measure up adequately to the changing tone of dissent that had become more earnestly politicized and radicalized and less concerned with the theatre of

exploration into inner space, the broad front of the underground (of which Project Sigma was a key part) had succeeded in both questioning and subverting power and its representations. It had shown that everybody could control the means of their expression by preserving 'the present against the past, against a future imposed teleologically ... at the beginning it is important to be wordless'.[41] Ultimately, Trocchi's belief that 'If one accepted "reality", whatever reality, one was already lost',[42] made possible the political dissent of 1968, in which the 'Reality Studio'[43] was stormed.

Andrew Wilson

1. Peter Stansill and David Zane Mairowitz, eds., *BAMN (By any means necessary): outlaw manifestos and ephemera, 1965–70*, Harmondsworth, Penguin, 1971, p.13.
2. Alexander Trocchi, 'The destruction of the object' [1962], 1 page ms note, Trocchi Estate.
3. This story of Walter Benjamin was alluded to by Herbert Marcuse, 'Liberation from the affluent society' in David Cooper, ed., *The dialectics of Liberation*, Harmondsworth, Penguin, 1968, p. 177. See also David Cooper, 'Beyond words', ibid., p. 202.
4. Regis Debray, *Révolution dans la révolution?*, Paris, Librarie François Maspero, 1967; Harmondsworth, Pelican, 1968.
5. Trocchi's phrase at a press conference (August 22) during the Writers Conference organized by John Calder, 1962 Edinburgh Festival. The audiotapes of this conference are in the National Sound Archive, London.
6. Ibid.
7. At this time both Gysin and Burroughs were living in Paris at 9 rue Git-le-

Coeur. Burroughs lived a peripatetic life in Tangier from 1954–9, staying in Paris intermittently between 1958 and 1959. He was in London in 1960 and 1962, Tangier again in 1960 and 1961, Marrakesh and Tangier in 1963 and 1964. He was in St Louis and New York between 1964 and 1965, London again in 1965 (with Christmas in Tangier) and then from 1966 until 1973. In January 1974 he moved to New York.

8. 1962 Writers Conference (August 24), see note 5. See William Burroughs and Brion Gysin, *The third mind*, New York, Viking, 1978, p.95.

9. The first instalment of 'The Moving Times', composed 10 February 1964 and published in *My own mag: William Burroughs Special/Special Tangier edition* [no.5, May 1964], is entitled 'We will Travel not only in Space but in Time as well'. When items cut up in 'The Burrough: Afternoon ticker-tape', *My own mag* [no.6, July 1964], were echoed in the *St Louis Globe Democrat* for 6 January 1965 Burroughs believed that such a connection illustrated 'how incidents were forecast in cross-column readings and cut-ups published in *My own mag* previously .... These are intersection points'. See 'The Moving Times: Tomorrow's news today' in *My own mag*, no.11 [February 1965].

10. The followers of this 11th-century Persian agitator, the Assassins, were fed on hashish. The first book of cut-ups quoted from Hassan's *Razor:* 'Not knowing what is and is not knowing, *I knew not'*, Burroughs, Gysin, Sinclair Beiles and Gregory Corso, *Minutes to go*, Paris, Two Cities, 1960, p.1.

11. Jacques Derrida, *La Dissémination,* Paris, 1972, pp. 217–18, in Gérard Georges Lemaire, '23 stitches taken' in *The third mind,* op. cit. p.20.

12. 1962 Writers Conference (August), see note 5.

13. Trocchi failed to notify the visa authorities of his use of narcotics. When he left the US for England in 1960–61 he was on the run, accused of supplying drugs to a minor: 'I came and went a criminal, or more exactly, a member of a new underground', autobiographical fragment, ts., *c.* 1970, Trocchi Estate.

14. [Alexander Trocchi], editorial, 'Words and war', *Merlin*, 23, summer–autumn, 1954, p.141.

15. Alexander Trocchi, *The Invisible insurrection & other notes (tactical prose of a contemporary pamphleteer)* [July 1966–71], unpub. ts., pp.3–4, Trocchi Estate.

16. Trocchi received *Potlatch* from July 1954 until October 1955. Issue no. 23 (13 October 1955) announced his resignation from *Merlin* and subsequent membership of the LI. He left for America very soon thereafter.

17. There are a number of letters from Debord to Trocchi in the Trocchi Estate, the earliest dated from March 1962. Trocchi was one of the four signatories to the 'Déclaration sur les procès contre l'Internationale Stuationniste en Allemagne Federale' (25 June 1962).

18. A letter (22 October 1962) from Debord to Trocchi, Trocchi Estate, accompanies the first translation of 'Technique du coup du monde' which he admitted to liking, while also suggesting some theoretical fine-tuning: 'I think only one thing needs to be made clear ... : it is that in their rebellion the intelligentsia can win the battle completely only by ultimately securing the disappearance of the separation between those who are currently artists and the non-creative population at large. And this concept can be expressed by adapting an old formula of Marx's as follows: the course of the intelligentsia must be a course "which in winning will lose" (which is the opposite of what has been done in the final analysis by the political bureaucracy made up of professional revolutionaries). I don't think that this goes against your ideas, does it?' Debord wanted Trocchi to attend the 1962 Antwerp conference, where he was made a member of the SI's Central Council and as such was on the editorial board of *Internationale Situationniste* for issue no.8 (January 1963) in which 'Technique du coup du monde' was published, pp.48–56.

19. 'Sur des publications de l'IS', *Internationale Situationniste*, no.10 (March, 1966), p.83, carries the note that since the appearance of Project Sigma's first publications 'it has been agreed by general consent that the *Internationale*

Situationniste could not be committed to such an open cultural research project .... It is no longer as a member of the Internationale situationniste that our friend Alexander Trocchi has since developed an activity several aspects of which we fully approve.'

20. Michèlle Bernstein, 'About the Situationist International', *Times Literary Supplement*, 31 September 1964, p.781: 'As a start they aimed to go beyond artistic specialisation – art as a separate activity – and delve beneath that whole movement for breaking-up of language and dissolution of forms.'

21. Alexander Trocchi, *Cain's book*, London, Calder & Boyars, 1966, p.45.

22. Copy of a letter from Trocchi to Burroughs (12 October 1963), p.2, Trocchi Estate.

23. Alexander Trocchi, 'Sigma: A tactical blueprint', *Sigma Portfolio*, no.3, p.1.

24. Alexander Trocchi, ed., *The Moving Times – Project Sigma*, London, [1964].

25. Alexander Trocchi, 'Invisible insurrection of a million minds', *Sigma, Portfolio* no.2, p.1.

26. Alexander Trocchi, *The decadence of a tradition,* unpub. ts., note c. 1964, Trocchi Estate.

27. 'Invisible insurrection ...', op. cit., p.1.

28. Ibid.

29. This event took ten days to prepare, attracted an audience of over 7000 to listen to Gregory Corso, Allen Ginsberg, John Latham, Paolo Leonni, Adrian Mitchell, Jeff Nuttall and Andrei Voznesensky among others, and take part in a 4-hour 'happening' for which the compère was Trocchi. A spontaneous invocation was composed at his flat by ten of the participants and later declaimed at a press conference at the Albert Memorial. One section of this text mapped the intersection points of an underground that was now recognized to be international, and moved freely through the fields of literature, drugs, theatre, art, pornography and social agitation: 'World declaration hot peace shower!.... Illumination, Now! Sigmatic New Departures Residu of Better Books & Moving Times in obscenely New Directions! Soul revolution City Lights Olympian lamb-blast! Castalia centrum new consciousness hungry generation Movement roundhouse 42 beat apocalypse energy-triumph! You are not alone!...'. 'International Poetry Incarnation', *Wholly Communion*, London, Lorrimer, 1965, p.9.

30. Jeff Nuttall, *Bomb culture*, London, MacGibbon & Kee, 1968, p. 135.

31. Gustav Metzger, *Auto-destructive art: Metzger at AA*, London, Destruction Creation, 1965, p.16.

32. Alexander Trocchi, untitled ms. notes (28 March 1963), 'Drowned in immaculate conception; Art as language', Trocchi Estate.

33. 'Invisible insurrection ...', op. cit., p. 3.

34. *Cain's book*, op. cit., pp.8 and 25–6.

35. Letter to Burroughs from Trocchi (8 June 1964), Trocchi Estate.

36. For contrasting descriptions of this meeting see *Bomb culture*, op. cit., pp. 221–7; John A. Walker, *John Latham*, London, Middlesex University Press, 1995, pp.71–3; Alexander Trocchi, *Junkie jottings,* unpub. ms., Trocchi Estate.

37. Letter to Trocchi from Berke (October 1964), Trocchi Estate.

38. Letter to Trocchi from Berke ('Sunday' [spring 1965]), Trocchi Estate.

39. *The Anti-University of London*, mimeographed course-catalogue [1968]. For Berke's part in the Anti-University and *FUNY*, see Joseph Berke, ed., *Counter-culture*, London, Peter Owen/Fire Books, 1969, pp. 12–34, 212–81.

40. Alexander Trocchi, 'MOB', *International Times*, no. 74 (14 March 1970).

41. *The decadence of a tradition*, op. cit.

42. Alexander Trocchi, 'Chapter 1 from his novel *The long book*', *Residu*, no. 2 (spring 1966), p. 11.

43. The banner that was carried by King Mob at the March 1968 demonstration in Grosvenor Square read 'Storm the Reality Studio and Retake the University'.

What are still called the 'events of 1968' for want of a better name, and very often reduced solely to their student and Parisian dimension and to the month of May 1968, are still the object of the most persistent truisms and are interpreted in ways that are very far removed from historical reality. It is true that the 'events of 1968' took place mainly during May and June, but they are part of an ongoing process, preceded by developments that took place slowly or rapidly and followed by profound changes: the '1968 years' had at their centre a powerful period which obscures what went before and after, though both are essential to understanding the phenomenon.[1] Young people and students were not the only social group participating in the process, and – not to mention movements that developed in other countries at a similar time – Paris did not monopolize protest within France.[2]

Like other countries, such as the United States and Britain in particular, France in the Sixties was marked by a cultural effervescence characterized simultaneously by the emergence of mass culture and the development of counter-cultures, with music playing a special role. But if these conflicting cultures were often mixed, especially among students, with protest movements, they were not confused with them. It would be historically mistaken to erase from the Sixties the truly political aspects of the social protest under the pretext of giving them a more consensual image. Nonetheless, it is difficult to locate the edges of what was political because protest movements of a traditional form and content – labour disputes, strikes, demonstrations – took place beside new kinds of movements with new themes; one of the crucial aspects of that modernity is the way private life invaded the political sphere, and in challenging society every dimension of life came under consideration. That is why it is useful to recall the themes of protest and the forms it took in that long decade starting at the beginning of the Sixties and ending in the mid-Seventies, in order to locate the networks and groups that initiated it, and possibly to conjure up some of the protagonists.

Before 1968: Isolated demonstrations

The decade opened with the last violent convulsions of the Algerian War; it should be remembered that violence in the streets started over the fighting in Algeria. Moreover, 1960 was an important turning-point in the reshaping of the French Left. In opposition to the Socialist Left wing which had been discredited by the colonial wars, a 'New Left' was founded based on the PSU (Parti socialiste unifié), and 121 intellectuals approved the refusal by conscripts to do military service. On 27 October 1960 the UNEF (Union nationale des étudiants de France) which then included one out of every two students organized the first united demonstration on a national scale against the Algerian War,[3] despite the shilly-shallying of the Confédération générale du travail (CGT – one of the main trade union congresses). So a whole generation of young people served their political and militant apprenticeship in the context of Algeria, a few in support of the FLN (Front de libération nationale – the Algerian freedom movement), many demonstrating in favour of peace in Algeria and against the OAS (Organisation armée secrète – French secret army organization). These demonstrations were usually banned by the government and often harshly repressed, like the demonstration on 8 February 1962 when the police caused the death of eight Communist demonstrators at Charonne Metro station. From the end of 1961 the FUA (Front universitaire anti-fasciste) federated the student anti-fascist committees formed to oppose the OAS, and fought Far Right groups backing a French Algeria for control of the Latin Quarter. Regarding the attitude of the leaders of the French Communist Party (PCF) as pusillanimous, the student organization of the party, the Union des étudiants communistes (UEC) entered a period of crisis that made it possible for Far Left political groups to emerge in the following years.

Once peace had been restored, social demands resurfaced. France witnessed rapid economic expansion, hectic urbanization and serious rural exodus. Living standards improved but not all French people benefited equally. Many workers were subject to conditions governed by a fairly strict application of Frederick Winslow Taylor's 'scientific management' theories, in cases where wages were going up less rapidly than the national wealth, or where company restructuring plans threatened their jobs. The year 1963 started with the most serious social unrest with the miners' strike, representing a grave setback for the social policy of the Pompidou government and expressing the resurgence of working-class militancy. A short time before, at the end

Communist Party poster, 1967. Musée d'Histoire contemporaine collection

The sixties, utopian years

of 1961, a strike by the Decazeville miners had not prevented the closure of their mine in Aveyron, but the long conflict at the Neyrpic company in Grenoble, apart from wage claims, had raised the problem of company management in terms close to those used by the 'New Left'. In 1964 at the end of a long process the CFTC (Confédération française des travailleurs chrétiens – Christian trade union

VIVE LA VOIE REVOLUTIONNAIRE BOLCHEVIQUE D'OCTOBRE 1917
PROLONGEE PAR LA
GRANDE REVOLUTION CULTURELLE PROLETARIENNE CHINOISE DE 1967
A BAS LE CAPITALISME! VIVE LE SOCIALISME!
Mouvement Communiste Français
(Marxiste-Léniniste)
26, Boulevard des Dames - MARSEILLE (2)
chaque semaine... Lisez l'Humanité nouvelle

congress) gave up its association with Christianity, changing its name to the CFDT (Confédération française démocratique du travail), while the CFTC survived as a rump for the minority who had opposed the change.

From the beginning of 1967 the social climate hardened. While the unions backed ritual 'national days of action', particularly opposing decrees relating to social security, young workers, many recent arrivals from the country, sometimes clashed with the forces of order and conflicts of a new kind appeared. The breach was opened in January at the Dassault factory in Bordeaux in a dispute over parity with Paris wages, then widened in February with a decision by the Rhodiaceta workers in Besançon and Lyons to occupy their factories in protest at working patterns. Again in Lyons, there was trouble at the Berliet factory, and the Lorraine miners protested over dismissals. At the Saint-Nazaire naval docks both staff and workers were on strike for two months. At Mulhouse, Le Mans and Lyons the traditional

union parades were punctuated by confrontations with the police. Old forms of action such as factory occupations resurfaced, and violence again erupted in labour disputes: wage claims, working conditions and hierarchical management structures were challenged and the unions were not always able to channel the militancy of young workers.[4]

New subjects of protest emerged. Universities were changing profoundly: there were over half a million students, a number that had more than doubled in seven years, and the traditional educational structures seemed ill-adapted to cope. *Les Héritiers* by Pierre Bourdieu and Jean-Claude Passeron, highlighting the workings of a class-bound education that replicated social divisions, quickly became a reference work for politically minded students. In the autumn of 1967 committees of action (CAL) were formed in the lycées (still equivalent to grammar schools). As for the UNEF, most of its representatives rejected both the traditional liberal university with its mandarin mentality and the Fouchet reform which was seen as technocratic: a second stage of that reform was due to be implemented at the start of the

OUI
créez
la révolution
continue

suffocating because of the strict moral code imposed by rules. For example, the Ministry for National Education decided that girls were allowed to visit boys in their rooms, the opposite not being allowed. From 1965 on there were incidents in the residences, often involving the police, at Montpellier and Antony in particular. The 1967 the disturbances spread, affecting Lille, Rennes and Nancy as well as Antony. At the university residences in Nanterre on 21 March a hundred or so male and female students occupied the girls' blocks, leading to police intervention. The press adopted an ironical attitude, generally failing to understand that the students wanted to be regarded as responsible adults, taking charge not only of their professional lives but their personal lives too.[7] In February 1968 the question was discussed at the Council of Ministers: freedom of movement within university residences was accorded only to those who had attained their majority, and

1967–8 academic year. The student union was also protesting against university selection, feeling that it would discriminate against students from disadvantaged social backgrounds. Though the UNEF was weakened and divided, it mobilized several thousand protestors on 9 November 1967. This was the first major mobilization by the UNEF since the Algerian War. In November a ten-day strike at the Nanterre faculty marked the beginning of a series of incidents on that campus, then still a building site.

In line with the thinking of the philosopher Henri Lefebvre and that of the Situationists who from 1966 had taken over the Association générale des étudiants at Strasbourg, private life erupted into the field of politics. For Lefebvre, 'daily life includes political life: political consciousness, the consciousness of belonging to a society and a nation, class consciousness .... And therefore criticism of daily life involves criticism of political life.'[5] In the programme distributed by the Situationists on the official first day of the academic year, like an echo we read: 'Students are a product of modern society, just like Godard or Coca-Cola. Their extreme alienation can only be countered by protesting against the whole of society.'[6] The closed world of the university residences which had shot up to house the growing numbers of students soon became

AVEC LE SECOURS ROUGE LUTTONS
POUR LA LIBERTE D'EXPRESSION
CONTRE LA REPRESSION POLICIERE

to minors under 21 who had obtained their parents' consent. The government was making itself the guardian of moral values that many of the students rejected.

Anti-imperialism and internationalism were also subjects of protest. Since the end of the war in Algeria, the Left and Far Left of the student movement had been observing anti-imperialist or revolutionary Third World movements which seemed to be opposed to the oppressive bureaucracy of the Soviet Union. The revolution in Cuba was enthusiastically supported, and the death of Che Guevara fighting with the Bolivian underground in 1967 turned him into a legend overnight. The break between People's China and the USSR and the Cultural Revolution which seemed to be challenging bureaucracy and the status of intellectual and manual work also aroused passions. Finally, as at the American

Militant magazines. The Trotskyist La Jeunesse communiste révolutionnaire *was founded in 1966.* **BDIC** *collection*

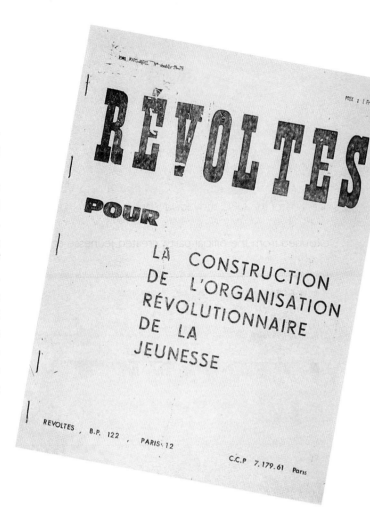

universities, in Germany, Italy or Japan, the Vietnam War touched the students' hearts; since 1966 the main student protests had been against American intervention in Vietnam, and they were all the more successful because they took place outside the traditional Left, which favoured a peace achieved by diplomatic means. At the end of 1966, at the behest of several intellectuals such as Jean-Paul Sartre, Alfred Kastler, Laurent Schwartz and Pierre Vidal-Naquet, a national Vietnam committee (CVN) was formed to support the action of the National Liberation Front (the Vietcong): the non-Communist Left, with the PSU at the forefront, and some members of the Far Left were active in it. At the beginning of 1967 Vietnam base committees (CVBs) were formed at the instigation of Marxist-Leninist militants. It was in the context of support for the Vietcong that international contacts were made and militant practices circulated from one country to another. A fairly small-scale demonstration at Liège in October 1966 was followed by a larger one in Berlin in February 1968 where French students learnt a lot from the SDS (Sozialistischer Deutscher Studentenbund – Socialist German students' union) militants.

Traditional organizations hardly seemed to react or came up with unsatisfactory responses; all of them were affected by crisis and dissidence. The PCF with a quarter of all voters was criticized for its rigidly doctrinal election tactics. Part of the UEC moved into open opposition in 1965. In the spring of 1966 some of those with Trotskyist leanings, excluded from the official party, created Jeunesse communiste révolutionnaire with Alain Krivine as its central figure.

was formed in 1967. Such anarchist groups as lasted acted as catalysts in putting forward certain demands, at Nanterre in particular. The crisis affecting organizations also touched religious youth movements: some students involved in the struggles left Jeunesse étudiante catholique to set up Jeunesse universitaire chrétienne, and many eventually joined Far Left organizations. Protestant students also went against the leaders of the Reformed Church by asserting the

Lithographs by Asger Jorn, co-founder of the Internationale situationniste, June 1968. Musée d'Histoire contemporaine collection

This movement joined already existing Trotskyist groups, such as Voix ouvrière and the Comité de liaison des étudiants révolutionnaires, which in 1968 changed its name to the Fédération des étudiants révolutionnaires. Other UEC dissidents with Maoist leanings founded the (Marxist-Leninist) Union des jeunesses communistes at the end of the same year. The Marxist-Leninist Communist Party of France

value of political awareness. The UNEF, now a battlefield for different political factions, was just a name, run in turn by various political trends (the Étudiants socialistes unifiés in 1967–8), but it could still organize united gatherings, and its structures on the ground were often very active. Despite a weak base among the students, the Far Left political groups helped to mobilize the student world.

1968: The protests crystallize

In March 1968 a famous article declared that 'the French are bored, they are not taking a close or a distant part in the great convulsions that are shaking the world' and that France had sunk into a 'state of melancholy'.[8] Yet two months earlier social struggles had broken out in Caen along the same lines as in the previous year: workers from Saviem, Jaeger and Sonormel went on indefinite strike, the town was shaken by virtual riots, and the action spread to other companies in the region. Here again the work patterns imposed by management and its authoritarian attitude were the cause. The students supported the workers' struggle and developed demands of their own.[9] There was unrest in other towns in the west during the first three months of 1968, e.g. Fougères, Redon, Honfleur and La Rochelle; the Channel fishermen were on strike throughout February.

In schools and universities all the latent subjects of protest in the previous years surfaced strongly at the same time. In January trouble started in the lycées; there were clashes with the police at the Nanterre faculty during a visit by François Misoffe, the Minister for Youth and Sport, challenged by Daniel Cohn-Bendit, a student of sociology, over the absence of young people's sexual problems from the *Livre blanc sur la jeunesse* (White Paper on youth). From the early days of February 1968, when the Vietcong launched their major Tet offensive, there was intensified mobilization in support of the Vietnamese. On 7 February the CVN demonstrated outside the American Embassy. On 21 February, a traditional day of struggle against colonialism and imperialism, the first 'occupation' of the year took place in the Latin Quarter, called for by the UNEF, the SNE Sup.,[10] the CVN and the CVBs. On 20 March during a lightning demonstration by the CVN the windows at the American Express building were smashed, which led to the arrest of a student from Nanterre. In response a hundred or so of his fellow-students occupied the administrative building at Nanterre to obtain his release and the right to express their political views. They decided to organize a day of political debate and hold a 'Journée Université critique' in imitation of the German SDS students; the links between them and a major part of the French student movement were strengthened during the international demonstration in Berlin on 18 February in support of the Vietcong. Named in an ironic reference to the Cuban Movement of 26 July, the Mouvement du 22 mars was created with Daniel Cohn-Bendit, a spokesman noted for his quick repartee, at its centre. The assassination attempt on Rudi Dutschke, the SDS leader, in Berlin on 11 April led to demonstrations, with lively clashes in the Latin Quarter, and a Mouvement du 25 avril was set up in Toulouse copying Nanterre's example. April saw an increasing number of incidents in Paris and the provinces between Far Left and Far Right militants, affecting only a minority. On 3 May while Georges Marchais in *L'Humanité* was denouncing 'the false revolutionaries who should be unmasked' and stigmatizing the 'Left-wing splinter groups', police intervention at the Sorbonne and the arrest of militants supporting Nanterre students summoned before the disciplinary council provoked massive, spontaneous reaction. The demonstrations of solidarity held in the following days grew and spread to the provinces; on the night of 10–11 May the barricades went up and police repression led to the unions, representing workers and teachers, calling a general strike for 13 May.

Silkscreen print from the Salon de la Jeune Peinture which in January 1969 presented 'La salle Rouge pour le Viêt-nam'. Musée d'Histoire contemporaine collection

le comité du salon de la jeune peinture presente :
manifestation de soutie au peuple vietnamien

'activities of the German anarchist Cohn-Bendit' — was a sign of apparent victory. Marches in provincial cities sometimes turned to violence: at Troyes, Clermont-Ferrand and Nantes, for example, where instructions for an indefinite strike were given. The following day the press underlined the size and the political dimension of the demonstrations,[11] so echoing the protest. What happened on 14 May then seemed like an obvious consequence: the screening on Channel 2 of the magazine programme *Zoom* for the first time giving air time to the student leaders, and the workers' occupation of the Sud-Aviation factory in Nantes[12] with the sequestration of the managing director and executive staff, as a prelude to a general strike. The student movement acted as a catalyst, making a new radicalism permissible.

That day has stuck in memories and history books as a turning-point; the general strike and the demonstrations apparently affected the alliance between workers and students. Work stoppages were restricted and no general instructions were given after the demonstration. On 13 May the regime was put on trial. 'Ten years is enough,' the demonstrators chanted in Paris and on the 164 marches in provincial towns, thus commemorating the putsch in Alger which had helped to bring General de Gaulle to power on 13 May 1958. The day before, Prime Minister Georges Pompidou had announced that the Sorbonne would reopen and that judicial proceedings would be halted: so it was also a victory march. The number of demonstrators in Paris varied: 176,000, reported the presenter of the 8 p.m. news on Channel 1; one million the organizers proclaimed; 300,000, said the Préfet de police. The war of numbers helped to trigger the strike at the ORTF (French radio and television), proof of French television's partisan attitude. The presence of Daniel Cohn-Bendit, a leader of the Mouvement du 22 mars, at the head of the Paris demonstration beside the national leaders of the major trade union movements — especially Georges Séguy, the secretary of the CGT and a French Communist Party member who had denounced the

Public proclamations, 13 May–16 June 1968

From 11 May, 800 students from the Arts faculty of Strasbourg university voted for the university to be autonomous and to be founded on direct democracy; on the evening of 12 May Paris students moved into the Censier faculty. But it is particularly the occupation of the Sorbonne from 13 May to 16 June that symbolizes that month of occupations and public proclamations,[13] together with the taking over of the Théâtre de l'Odéon on 17 May, which added a cultural and political dimension. For a month these two permanent forums in the Latin Quarter brought together orators of every origin, who inaugurated a new style of intervention in public areas, bypassing the normal systems of representation based on delegation. Written slogans on the wall and posters, discussed at general meetings and not signed, from the people's studio at the École des beaux-arts,[14] which had been occupied since 15 May, were also symbolic works, protesting through drawings and words, often humorous or mocking. The occupation of factories spread from 14 May throughout France, and the strike as it became general paradoxically led to a provisional exit from the protest. The two days of 24 and 25 May were another turning-point; the failure of De Gaulle's speech, the violent demonstrations on 24 May – a police inspector was killed in Lyons, and the Paris Bourse was set on fire – the television journalists' strike and the opening of the Grenelle negotiations between the government, the unions and the employers' organizations, these events began the isolation of the protestors. General de Gaulle's speech on 30 May, after support from several hundred thousand people, helped to find a solution for the crisis by holding elections. The centre of interest shifted to the ballot box. Strikers who persisted in occupying their work-places more frequently came into conflict with the forces of order, as at the Renault-Flins and Peugeot-Sochaux plants, where the first protestors died. The image of a whole generation of rebellious, generous young people was supplanted in public opinion by that of isolated subversive elements threatening the unity of the nation. The dissolution of the Far Left organizations on 12 June, the end of the ORTF strike[15] and the overwhelming victory of the Gaullist majority at the elections held on 23 and 30 June were milestones in what seemed to be a restored consensus.

The widespread protest of the 1968 years

The crisis that occurred in May and June 1968 in fact shook the foundations of political power. The reform proposals put forward by De Gaulle, who resigned in April 1969, then those of Jacques Chaban-Delmas, Georges Pompidou's Prime Minister from 1969 to 1972, came into conflict on the one hand with the party of law and order as embodied by Raymond Marcellin, the Minister of the Interior, and on the other with a widespread protest which destabilized several Establishment institutions, such as national education, the army and the law. The intelligentsia were on the streets alongside Far Left groups who had one common objective, whether they were of an anarchist, Maoist or Trotskyist persuasion: to transform the world and change life; they expressed themselves through symbolic or violent action, particularly against Far Right groups. In this 'decennial frenzy of politicization'[16] new social movements such as the women's movement or regional and ecology movements contributed to profound evolutionary changes in French society in the Seventies.

The Centre expérimental of Vincennes which was set up in the autumn of 1968 seemed like a show-case, but was also seen as an abscess on which protest could centre, at the same time as being a laboratory for new teaching methods in universities, which had themselves been radically reorganized by the Edgar Faure reform.[17] Unrest among lycée pupils and university students continued, with a refusal to participate and a questioning of the school and university establishment, which was also a rejection of society. The arrest of an ordinary lycée pupil in 1971 which was seen as unjust resulted in tens of thousands of lycée pupils marching on the streets. Two years later when the Debré law enacted in June 1970 limiting deferments of military service was implemented both girls and boys demonstrated. Their watchword, 'You've had five years! Cuckoo, we're back!', established their kinship with the '68 protest. In industrial enterprises protest against the Taylor-inspired 'scientific management' of labour was highlighted by moves originated by semi-skilled workers starting in April 1971 at the Renault factory in Le Mans. Confronted with this militancy on the part of the workers, which also involved young people, women and immigrants, the union movements were divided: while

chroniques de
l'art vivant

N°18 Mars 1971 Prix 3f

ACTUEL
novapress

MENSUEL 3F
35 F. belges

N°15 Décembre 1971

entretien avec marcuse et 72 pages de BANDES DESSINEES

la cause du peuple

journal de front populaire   n°17 16.17 juin 1968 .50 c

LEUR CAMPAGNE COMMENCE

3

NOTRE LUTTE CONTINUE

suite p.4

VIVE LA REVOLUTION

NOUVELLE SERIE DE « VIVE LE COMMUNISME »   N° 6 – 5 Juin 1970

journal marxiste-léniniste-maoïste

qui a peur de qui ?

1f 50

TOUT !

CE QUE NOUS VOULONS : TOUT 12

bimensuel 23 AVRIL 71

y en a plein le cul !

LIBRE

DISPOSITION

DE

NOTRE

CORPS

Actuel was edited by
Jean-François Bizot,
Tout! and *La Cause du*
peuple by Jean-Paul
Sartre, *Vive la Révolution*
by Lecardonnel and
Chroniques de l'art Vivant
by Aimé Maeght and
Jean Clair.
Private collection

the CFDT supported it, the CGT spoke of 'Left-wing adventurism'. Some of these 'Left-wingers' – about 2000 – had 'infiltrated' factories between 1967 and 1975 to bring together and support, so they said, the elements of revolutionary consciousness present in a working class that had in fact become the subject of myth.[18] In February 1972 the death of a young Maoist worker at the gates of the Renault-Billancourt plant, killed by a night watchman working for the company, was the tragic culmination of that movement towards fusion with the working classes: between 100,000 and 200,000 people followed the funeral cortège in Paris. Renowned intellectuals such as Simone de Beauvoir, Jean-Paul Sartre, Michel Foucault, Jean-Pierre Faye, Maurice Clavel and Claude Mauriac intervened to support workers injured in accidents at work, to protest against the ban on Far Left newspapers (*La Cause du peuple*, *Vive la révolution*), defend freedom of speech, and argue that groups excluded from society such as prisoners should be given a voice. In February 1971 Michel Foucault set up the Groupe Information Prison (GIP) which denounced prisons as instruments of social repression.[19] The Groupe Information Santé and the Groupe d'information et de soutien des travailleurs immigrés (GISTI) were set up along the same lines.

Protest against the prevailing norms and values could also be seen in the women's and gay movements. From the summer of 1968 some individuals withdrew from the industrial, urban consumer society, trying to build alternative living places, associations, groups outside the commercial circuits. Newspapers such as *Actuel* or *La Gueule ouverte* were collective organizers, helping individuals to make contact and setting up barter networks. These often ephemeral aspirations coincided with the preoccupations of the regionalist movements rebelling against Parisian centralism. Brittany, Corsica and Occitania (south-west France) witnessed the formation of groups, the most famous rejecting plans to extend the military camp at Larzac; on the initiative of peasant farmers attached to their land, it brought together Occitans wanting to live in their country, anti-militarists and ecologists.[20] It was a motley collection, but they held on until 1981, so benefiting from the change in political power and attaining their stated objective.

Protest at the concept of the couple and the family, and the movement for freedom for the body, made the largest

Silkscreen-printed poster. Musée d'Histoire contemporaine collection

contribution towards the transformation of society, radicalizing and effecting profound changes from the mid-Sixties on. From 1970 a handful of women rejected the concept and frontiers of what was seen as political, declaring that 'the private is political', and fighting for the right to contraception and abortion. Spectacular actions such as the 'Manifeste de trois cent quarante-trois femmes' in which 343 women, most of them very well known, including writers, actresses and journalists, admitted having had abortions were a radical challenge to the repressive law of 1920. They compelled the government to issue decrees implementing the Neuwirth law on the free availability of contraception, enacted in 1967 but never applied. Within the movement for freedom in abortion and contraception (MLAC) set up in April 1973, doctors and women defied the law and the doctors' association by carrying out the forbidden abortions, at first secretly then openly. Feminism had adopted the discourse and practices of radicalism, leading to the acceptance of the Veil law in 1975.[21] Thus the utopia of action turned out to be a detour leading to integratory reforms in 1974–5 at the start of Valéry Giscard d'Estaing's seven-year term as president. The economic crisis that gradually became a fact of life and the crumbling of the Marxist model contributed towards the gradual breaking-up of individual and collective protest movements in France.

Geneviève Dreyfus-Armand and
Michelle Zancarini-Fournel

1. The expression 'the '68 years' in the sense that it is used here refers to a research and teaching seminar organized at the Institut d'histoire du temps présent (IHTP) starting in 1994, with Robert Frank (Université de Paris-I), Marie-Françoise Lévy (IHTP) and the authors of this article in charge, and with Maryvonne Le Puloch (IHTP) collaborating. See *Mémoires de 68. Guide des sources d'une histoire à faire*, Paris, Association Mémoires de 68/BDIC-Verdier, 1993.
2. For a bibliography on protest movements in France, see *Bulletin de l'IHTP*, no. 58, December 1994, pp. 46, 74.
3. Alain Monchablon, *Histoire de l'UNEF de 1956 à 1962*, Paris, PUF, 1983.
4. Alain Delale and Gilles Ragache, *La France de 68*, 1st edn 1978; Paris, Le Seuil, 1988.
5. Henri Lefebvre, *Critique de la vie quotidienne*, Paris, Grasset, 1947; 2nd edn, L'Arche, 1958.
6. *De la misère en milieu étudiant considérée sous ses aspects économique, politique, psychologique, sexuel et notamment intellectuel et de quelques moyens d'y*

Silkscreen-printed
poster, 1973.
Musée d'Histoire
contemporaine
collection

remédier, by members of the Internationale Situationniste and students at Strasbourg, AFGES (Association fédérative générale des étudiants de Strasbourg), 1966.
7. *Le Monde*, 25 April 1967, p. 11.
8. Pierre Viansson-Ponté, 'Quand la France s'ennuie...', *Le Monde*, 15 March 1968.
9. Gérard Lange, 'L'exemple caennais. in *Mai 68. Les Mouvements étudiants en France et dans le monde*, Nanterre, BDIC, 1988.
10. Syndicat national de l'enseignement supérieur (National union of teachers in higher education).
11. Danielle Tartakowsky, 'Les Manifestations de mai-juin 68 en province' in *68. Exploration du mal français*, vol. 1, *Terrains*, Paris, L'Harmattan, 1992.
12. François Le Madec, *L'Aubépine de Mai. Chronique d'une usine occupée, Sud-Aviation, Nantes, 1968*, Nantes, CDMOT, 1988.
13. Michel de Certeau, *La Prise de parole et autres écrits politiques*, Paris, Le Seuil, 1994.
14. 'L'Atelier populaire de l'ex-École des beaux-arts', conversation between Gérard Fromanger and Laurent Gervereau, in *Mai 68. Les Mouvements étudiants en France et dans le monde*, op. cit.
15. *Mai 68 à l'ORTF*, Paris, INA/Comité d'histoire de la télévision française/La Documentation française, 1987.
16. Pascal Ory, *L'Aventure culturelle française, 1945–89*, Paris, Flammarion, 1989.
17. Antoine Prost, '1968: mort et naissance de l'Université française', *Vingtième siècle*, no. 23, July–September 1989.
18. Robert Linhart, *L'Établi*, Paris, Éditions de Minuit, 1978.
19. Michel Foucault, *Dits et écrits*, Paris, Gallimard, 1994, vol. II, pp. 174, 175.
20. Bernard Lacroix, *L'Utopie communautaire. Histoire sociale d'une révolte*, Paris, PUF, 1981.
21. Françoise Picq, *Libération des femmes. Les années-mouvement*, Paris, 1993.

Left:
Small poster by
Wolinski for *Hara-Kiri
Hebdo*, banned in
1970 when it became
Charlie-Hebdo.
Musée d'Histoire
contemporaine
collection

273

The Sixties in Britain
by David Alan Mellor

1962

October

5. Release of the first Beatles record, a 45 rpm with *Love me do* on side A and *P.S. I love you* on side B.

22. The Soviet spy John Vassal is found guilty of spying at the Old Bailey in London.

President Kennedy announces that Soviet missiles have been detected on Cuba.

24. Fluxus artists construct environments at Gallery One, London.

November

Telstar by the Tornados is no. 1 on the hit parade.

24. First screening of the BBC's satirical programme, *That was the week that was*, 'the most hypnotically watched TV programme in history', attacking Harold Macmillan's ruling Conservative government using a mixture of comic sketches, songs, graphic innovations and cabaret numbers.

December

Lectures by Gustav Metzger at Ealing School of Art on auto-destructive art; Pete Townsend, who later formed part of the Who Pop group, was in the audience.

Premiere of *Doctor No*, the first James Bond film.

At the Edinburgh Festival Mark Boyle and Joan Hills produce *Big Ed*, their first remarkable theatrical event, provoking outrage.

Britain and France decide to collaborate on a supersonic passenger plane.

Execution of James Hanratty, found guilty of the 'A6 murder'.

Uganda, Jamaica, Trinity and Tobago, former British colonies, achieve independence.

Opening of the Hilton Hotel on Park Lane.

3536 women use the Pill after permission to market it was given the previous year.

Publication of *The voices of time*, short stories by J.G. Ballard.

Series of pictures by Richard Hamilton, *Towards a definitive statement on the coming trends in menswear*.

1963

January

18. Death of Hugh Gaitskell, opposition leader of the Labour Party, succeeded by Harold Wilson (14 February).

29. General de Gaulle votes against Britain's entry into the Common Market.

February

14. Second Beatles record, *From me to you*, enters the British hit parade.

March

21. *Paintings as photographs* exhibition at St Martin's School of Art: Gerald Laing exhibits hyper-realist portraits of Brigitte Bardot and Anna Karina.

27. The Beeching Report recommends cutting down the extent of the British Rail railway network.

Lewis Morley photographs Christine Keeler.

Publication of *Honest to God* by the Bishop of Woolwich, about the secularization of religion, which creates a great stir.

April

12. The militant disarmament organization 'Spies for peace' reveals the government's secret storage site for nuclear bombs.

The British Pop artists Blake, Hockney, Jones, Laing, Boshier and Phillips go to Paris for the 3rd Biennale of young artists.

That was the week that was attracts a viewing audience of 12 m.

May

2. *From me to you*, first Beatles song to reach no. 1 on the British hit parade.

June

4. John Profumo, Secretary of State for War, resigns from the Conservative government because of his affair with Christine Keeler.

David Bailey meets Andy Warhol during his second visit to New York.

August

8. Great Train Robbery: 'Buster' Edwards, Bruce Reynolds, Ronny Biggs and their gang steal £2,500,000 from British Rail and the Bank of England.

First television showing of *Ready, Steady, Go!*, a Pop programme for young people.

September

10. One-man show by Pauline Boty (Grabowsky Gallery).

Independence for Malaysia.

October

18. Harold Macmillan resigns as Prime Minister

and is replaced by Sir Alec Douglas-Home.

Chris Blackwell creates the first independent record company, Island, specializing in Afro-Caribbean, soul, and rhythm and blues.

13,670 women use the Pill.

Richard Hamilton starts studies for his *Portrait of Hugh Gaitskell as a famous monster of Filmland* (finished 1964).

1964

March

30. Tribal street battles between mods and rockers in the south coast resorts.

Mark Boyle produces the first happenings, *Shepherd's Bush TV frame works*.

April

Launch of BBC2, third TV channel using 26-line high definition.

June

8–9. *The Dennison Hall happenings* in London: performances and events involving J.J. Lebel, Mark Boyle and Joan Hills.

The Beatles' manager, Brian Esptein, invites Robert Whitaker to come back from Australia and work with him as artistic adviser and occasionally as a photographer.

July

9. *House of the rising sun* by the Animals is no. 1 on the hit parade.

A hard day's night by Richard Lester premiered in Liverpool.

October

15. Harold Wilson leads the Labour Party to electoral victory for the first time in thirteen years.

Paintings etc: 54–64, Richard Hamilton exhibition (Hanover Gallery). The *Daily Express* expresses outrage at the purchase of Richard Hamilton's painting *Portrait of Hugh Gaitskell as a famous monster of Filmland* by the Arts Council.

The British colony of Northern Rhodesia becomes independent, adopting the name Zambia. Tanzania, made up of the former British colonies of Tanganyika and Zanzibar, achieves independence.

Biba, a clothes shop owned by Barbara Hulanicki, opens in Abingdon Road, Kensington.

Ossie Clark and Alice Pollock open the Quorum boutique in Chelsea.

44,000 women in Britain use the Pill.
Publication of J.G. Ballard's *The terminal beach*.

1965
January
24. Death of Winston Churchill.
February
18. *I can't explain* by The Who is no. 8 on the hit parade.

The Labour Minister Jennie Lee argues in favour of a 'brighter and more cultured' Britain, and the budget for the arts set at £285,000 pa.
February and March
One year after the Beatles' 'cultural conquest' of the United States, British artists achieve recognition through exhibitions in New York (Bridget Riley, Gerald Laing, Peter Phillips) and Minneapolis with *London: The new scene* at the Walker Arts Center.
March
First issue of *Nova*, a magazine aimed at the 'thinking woman'.
May
4. Electo publishes a collection of silkscreen prints by Eduardo Paolozzi, *As is when*, so starting a boom in contemporary prints.
June
Gathering of 'beat' poets at the Royal Albert Hall with Ginsberg, Alexander Trocchi and patients from R.D. Laing's Kingsley Hall community among those present.
July
Creation of the BEV art studio (associating Douglas Binder, Dudley Edwards and David Vaughan) opposite David Bailey's home in Camden Town.
13. Abolition of the death penalty after a free vote in the House of Commons.
September
9. *I can't get no satisfaction* by the Rolling Stones is no. 1 on the hit parade.
October
8. The Central Post Office tower opens, a symbol of Swinging London and its technological decor.
20. Peter Blake exhibits at the Robert Fraser Gallery.
November
4. *My generation* by The Who is no. 2 on the hit parade.
11. The most serious crisis of decolonization: white politicians seize power in Southern Rhodesia and declare 'unilateral independence', refusing to give black majority the vote.

David Bailey publishes *A box of pin-ups*, portraits of London celebrities including the Beatles, Cecil Beaton and the Kray twins, Ronnie and Reggie.
December
16. *Day tripper* by the Beatles is no. 1 on the hit parade.
22. *The Sun* publishes an article on the first proto-psychedelic mural painted by BEV on the wall of the Main Wolff Partnership building at 81 Parkway, Camden Town, London.

1966
April
Michelangelo Antonioni starts shooting the film *Blow-up* in the studio of the photographer John Cowan in London, using David Bailey's life as his inspiration.
June
The Victoria and Albert Museum stages an Aubrey Beardsley retrospective which influences the resurgence of Art Nouveau in graphic art.
Publicity for the Beatles' *Paperback writer* includes a 'auto-destructive' session of poses directed by Stuart Brisley and photographed by Bob Whitaker.
Richard Hamilton organizes a Marcel Duchamp retrospective (Tate Gallery), reconstructing *The bride stripped bare...*
Exhibition by the Groupe de la Recherche d'art visuel (GRAV), Indica Gallery.
July
20. Prime Minister Harold Wilson 'freezes' prices and incomes to deal with the economic crisis resulting from attacks on the pound. End of the period of 'swinging' cultural optimism.
September
15. *All or nothing* by the Small Faces is no. 1 on the hit parade.
An AC Cobra sports car decorated by BEV on display at the Robert Fraser Gallery.
'Destruction in Art' Symposium (DIAS) in London, opening with *Son et lumière for insects, reptiles and water creatures* by Mark Boyle and Joan Hills.
October
Arrival from Australia of Richard Neville and Martin Sharp who prepare to publish a London edition of the magazine *Oz*.
15. Arrest of Ian Brady and Myra Hindley for the Moors murders.
Richard Hamilton exhibits reliefs by Guggenheim (Robert Fraser Gallery).
In the second issue of *The International Times (IT)*, an *avant-garde* underground cultural newspaper published in London, Pete Townsend recognizes

the influence of 'Auto-destructive art' and Gustav Metzger on the Who and on him personally.
Nigel Weymouth and Michael English carry out the decoration of the shops Granny Takes a Trip and Hung On You.
November
4. Gabriel Weissmann exhibits psychedelic paintings at R.D. Laing's Kingsley Hall community.
December
23. First psychedelic evening *Nitetripper* by the UFO at the Barney Club, Tottenham Court Road, London.
Britain grants independence to Guyana, Lesotho and Botswana.
Foundation of the Track Records record company by Chris Stamp and Kit Lambert; they sign up Jimi Hendrix, The Who and the Crazy World of Arthur Brown.
In Britain 800,000 women use the Pill.

1967
January
29. Formation of the Northern Ireland Civil Rights Association (NICRA) protesting against undemocratic rule.
February
12. Police raid on Keith Richards of the Rolling Stones followed by his arrest and that of Mick Jagger and Robert Fraser, owner of the Robert Fraser Gallery.
17. 'Light show' by Mark Boyle and Joan Hills at the *Love festival* of the UFO club, with Soft Machine.
Joe Boyd and John Hopkins set up Osiris Visions to sell UFO and *IT* posters by Michael English and Nigel Weymouth (also known as Hapshash and The Coloured Coat) from the Indica Bookshop.
March
30. Peter Blake, Jan Haworth and Michael Cooper make the *Sergeant Pepper* picture for the sleeve of the Beatles' *Sergeant Pepper* album.
BEV finish decorating the Lord John shop in Carnaby Street.
Hapshash's 'UFO Mark II' poster is put up illegally at a block of flats under construction in Bayswater.
April
29. 'The 14-hour technicolor dream', a festival of events and happenings, held at Alexandra Palace ,with a poster by Michael McInnerney.
May
25. Delivery of John Lennon's psychedelically decorated Rolls Royce.

Creation of the Artist's Placement Group (APG) on the initiative of John Latham.

June

1. *Sergeant Pepper* released in Britain.

4. Yoko Ono flies her *Be-in* kite at Parliament Fields.

28. Mick Jagger and Robert Fraser appear in handcuffs and are sentenced for infringing the laws on drugs at Chichester.

29. Pete Townsend takes a full page of the *Evening Standard* to protest that Mick Jagger and Robert Fraser have been used as scapegoats.

The Richardson brothers, Charles and Eddy, are given long prison sentences for violence and robbery in south London.

July

16. Demonstration supporting the legalization of cannabis in Hyde Park, posters by Martin Sharp and Michael McInnerney.

19. *All you need is love* by the Beatles is no. 1, after the worldwide satellite screening of the 25 June programme.

24. Famous members of the intelligentsia and celebrities including John Lennon, Paul McCartney and Richard Hamilton sign an appeal designed by Michael McInnerney and published as a full-page advertisement in *The Times* calling for the laws on the use of marijuana to be liberalized.

A conference entitled 'Dialectics of liberation' held in London with Herbert Marcuse, Michael X and R.D. Laing.

Richard Hamilton organizes the reopening of the Robert Fraser Gallery while Fraser is in prison.

Carolin Coon creates Release, an information bureau on drugs for young people.

Publication of 5th issue of *Oz*, 'Plant a flower child', the first magazine made up of posters designed by Robert Whitaker and Martin Sharp.

Polydor, a subsidiary of Track Records, starts to rationalize silkscreen poster production by Osiris Visions (also producing offset-litho prints) to recover the money it has invested.

August

Death of Brian Epstein, the Beatles' manager.

September

London Situationists translate and reprint comic-strip posters made by Strasbourg Situationists, and use them to cover walls.

October

The cover of the 7th issue of *IT* designed by Martin Sharp depicts Bob Dylan as an icon. It will become the most widely sold poster of the period, 'Blowing in the mind'.

November

Omtentacle, a new poster-production company (Dudley Edwards and Michael McInnerney), commissioned by John Esam, editor of *Image*, to produce the poster for 'La Fenêtre Rose', at the Palais des Sports, Paris, with Soft Machine, Mark Boyle, Joan Hills, Spencer Davis and David Medalla.

Four pirate versions of Osiris Visions' poster of 'Che Guevara' have been brought out since the spring.

December

2. First colour television programmes broadcast on BBC2.

7. The Beatles open the Apple shop in Baker Street selling clothes and drawings by The Fool (Marijke Koger and Simon Posthuma) who also created the shopfront.

27. Opening of the Fulham Gallery selling only psychedelic posters.

Peter Lederbore makes 'Big O' posters a subsidiary of *Oz* publications.

Work starts on decorating Pussy Weber's Flying Dragon, a macrobiotic restaurant at 436 Kings Road, Chelsea.

The withdrawal of the British Empire from east of Suez is completed with the independence of Aden and the Protectorate of South Arabia.

Lee Bender opens the shop Bus Stop in Kensington Church Street.

The Carnaby Street shop Gear sells 300,000 posters in 1967.

1968

January

Galerie 5 in Geneva stages an exhibition of psychedelic posters from London by Hapshash and Omtentacle.

February

Jeremy Fry sets up Unlimited to produce and sell multiple works of art. Omtentacle finishes decorating Flying Dragon restaurant.

March

5. César makes plastic extrusions at the Tate Gallery; Stuart Brisley burns rubbish.

April

20. Enoch Powell makes an openly racist speech, 'Rivers of blood', obtaining the backing of the London dockers and Smithfield porters who march on Parliament in his support.

May

9. The Kray twins, Reggie and Ronnie, are arrested for the murders of George Cornell, 'Jack the hat' McVitie and 'Mad axe man' Frank Mitchell.

Ronan Point council estate's tower block collapses in London.

28. Inspired by militant students in France, the students of Hornsey College of Art occupy the lecture rooms.

Exhibition of poetry posters at Brighton Festival.

Start of the television series *Civilisation* with Kenneth Clark.

Mark Boyle and Joan Hills accompany Jimi Hendrix on his US tour, looking after the lighting.

Big O arranges distribution outlets for its psychedelic posters in Paris and Barcelona.

June

Release of Jean-Luc Godard's film *One plus one* with the Rolling Stones and the Notting Hill Black Panthers.

July

22. Exhibition, *Are you here?*, of John Lennon's work (Robert Fraser Gallery).

August

14. *Fire* by the Crazy World of Arthur Brown at no. 1 on the hit parade.

24. NICRA organizes the first large-scale march in support of civil rights to Dungannon, Northern Ireland.

Richard Hamilton produces the record sleeve of the Beatles *White album*.

Nicholas Roeg starts shooting the film *Performance* in Notting Hill.

Richard Hamilton starts *Swinging London* series with the trial of Mick Jagger and Robert Fraser in 1967 as its axis.

October

27. Anti-American demonstration in Grosvenor Square is the culmination of opposition to the Vietnam War in the Britain.

November

Martin Sharp publishes the issue of *Oz* entitled 'Magic theatre'.

1969

January

4. Civil rights march organized by NICRA is ambushed by Protestant extremists at Burntollet Bridge, Northern Ireland.

March

2. First flight of the prototype Concorde at Toulouse.

Release of *Tommy*, a rock opera by The Who, record sleeve by Michael McInnerney.

April

16. *Israelites* by Desmond Dekker is first Afro-Caribbean no. 1 on the hit parade.

May

Ettore Sotsass visits London to study psychedelic decorations and meets Martin Sharp and Michael McInnerney. He publishes his findings in an article, 'Negozi a Londra', in *Domus*, no. 480.

June

25. *Environmental reversals* at Camden Arts Centre.

July

Death of Brian Jones of the Rolling Stones.

August

12 to 15. Conflict between Londonderry Protestants and Catholics leads to British Army troops being deployed in the town.

September

26. Eradication of stage censorship with abolition of the Lord Chamberlain's office.
Premiere of the revue *Oh Calcutta!* by Kenneth Tynan.

October

Seeds for a random garden, show by Joan Hills.

November

13. Opening of the first Peter Blake retrospective in Bristol (City Art Gallery).

December

The Provisional Irish Republican Army (PIRA), wanting to use more militant strategies against the British government in Northern Ireland, breaks away from the IRA.
Table by Allen Jones.
Snow white and the black dwarf by Joe Tilson.
Fashion plate, a series by Richard Hamilton.
Biba moves to larger premises in Kensington High Street.
Opening of Yves Saint Laurent boutique in Bond Street.
1,250,000 women use the Pill in Britain.

1970

March

12. Opening of the Richard Hamilton retrospective (Tate Gallery).

April

18. *All kinds of everything* by Dana is no. 1 on the hit parade.

June

General election; Edward Heath forms a Conservative government.
27. Start of military action by the Provisional IRA in Belfast district of Short Strand against Protestants.

September

Death of Jimi Hendrix.
Publication of *Playpower* by Richard Neville.

Publication of *The female eunuch* by Germaine Greer, translated into French in 1972.
Publication of air-brush paintings by Michael English.
Start of series by Mark Boyle and Joan Hills.
Martin Sharp produces the *Smartiples* series of posters on plasticized paper for Big O; buyers use them as blinds.
Big O is run from a stall at Kensington Market under the name 'Printmint'. Peter Lederbore and Roger Dean become partners.
David Hockney retrospective (Whitechapel Art Gallery).
The British manufacturer of throw-away clothes, Goujon Paprelogs Ltd, predicts that 10% of the population will adopt this type of clothing.
Publication of *The atrocity exhibition* by J.G. Ballard.

1971

January

Introduction of decimal coinage to Britain.

July

10. *Won't get fooled again* by The Who is no. 9 on the hit parade.
24. *Get it on* by T. Rex is no. 1 on the hit parade.

August

After appealing against the verdict in the longest obscenity trial in British history, Richard Neville and Felix Dennis, who are in charge of *Oz,* are imprisoned for publishing no. 28. An effigy of Judge Argyle is burnt outside the Old Bailey.
9. The imprisonment of Catholics in Northern Ireland leads to prolonged rioting.

Winter

The Angry Brigade, a London-based armed terrorist group, tries to blow up the Central Post Office Tower.
To try and accelerate economic growth the Conservative government instigates the 'Barber boom', called after the Chancellor of the Exchequer, with his policy of fiscal suppleness and credit.
Margaret Thatcher is appointed Secretary of State for Education; she discontinues free milk for schoolchildren.
The census confirms that $1\frac{1}{2}$ million Commonwealth immigrants live in Britain.

1972

January

30. 'Bloody Sunday'; British troops kill thirteen people in Londonderry during a civil rights march.

February

The National Union of Mineworkers (NUM) win

their strike against the Conservative government.
5. Mark Bolan's group T. Rex reaches no. 1 on the hit parade with *Telegram Sam*.

July

31. The British forces occupy 'no-go' areas in Catholic districts of Londonderry and Belfast in the Motorman operation.

Summer

Arrival of Ugandan Asians expelled from Uganda by Idi Amin.
Richard Hamilton finishes the series *Soft pink landscape.*

1973

January

Britain enters the Common Market.

February

Oppositing leader Harold Wilson and the trade unions agree a joint policy, the 'Social Contract'.

March

The Provisionals start a campaign in London of blowing up cars in mainland Britain.

July

28. Gary Glitter is no. 1 on the hit parade with *I'm the leader of the gang (I am)*.

October

Prime Minister Edward Heath rejects a request from President Nixon to use British-based planes for ferrying US supplies to Israel during the Yom Kippur War.

November

The Conservative government declares a state of emergency.
Energy and electricity in Britain are threatened simultaneously by the NUM, which declares a ban on overtime in its fight for higher wages, and by the disruption of oil supplies following the Yom Kippur War, after the Arab attack on Israel.
Fall in the Stock Market when the economic bubble created by the Barber boom bursts.
Bankruptcies hit real estate and financial companies.

December

13. Rationing of power supplies for industrial and domestic users. Introduction of the three-day working week to save energy.
Sculpture of *An oak tree* by Michael Craig Martin.
Publication of Martin Amis's novel *Dead babies*.
Publication of *Crash* by J.G. Ballard.
Skin series by Mark Boyle: cytograms of the artist's body.
Biba moves into huge premises formerly occupied by Derry & Toms department store in Kensington.

And in France, 1962–73, by Laurence Bertrand Dorléac

1962

October
28. 'Yes' vote wins referendum on reforming the constitution.

November
18. Parliamentary elections with victory for the Gaullists.

1962

Filipacchi launches the magazine *Salut les copains*. The wearing of cassocks becomes optional in most dioceses.

Essays: *L'Afrique noire est mal partie* by René Dumont; *Vers une civilisation du loisir* by Joffre Dumazedier; *La Pensée sauvage* by Claude Lévi-Strauss; *Nietzsche et la philosophie* by Gilles Deleuze; *La République moderne* by Pierre Mendès-France.

Literature: *Mobile* by Michel Butor; *Le Palace* by Claude Simon; *Les Fruits d'or* by Nathalie Sarraute. Prizes: *Les Bagages de sable* by Anna Langfus (Goncourt); *Le Veilleur de nuit* by Simone Jacquemard (Renaudot); *Le Sud* by Yves Berger (Fémina).
Bestsellers: *Les Prétoriens* by Jean Lartéguy; *La Foire aux cancres* by Jean-Charles; *L'Île* by Robert Merle; *Journal à quatre mains* by Benoîte and Flora Groult; *Le Désastre de Pavie* by Jean Giono.

Town planning, architecture: Tower-block estate at Meudon-la-Forêt (1959–62); 'Ensemble des Bluets' by Paul Bossard at Créteil (1961–2).

Arts: Major exhibitions: *Figures de Corot*; *Picabia*; *Atelier Brancusi*; *Le Corbusier*; *Art mexicain, Gustave Moreau et ses élèves*; *Giacometti*.
First Fluxus festival in France (American Center) with seven concerts.
Foundation of Panique group with Arrabal, Gironella, Jodorowsky, Olivier, Steinberg and Topor.
Christo erects *Rideau de fer* in the rue Visconti in Paris.
Antagonismes II l'objet (Musée des Arts décoratifs): 500 artists exhibit objects; *Nouvelle figuration II* (Galerie Mathias Fels & Cie) with Baj, Christoforou, Hultberg, Messagier, Petlin, Rebeyrolle, Salles, Tal-Coat.

Comic strip: Inception of the Club des bandes dessinées.

Cinema: *Vivre sa vie* by Jean-Luc Godard; *Cléo de 5 à 7* by Agnès Varda; *Les Dimanches de Ville-d'Avray* by Serge Bourguignon.
Prizes: *La Parole donnée* by Anselmo Duarte (Palme d'Or, Cannes Film Festival); *Le Soupirant* by Pierre Étaix (Louis Delluc).
Released in France: *Eva* by Joseph Losey; *Eclipse* by Michelangelo Antonioni; *Divorce Italian style* by Andrei Tarkovski; *Lolita* by Stanley Kubrick; *The trial* by Orson Welles; *West Side story* by Robert Wise and Jerome Robbins; *The longest day* by Darryl F. Zanuck.

Theatre: *L'Alcade de Zalamea* by Calderon (TNP); *Un otage* (*The hostage*) by Brendan Behan (Odéon); *Les Rustres* (*I Rusteghi*) by Goldoni (TNP).

Music: Homage to Claude Debussy; Darius Milhaud and Arthur Honegger festivals.

Media: Television: 3,425,839 sets; first mondovision spectacle by Telstar.
Intervilles by Guy Lux; *Le Dialogue des Carmélites* by Georges Bernanos, produced by Georges Folgoas; *Thierry la Fronde*; *Bonne nuit les petits*.
Publishing: New paperback collection: 'Le monde en 10/18' (Plon).

Sport: Victories for Michel Jazy and Claude Piquemal (athletics), Jacques Anquetil (cycling), Christine Caron and Alain Gottvalès (swimming), Marielle Goitschel (skiing).

Deaths: Jean Amrouche, Gaston Bachelard, Pierre Benoît, Alfred Cortot, Daniel Halévy, Jacques Ibert, René Julliard, Yves Klein, Louis Massignon, Roger Nimier, Daniel Sorano, Bruno Walter.

1963

January
14. General de Gaulle officially announces his opposition to the entry of Britain to the Commom Market and his support for retaining a national strike force.
22. Signature of the Franco-German Treaty of Co-operation.

February
14. Arrest of several officers accused of plotting against General de Gaulle.

March
1. Start of miners' strike.
4. Failure of miners' demands; widely observed general strike.

April
5. Following negotiations, miners return to work.

June
22. Night of *Salut les copains* at Place de la Nation, with Pop-star idols.

July
27. Law regarding advance notification of strikes.
29. General de Gaulle reaffirms France's independence *vis-à-vis* the USA and the primacy of the Franco-German treaty over the Common Market.

October
Véronique rocket, carrying the first 'space' cat which is recovered by parachute, is launched at Hammaguir base.

November
25. Demonstrations against the strike force.

1963

Opening of the first Carrefour hypermarket at Sainte-Geneviève-des-Bois.
First Kodak Instamatic cameras.
Start of serial production of atomic bombs; Super Frelon, a new French helicopter, beats world speed record.
One out of four students belongs to the UNEF (Students' Union).

Essays: *La Philosophie critique de Kant* by Gilles Deleuze; *Sur Racine* by Roland Barthes; *Pour un nouveau roman* by Alain Robbe-Grillet; *La Nouvelle Classe ouvrière* by Serge Mallet; *La Place de l'homme dans la nature* by Pierre Teilhard de Chardin; French translation of *Eros and civilization* by Herbert Marcuse.

Literature: *Oh! les beaux jours* (*Happy days*) by Samuel Beckett; *Le Fou d'Elsa* by Louis Aragon; *La Force des choses* by Simone de Beauvoir.
Bestsellers: *Sang d'Afrique* by Guy des Cars; *Hortense* by Cecil Saint-Laurent; *Tous n'étaient pas des anges* by Joseph Kessel; *Stances à Sophie* by Christiane Rochefort; *Une Journée d'Ivan Denissovitch* (*One day in the life of Ivan Denisovich*) by Alexander Solzhenitsyn; *Le Daniscope* by Pierre Daninos; *La Motocyclette* by André Pieyre de Mandiargues.
Prizes: *Quand la mer se retire* by Armand Lanoux

(Goncourt); *Le Procès-verbal* by J.M.G. Le Clézio (Renaudot); *Un chat qui aboie* by Gérard Jarlot (Médicis).

Town planning, architecture: 'Le Wiseberg' tower-block estate by Émile Aillaud at Forbach (1961–3); CIMT headquarters by Jean Prouvé at Neuilly; 'La Courneuve' tower-block estates for 4000 by Delacroix and Tambuté at Aubervilliers (1956–63).

Arts: Major exhibitions: Delacroix and Kandinsky, *Gromaire*. Musée Matisse opened in Nice. *Art contemporain* (Grand Palais): modern works, 1910–60; *La Grande Aventure de l'art au XXe siècle* (Château des Rohan); 3rd Paris Biennale, the works of GRAV (Groupe de Recherche d'art visuel) exhibited in entrance hall – French selection: Aillaud, Buraglio, Christo, Deschamps, Erró, Rancillac, Saint-Phalle, Skira, Spoerri – British selection: Blake, Boshier, Hockney, Jones, King – Japanese: Kudo; 31 American painters (American Cultural Center); American Pop art (Galerie Sonnabend); *Donner à voir 3* (Galerie Cruze) selected by G. Gassiot-Talabot, J.-C. Lambert, J.-J. Lévêque, R.-J. Moulin and J. Pierre.

Fluxus festival in Nice: street demonstrations by Ben Vautier, Brecht, La Monte Young, Maciunas and Paik.

Cinema: *Le Mépris* by Jean-Luc Godard; *Le Procès de Jeanne d'Arc* by Robert Bresson; *Muriel* by Alain Resnais; *Le Feu follet* by Louis Malle; *Le Joli mai* by Chris Marker; *L'Immortelle* by Alain Robbe-Grillet.

Prizes: *The leopard* by Luchino Visconti (Palme d'Or, Cannes Film Festival).

Released in France: *Otto e mezzo* by Federico Fellini; *Main basse sur la ville* by Francesco Rosi; *The Birds* by Alfred Hitchcock; *The Silence* by Ingmar Bergman.

Theatre: *Galileo Galilei* by Bertold Brecht (TNP); *Divine Paroles* by Ramón Maria del Valle-Inclán (Odéon); *Oh! Les beaux jours* (*Happy Days*) by Samuel Beckett (Odéon).

Music: *Wozzeck* (Paris Opéra), conducted by Pierre Boulez, directed by Jean-Louis Barrault, set design by André Masson; *Pacem in terris* by Darius Milhaud; *Musiques formelles* by Iannis Xenakis.

Media: Television: 4,440,278 sets.

Jacques le Fataliste by Diderot, directed by Pierre Cardinal; *Les Raisins verts* by Jean-Christophe Averty.

Sport: Victories for Yves Saint-Martin (horse-riding), Michel Jazy and Claude Piquemal (athletics), Jacques Anquetil (cycling), Jean-Claude Magnan (fencing), Alain Gottvalès (swimming), Annie Famose and François Bonlieu (skiing), Guyonne Dalle (water-skiing).

Deaths: Hans Arp, Georges Braque, Jean Cocteau, Édith Piaf, Francis Poulenc, Tristan Tzara, Jacques Villon.

1964

January

France recognizes the People's Republic of China.

April

Survey in *Paris-Match* on the new young generation in France. Diagnosis: 'Not much interest in politics, a decline in religious feeling, dreams of cars, record-players and TV'.

May

29. The Assemblée nationale approves the statute creating the ORTF (French radio and television).

August

15. General de Gaulle presides over the 20th anniversary of the Allied landing in Provence. An unsuccessful attempt is made on his life.

October

22. Jean-Paul Sartre refuses Nobel Prize for Literature.

November

7. Split within the CFTC (Catholic trade union movement), with majority forming the new CFDT.

December

16–17. Parliament declares that crimes against humanity cannot be limited by prescription.

1964

Jean Moulin is interred at the Panthéon.

Essays: *Parlez-vous franglais?* by Étiemble; *Les Mots* by Jean-Paul Sartre; *Proust et les signes* by Gilles Deleuze; *Le Geste et la parole* by André Leroi-Gourhan; *Essais critiques* by Roland Barthes; *Le Cru et le cuit* by Claude Lévi-Strauss; *Les Héritiers* by Pierre Bourdieu and Claude Passeron.

Literature: *Journal 1953–1956* by Witold Gombrowicz; *Le Ravissement de Lodl V. Stein* by Marguerite Duras; *Une Mort très douce* by Simone de Beauvoir; *Le Pont de Londres* by Louis-Ferdinand Céline.

Bestsellers: *Pour l'honneur* by Joseph Kessel; *Snobissimo* by Pierre Daninos; *Les Sultans* by Christine de Rivoyre; *L'Espion qui venait du froid* (*The spy who came in from the cold*) by John Le Carré.

Prizes: *L'État sauvage* by George Conchon (Goncourt); *L'Écluse* by Jean-Pierre Faye (Renaudot); *L'Opoponax* by Monique Wittig (Médicis).

Town planning, architecture: First exhibition of work by Jean Prouvé (Musée des Arts décoratifs), Paris.

Arts: Major exhibitions: *Toulouse-Lautrec*; *Les Hittites*; *L'Art copte*; *Chefs d'oeuvre de la sculpture dans les musées de Province*; *Cinquante ans de 'collages': Papiers collés, assemblages, collages, du cubisme à nos jours* at Saint-Étienne; *Nouvelles tendances: Propositions visuelles du mouvement international* (Musée des Arts décoratifs) with Cruz-Diez, Debourg, Demarco, Hacker, Miranda, Reinhartz, Richter, Talman, Tomasello, Vardanega, Zehringer ...; *L'Écriture du peintre* with Degottex, Giacometti, Hantaï, Hartung, Mathieu, Michaux, Tobey; 20th 'salon de mai' (Musée d'Art moderne de la Ville de Paris) with New Realists, American Pop artists and Italian neo-Realists; 1st *Festival de la Libre Expression* (American Cultural Center) with Jean-Jacques Lebel, Ben, Filliou, Kudo, Pomereulle, Williams; *Mythologies quotidiennes* (Musée d'Art moderne de la Ville de Paris) with Arnal, Arroyo, Berni, Bettencourt, Cremonini, Dado, Foldes, Golub, Monory, Pistoletto, Rancillac, Raynaud, Raysse, Réchiquot, Saint-Phalle, Télémaque, Voss; *Art USA New: The Johnson collection of contemporary American painting* (Musée d'Art moderne de la Ville de Paris); *Huit ans d'agitation, 1956–64* , final exhibition at the Galerie Daniel Cordier; *Hard-edge* (Galerie Denise René) with Albers, Arp, Baertling, Herbin, Liberman, Lhose, Mortensen, Taeuber-Arp, Vasarely; *Lettrisme et hypergraphie* (Galerie Stadler) with Altman, Brau, Dufrêne, Isou, Lemaître, Naves, Pomerand, Sabatier, Voronsky, Wolman; *Mouvement 2* (Galerie Denise René) with Cruz-Diez, Demarco, Le Parc, Morellet, Mortensen, Novac, Rickey, Seuphor, Tinguely, Tomasello, Yvaral.

Chagall paints the ceiling of the Opéra.

Official opening of Fondation Maeght at Saint-Paul-de-Vence.

Comic strip: *Barbarella*, first comic-strip album 'for adults'.

Cinema: *La Peau douce* by François Truffaut; box-office success of *Le Gendarme de Saint-Tropez* by Jean Girault.

Prizes: *Les Parapluies de Cherbourg* by Jacques Demy (Palme d'Or, Cannes Film Festival); *Le Bonheur* by Agnès Varda (Louis Delluc).

Released in France: *The servant* by Joseph Losey; *Quatre garçons dans le vent* (*A hard day's night*) by

Richard Lester; *The diary of a chambermaid* by Luis Buñuel; *Les Monstres* by Dino Risi; *Doctor Strangelove* by Stanley Kubrick; *America, America* by Elia Kazan.

Theatre: *Le Dossier Oppenheimer* by Jean Vilar (Athénée); *Zoo* by Vercors (TNP); *Sainte-Jeanne (Saint Joan)* by George Bernard Shaw, staged by G. Neveux; Montparnasse, the Piccolo Teatro of Milan with *Les Deux Jumeaux* by Goldoni.

Music: *La Famille Bach* (France-Musique); the Beatles give their first Paris performance, sharing the bill with Sylvie Vartan and Trini Lopez; the Rolling Stones at the Olympia: 40 arrests.

Media: Television: 5,235,270 TV sets. Creation of the second TV channel. First American serial on television. First screenings of: *La Caméra invisible* by Pierre Bellemare and *Les Femmes aussi* by Éliane Victor; *Zorro*; *Belphégor*; *Le Ménage enchanté*.

Sport: Victories for Jacques Anquetil (cycling), Jean Guichet (motor-racing), Alain Gottvalès (swimming), Éric Tabarly (sailing), the Goitschel sisters (skiing).

Deaths: Alexandre Archipenko, Roger Bissière, Brendan Behan, Pierre Brisson, Gaston Chaissac, Raoul Dufy, Jean Fautrier, Michel Larionov, Giorgio Morandi, Gaby Morlay, Maurice Thorez.

1965

January

27–8. Public services on strike.

February

11. France leaves the Gold Exchange Standard and invites the 'great powers' to follow.

March

Left's improved standing is confirmed at the municipal elections.

July

1. France embarks on an 'empty chair' policy in Brussels.

September

9. François Mitterand announces his candidacy for the Presidential elections.

10. Foundation of the Fédération de la gauche démocrate et socialiste by the SFIO (French section of the Workers International), the Radical party and certain clubs.

October

23. French bishops permit priests to work full time in factories under certain circumstances.

29. Mehdi Ben Barka is kidnapped.

December

19. General de Gaulle wins the second round of the presidential election (polling 55.19% of the votes, as against 44.8% polled for François Mitterand).

1965

The Nobel Prize for Medicine awarded to Jacques Monod, André Lwoff and François Jacob.

Essays: *Lire 'le Capital'* by Louis Althusser; *Nietzsche* by Gilles Deleuze; translation of *Essay on the theory of science* by Max Weber.

Literature: *Quelqu'un* by Robert Pinget; *La Fièvre* by Jean-Marie Gustave Le Clézio; *Le Procès de Gilles de Rais* by Georges Bataille.

Bestsellers: *L'Astragale* by Albertine Sarrazin; *La Mise à mort* by Louis Aragon; *Les Eygletières* by Henri Troyat; *Féminin pluriel* by Benoîte and Flora Groult; *La Chamade* by Françoise Sagan.

Prizes: *L'Adoration* by Jacques Borel (Goncourt); *Les Choses: Une histoire des années soixante* by Georges Pérec (Renaudot); *Quelqu'un* by Robert Pinget (Fémina); *La Rhubarbe* by René Victor Pilhes.

Town planning, architecture: 'La Duchère' tower-block estate by Cottin, Novarina near Lyons; Le Haut-le-Lièvre slab-block estate by Zehrfuss in Nancy (1947–65).

Villa Savoye by Le Corbusier is listed as a historic monument.

Arts: Major exhibitions: *Trésors des églises de France*; *Le Danemark, ses trésors et son art*; *Maîtres de la peinture contemporaine* at the Musée d'Art et d'Industrie, Saint-Étienne, and Musée Fabre, Montpellier; 16th Salon de la Jeune Peinture (Musée d'Art moderne de la Ville de Paris) with British Pop artists, Spanish Equipo Cronica artists, German Spur group artists – Aillaud, Arroyo, Cueco, Parré, Recalcati and Tisserand all exhibit works in green and with the same dimensions; *Un groupe 1965* (Musée d'Art moderne de la Ville de Paris) with Alechinsky, Arman, Balthus, Bury, Degottex, Duchamp, Étienne-Martin, Fautrier, Jorn, Lapicque, Matta, Rebeyrolle, Stahly, Tal-Coat, Tinguely, Bram Van Velde; *États-Unis, sculptures du XXᵉ siècle* (Musée Rodin); *Hommage a Nicéphore Niepce* (Galerie J); 4th Paris Biennale (Musée d'Art moderne de la Ville de Paris); *La Figuration narrative dans l'art contemporain* (Galerie Creuze); *Pop porn, Pop corn, Corny* (Galerie Larcade) with Arman, Duchamp, Dali, Ernst, Fontana, Hains, Klein, Miró, Picabia, Rauschenberg, Raynaud, Rivers, Tinguely; *L'Écart absolu: XIᵉ exposition internationale du surréalisme* (Galerie de l'Oeil); *Les objecteurs* with

Raynaud (Galerie Larcade), Pommereulle (Galerie Ranson), Arman and Kudo (Galerie J).

André Masson decorates the ceiling of the Odéon theatre.

Cinema: *Pierrot le fou* and *Alphaville* by Jean-Luc Godard; *La Vieille Dame indigne* by René Allio; *Viva Maria* by Louis Malle.

Box-office successes: *Le Corniaud* by Gérard Oury; *La 317ᵉ section* by Pierre Schoenderffer.

Prizes: *Le Knack (The knack)* by Richard Lester (Palme d'Or, Cannes Film Festival); *La Vie de château* by Jean-Paul Rappeneau (Louis Delluc).

Released in France: *Pour l'exemple (For king and country)* by Joseph Losey; *Goldfinger* by Guy Hamilton; *Giulietta degli spiriti* by Federico Fellini; *Les Amours d'une blonde* by Milos Forman.

Theatre: *Maître Puntila et son valet Matti (Puntilla)* by Bertold Brecht, staged by Georges Wilson (TNP); *Les Troyennes (Trojan Women)* by Euripedes, staged by Jean-Paul Sartre; *La Musica: Les eaux et forêts* by Marguerite Duras (Champs-Élysées studio); *Le Cercle de craie caucasien (The Caucasian chalk circle)* by Bertold Brecht (Aubervilliers).

Music: *La Tosca* with Maria Callas and Tito Gobbi (Opéra).

Media: Television: 6,493,943 sets.

Sport: Victories for Michel Jazy (athletics), Jacques Anquetil (cycling), Jean-Claude Magnan (fencing), Christine Caron (swimming), Alain Calmat (ice-skating), Jean-Claude Killy (skiing).

Deaths: Jacques Audiberti, Daniel-Rops, Gaston Dominici, Le Corbusier, Roger Vailland, Edgar Varèse.

1966

March

France withdraws from NATO.

May

17. General strike in the public and private sectors.

July

2. First French nuclear explosion in Polynesia at Mururoa.

October

French bishops meeting at Lourdes decide to discontinue abstinence on Fridays, adopt a new presentation of the catechism and accept the principle of married deacons.

November

Nobel Prize for Physics awarded to Alfred Kastler.

Colloquium in Caen on French universities.

Call for a major reform of the French system.

December

Kosygin visits France.

1966

Essays: *Les Mots et les choses* by Michel Foucault; *Écrits* by Jacques Lacan; *Le Bergsonisme* by Gilles Deleuze; *La Mort* by Vladimir Jankélévitch.

Literature: *Les Mangeurs d'étoiles* by Romain Gary; *Le Déluge* by Jean-Marie Gustave Le Clézio. Bestsellers: *Papillon* by Henri Charrière; *Deux Cavaliers de l'orage* by Jean Giono; *Les Comédiens* (*The comedians*) by Graham Greene; *La Quarantaine* by Jean-Louis Curtis.
Prizes: *Oublier Palerme* by Edmonde Charles-Roux (Goncourt); *La Bataille de Toulouse* by José Cabas (Renaudot); *Une saison dans la vie d'Emmanuel* by Marie-Claire Blais (Médicis).

Arts: Major exhibitions: *Vermeer*; Dada retrospective; Picasso retrospective (Grand Palais), 403,000 visitors (record attendance for a living artist); *Dix ans d'art vivant 1945–55* (Fondation Maeght); *Climat 1966*, Musée de Peinture et de Sculpture, Grenoble, with Debré, Degottex, Dewasne, Hantaï, Jacobsen, Jorn, Lanskay, Lardera, Manessier, Masson, Mathieu, Riopelle, Soulages, Tapies, Tal-Coat, Tomasello, Vasarely; *Le Musée dans l'usine: Collection Peter Stuyvesant* (Pavillon Marsan); *Gutaï* (Galerie Stadler) with Murakami, Shiraga, Yoshihara; *Exposition en forme de triptyque* (Galerie Jean Fournier) with Buraglio, Buren, Hantaï, Meurice, Parmentier, Riopelle, Tapies; *Onze lettristes* (Galerie Stadler); *Happenings* (Galerie Ileana Sonnabend). Reopening of the Orangerie; GRAV organizes a day of action in the streets of Paris.

Cinema: *Masculin-Féminin* by Jean-Luc Godard; *Fahrenheit 451* by François Truffaut; *Paris brûle-t-il?* by René Clément; *Le Deuxième souffle* by Jean-Pierre Melville; *Cul-de-sac* by Roman Polanski. Box-office successes: *La Grand Vadrouille* by Gérard Oury.
Prizes: *Un homme et une femme* by Claude Lelouch (Palme d'Or, Cannes Film Festival); *La guerre est finie* by Alain Resnais (Louis Delluc); *La Bataille d'Alger* by Gillo Pontecorvo (Lion d'Or). Released in France: *Modesty Blaise* by Joseph Losey; *The spy who came in from the cold* by Martin Ritt; *Doctor Zhivago* by David Lean.

Theatre: *Les Paravents* by Jean Genet causes a scandal at the Odéon; *Le Grand cérémonial* by Fernando Arrabal (Les Mathurins); *Le Roi se meurt* by Eugène Ionesco revived at the Athénée.

Music: *Éclat* by Pierre Boulez.

Media: Television: 7,471,192 sets. *Marie Tudor* by Victor Hugo, produced by Abel Gance; *La tour Eiffel qui tue* by Guillaume Hanoteau, produced by Michel de Ré.
Radio: *Pop club* created by José Artur (France Inter), *Super Hit-Parade* created by Fabrice (RTL). Press: *Hara-Kiri* is censored; *Jazz Hot* produces a special issue called 'Rock & Folk', which became a monthly from 1967.

Sport: Victories for Roger Bambuck and Michel Jazy (athletics), Jacques Anquetil, Bernard Guyot, Pierre Trentin and Daniel Morelon (cycling), Alain Mosconi (swimming), Jean-Claude Killy, Guy Périllat, Annie Famose and Marielle Goitschel (skiing).

Deaths: Vincent Auriol, Victor Brauner, André Breton, Julien Carette, Pierre Descaves, Georges Duhamel, Célestin Freinet, Jean Galtier-Boissière, Alberto Giacometti, Jean Lurçat, Violette Nozières, Cécile Sorel.

1967
February

3. School leaving age raised from fourteen to sixteen.
Strikes.

March

5–12. Parliamentary elections. Perceptible revival of support for the Left.
29. First French atomic submarine, *Le Redoutable*, launched at Cherbourg.

April

9. Oil pollution on the Cotentin coastline and later on the Brittany beaches.
Strike in the Lorraine iron mines.

June

2. Jacqueline Dubut is the first female commercial air-line pilot (at Air Inter).
Six-Day Arab-Israeli war: solidarity movement supporting Israel.

July

12. Creation of the Agence nationale pour l'emploi (national labour exchange).
31. General de Gaulle states that France will help the French Canadians achieve 'the liberation goals they themselves have set'.

August

18. Regulations on employee profit-sharing published.

September

Violent demonstrations by peasants in Brittany.

November

3. Birth of the fifty millionth French national.

25. Week-long strike at Nanterre university.
December

19. Neuwirth law authorizing contraception approved.
Unemployment an issue: 226,000 unsatisfied job-seekers this month. Comités d'action lycéens created by Trotskyist militants.

1967

First heart transplant by Professor Christian Barnard, South Africa.
CNEXO: first French nuclear submarine.
Emergence of committees opposing Vietnam War.

Essays: *La Société du spectacle* by Guy Debord; *Système de la mode* by Roland Barthes; *L'Écriture et la Différence* by Jacques Derrida; *Tombeau pour 500,000 soldats* by Pierre Guyotat; *Le Traité de savoir-vivre à l'usage des jeunes générations* by Raoul Vaneigem.
Bestsellers: *Le Défi américain* by Jean-Jacques Servan-Schreiber; *Où tu porteras mon deuil* by Dominique Lapierre and Larry Collins.

Literature: *Blanche ou l'oubli* by Louis Aragon; *Les Belles Images* by Simone de Beauvoir; *La Traversière* by Albertine Sarrazin; *La Plaisanterie* by Milan Kundera.
Bestsellers: *Le Matrimoine* by Hervé Bazin; *Antimémoires* by André Malraux; *Élise ou la vraie vie* by Claire Etcherelli.
Prizes: *La Marge* by André Pieyre de Mandiargues (Goncourt); *Histoire* by Claude Simon (Médicis).

Town planning, architecture: Palais Alpexpo by Jean Prouvé at Grenoble; La Maison de l'Iran, Cité universitaire, by Claude Parent (1965–7).

Arts: Major exhibitions: *Toutankhamon*; *Bonnard*; *Art russe*; *Ingres*; *Chagall*; *Lumière et mouvement*. *Bande dessinée et figuration narrative* (Musée des Arts décoratifs); *Une Aventure de l'art abstrait 50–57/67* (Musée Galliera); *L'Art brut* (selection by Dubuffet from the collections of the Compagnie de l'art brut); *Dix Ans d'art vivant, 1955–65* (Fondation Maeght); *L'Art pour la paix au Viêt-nam* (Galerie Creuze); *BMPT* in the auditorium (Musée des Arts décoratifs) with Buren, Mosset, Parmentier, Toroni; *Le monde en question (ou vingt-six peintres de contestation)* at the ARC, with Arroyo, Berni, Cremonini, Golub, Kudo, Matta, Millares, Petlin, Rancillac, Recalcati, Sarkis, Equipo cronica; 18th Salon de la Jeune Peinture (Musée d'Art moderne de la Ville de Paris); *La cédille qui sourit* (Galerie Jacqueline Ranson). Creation of the ARC (Animation Recherche Confrontation) at the Musée d'Art moderne de la

Ville de Paris; foundation of the CNAC (Centre national d'art contemporain) by the Ministry for Culture. Demonstration by the BMPT artists who remove their paintings from the walls.

Comic strip: *Valérian* by J.-C. Mézière, text by Christian; rediscovery of *Tarzan*.

Cinema: *Weekend*, *La Chinoise*, *Made in USA* and *Deux ou trois choses que je sais d'elle* by Jean-Luc Godard; *Le Vieil Homme et l'enfant* by Claude Berri; *Mouchette* by Robert Bresson; *Les Demoiselles de Rochefort* by Jacques Demy; *La Musica* by Marguerite Duras; *Vivre pour vivre* by Claude Lelouch; *Le Samouraï* by Jean-Pierre Melville; *La Chasse au lion* by Jean Rouch; *La Religieuse* by Jacques Rivette (censored).
Prizes: *Blow-up* by Michelangelo Antonioni ('grand prix', Cannes Film Festival); *Belle de jour* by Luis Buñuel (Lion d'Or, Venice Film Festival).
Released in France: *Accident* by Joseph Losey; *Marat-Sade* by Peter Brooks; *Chronique d'Anna Magdalena Bach* by J.-M. Straub; *Who's afraid of Virginia Woolf?* by Mike Nichols.

Theatre: *La Cuisine* (*The kitchen*) by Arnold Wesker, adapted by P. Léotard, directed by Ariane Mnouchkine.
The Avignon Festival opens its doors to dance. First fringe shows.

Dance: *Messe pour le temps présent* by Pierre Henry and Maurice Béjart.

Music: *Pli selon pli* by Pierre Boulez; *Hymnen* by Karlheinz Stockhausen.
Creation of the Orchestre de Paris conducted by Charles Munch.

Media: Television: *Les Chevaliers du ciel* serial; *Les Dossiers de l'écran* by Armand Jammot. Colour television launched.
Press: Creation of *Opus* and *Robho* magazines; monthly magazine *Photo* and *Historia Magazine* launched.

Sport: Victories for Roger Bambuck, Marc Bergé, Jocelyn Delecour, Claude Piquemal and Hervé d'Encausse (athletics), Roger Pingeon (cycling), Daniel Robin (wrestling), Jean-Claude Killy (skiing), Françoise Durr (tennis).

Deaths: Marcel Aymé, Françoise Dorléac, Jean Duvivier, Maurice Garçon, Roger Ferdinand, André Maurois, Field-Marshall Juin, Henri Perruchot, Albertine Sarrazin, Ossip Zadkine.

1968

January

26. Workers' demonstrations in Caen.
Incidents at Nanterre university.

February

6. Opening of the Winter Olympics held at Grenoble.
9. Henri Langlois, director of Cinémathèque, is replaced; protests lead to his reinstatment on 22 April.
14. Student demonstrations against rules in student hostels.

March

22. Incidents at Nanterre university.
28. Dean of the arts faculty at Nanterre suspends classes for four days.

May

From 2 May. Riots, student demonstrations, clashes with the CRS (riot squad).
10. A night of rioting in the Latin Quarter.
15. Occupation of the Odéon theatre and the Renault factory at Cléon. Strikes spread.
19. General de Gaulle declares: 'Reform, yes; lawlessness, no'.
24–5. Renewed confrontations.
Fire started at the Paris Bourse.
Start of the ORTF (radio and television) strike.
Start of Grenelle negotiations between Georges Pompidou and the 'social partners'.
27. Draft agreement is turned down by the workers. Demonstration at the Charléty stadium without the Communists.
29. General de Gaulle leaves for Baden Baden. Large CGT (trade union movement) demonstration in Paris.
30. Broadcast message from General de Gaulle dissolving the Assemblée nationale.

June

23–30. Victory by Gaullist majority at parliamentary elections.
Gradual resumption of work and university classes during the month.

July

8. Official summary of the May disturbances in Paris: 1910 policemen and 1459 demonstrators injured; damage costing FF 2.5 million on the public highway.
10. Georges Pompidou resigns as Prime Minister. Maurice Couve de Murville is appointed to replace him.
24. Law grants an amnesty for actions carried out in the context of the Algerian War.
31. The ORTF is reorganized: 200 journalists sacked following the May events.

September

2. Jean-Louis Barrault is dismissed as director of the Odéon theatre.

13. Creation of university centres at Vincennes and Dauphine.

October

11. Law on direction and aims of higher education (Edgar Faure).
21. Central Committee of the French Communist Party publicly condemns Roger Garaudy's opposition to Soviet intervention in Czechoslovakia.
31. Dissolution of the Far Right 'Occident' movement.

December

12. Renewed disturbances at Nanterre.
31. General de Gaulle declares: 'So let us bury the devils that have tormented us during the year that is coming to an end'.

1968

First French H-bomb exploded at the experimental centre in the Pacific.
First heart transplants in France.
World record in speleology.
Gabrielle Russier affair.
Official opening of the Maison de la Culture in Grenoble; inception of the Société des réalisateurs français (SRF).

Essays: *Le Système des objets* by Jean Baudrillard; *Le Movement de mai 68* by Alain Touraine; *La Révolution introuvable* by Raymond Aron; *Asphyxiante culture* by Jean Dubuffet; *Pouvoir politique et classes sociales* by Nikos Poulantzas.
Bestsellers: *Les Américains* by Roger Peyrefitte.
First translations of books by McLuhan: *La Galaxie Gutemberg* (*The Gutemberg galaxy*) and *Pour comprendre les médias* (*Understanding media*).

Literature: *La Femme rompue* by Simone de Beauvoir; *Battre la campagne* by Raymond Queneau; French translation of *Cent ans de solitude* (*One hundred years of solitude*) by Gabriel Garcia Marquez.
Bestsellers: *Les Guerilleros* by Jean Lartéguy; *Le Pavillon des cancéreux* (*Cancer ward*) by Alexander Solzhenitsyn; *Le Singe nu* (*The naked ape*) by Desmond Morris.
Prizes: *Belle du Seigneur* by Albert Cohen (Académie française 'grand prix du Roman'); *Les Fruits de l'hiver* by Bernard Clavel (Goncourt); *Le Devoir de violence* by Yambo Ouloguem (Renaudot); *Le Mendiant de Jérusalem* by Élie Wiesel (Médicis); *L'Oeuvre au noir* by Marguerite Yourcenar (Fémina); *Le Petit Matin* by Christine de Rivoyre (Interallié).

Architecture: Crisis over teaching at the École

nationale supérieure des beaux-arts; *Publication des Mémoires d'un architecte* by Pouillon; reform of teaching of architecture.

Arts: Major exhibitions: *L'Art des Mayas du Guatemala*; *Miró*; *Baudelaire*; *Le Décor quotidien de la vie en 1968*.

Aspects de la figuration depuis la guerre, Musée d'Art et d'Industrie, Saint-Étienne; *Trois sculpteurs*, first CNAC exhibition, rue Berryer, with Brown, Étienne-Martin, Mason; *Totems et tabous: Lam, Matta, Penalba* (Musée d'Art moderne de la Ville de Paris); *Cinétisme-Spectacle-Environnement*, Maison de la Culture, Grenoble; *Peintres européens d'aujourd'hui*.

Opening of a 'salle lettriste et hypergraphique', Musée national d'Art moderne; establishment of studios for making posters, École nationale supérieure des beaux-arts and École des Arts décoratifs.

Comic strip: Wolinski and Siné create *L'Enragé*.

Cinema: *Je t'aime, je t'aime* by Alain Resnais; *Les Biches* by Claude Chabrol; *Barbarella* by Roger Vadim.

Prizes: *Baisers volés* by François Truffaut (Louis Delluc).

Released in France: *Boom* by Joseph Losey; *Space Odyssey 2001* by Stanley Kubrick; *Le Bal des vampires* and *Rosemary's baby* by Roman Polanski; *Bonnie and Clyde* by Arthur Penn.

Theatre: Opening of Théâtre de la Ville in Paris with *Six personnages en quête d'auteur* (*Six characters in search of an author*) by Luigi Pirandello; New 'Jeune Théâtre' festival in Nancy; 'Living Theater' play at the Palais des Papes, Avignon.

Music: Varèse, Xenakis, Berio and Pierre-Henry at the 'Journées internationales de musique', Paris; 'Grand prix national' for music awarded to Marius Constant; *Turangalila* by Olivier Messiaen turned into a ballet by Roland Petit at the Opéra; *Éclat, Figures, Doubles et Prismes* by Pierre Boulez.

Dance: Carolyn Carlson at the Paris 'Festival de la Danse'.

Media: Television: *En direct de l'Assemblée nationale* produced by Igor Barrère and Raoul Sangla; *La Chute de Berlin* produced by Frédéric Rossif; first broadcast of commercial advertising. Press: Launch of *Les Chroniques de l'art vivant*.

Sport: Victories for Jean-Claude Killy (skiing), Roger Bambuck (athletics), Catherine Lacoste (golf).

Deaths: Louis Aubert, Mireille Balin, Guy Boniface, Jacques Chardonne, Marcel Duchamp,

Fontana, Foujita, Mauricet, 'la Môme Moineau', Charles Munch, Jean Paulhan, Maurice Rostand, Survage, Van Dongen, Jean Yonnel.

1969

January

6. Total embargo on the supply of French arms to Israel.

8. Fourteen members of the Brittany Liberation Front, accused of involvement in attacks, are brought before the National Security Court.

February

2. 34 students expelled from university for occupying the Rector's offices.

March

5. First strike by small shopkeepers in Paris; during coming months they continue to demonstrate.

April

27. 'No' vote wins referendum on regionalization and Senate reform.

28. General de Gaulle leaves office.

29. Approval of law giving a fourth week of annual paid holiday.

30. Minister for the Interior bans May Day processions in Paris.

May

1. 700 precautionary arrests at Belleville where the Far Left had decided to demonstrate.

2. A Far Right commando group enters the lycée Louis-le-Grand in Paris where a pupil loses his fingers after a grenade attack.

June

15. George Pompidou is elected President of the Republic.

August

8. The franc is devalued.

September

16. Speech by the Prime Minister, Jacques Chaban Delmas, on the 'new society' that should replace the 'blocked society'.

November

15. Demonstrations against Vietnam War; many arrests.

16. Demonstrations by farmers; Minister Olivier Guichard is kept for three hours at a farm near Nantes.

26. Arrest of Gérard Nicoud, leader of shopkeepers' protest movement.

1969

Student disturbances continue. Edgar Faure brings autonomy and participation to universities.

First flights by Concorde. Official opening of the

first section of the RER.

First MacDonald's restaurant opens in France.

First ecological campaign defending Parc national de la Vanoise.

Essays: *L'Archéologie du savoir* by Michel Foucault; *Différence et répétition* and *Logique du sens* by Gilles Deleuze; *Figures (III)* by Gérard Genette; *La Rumeur d'Orléans* by Edgar Morin; *Scénographie d'un tableau* by Jean-Louis Schefer; *Écrits sur l'histoire* by Fernand Braudel.

Translation of *Vers la libération* by Marcuse; success of *Dieu existe, je l'ai rencontré* by André Frossard; final issue of the *Internationale situationniste*.

Literature: *Détruire, dit-elle* by Marguerite Duras; *La Disparition* by Georges Pérec; *Ronde de nuit* by Patrick Modiano.

Bestsellers: *Printemps au parking* by Christiane Rochefort; *Les Chemins de Katmandou* by René Barjavel; *Les Allumettes suédoises* by Robert Sabatier.

Prizes: *Creezy* by Félicien Marceau (Goncourt); *Dedans* by Hélène Cixous (Médicis); *La Deuxième Mort de R. Mercader* by Jorge Semprun (Fémina).

Town planning, architecture, design: Tour Nobel by Mailly and Dépussé at La Défense; start of new town of Vaudreuil by the Atelier de Montrouge team; renovation of Ivry-sur-Seine by Jean Renaudie; work begun on Roissy airport by Paul Andreu; opening of Centre de création industrielle (CCI) within the Musée des Arts décoratifs: *Qu'est-ce que le design?* , exhibits by Joe C. Colombo, Charles Eames, Fritz Eichler, Roger Tallon.

President Pompidou announces a cultural centre at Beaubourg. Paris wholesale market (Les Halles) transferred to Rungis.

Arts: Major exhibitions: *Miró*; *Delvaux*; *Chagall*; *Klee*; *Giacometti*.

Distances (ARC) with Adami, Bertholo, Kermarrec, Klapheck, Monory, Poli, Stämpfli, Télémaque, Titus-Carmel; *Alocco, Dezeuze, Dolla, Pagès, Pincemin, Saytour, Viallat* (École spéciale d'architecture); Salon de la Jeune Peinture on the theme of *Police et culture*; *Work in progress* (American Cultural Center) with Ben, Boltanski, Brusse, Cadare, Dietman, Gette, Gilli, Kirili, Miralda; works by Dezeuze, Pagès, Saytour and Viallat exhibited at Coaraze (Alpes Maritimes); exhibitions by Sieff and Sudre; 'Salle rouge pour le Viêt-nam' installed by the Salon de la Jeune Peinture (ARC) with Aillaud, Alleaume, Arroyo, Baratella, Buraglio, Cane, Cueco, Rieti, Schlosser, Tisserand; foundation of the Rencontres photographiques internationales of Arles.

Comic strip: Children's weekly publication *Vaillant* becomes *Pif gadget*; rediscovery of *Little Nemo*; first feminist comic strips by Claire Bretécher; first issue of *Cahiers de la bande dessinée*.

Cinema: *Z* by Costa-Gavras; *Ma Nuit chez Maude* by Éric Rohmer; *Pierre et Paul* by René Allio; *La Fiancée du pirate* by Kaplan; *Un homme qui me plaît* by Claude Lelouch; *Calcutta* by Louis Malle.

Prizes: *L'Enfance nue* by Nelly Maurice Pialat (Jean Vigo); *Les Choses de la vie* by Claude Sautet (Louis Delluc).

Released in France: *Midnight cowboy* by John Schlesinger; *Satyricon* by Federico Fellini.

Theatre: *Orden* produced by Georges Lavelli; *Bérénice* directed by Roger Planchon; *La Résistible Ascension d'Arturo Ui* (*Der aufhaltsame Aufstieg von Arturo Ui*) directed by Georges Wilson; *Les Clowns* directed by Ariane Mnouchkine.

Avignon Festival includes fine arts. Peter Brook settles in France. Success of café theatre with Le Lucernaire, the Splendid, Le Café de la Gare (Romain Bouteille).

Music: Karlheinz Stockhausen (TNP and Fondation Maeght); *Nomos Gamma* by Ianis Xenakis; *Requiem* by György Ligeti; *Méditations sur le mystère de la Sainte-Trinité* by Olivier Messiaen; *Hair* (Théâtre de la Porte-Saint-Martin). First regional opera house opens.

Celestial Communication Orchestra started by Alan Silva.

First Pop festival in France at Amougies.

Dance: *Dances at a gathering* by Jerome Robbins.

Media: Launch of magazines *Charlie mensuel* and *Hara-Kiri Hebdo*.

Deaths: Emmanuel d'Astier de la Vigerie, Edouard Goerg, Joseph Kosma, Serge Poliakoff, André Salmon, Louise de Vilmorin.

1970
March
2–3. Violence on the Nanterre campus; 30 to 40 people injured.
April
29. Girls may now attend the École polytechnique.

30. Assemblée nationale adopts 'anticasseurs' law (outlawing the use of violence in protests).
May
27. Dissolution of the Proletarian Left; its leaders

indicted: demonstration and clashes.

August
26. First demonstration by the Mouvement de libération de femme (MLF; Women's Liberation Movement) .

November
9. Death of General de Gaulle; he is buried at Colombey on 12 November.

1970
Disturbances involving students and lycée pupils continue. Monseigneur Lefebvre rejects Vatican II and founds the Fraternité sacerdotale Saint-Pie X. Launch of the *Péole* satellite in Guyana. First Paris-Cherbourg turbo-train.

Essays: *Capitalisme et schizophrénie* by Gilles Deleuze and Félix Guattari; *La Forme de l'intelligence* by Robert Klein; *Marx est mort* by Jean-Marie Benoist; *La Reproduction* by Pierre Bourdieu and Jean-Claude Passeron; *Du Sens* by Algirdas-Julien Greimas; *La Société bloquée* by Michel Crozier; *Libres Enfants de Summerhill* (*Summerhill*) by A.S. Neill.

Bestsellers: *Le Duel de Gaulle-Pompidou* by Philippe Alexandre; *Le Hasard et la nécessité* by Jacques Monod; first volume of *Les Mémoires d'espoir* by Charles de Gaulle.

Literature: *Où* by Michel Butor; *La Guerre* by Jean-Marie Gustave Le Clézio.

Bestsellers: *Love story* by Éric Segal; *Le Parrain* (*The Godfather*) by Mario Puzo; *Chien blanc* by Romain Gary; *Le Talisman* by Marcel Dassault.

Prizes: *Le Roi des Aulnes* by Michel Tournier (Goncourt); *Sélironte ou la chambre impériale* by Camille Bourniquel (Médicis); *Les Poneys sauvages* by Michel Déon (Interallié); *La Crève* by François Nourissier (Fémina).

Town planning, architecture: Pont de la Bourse, Le Havre, by Guillaume Gillet; decoration of La Défense esplanade by Agam, Dubuffet and Miró; 'ZUP le Mirail' tower-block estate for 100,000 by Candilis, Woods and Josic; work starts on Villeneuve tower-block estate, Grenoble, the first megastructure, by Georges Loiseau and Jean Tribel.

Art et architecture: Bilans et problèmes du 1%, Halles centrales de Paris; 'Prix de Rome' for architecture discontinued; Paris City Council accepts scheme for redesigning Les Halles area; competition for the future Centre Georges-Pompidou launched.

Arts: Major exhibitions: *L'Art flamand de Ensor à Permeke*; *Goya*; *Rembrandt*; *Matisse*; *Klee*; *Picasso*;

Hélion.

Salon de la Jeune Peinture, *Qui tue?*, collective work based on the Gabrielle Russier affair; *Image/dessin* (ARC); *18 Paris IV 70*, 66 rue Mouffetard, Paris, exhibition of Conceptual art; *Cent artistes dans la ville* at Montpellier with Ben, Boltanski, Castro, Dezeuze, Dolla, Kiefer, Pincemin, Rouan, Saytour, Viallat; *Supports-Surfaces* (ARC) with Bioulès, Devade, Dezeuze, Saytour, Valensi, Viallat; *L'Art vivant aux États-Unis* (Fondation Maeght); 3rd international salon of Galeries pilotes; *Artistes et découvreurs de notre temps* (Musée d'Art moderne de la Ville de Paris); *Concept-Théorie* (Galerie Daniel Templon) with Art & Language, Atkinson, Bainbridge, Baldwin, Burgin, Burn, Hurrel, Kirili, Koslow, Kosuth, Prini, Ramsden, Venet.

'Prix de Rome' awards discontinued. Creation of the magazine *VH 101*.

Comic strip: First album of *Valérian*, spatio-temporal agent; rediscovery of *Prince Vaillant*; first thesis devoted to Hergé.

Cinema: *L'Aveu* by Costa-Gavras; *Borsalino* by Jacques Deray; *Le Cercle rouge* by Jean-Pierre Melville; *Le Genou de Claire* by Éric Rohmer; *Élise ou la vraie vie* by Michel Drach; *Elle boit pas, elle fume pas mais elle cause* by Michel Audiard; *L'Enfant sauvage* by François Truffaut.

Prizes: *Moa Bish* by Raoul Contard (Jean Vigo), *Mash* by Robert Altman (Palme d'Or, Cannes Film Festival).

Released in France: *Tristana* by Luis Buñuel; *The damned* by Visconti; *Zabriskie Point* by Michelangelo Antonioni; *Woodstock* by Richard Wadleigh.

Theatre: *1789* by Ariane Mnouchkine; *Bérénice* by Racine staged by the Roger Planchon company; *Orlando furioso* by Luca Ronconi. 'Grand Prix national' for theatre awarded to Jean Dasté. Creation of the Centre national de la marionnette; first Charleville-Mézières festival.

Music: Sun Râ concert (Fondation Maeght); *Tout un monde lointain* by Henri Dutilleux; *Faisceaux, diffraction* by J.-C. Eloy.

Failure of Biot and Aix-en-Provence Pop festivals.

Dance: *Ballet du XXᵉ siècle* by Maurice Béjart at Chaillot.

Media: Television: 10,967,913 sets. *À Armes égales* (first programme between Michel Debré and Jacques Duclos); *Alain Decaux raconte*; *Le Club de la presse*; *La Dynastie des Forsyte* (*The Forsyte Saga*).

Radio: *Campus* by Michel Lancelot (Europe 1).

Publishing: Launch of the paperback collection 'Points' by Éditions du Seuil; creation of the 'Champ libre' publishing company; start of the magazines *La Recherche*, *Rock & Folk* and *Actuel*.

Sport: Victories for Jean Wadoux (athletics), Janou Lefebvre (equestrian sport).

Deaths: Emmanuel Berl, Bourvil, René Capitant, Samson François, Jean Giono, Félix Gaillard, Charles de Gaulle, Jacques Hébertot, Henri Jeanson, Pierre Mac Orlan, Henri Massis, François Mauriac, Marie-Laure de Noailles, Henri Queuille, Théo Sarapo, Raymond Subes, Elsa Triolet.

1971

February

Lycée pupil Gilles Guiot found guilty; start of disturbances in lycées.

March

14–21. Municipal elections.
The opposition makes progress.

April

4. Manifesto supporting abortion by 343 prominent women who admit to having had abortions.
29. Clashes at Renault.

June

2. 300 journalists demonstrate the use of third degree and excesses by the police.
5. Violent incidents in the Latin Quarter.
11–13. New Socialist Party conference at Épinay: François Mitterand becomes party's First Secretary.

July

16. Law about continuing training.

October

6. Approval for bill abolishing distinction between legitimate, natural and adulterous parenthood.
25–30. Brezhnev visits France (his first journey to the west).

November

19. Lycées demonstrate against Guichard circular recommending heads to act firmly.

1971

Disturbances involving lycée pupils and students continue; formation of the Front homosexuel d'action révolutionnaire (FHAR; Revolutionary Gay Rights Movement); formation of the Groupe d'information sur les prisons (GIP; Prison Information Group) centred on Sartre, Foucault and Vidal-Naquet.

Creation of the first ecological museum, Écomusée du Creusot Montceau-les-Mines.

Jacques Duhamel appointed Minister for Cultural Affairs.

Essays: *L'École capitaliste en France* by Christian Baudelot and Roger Establet; *Une Société sans école* by Ivan Illitch; *Pour décoloniser l'enfant* by Gérard Mendel; *Les Enfants du rêve* by Bruno Bettelheim; *Sade, Fourier, Loyola* by Roland Barthes; *L'Idiot de la famille* by Jean-Paul Sartre; *Comment on écrit l'histoire* by Paul Veyne; *La Politique du mâle* (*Sexual politics*) by Kate Millett.

Literature: Bestsellers: *O Jérusalem* by Lapierre and Collins; *Les Chênes qu'on abat* by André Malraux; *Les Mots* by Jean-Paul Sartre; *Mourir d'aimer* by Duchesne; *Sur la route* (*On the Road*) by Jack Kerouac; *Do it* by Rubin.
Prizes: *Les Bêtises* by Jacques Laurent (Goncourt); *L'Irrévolution* by Pascal Laîné (Médicis); *La Gloire de l'Empire* by Jean d'Ormesson (Académie française 'grand prix du roman').

Town planning, architecture: Architects Piano and Rogers win competition to build Centre Georges-Pompidou; Niemeyer, Deroche and Chemetov finish Communist Party headquarters on Place du Colonel-Fabien, Paris; faculty building at Jussieu by Édouard Albert (1964–71); 'La Grande Borne' tower-block estate at Grigny (1964–71); competition for the centre of Évry new town (1971–2); University of Lyons II at Bron ('proliferating' architecture) by Dottelongue and Petroff (1969–71); Les Halles designed by Baltard in Paris demolished; big demonstration on bicycles in Paris; start of the 'Plan Construction' by Paul Delouvrier and Robert Lion.

Arts: Major exhibitions: *Picasso*; *Monet*; *Bacon*; *Léger*; *Max Ernst*; *Rouault*; *L'Art en Yougoslavie de la préhistoire à nos jours*.
L'image en question: Leonardo Cremonini, Alain Jacquet, Bernard Moninot, Jacques Monory, Peter Stämpfli, Harold Stevenson, Maison de la Culture et des Loisirs at Saint-Étienne; *Supports/Surfaces* (theatre, Cité universitaire) with Bioulès, Devade, Dezeuze, Saytour, Valensi, Viallat – artists invited: Arnal, Cane, Dolla, Pincemin; *Peintures et objets* with Adzak, Arroyo, Barré, Bettencourt, Cruz-Diez, Cueco, Degottex, Francken, Hamisky, Morellet, Raynaud, Rouan ...; 7th Paris Biennale where works grouped by trend and not by country: Conceptual art, hyper-realism, objects sent by post, interventions; 22nd Salon de la Jeune Peinture (Grand Palais); fourteen painters exhibit works on 'Life and death of a miner'; works from summer 1970 and a photographic summary (Galerie Jean Fournier) with Dezeuze, Saytour, Valensi, Viallat. *L'enseignement de la*

peinture by Marcelin Pleynet; foundation of the magazines *Peintures cahiers théoriques* and *Artitudes*.

Comic strip: First comic-strip fair at La Mutualité.

Cinema: *Les Deux Anglaises et le Continent* by François Truffaut; *La Veuve Couderc* by Pierre Granier-Deferre; *Mourir d'aimer* by André Cayatte; *Le Chagrin et la Pitié* by Marcel Ophuls; *Le Souffle au coeur* by Louis Malle.
Prizes: *Le Messager* by Joseph Losey (Palme d'Or, Cannes Film Festival); *Rendez-vous à Bray* by André Delvaux (Louis Delluc).
Released in France: *Death in Venice* by Luchino Visconti; *Les Clowns* by Federico Fellini; *Sacco e Vanzetti* by Giuliano Montaldo; *The Decameron* by Pier Paolo Pasolini; *La Salamandre* by Alain Tanner; *Il Conformista* by Bernardo Bertolucci; *Love story* by Arthur Miller; *Taking off* by Milos Forman; *Un été 42* by Robert Mulligan.

Theatre: Inception of Nancy 'Festival du Jeune Théâtre'; discovery of Bob Wilson (*Le Regard du sourd*); *C'était hier* (*Old Times*) by Harold Pinter. J.-P. Vincent stages Brecht's *Tambours et trompettes* and *La Cagnotte* by Labiche; *Zartan fils aîné de Tarzan* by the Jérôme Savary's Grand Magic Circus.
Creation of the *Cahiers de la production théâtrale*.

Dance: *Nijinsky, clown de Dieu* by Maurice Béjart; *The sleepers* by Falco.

Music: *Songe à nouveau rêvé* by André Jolivet; *Opéra électronique* by E. Jünge and A. Almuro; *Kamakala* by J.-C. Eloy; Rolf Liebermann appointed to the Paris Opéra.
Soft Machine concert at the Palais des Sports ends in clashes between the police and spectators; incidents marr concert by Santana at Olympia which closes its doors to rock; Auvers-sur-Oise festival ends in mud and unruliness. End of Pop festivals in France.

Media: Television: *Les Nouvelles Aventures de Vidocq*; *Le Troisième Oeil* by René Marchand.
Radio: Creation of FIP (France Inter); *Nouveau répertoire* (France Culture) by Lucien Attoun.
Press: Foundation of the Libération press agency by Maurice Clavel and Jean-Paul Sartre; creation of France-Loisirs, mass direct-selling club.

Sport: Victories for François Cevert (motor-racing), Jean-Claude Bouttier and Joe Frazier (boxing), Jacqueline Rouvier and Michèle Jacot (skiing).

Deaths: Coco Chanel, Raymond Escholier, Fernandel, Jean Follain, Jean Grenier, René Simon, Alexandre Vialatte, Jean Vilar, Charles Vildrac.

1972

January
19. First prison reform measures.

February
25. Scuffles outside Renault factory, Billancourt. Death of the Far Left militant Pierre Overney.

April
23. Referendum on enlarging the EEC.

June
26. Signature of the joint programme for Left-wing government.

29. Buffet and Bontemps condemned to death for their double crime (executed on 28 November at La Santé prison).

July
5. Pierre Messmer is appointed Prime Minister.
12. Left-wing radicals support joint Left-wing programme of the Communist and Socialist parties.

October
11. Trial and release of a 17-year-old girl at Bobigny for abortion. The day before a large demonstration in Paris supports abortion 'free and on demand'.

November
1. Third rise in SMIC (basic minimum wage) in the year.

1972

After a long delay the Neuwirth law on contraception is brought into force.
Prototype TGV (high-speed train) is presented.
First flight by Airbus.
Inception of the Mouvement Choisir and the Comité d'action des prisonniers (CAP; Prisoners' Action Committee).

Essays: L'Anti-Oepide by Gilles Deleuze and Félix Guattari; Naissance de la clinique by Michel Foucault; Lénine et la philosophie by Louis Althusser; Théorie du nuage by Hubert Damisch; La Dissémination by Jacques Derrida.
Bestseller: Si je mens by Françoise Giroud.

Literature: Correspondance générale by Paul Léautaud; Cicatrices du soleil by Tahar Ben Jelloun; Vous les entendez by Nathalie Sarraute; O vous frères humains by Albert Cohen; Nada by Jean-Patrick Manchette.
Bestsellers: Chocolats de l'entracte by Françoise Chalais; Seigneur du fleuve by Bernard Clavel; Manouche by Roger Peyrefitte; Trois sucettes à la menthe by Robert Sabatier.
Prizes: L'Épervier de Maheux by Jean Carrière (Goncourt); Le Tiers des étoiles by Maurice Clavel

(Médicis); Les Boulevards de ceinture by Patrick Modiano (Académie française 'grand prix du roman').

Town planning, architecture: Tour Maine-Montparnasse by Baudoin, Cassan, Hoyme de Marian and Saubot; Tour du Gan at La Défense by Gaudin; holiday home development by François Spoerry at Port-Grimoud (1966–72); Sarcelles tower-block estate by Boileau and Labourdette (1955–72).

Arts: Major exhibitions: École de Fontainebleau; La Tour; Van Gogh; Brauner; Chaissac; Man Ray; Agam.
72. Douze ans d'art contemporain en France (Grand Palais) – police intervene at official opening and artists withdraw their works: Alechinsky, Dufrêne, Étienne-Martin, Les Malassis, Villeglé; creation of Galerie des Locataires (no fixed premises) by I. Briard, with participation by Boltanski, Borgeaud, Buren, Cadere, Fleischer; official opening of the new Musée des Arts et Traditions populaires at Porte Maillot; Yvon Lambert: Actualité d'un bilan (Galerie Yvon Lambert).

Comic strip: First issue of the magazine L'Écho des Savanes with Bretécher, Gotlib, Mandryka.

Cinema: L'Aventure, c'est l'aventure by Claude Lelouch; Nous ne vieillirons pas ensemble by Maurice Pialat; Avoir vingt ans dans les Aurès by René Vautier; L'Attentat by Yves Boisset; L'Amour l'après-midi by Éric Rohmer; Les Fous du stade by Claude Zidi.
Prizes: L'Affaire Mattei by Francesco Rosi (Palme d'Or, Cannes Film Festival); État de siège by Costa Gavras (Louis Delluc); César et Rosalie by Claude Sautet ('grand prix du Cinéma français').
Released in France: La Bataille d'Alger by Gilla Pontecorvo; Family life by Ken Loach; Harold et Maude by Hal Ashby; La vraie nature de Bernadette by Gilles Carle; Last Tango in Paris by Bernardo Bertolucci; Fellini Roma by Federico Fellini; La Grande Bouffe by Ferreri; The discreet charm of the bourgeoisie by Luis Buñuel; The wedding by Andrzej Wajda; Everything you always wanted to know ... by Woody Allen; Clockwork orange by Stanley Kubrick; Cabaret by Bob Fosse; Deliverance by John Boorman; The godfather by Francis Ford Coppola; Trash by Andy Warhol and Paul Morissey.

Theatre: TNP (Patrice Chéreau and Roger Planchon) transfers to Villeurbanne; foundation of the 'Festival d'Automne'; La Colonie by Resvani; 1793 by Ariane Mnouchkine (Cartoucherie de Vincennes); Où boivent les vaches by Roland

Dubillard; Dans la jungle des villes by Bertold Brecht produced by J.-P. Vincent.

Dance: Stimmung, music by Karlheinz Stockhausen, choreography by Maurice Béjart.

Music: Polytope (light and music) by Ianis Xenakis; Exotica by Moricio Kagel; success of Alan Stivell at the Olympia.

Media: Television: Law on the new statute for the ORTF; start of third channel. La Légende du siècle by Claude Santell; Les Rois maudits by Maurice Druon.
Radio: Non-stop by Philippe Bouvard (RTL); Cosmos by Jean-Jacques Vierne (France Culture). Creation of Viva photographic agency.
Publishing: Guide Gault et Millau; the magazine Artpress; the monthly ecological magazine La Gueule ouverte; closure of the weekly Les Lettres françaises; start of 'Folio' collection (Gallimard).

Sport: Victories for Alain Colas (sailing), Jean-Paul Coche and Jean-Jacques Mounier (judo), Jean-Pierre Beltoise (motor-racing).

Deaths: Pierre Brasseur, Jean Casadesus, Maurice Chevalier, Bobby Lapointe, Pierre Lazareff, Violette Leduc, Henry de Montherlant, Joseph Paul-Boncour, Jacques Pirenne, Lucien Rebatet, Jules Romains, Raymond Souplex.

1973

February
6. Arson attack on Pailleron secondary school in Paris, a prefabricated building: 20 victims.

March
4–11. Parliamentary elections give victory to the party leaving power.
23. Demonstration by lycée pupils against Debré law on national service.

June
18. Workers at Lip factories in Besançon take over the manufacture of watches.

August
14. The Lip premises evacuated by the police.
26. Demonstration at Larzac against extending the army camp.

September
29. National march in support of Lip workers.

December
6. General strike.

1973

First 'petrol crisis'.
First phase of the Franco-American FAMOUS (French American Mid Oceanic Undersea Survey) programme.

Maurice Druon appointed Minister for Cultural Affairs.

Ministry for National Education brings in sex education in schools.

Essays: *L'Utopie ou la mort!* by René Dumont; first volume of *Séminaire* by Jacques Lacan; *Le Plaisir du texte* by Roland Barthes; *Des Choses cachées depuis la fondation du monde* by René Girard; *Le Territoire de l'historien* by Emmanuel Le Roy Ladurie; *La Cause des femmes* by Gisèle Halimi; *Croissance zéro* by Alfred Sauvy. Bestsellers: *Quand la Chine s'éveillera* by Roger Peyrefitte; *Le Temps qui reste* by Jean Daniel; *Malraux* by Jean Lacouture.

Literature: *Triptyque* by Claude Simon; *Intervalle* by Michel Butor; *La Boutique est ailleurs* by Georges Pérec.

Bestsellers: *L'Archipel du Goulag* (*The Gulag Archipelago*) by Alexander Solzhenitsyn; *Le Grand Secret* by René Barjavel; *Le Livre de la vie* by Martin Gray.

Prizes: *L'Ogre* by Jacques Chessex (Goncourt); *Paysage de fantaisie* by Tony Duvert (Médicis); *Un taxi mauve* by Michel Déon (Académie française 'grand prix du roman'); *La vie est ailleurs* by Milan Kundera (Médicis for a foreign writer).

Arts: Major exhibitions: *Pompéi; Soutine; Braque; Dubuffet; Trésors d'art chinois; La Tapisserie du XIVᵉ au XVIᵉ siècle; Futurisme.*

Creation of the Centre d'arts plastiques contemporains (CAPC), under director Jean-Louis Froment; *Michel Butor et ses peintres*, Musée des Beaux-Arts, Le Havre; *La Peinture anglaise aujourd'hui* (Musée d'Art moderne de la Ville de Paris) with Abrahams, Blake, Buckley, Hamilton, Hockney, Riley, Scully, Smith; 8th Paris Biennale: 98 artists invited by 52 international correspondents and a committee of 12 experts; *Réalité-Réalités-Réalité*, Musée d'Art et d'Industrie in Saint-Étienne, with Bechtle, Bertholin, Boltanski, Cane, Judd, Le Gac, Messagier, Meurice, Salt, Stella, Viallat; *Grands maîtres; Hyperréalistes américains* (Galerie des 4 mouvements); *Une exposition de peinture réunissant certains peintres qui mettraient la peinture en question* at 16 place Vendôme, with Buren, Charlton, Griffa, Lohaus, Marden, Martin, Palermi, Ryman, Toroni; *Peinture* (Galerie Jean Fournier) with Bishop, Degottex, Francis, Hantaï, Jaffe, Mitchell, Viallat.

Cinema: *La Nuit américaine* by François Truffaut; *Elle court elle court la banlieue* by Gérard Pirès; *La Maman et la Putain* by Jean Eustache; *RAS* by Yves Boisset; *Le Train* by Pierre Granier-Deferre; *Pleure pas la bouche pleine* by Pascal Thomas; *La Planète sauvage* by René Laloux and Roland Topor. Box-office successes: *Français, si vous saviez* by Harris and Sedouy; *Les Aventures de Rabbi Jacob* by Gérard Oury; *Un flic* by Jean-Pierre Melville. Prizes: *L'Horloger de Saint-Paul* by Bernard Tavernier (Louis Delluc); *Projection privée* by François Leterrier ('grand prix du Cinéma français').

Released in France: *Themroc* by Claude Faraldo; *Mean streets* by Martin Scorsese; *Aguirre* by Werner Herzog; *Nos plus belles années* by Sydney Pollack.

Theatre: Grotowski stars in Paris; *Rosa collective* by Rezvani and Gatti; *La Dispute* by Marivaux staged by Patrice Chéreau; *En r'venant de l'Expo* by Grumberg.

Success of *La Cage aux folles* with Jean Poiret and Michel Serrault.

Music: *La Traviata* by Verdi produced by Maurice Béjart; *Concerto pour deux pianos* by Luciano Berio; *Kyldex 1* by P. Henry, P. Schaeffer and A. Nikolaïs.

Dance: *Un jour ou deux* (John Cage) by Merce Cunningham; *Golestan ou le jardin des roses* (traditional Iranian music) by Maurice Béjart.

Media: Television: The ORTF is dismantled; 14,046,101 sets, 1,091,588 of them colour. *Les Thibault.*

Radio: Pirate radio stations: Rennes, Radio B. Sud; *Les conteurs ont la parole* by Pierre Sipriot (France Culture).

Press: Disappearance of *La Cause du peuple* and creation of *Libération* controlled by Maoists, including Serge July; *Le Monde, dossiers et documents; Play-Boy*, French edition; *Le Guide du routard.*

Foundation of the Sygma, Sipa Press and Fotolib photographic agencies.

Sport: Victories for Henri Pescarolo and Gérard Larousse (motor-racing), Luis Ocaña (cycling), Christian Noël (fencing with foils).

Deaths: Marc Allégret, Alexandre Arnoux, André Barsacq, Roland Dorgelès, Gabriel Marcel, Jacques Maritain, Pablo Picasso, Fernand Raynaud, Jean-Marie Serreau, Albert Skira.

Record sleeve for the Beatles' *Sergeant Pepper* album, designed in 1967 by Peter Blake. © DACS 1997 All rights reserved DACS.

To the right, a bust of Richard Lindnes (one of the very few busts made for the occasion that was not destroyed) preserved by the artist.